Improving School Climate

Improving School Climate provides evidence-based and practical strategies for cultivating a healthy school environment, while also avoiding behavior problems.

The book is packed with strategies centered on key components and conditions for a positive school climate, such as positive teacher-student relationships, positive student-student relationships (including absence of bullying), supportive home-school relationships, student engagement, effective classroom management and school discipline, school safety, and student self-discipline.

This text is an important inclusion for educators and school psychologists who prefer a structured, evidence-based, and practical approach for improving school climate, while also promoting students' academic achievements, preventing behavior problems, and fostering students' social and emotional competencies.

George G. Bear, PhD, is a professor of school psychology at the University of Delaware. He has published over 100 book chapters and articles in peer-reviewed journals, and 8 books. As a member of four editorial boards of leading journals in school psychology, he has frequently reviewed articles on school climate. He worked as a school psychologist and school administrator and continues to serve as a consultant to the state's School-Wide Positive Behavior Supports and school climate initiatives, including Delaware's School Climate Transformation Grant.

Improving School Climate

Practical Strategies to Reduce Behavior Problems and Promote Social and Emotional Learning

George G. Bear

First published 2020
by Routledge
52 Vanderbilt Avenue, New York, NY 10017

and by Routledge
2 Park Square, Milton Park, Abingdon, Oxon, OX14 4RN

Routledge is an imprint of the Taylor & Francis Group, an informa business

© 2020 Taylor & Francis

The right of George G. Bear to be identified as author of this work has been asserted by him in accordance with sections 77 and 78 of the Copyright, Designs and Patents Act 1988.

All rights reserved. No part of this book may be reprinted or reproduced or utilised in any form or by any electronic, mechanical, or other means, now known or hereafter invented, including photocopying and recording, or in any information storage or retrieval system, without permission in writing from the publishers.

Trademark notice: Product or corporate names may be trademarks or registered trademarks, and are used only for identification and explanation without intent to infringe.

Library of Congress Cataloging-in-Publication Data
Names: Bear, George G., author.
Title: Improving school climate : practical strategies
  to reduce behavior problems and promote social and emotional
  learning / George G. Bear.
Description: New York : Routledge, 2020. | Includes bibliographical
  references and index. |
Identifiers: LCCN 2019052656 (print) | LCCN 2019052657 (ebook) |
  ISBN 9780815346388 (hardback) | ISBN 9780815346401
  (paperback) | ISBN 9781351170482 (ebook)
Subjects: LCSH: School environment. | Teacher-student relationships. |
  Classroom management. | Educational psychology. | Social learning.
Classification: LCC LC210 .B42 2020 (print) | LCC LC210
  (ebook) | DDC 371.102/4—dc23
LC record available at https://lccn.loc.gov/2019052656
LC ebook record available at https://lccn.loc.gov/2019052657

ISBN: 978-0-815-34638-8 (hbk)
ISBN: 978-0-815-34640-1 (pbk)
ISBN: 978-1-351-17048-2 (ebk)

Typeset in Sabon
by Swales & Willis, Exeter, Devon, UK

Dedicated to

Debby Boyer, Sarah Hearn, and Linda Smith
Without their support, collaboration, and commitment to improving school climate in Delaware this book would never have been written.

CONTENTS

	Illustrations	viii
	Preface	ix
	Acknowledgements	xi
	Contributing Author	xii
1	School Climate: An Albatross, Unicorn, or Phoenix?	1
2	Promoting Positive Teacher-Student Relationships	21
3	Promoting Positive Student-Student Relationships	34
4	Developing Social and Emotional Competencies and Self-Discipline CO-AUTHORED WITH ANGELA SOLTYS	47
5	Teacher-Centered Strategies for Preventing Behavior Problems	67
6	Correcting Behavior Problems	89
7	Fostering Student Engagement	114
8	Preventing and Reducing Bullying	129
9	School Safety: What Works and What Doesn't	147
10	Assessing School Climate and Linking Results to Effective Practices	167
	References	187
	Index	224

ILLUSTRATIONS

Figures

1.1	U.S. Department of Education's Model of School Climate	4
1.2	Conceptual Framework of School Climate	9

Tables

10.1	Scales and Subscales of the Delaware School Surveys (number of items is in parentheses)	170
10.2	Items on the Delaware School Climate Scale (Student Version)	172
10.3	Items on the Positive, Punitive, and SEL Techniques Scale	176
10.4	Items on the Delaware Bullying Victimization Scale	177
10.5	Items on the Delaware Student Engagement Scale (Student Version)	178
10.6	Items on the Delaware Student Social and Emotional Competencies Scale	179

PREFACE

When schools in Delaware first began implementing Schoolwide Positive Behavioral Supports and Interventions (SWPBIS) almost 20 years ago it quickly became evident to some of us working with that project that a reduction in office disciplinary referrals (ODRs) and suspensions and an increase in the distribution of tokens to students for good behavior did not necessarily indicate a positive school climate. Undoubtedly, reduced ODRs and suspensions and greater positive reinforcement of desired behavior were certainly needed in many schools. But, we soon recognized that there was much more to improving school climate than simply telling teachers to quit sending kids to the office for minor behavior problems and having them disseminate tokens for good behavior. Although those two indicators provided objective data that were easy to count, neither one informed schools if students actually improved in their behavior, or more importantly viewed their schools favorably. Did it matter much if a school had low ODRs and teachers distributed a lot of tokens if students thought that teachers were uncaring, if students did not get along with one another, if bullying was common, if students were not engaged, if students were not taught social and emotional skills, or if students and staff felt unsafe?

Supported by a wealth of research, as presented throughout this book, we thought that student perceptions in areas of school climate were more important than ODRs and other sources of data that schools were then using to gauge school improvement and to determine if their school was "positive." We observed a great need for valid and practical tools to assess important dimensions of school climate. We also observed the need for positive interventions and supports that went beyond the frequent and systematic use of positive reinforcement, especially distributing tokens for good behavior. The need for additional evidence-based strategies and interventions for developing social and emotional competence was evident in many schools, especially those where school climate was poor.

In response to those observations, over the past 15 years colleagues and I working at the University of Delaware's Center for Disabilities (CDS; and more specifically the SWPBIS and school climate projects) and with the Delaware Department of Education have developed and validated tools that assess multiple aspects of school climate and related constructs. They include the assessment of how students, teachers/staff, and/or parents perceive teacher-student relationships, student-student-relationships, student engagement, school safety, bullying, students' social and emotional competence, and teachers' use of techniques to prevent and correct behavior problems and to develop social and emotional competences.

This work has been supported with ongoing funding from the Delaware Department of Education and more recently with funding from a five-year School Climate Transformation Grant from the U.S. Department of Education. This grant has allowed us to focus not only on assessing school climate, but also on helping schools link assessment results to evidence-based practices for improving school climate. This book emanated from much of that work, but greatly expands on it by providing a strong theoretical and research foundation for improving school climate and by presenting educators with a wider range of evidence-based and practical interventions for improving school climate while simultaneously preventing and reducing behavior problems and fostering students' social, emotional, moral, and academic development. The strategies and interventions are grounded in an authoritative approach to classroom management, school discipline, and school climate that emphasizes the critical importance of social-emotional support and structure. The approach integrates strategies and interventions commonly found in the SWPBIS and Social and Emotional Learning (SEL) initiatives, while drawing from the strengths of each of those approaches and addressing its weaknesses. As seen throughout this book, such a comprehensive and integrative approach characterizes the most effective classroom teachers and schools.

ACKNOWLEDGEMENTS

I would like to acknowledge and thank the many individuals I have worked with in efforts to improve school climate in Delaware schools, each of whom contributed to this book in one way or another. Primary among them are my two principal collaborators for over 15 years at CDS (and the best bosses one can have): Debby Boyer, PBS Co-Project Director, and Sarah Hearn, PBS Project Coordinator. Of equal importance in the success of Delaware's school climate improvement efforts has been the support of Linda Smith (PBS Co-Project Director) and Mary Ann Mieczkowski (Director of Exceptional Children Resources) at the Delaware Department of Education.

I also would like to thank Megan Pell (Instructional Coach at CDS) and multiple doctoral students, past and present, who helped develop school climate assessment tools and intervention training modules, and consistently created a wonderful climate to work: Jessica Slaughter, Lindsey Mantz, Chunyan Yang, and Angela Soltys (Harris). Their time, creative energy, and wonderful dispositions have been greatly appreciated. Special thanks also go to the graduate research assistants in our educational specialist program in school psychology who spent hours and hours searching and carefully citing and editing references for the book: Natali Munoz and Fiona Lachman.

Finally, for their caring, listening, and other emotional support while writing this book I thank my wife (and exemplar of the authoritative approach to classroom management and parenting), Patti Bear, and our always attentive and loving two-year old golden retriever, Winnie the Pooh. Winnie was next to me in writing almost every word. I wish she could read what we wrote together.

CONTRIBUTING AUTHOR

Angela Soltys, MA, is a doctoral student in the school psychology program at the University of Delaware. Her research interests are in the areas of school climate, student engagement, social and emotional competence, and classroom management and disciplinary techniques. Angela co-authored Chapter 4, but also contributed to all other chapters by helping review and integrate the research literature.

CHAPTER 1

SCHOOL CLIMATE
An Albatross, Unicorn, or Phoenix?

In a comprehensive and classic review of the literature on school climate almost 40 years ago, Anderson (1982) posed a question that resonates today: Is school climate best viewed as an albatross, a unicorn, or a phoenix? As an albatross, school climate would be viewed as something undesirable—as "a burden" to policymakers "who need information on mechanisms that can be easily manipulated to affect student outputs" (p. 371). School climate, especially when viewed at that time by many as an unidimensional construct, failed to provide much guidance for school improvement. As a unicorn, however, school climate would be viewed by policymakers as something desired, yet unattainable, as something "to be hoped for and dreamt about but one which can never be found" (p. 371). If viewed as either an albatross or unicorn, it would be best for researchers to avoid school climate. This was because of unclear and inconsistent definitions and the lack of theoretical conceptualizations, measures, and guiding theories; difficulties with statistical analyses; and little research demonstrating the value of school climate and the effort for improvement. Researchers would be better off focusing on classroom effects on student behavior since they had been shown to be much greater than school level effects—a finding that is still true today (e.g., Bierman et al., 2007).

Instead of an albatross or unicorn, Anderson (1982) suggested that more optimistic educators and researchers might view school climate as a phoenix, as something desired and possible—"born of the ashes of past school effects research" (p. 372). But as a phoenix, school climate would need to be conceptualized not as a unidimensional, or singular, construct but as a multidimensional construct consisting of a combination of interrelated school characteristics shown to determine student learning and behavior, and ones that schools could successfully target for change. Those characteristics would be schoolwide, beyond the individual and classroom levels, reflecting the overall school environment. For a phoenix to arise, the greatest challenge to researchers was to address major shortcomings of earlier research on school climate. This called for (a) more clear and consistent definitions, conceptualizations, and measures of school climate; (b) theoretical frameworks to guide school climate research and practice, including how it is conceptualized and measured; (c) psychometrically sound measures of school climate; and (d) empirical research identifying domains or dimensions of school climate that schools could target for improvement to help achieve educationally important outcomes.

Rising of a Phoenix

At the time of Anderson's (1982) review of the literature, it is likely that a greater number of researchers and policymakers viewed school climate as an albatross or unicorn than a phoenix, as during that period school climate received little attention in educational research and practice. More recently, however, a phoenix has arisen, largely due to the great strides researchers and policymakers have made in addressing the major shortcomings of earlier research, as listed above. This is reflected in a rapidly growing body of research on school climate, as seen throughout this book, and in school climate being a focus of schoolwide programs for improving academic achievement, preventing behavior problems, and promoting social and emotional well-being. Those programs include universal-level social and emotional learning (SEL) programs that target the development of a wide range of social and emotional competencies, such as self-management, social awareness, and responsible decision-making (see Chapter 4); School-Wide Positive Behavioral Interventions and Supports (SWPBIS), which tend to focus more on the direct teaching and reinforcement of specific and desired student behaviors for improving school climate (Sailor, Dunlap, Sugai & Horner, 2009); and programs that are directed toward more specific problems or concerns, such as bullying (Swearer & Hymel, 2015) and on school violence and safety (Borum, Cornell, Modzeleski, & Jimerson, 2010).

Recognition of the importance of school climate also is seen in the following actions taken and funding and resources provided by the United States Department of Education (U.S. DOE):

- The Every Student Succeeds Act requiring that schools use a minimum of four accountability indicators, with one such indicator being school quality, which may consist of "school climate and safety" (see www.ed.gov/essa).
- Beginning in 2014 and continuing annually, the Office of Elementary and Secondary Education providing states and local education agencies with School Climate Transformation Grants to improve (and assess) school climate.
- Developing the web-based ED School Climate Survey (EDSCLS; U.S. DOE, Office of Safe and Healthy Schools, 2019a) for states and schools to assess students' perceptions of school climate in middle and high school, examine national data, and receive scores in real time.
- Developing a compendium of school climate measures for schools to draw from (see https://safesupportivelearning.ed.gov/topic-research/school-climate-measurement/school-climate-survey-compendium).
- Creating and disseminating school climate materials and resources to schools, including a *Quick Guide on Making School Climate Improvements* (U.S. DOE, Office of Safe and Healthy Students, 2016) and the *Parent and Educator Guide to School Climate Resources* (U.S. DOE, Office of Elementary and Secondary Education, 2019). These documents explain the concept of school climate, offer suggestions for improving school climate, and provide parents and educators with additional school climate resources.

How School Climate is Commonly Defined, Conceptualized, and Measured

How school climate is defined, conceptualized, and measured varies greatly in research, policy, and practice. Definitions of school climate differ in abstractness and the extent to which they recognize multiple domains and dimensions of school climate, and which ones are included and excluded. For example, among popular definitions appearing in the literature, Haynes, Emmons, and Ben-Avie (1997) defined school climate in rather general and abstract terms, with a specific focus on interpersonal relationships, or interactions, that influence children. That is, they defined school climate as "the quality and consistency of interpersonal interactions within the school community that influence children's cognitive, social, and psychological development" (p. 322). Placing greater emphasis on school safety, Cohen, McCabe, Michelli, and Pickeral (2009) defined school climate as "the quality and character of school life" that includes "norms, values, and expectations that support people feeling socially, emotionally, and physically safe" (p. 182).

In fairness to both of these teams of researchers, whereas their definitions were largely unidimensional, they conceptualized and measured school climate as a multi-dimensional construct. The School Climate Scale developed by Haynes, Emmons, and colleagues (Emmons, Haynes, & Comer, 2002; Haynes, Emmons, & Comer, 1994) includes the following six subscales: Student Interpersonal Relations, Student-Teacher Relations, Parent Involvement, Order and Discipline, Fairness, and Sharing of Resources. Likewise, Cohen et al. (2009), together with the National School Climate Council and the National School Climate Center (NSCC), conceptualized school climate as consisting of four major domains: relationships, safety, teaching and learning, and institutional environment. The NSCC (2019) also recently added leadership and professional relations and social media as additional domains of school climate (assessed on the teacher survey), although it is unclear why these two were added. The measure of school climate developed by the NSCC, the Comprehensive School Climate Inventory (NSCC, 2019b), includes 13 subscales: Rules and Norms, Sense of Physical Security, Sense of Social-Emotional Security, Support for Learning, Social and Civic Learning, Respect for Diversity, Social Support-Adults, Social Support-Students, School Connectedness/Engagement, Physical Surroundings, Social Media, Leadership, and Professional Relationships.

More recently, the National Center on Safe Supportive Learning Environments (2019) defined school climate as: "a broad, multifaceted concept that involves many aspects of the student's educational experience" while noting that a positive school climate is "the product of a school's attention to fostering safety; promoting a supportive academic, disciplinary, and physical environment; and encouraging and maintaining respectful, trusting, and caring relationships throughout the school community no matter the setting—from Pre-K/Elementary School to higher education."

In its *Parent and Educator Guide to School Climate Resources* (U.S. Department of Education, Office of Elementary and Secondary Education, 2019), and drawing from a description of school climate by the National Center on

4 *School Climate*

Safe and Supportive Learning Environments, the U.S. DOE recently characterized school climate as follows:

> School climate reflects how members of the school community experience the school, including interpersonal relationships, teacher and other staff practices, and organizational arrangements. School climate includes factors that serve as conditions for learning and that support physical and emotional safety, connection and support, and engagement. ... A positive school climate reflects attention to fostering social and physical safety, providing support that enables students and staff to realize high behavioral and academic standards as well as encouraging and maintaining respectful, trusting, and caring relationships throughout the school community.
>
> (p. 2)

This description emphasizes three general domains of school climate: connectedness and support (or relationships), safety, and engagement. These three domains also are found in the U.S. DOE's Safe and Supportive School Model of School Climate developed by a national panel of researchers and other experts on school climate for the U.S. DOE. That model was developed to guide schools in identifying key areas for creating "safe and supportive climates in their schools" (National Center on Safe Supportive Learning Environments, 2019). It now serves as the framework for the web-based ED School Climate Survey (EDSCLS; U.S. DOE, Office of Safe and Healthy Students, 2019), which is used by states, local education agencies, and schools to assess school climate. However, instead of calling categories connectedness and support, safety, and engagement, the three main categories are called engagement, safety, and environment. As shown in Figure 1.1, the model includes 13 domains subsumed under these three categories.

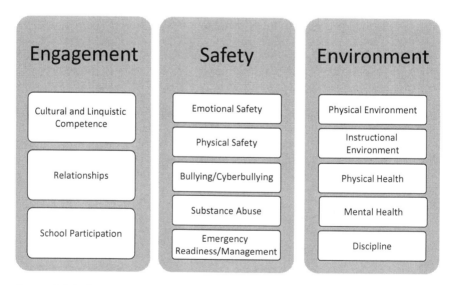

Figure 1.1 U.S. Department of Education's Model of School Climate

It is unclear how these domains and their contents originated, and why the contents were assigned to the given categories. For example, it is perplexing that the category of engagement includes relationships and school participation but excludes other elements of engagement commonly recognized among researchers, particularly cognitive and behavioral engagement. Instructional environment, which might be viewed as encompassing those two forms of engagement, is grouped under the category of environment which seems to consist of a hodgepodge of school environmental characteristics (i.e., physical environment, instructional environment, discipline) and other factors that are typically viewed by researchers as *outcomes* of those and other characteristics of school climate (i.e., mental health, physical health). It also is unclear why substance abuse is viewed as a distinct dimension of school climate (might one also include weapons?) and why there is a need to include five separate dimensions of safety (which are likely closely correlated, and unlikely distinct).

Perhaps most baffling is why the three categories for assessing school climate (engagement, safety, environment) differ from the three categories of school climate recognized elsewhere by the U.S. DOE as constituting school climate—connectedness and support, safety, and engagement. As discussed later, the latter three categories represent the three domains most widely recognized by researchers as representing the construct of school climate. Unfortunately, no supporting research is currently given in the technical manual (or on the government websites) to justify the inclusion of these three domains and what they comprise.

Common Domains of School Climate

As seen in the 13 subscales of the National Center for School Climate's Comprehensive School Climate Inventory and the 13 domains of school climate assessed in the U.S. DOE's Safe and Supportive School Model of School Climate (2019), measures and conceptualizations of school climate are often quite broad and vary greatly in what they include. Cornell and Huang (2019) note that such broad conceptual models and measures of school climate

> have the virtue of being comprehensive but may risk overinclusiveness and lose meaningfulness. If every aspect of a school is part of its climate, then it is not clear what the concept means and how it can be related to other important school characteristics.
>
> (p. 159)

They further comment that "The school's climate should be distinguishable from other elements of the school environment, such as the condition of the building, the quality of its teachers, its curriculum, or the demographics of its students. Otherwise, the term *school climate* means little more than 'the school'" (p. 159).

Fortunately, reviews of the research literature have identified a small number of domains, typically four or five, that are common across measures of school climate. Zullig, Koopman, Patton, and Ubbes (2010) identified five domains: (1) social relationships (teacher-student and student-student); (2) order, safety, and discipline; (3) academic outcomes; (4) school facilities; and (5) school connectedness (e.g., liking of school). Note that the domain of school connectedness is often included on other measures under the domain of relationships or community; thus, one might argue that the review identified four, not five, domains.

In their review of measures of school climate, Ramelow, Currie, and Felder-Puig (2015) found that of the four domains of school climate identified by Cohen et al. (2009) (i.e., relationships, safety, teaching and learning, and institutional environment) the domains of relationships and safety (which included rules and expectations) were most often found on measures of school climate, whereas the domain of teaching and learning and the domain of environmental-structural were found the least. Interestingly, they found no measure that included all four domains.

In a more comprehensive review of the research literature, which included 297 empirical studies, Wang and Degol (2016) concluded that school climate was best conceptualized as comprised of four broad domains: community, safety, academic, and institutional environment. Within those four domains they further identified 13 more specific dimensions, with the community domain consisting of quality of relationships (teacher-student and teacher-staff), connectedness (i.e., sense of belonging), respect for diversity (including fairness and autonomy), and partnership (i.e., parent involvement); the safety domain consisting of social/emotional safety (including lack of bullying), discipline and order (including fairness and clarity of school rules), and physical safety; the academic domain consisting of teaching and learning, professional development, and administrative leadership; and the institutional environment consisting of structural organization (e.g., class size, school size, ability grouping) and availability of resources (i.e., supplies, materials, equipment). The authors cited research linking each of the four domains to valued academic, behavioral, and psychological and social outcomes for students, while recognizing that the research base is stronger for the academic and community domains than for the safety and institutional environment domains. They also found that few measures included the institutional environment domain.

In sum, although there is no one commonly recognized definition of school climate and reviews of the literature find that measures of school climate vary greatly in their composition, there is growing consensus among researchers that school climate includes four broad domains: (1) interpersonal relationships (also referred to as social support, connectedness, and community); (2) safety, order, and discipline (also referred to as structure); (3) engagement (also referred to as academics or teaching and learning); and (4) institutional environment (also called school facilities, environmental-structural). Reviews conclude, however, that the fourth domain is seldom found on measures of school climate, and when found it varies greatly as to what aspects of the institutional environment are assessed.

Several other conclusions are commonly shared by reviewers of the literature (Anderson, 1982; Cornell & Huang, 2019; Ramelow et al., 2015; Wang & Degol, 2016)—conclusions that should guide the development, or a school's choice, of school climate measures. First, very few measures have been guided by a theoretical framework. Models and measures of school climate vary greatly in the number and type of domains or dimensions included, and it is often unclear theoretically why some school characteristics or domains are included or excluded and how those included are related to one another and to valued educational and student outcomes. Second, many measures also lack sufficient evidence of validity and reliability. This includes the frequent lack of empirical evidence supporting how the measure is conceptualized and documenting that its various dimensions are not measuring one and the same thing (e.g., demonstrating via factor analysis that respect for diversity is not the same as positive student-student relationships, or that emotional safety and mental health are not the same).

Third, a major purpose of assessing school climate should be to guide school improvement efforts. As such, school climate measures should focus on those aspects of school climate that are most malleable, and ones that researchers have shown can readily and effectively be targeted for improvement. As noted by Cornell and Huang (2019):

> A useful conception of school climate should provide a model of how features of school climate interact with one another, how school climate relates to independent student and school outcomes, and, most important, how school personnel can take action to improve school climate and generate more favorable outcomes for their students. Favorable outcomes should include both academic and nonacademic benefits, such as higher academic achievement and employment, healthy social-emotional adjustment, and development of good citizenship and character reflecting individual responsibility and respect for others.
>
> (p. 162)

Proposed Definition and Theoretical Framework

Avoiding the common mistake of defining school climate too abstractly or too broadly, in this book school climate refers to four interrelated and malleable characteristics of a school that foster students' academic achievements and their social and emotional development:

- *social and emotional support*, as seen in caring and respectful interpersonal relationships and responsiveness to students' basic psychological needs
- *structure*, as seen as high behavioral expectations, fair disciplinary practices, and an orderly and safe learning environment
- *student engagement*, as seen in students being emotionally, cognitively, and behaviorally engaged in school
- *safety*, as evidenced by students and teachers/staff feeling safe (which includes the absence of bullying)

As shown previously, these four domains are commonly found in models and popular measures of school climate. More so than other domains found in the literature, they also are more consistently shown to be related to two of the foremost aims of education: academic achievement and social and emotional development or competence of students. As illustrated in Figure 1.2, the four domains are interrelated, influencing one another in a dynamic and bidirectional fashion. Although interrelated, the four domains are conceptually distinct, as supported in a number of research studies on measures of school climate that included factors corresponding to the four domains. Studies tend to report moderate correlations between the factors, which indicate that they tap into a similar global construct (i.e., school climate). Yet, as revealed in results of confirmatory factor analyses, the four domains and dimensions within them are conceptually distinct (e.g., Bear, Gaskins, Blank, & Chen, 2011; Bear et al., 2019; Brand, Felner, Shim, Seitsinger, & Dumas, 2003). In practice, examples of viewing the domains as closely related but separate would include the recognition that although both high social-emotional support and structure characterize the most effective teachers and schools, it is not uncommon to find a teacher or school lacking in one of those two domains. This is often seen in teachers and schools with an authoritarian, or zero-tolerance, approach to school discipline that emphasizes structure, using harsh practices, while neglecting social-emotional support (Bear, 2010). Viewing the domains as interrelated yet distinct also would include the understanding that while social and emotional support and structure largely determine student engagement, they do not ensure it, as many other factors, including individual child, peer, and home factors, greatly influence the extent to which students are emotionally, cognitively, or behaviorally engaged in school.

Although the framework focuses on the school, or students in aggregate, it also applies to individual students. It recognizes that at both the school and individual levels the effects between the four domains are multidirectional, and that those effects, separately or combined, also influence academic achievement and social and emotional development in a bidirectional manner. For example, just as social-emotional support and structure influence engagement and perceptions of safety, so too can engagement and perceptions of safety influence social-emotional support and structure. This is seen in a lack of student engagement harming interpersonal relationships and influencing a teacher's responsiveness to a student's psychological needs. Likewise, a bidirectional relation exists between student engagement and the valued outcomes of academic achievement and social and emotional development. For example, student engagement largely determines academic achievement at the school and individual student levels, but so is student engagement influenced by beliefs, values, and competencies of students at the school and individual student levels.

The framework is not intended to include all factors that are viewed as parts of school climate or are known to influence academic achievement and students' social and emotional development. Thus, demographic factors (e.g., gender, race, socioeconomic status, urban vs rural, school size), the physical environment of the school, administrative leadership and organization, the mental health and training of teachers and staff, and factors outside of the school are deliberately excluded. This is to avoid the mistake, as warned by Cornell and Huang (2019), of construing school climate so broadly that it loses meaningfulness. Those factors also are excluded, however, because they are difficult to change (e.g., demographic factors, factors outside of school), their relation to valued outcomes is debatable or minimal (physical environment of the school), or they constitute factors that few school climate intervention teams that examine school climate data would care or be qualified to address (e.g., administrative leadership, the mental health of teachers and staff).

The theoretical framework for conceptualizing school climate as consisting primarily of social and emotional support, structure, student engagement, and safety emanates from research and current theories of human development, as discussed in the following three sections, that support the importance of each

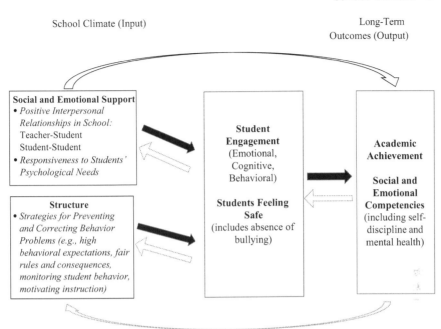

Figure 1.2 Conceptual Framework of School Climate

domain in academic achievement and social and emotional development. In the first section, each of the four domains is described and research is summarized that links it with students' academic achievement and social and emotional development. Next, the authoritative approach to parenting, classroom management, and school discipline is discussed and applied to school climate. Supported by research and theory, this approach serves as a foundation for the framework and its emphasis on social-emotional support and structure. It also forms the basis of many practices recommended throughout the book for improving school climate, including practices for preventing and correcting behavior problems and developing social and emotional competencies. Finally, developmental theories supporting the framework are presented.

Social and Emotional Support

This domain incorporates two closely related dimensions: interpersonal relationships (teacher-student and student-student) and responsiveness to students' basic psychological needs of relatedness, competence, and autonomy.

Interpersonal relationships. In school this refers to how students, teachers, and staff relate to one another. It is widely recognized as a critical component of school climate, as seen previously in all reviews of the literature identifying it as such. As reviewed in Chapter 2 on teacher-student relationships, a wealth of research shows students' perceptions of their teachers as caring, respectful, supportive, and accepting are associated with multiple positive outcomes, including greater academic engagement and achievement (Fredricks, Blumenfeld, & Paris, 2004), greater prosocial behaviors (Luckner & Pianta, 2011; Obsuth et al., 2017), and fewer antisocial and aggressive behaviors (Obsuth et al., 2017). When such perceptions exist, students are more willing to cooperate with school rules and adult expectations out of respect and a desire to maintain the positive teacher-student relationship rather than fear of punishment or promise of rewards (Wentzel, 1997, 2006). Likewise, as reviewed in Chapter 3, a number of positive outcomes are associated with supportive student-student relationships. They include less acting out, aggression, and delinquent behaviors (Brand et al., 2003; Demaray & Malecki, 2002; Sturaro, van Lier, Cuijpers, & Koot, 2011), and fewer internalizing problems, such as loneliness, low self-esteem, depression, and suicide (Brand et al., 2003; Spilt, van Lier, Leflot, Onghena, & Colpin, 2014). When poor peer relationships exist, students are at much greater risk for low academic achievement (Buhs, Ladd, & Herald, 2006; Perdue, Manzeske, & Estell, 2009), avoiding school (Buhs et al., 2006), and not completing school (French & Conrad, 2003). Bullying also is much more to likely to occur in classes and schools where peer support, respect, and acceptance are lacking (Jenkins & Demaray, 2012; Wang, Iannotti, & Nansel, 2009). Furthermore, as with teacher-student relationships, when students view student-student relationships as caring and supportive, students are more likely to stand up against bullies, and bystanders are more likely to intervene (Rigby & Johnson, 2006; Saarento, Kärnä, Hodges, & Salmivalli, 2013).

Responsiveness. Support from teachers and peers entails not only social support in meeting the need for relatedness, but additional forms of support (referred to as responsiveness) are necessary to meet additional needs in areas of social and emotional development, especially those of autonomy and competence. Positive interpersonal relationships certainly help meet those two needs, but they are not sufficient. For example, students might feel that others accept, respect, and care about them but nevertheless fail to experience a sense of autonomy and competence. Autonomy refers to one's belief that he or she chooses, controls, and determines his or her own behavior. Competence refers to feeling successful in areas that one values, which among students typically include interpersonal relations, academics, and behavioral conduct (Harter, 2006). Positive self-worth, or self-esteem, and motivation require that individuals experience a healthy balance of social support (or relatedness), autonomy, and competence (Ryan & Deci, 2017).

An emphasis on responsiveness to students' developmental needs, which extends beyond responsiveness to the need for relatedness, is supported by the classic work on parenting by Baumrind (1971, 2013). As discussed later in this chapter, Baumrind found that what she labeled *responsiveness*, and when combined with *demandingness* (similar to what is referred to as structure in school climate), characterizes the most effective style of parenting. As described by Baumrind (2013, p.26): "*Responsiveness* refers to parents' emotional warmth and supportive actions that are attuned to children's vulnerabilities, cognitions, and inputs and are supportive of children's individual needs and plans."

Warmth and caring are certainly part of social and emotional support but are insufficient for meeting children's psychological needs. Social and emotional support requires more deliberate and direct actions, within the context of supportive relationships, that teach and promote competencies of social, emotional, and moral development, such as social perspective-taking, empathy, and responsible decision-making. Actions for developing those competencies are the focus of Chapter 4. That chapter includes research linking social and emotional competence to highly valued outcomes which include student engagement, academic achievement, prosocial behavior, and mental health.

Structure

Structure, or what Baumrind (2013) called *demandingness*, refers to adults presenting clear and high behavioral and academic expectations; providing necessary supervision and monitoring of student behavior; and having fair rules, while enforcing them consistently and fairly. When correcting misbehavior, persuasion, guidance, and reasoning is preferred over punishment and external control, but the latter are used when needed. In the context of school, structure includes teaching that is motivating and promotes student engagement and academic achievement. Research shows that such preventive and corrective actions, especially when combined with responsiveness, characterize not only the most effective parents (Baumrind, 2013), but also the most effective teachers and schools (Arum, 2003; Bear, 2005, 2015; Brophy, 1996). Students' perceptions of clear and fair behavioral expectations, rules, and consequences are associated with greater prosocial behavior (Bradshaw, Waasdorp, & Leaf, 2012), greater student engagement and academic achievement (Benner, Graham, & Mistry, 2008; Welsh, 2000, 2003), and fewer behavior problems and disruptive behavior (Arum, 2003; Bradshaw et al., 2012; Gottfredson, Gottfredson, Payne, & Gottfredson, 2005; Welsh, 2000, 2003), including bullying and peer victimization (Gregory, Skiba, & Noguera, 2010; Waasdorp, Bradshaw, & Leaf, 2012).

Engagement

As discussed in Chapter 7, student engagement refers to the extent to which students value and are involved in academic and social activities in school (Li & Lerner, 2013; Reeve, 2013). Student engagement exists in three forms: emotional, behavioral, and cognitive (Fredricks et al., 2004; Lee & Shute, 2010; Reschly & Christenson, 2013). In general, emotional engagement refers to students' positive and negative affective reactions and feelings toward school, behavioral engagement to behaviors that indicate that students follow school rules and are actively involved in academic and other school-related activities, and cognitive engagement to the desire and willingness among students to exert their best effort toward learning (Fredricks et al., 2004; Lee & Shute, 2010). As reviewed in Chapter 7, a wealth of research shows that social-emotional support and structure foster student engagement (e.g., Cornell, Shukla, & Konold, 2016) and that student engagement leads to greater academic achievement and fewer behavior problems (Baroody, Rimm-Kaufman, Larsen, & Curby, 2016; Wang & Eccles, 2012a) as well as overall social-emotional well-being (Osterman, 2000).

Feelings of Safety

Feelings of safety are closely related to behavioral, cognitive, and emotional engagement, and especially the latter. Emotional engagement entails liking and enjoying school. It is difficult to imagine a student feeling unsafe but liking and enjoying school. However, feeling safe does not ensure student engagement, as many students feel safe but are lacking in cognitive, behavioral, and emotional engagement. Thus, safety and engagement are viewed in the framework as two separate yet interrelated constructs.

Feeling safe, or emotional safety, also is viewed as separate from physcial safety. Physical safety generally refers to actions, including structure-based practices, taken by schools with the intention of increasing the actual safety of students. The effectiveness of those actions is typically measured by indicators assessing violent and criminal activities (and often with little concern about emotional safety). As discussed in Chapter 9 on safety, many actions taken by schools with the intent to ensure physical safety do not enhance students' perceptions of safety. Indeed, as discussed in that chapter, too often safety measures have the opposite effect, leading students to experience greater anxiety and fear about their safety, to feel less safe, and to dislike school. This is seen in a zero tolerance approach to school discipline that emphasizes suspensions and the pervasive use of security measures such as school resource officers, cameras, and metal detectors (especially when not needed, such as in schools with no history of violence). As discussed and recommended in Chapter 9, it is a combination of practices associated with social-emotional support and structure that lead to both greater physical and emotional safety.

Academic Achievement and Social and Emotional Development as the Primary Aims of Education

As reflected in the last panel of the framework presented in Figure 1.2, school climate, consisting of four domains, is associated with two highly valued educational outcomes commonly targeted in school improvement efforts: academic achievement and social and emotional development (or competence). Academic achievement, as typically assessed by standardized tests, is fairly self-explanatory and thus will not be discussed here. As mentioned previously, and documented throughout this book, ample research shows that social-emotional support and structure determine student engagement, which in turn, determines academic achievement. Because the category of social and emotional development is less clear and more encompassing, it requires greater attention.

In the framework, social and emotional competence is used as a general term that refers to knowledge, beliefs, values, and behaviors associated with self-discipline and mental health (or emotional well-being). In education the term is often used interchangeably with self-discipline, civic responsibility, and mental health. As used in this book, social and emotional development subsumes the five social and emotional learning (SEL) competencies recognized by the Collaboration for Social and Emotional Learning (CASEL; see www.casel.org). Those five competencies underlie self-discipline. For centuries, educators have viewed self-discipline as critical to American democracy grounded in individual rights and self-governance (Bear, 2005; McClellan, 1999). In support of self-discipline as a primary aim of education, a 2000 Gallup poll found that the general public believed that the most important purpose of public education is "to prepare students to be responsible citizens" (Rose & Gallup, 2000). Self-discipline refers to students regulating their own behavior with minimal adult monitoring and control (Bear, 2005, 2010). It includes a moral component—more than positive social relationships or getting along with others. That is, it entails knowing what's right, desiring to do what is right, and doing what is right (Bear, 2005; Rest, 1983). This includes inhibiting or regulating antisocial, disrespectful, harmful behavior and assuming responsibility for one's actions. But, it also includes exhibiting prosocial behaviors such as helping, respecting, and caring about others (Bear, 2005). Adding the moral component highlights that self-discipline and civic responsibility should not be driven by self-centered or hedonistic moral reasoning based on external rewards or fear of punishment but instead on understanding the impact of one's behavior on others (individually and collectively), the anticipation of feelings of guilt, and an appreciation of rules, laws, property rights, and moral principles of trust, respect, and honesty.

In the framework, social and emotional competence includes mental health. Mental health consists of the absence of mental or behavioral disorders; the presence of subjective well-being, or happiness and life satisfaction; and the ability to cope with adversity (National Research Council and Institute of Medicine, 2009). Consistent with self-determination theory (Ryan & Deci, 2017), as discussed later in this chapter, mental health requires that students' psychological needs of relatedness, competence, and autonomy be met. Indeed, mental health is largely defined by individuals interacting positively with others and feeling a sense of belongingness or connectedness with others, feeling competent in areas of importance in their lives, and experiencing a sense of autonomy.

Students' social and emotional competence, or mental health, is positively related to their academic achievement, although the association tends to be small (O'Connor, Cloney, Dvalsvig, & Goldfeld, 2019). Both variables are influenced by multiple factors in students' lives and school climate is among them. As illustrated in Figure 1.2, social-emotional support and structure influence academic achievement and social and emotional competence directly and indirectly through their impact on engagement and feelings of safety. Supported by longitudinal studies examining relations between domains of school climate and valued outcomes (e.g., Jiang, Huebner, & Siddall, 2013; Wang & Eccles, 2012a), the framework also recognizes that the relations are bidirectional but with the influences of the four domains of school climate on academic achievement being stronger than that of academic achievement and social and emotional competence on school climate.

Authoritative Approach to Parenting, Classroom Management, and School Discipline Applied to School Climate

An emphasis on social and emotional support, and particularly responsiveness, and on structure, follows from the classic work on parenting by Diana Baumrind (1971) first published over half a decade ago. Baumrind identified three styles of parenting and the behaviors of children associated with each style. Since then a wealth of research has supported and extended her findings (see Baumrind, 2013 for review). The three styles are *authoritative*, *authoritarian*, and *permissive*.

A fourth style, *uninvolved* or *neglectful*, was identified later by researchers, but is not included here since it pertains very little to school climate and school discipline. Baumrind found that what largely differentiates the three styles is the extent to which each style is characterized by a combination of responsiveness and demandingness. The least effective styles of parenting are authoritarian and permissive, with authoritarian parents being high in demandingness but low in responsiveness, and permissive parents being high in permissiveness and low in demandingness. Authoritative parents are high in both qualities. Compared to children of permissive and authoritarian parents, children of authoritative parents have greater academic achievement, and exhibit more prosocial behaviors and fewer antisocial behaviors (Dornbusch, Ritter, Leiderman, Roberts, & Fraleigh, 1987; Steinberg, Elmen, & Mounts, 1989).

As noted previously, and discussed further in Chapters 5 and 6, research in the areas of classroom management and school discipline have consistently supported an authoritative approach (Bear, 2015). Authoritative teachers and staff strive to build and maintain positive and supportive relationships with students, between students, and between the home and school. Additional and deliberate actions are taken to be responsive to students' needs, which include developing social and emotional competencies that underlie self-discipline.

Authoritative adults expect students to exhibit self-discipline, and they *demand* appropriate behavior. They understand that social-emotional support and structure are intertwined and dependent on one another, and that a healthy balance of the two is required for effective classroom management and school discipline. They recognize that when students perceive teacher-student and student-relationships favorably, they are much more motivated to follow rules and to internalize the prosocial values and norms that schools aim to communicate (Hughes, 2002; Wentzel, 2002). Authoritative adults also recognize that when structure is lacking, as seen in low behavioral expectations and unfair rules and consequences, students tend to have little respect for their teachers (McKnight, Graybeal, Yarbro, & Graybeal, 2016).

Responsiveness and demandingness (or structure) refer not only to environmental conditions that foster self-discipline but also to student-centered strategies that parents and educators use to develop children's social and emotional competencies. For example, whereas demandingness includes structures such as high expectations, fair rules, and monitoring student behavior, another key component is *confrontative control*. Confrontative control is not to be confused with coercive control. As noted by Baumrind (2013, p. 19), "Confrontative control is demanding, firm, and goal-directed, whereas coercive control is intrusive, manipulative, punitive, autonomy undermining, and restrictive (Patterson, 1982)." Whereas confrontative control is intended to bring about willing compliance, coercive control brings about grudging compliance and at times outright disobedience. Confrontative control challenges ways of thinking and emotions, as well as the lack of thinking and emotions, associated with antisocial behavior such as blaming others and making excuses, acting impulsively or in anger, failing to apply skills in one's repertoire, and not accepting responsibility for one's actions. It is intended to help develop thought patterns and emotions that inhibit antisocial behavior and promote prosocial behavior, in hopes that they will be applied in the future. Although students are encouraged to express their own opinions and actively participate in decision-making, and autonomy is highly valued, harmful actions are never accepted. Instead, they are always challenged, and sanctions are imposed when students fail to act in a morally responsible manner (Morris, Cui, & Steinberg, 2013).

Authoritative Approach Applied to School Climate

Applied to a model of school climate, an emphasis on responsiveness and demandingness was seen in Stockard and Mayberry's (1992) theoretical framework of school climate. However, Stockard and Mayberry did not draw from or base their framework on Baumrind's research. They conducted a comprehensive review of the sociological, psychological, and economic theories and research of organizations, which included the effective schools and school climate literatures. Based on their review, they concluded that school climate is best conceptualized as consisting of two broad dimensions: *social action* and *social order*. Social action is similar to responsiveness, or social support, in authoritative discipline theory, with its emphasis on the everyday social interactions among teachers, staff, and students (i.e., the presence of caring, understanding, concern, and respect). Social order is similar to demandingness, or structure, with its primary goal being to curtail behavior problems and promote safety.

Although studies of school climate in general support Stockard and Mayberry's school climate framework, very few have focused specifically on social action and social order as conceptualized in the framework. Exceptions, however, are several studies conducted by Griffith (1995, 1997) which found that elementary school students' perceptions of social action and social order, and particularly the former, were related to their self-reports of academic performance and satisfaction.

Only recently has the authoritative discipline approach been applied more specifically to school climate, with social support and structure recognized as its two primary components, as found on the Delaware School Climate Survey-Student (DSCS-S) Bear et al., 2011, Bear et al., 2019) and the Authoritative School Climate Scale (Cornell, 2015). On both measures, structure is quite similar to Baumrind's demandingness. However, social support differs from Baumrind's responsiveness in placing almost exclusive emphasis on interpersonal relations while not recognizing other ways in which adults are responsive to the social and emotional needs of students.

When applied to school climate, an authoritative school climate has been found to be associated with the following:

- fewer behavior problems (Bear et al., 2011; Wang, Selman, Dishion, & Stormshak, 2010)
- fewer school suspensions from school (Bear et al., 2011, 2019; Gregory, Cornell, & Fan, 2011; Huang & Cornell, 2018)
- less bullying and bullying victimization (Cornell, Shukla, & Konold, 2015; Gregory et al., 2010)
- less student aggression toward teachers (Berg & Cornell, 2016; Gregory, Cornell, & Fan, 2012)
- less risk behavior, including weapon carrying and substance use (Cornell & Huang, 2016)

- less truancy and dropping out (Pellerin, 2005)
- greater engagement (Cornell et al., 2016; Lee, 2012)
- greater academic achievement (Bear et al., 2011; Gregory et al., 2010; Konold et al., 2014; Lee, 2012)

Theoretical Support for the Framework in This Book

Although it is well established that school climate, irrespective of how it is defined or conceptualized, is related to the academic achievement and social and emotional adjustment of students, the processes that account for the effects of school climate are much less clear. This includes how social support and structure foster engagement and feelings of safety and, in turn, academic achievement and social and emotional adjustment. Five theories, models, and frameworks in educational, social, and developmental psychology provide explanation and have guided much of the research related to school climate: the bioecological model, social control theory, attachment theory, social cognitive theory, and self-determination theory. Each is discussed briefly below.

Bioecological Model, or Ecological Systems Theory, of Human Development.
The most popular theory or model for explaining the impact of school climate on student behavior has been Bronfenbrenner's model or theory of human development (Bronfenbrenner, 1979; Bronfenbrenner & Ceci, 1994). Calling it an ecological systems theory of human development earlier in his career, and with a primary focus on environmental and social factors influencing behavior, Bronfenbrenner later labelled it a bioecological model in greater recognition of the important role of individual influences on behavior as well as on one's environment. As noted by Wang and Degol (2016) in their review of the measures of school climate, Bronfenbrenner's model is "one of the theoretical pillars of school climate research" (p. 319).

Bronfenbrenner first developed his ecological systems theory of human development to explain how poverty and other environmental factors influenced children's development (and the need for early intervention programs such as Head Start). At the core of the theory is that human behavior is influenced by the dynamic interaction of multiple environmental, societal, and individual factors. The factors operate and interact at different systemic levels, ranging from the home, community, and society to the more immediate school or classroom environment (i.e., the microsystem). Factors influence one another in an ongoing, dynamic, bidirectional or multidirectional, and contextual-specific fashion. The theory recognizes that whereas multiple systems of the environment influence how students think, feel, and act, students also influence their environments. Applied to school climate, the theory would posit that support and structure are among multiple factors that determine if students are academically engaged and if prosocial or antisocial behavior is more prevalent, but also would recognize that student engagement and behavior influence support and structure. For example, when students are engaged and self-discipline is evident, less structure is needed and the social support of peers and adults is often more readily provided.

The model clearly recognizes that multiple distal and proximal factors influence student behavior. Within the context of school climate, emphasis is placed on social relationships (e.g., a student's relationship with the teacher, peers, and family) and on values and norms that influence how students think and act (Swearer & Hymel, 2015).

Social Control Theory. The bioecological model and social control theory share many of the same tenets, with an emphasis on multiple environmental determinants of behavior. They differ, however, in that the bioecological model was intended to be a more general theory of human development, whereas the latter was intended to explain delinquent acts. Hirschi's (1969) social control theory emphasizes the influence of social bonds, which are of four types: attachment, commitment, involvement, and belief. Individuals are most likely to break social norms and commit delinquent acts when one or more of those social bonds are lacking or are broken. For example, when relationships are close and supportive (i.e., the social bond of attachment to others, and school, exists), students are more likely to internalize values and moral codes shared by teachers and classmates. They also more willingly refrain from harmful and deviant behavior because they want to maintain the bond of attachment with others. Similarly, when students feel committed and actively involved, or engaged, in school activities, they are less likely to exhibit delinquent behaviors. The same applies to students believing that rules are fair and feeling committed to following them: Under those conditions students are more likely to exhibit normative behavior and to inhibit delinquent behaviors.

Attachment Theory. Another theory that emphasizes the importance of relationships and social-emotional support in deterring behavior problems and fostering engagement and psychological well-being is attachment theory (Ainsworth, 1989; Bowlby, 1969). According to this theory, it is through their early interactions with caregivers that children create *internal working models of attachment*. Those working models determine how children relate to others in the future, feelings of safety, and the degree to which behavior is independent/autonomous or dependent on others. Whereas secure attachments foster close and trusting relationships with others, feelings of safety, independent/autonomous behavior, and positive self-esteem, insecure attachments lead to the opposite and thus are associated with multiple negative social, emotional, and academic outcomes, including delinquency (Fearon, Bakermans-Kranenburg, van IJzendoorn, Lapsley, & Roisman, 2010).

Although attachment theory has most commonly been applied to parenting, and especially parenting during infancy and early childhood, it also applies to teacher-student relationships and students of all ages (Pianta, 1999). When teacher-student relationships are positive, or secure, the psychological needs of students are likely to be met, as students can count on their teachers providing necessary social and emotional support. For example, students are more inclined to talk to their teachers when they have problems, such as when being bullied (Eliot, Cornell, Gregory, & Fan, 2010). Additionally, when relationships are positive and students feel secure, they experience less stress and greater self-confidence, self-efficacy, and engagement in learning and are less likely to violate existing norms (Ahnert, Harwardt-Heinecke, Kappler, Eckstein-Madry, & Milatz, 2012).

Social cognitive Theory. As with the theories discussed above, and applied to school climate, social cognitive theory emphasizes the dynamic and reciprocal interaction of the student (including the student's cognitions and emotions), the environment, and behavior. However, it provides greater guidance as to the self-regulatory thought processes (and to a lesser extent emotions) of students that programs might address for promoting prosocial behavior and a positive school climate. Among the additional contributions of social cognitive theory to explaining how school climate influences student behavior (and vice versa) is recognition of the influences of internal and external reinforcement, observational learning and modeling, and self-regulatory systems, especially goals and expectations, self-efficacy (i.e., one's competence in successfully performing a behavior), and mechanisms of moral disengagement. Mechanisms of moral disengagement, as discussed in Chapter 4, are unique to cognitive-behavior theory, and help explain why students often commit immoral acts, such as bullying, lying, stealing, and cheating, despite being taught and knowing why they are wrong.

Self-determination Theory. As noted earlier in this chapter, self-determination theory emphasizes the importance of meeting three basic psychological needs for children to be motivated and engaged in learning and to be socially and emotionally adjusted. Those needs are relatedness, confidence, and autonomy. In school, each of those needs is met in the context of supportive teacher-student and student-student relationships. It is interactions with teachers and peers that largely determine not only if students experience a sense of belonging, or relatedness, but also feelings of competence and autonomy. Structure also is important, however, as students are unlikely to feel competent and experience a sense of autonomy, irrespective of supportive relationships, in schools that emphasize external control of behavior, especially with harsh punitive practices, and fail to develop students' social and emotional competencies.

Positive school climates help meet students' psychological needs by promoting higher self-esteem, self-confidence, and satisfaction with school (Croninger & Lee, 2001; Demaray & Malecki, 2002; Jiang et al., 2013; Spilt et al., 2014), as well as greater academic engagement and achievement (Danielsen, Wiium, Wilhelmsen, & Wold, 2010; Wentzel, Barry, & Caldwell, 2004). These student characteristics have been shown to serve as major protective factors in bullying and bullying victimization (Zych, Farrington, & Ttofi, 2018).

Closely associated with self-determination theory is stage-environment fit theory (Eccles & Midgley, 1989). It too recognizes the critical importance of the environment (e.g., school) meeting the psychological needs of students, especially during the transition from elementary to middle school. Students are academically motivated and engaged when the school environment fits their psychological needs, which includes the needs for autonomy, competence, and relatedness (Zimmer-Gembeck, Chipuer, Hanisch, Creed, & Mcgregor, 2006).

In sum, the five theories above explain the dynamic and reciprocal effects between school climate and student behavior while highlighting multiple influencing factors at the school level that are malleable and align with the four domains of school climate emphasized in the model presented in this chapter. Whereas each theory helps explain how support, structure, engagement, and safety influence academic achievement and social, emotional, and moral development, they vary in the attention given to each domain and the mechanisms of influence. For example, attachment theory, self-determination theory, and social control theory place great emphasis on the importance of interpersonal relationships and responsiveness (i.e., the social and emotional support domain). In addition to the social and emotional domain, social control theory also emphasizes the critical role of student engagement, whereas self-determination theory and social-cognitive theory, which are more cognitively-based, emphasize that actions within the domains of structure, engagement, and safety are necessary to help meet students' psychological needs. Bioecological theory, the more general of the five theories, supports the importance of each of the four domains, recognizing that multiple factors at multiple system levels influence school climate and student behavior.

Although emphasized more so in bioecological and social-cognitive theories than the other two theories, each of the five theories share the view that multiple environmental factors influence student behavior, but it is how students perceive those environmental factors, rather than objective reality per se, that matters the most. This applies to school climate and each of its four domains and to the impact of school climate on the academic achievement and social, emotional, and moral development. For example, a school might document actions based on objective criteria or subjective opinion that it believes show that teachers and staff are caring, supportive, and responsive to students' needs; that rules and expectations are clear; that the curriculum is motivating and challenging (based on claims of teachers); and that the school is safe (as seen in security measures being in place, or by suspending students who are viewed as threatening school safety). But if students fail to *perceive* those actions the same way and view the school climate unfavorably then it is the students' perceptions rather than what is reported by the school that will best predict student academic achievement and student behavior. Because students' perceptions of school climate are the best predictors of their behavior, most studies, about 90%, use student surveys to measure school climate (Wang & Degol, 2016).

Conclusion and Implications for Practice

In this chapter it was argued that instead of viewing school climate as an albatross or unicorn, it should be viewed as a phoenix—with school climate demonstrating new life and promise. Its regeneration has been fanned by a wealth of new measures and research documenting that school climate is related to multiple valued outcomes, including students' academic achievement, behavior, and mental health, and by major initiatives of the U.S. Department of Education to encourage schools to target school climate in school improvement efforts. How long it will be before the phoenix returns again to its ashes will likely be determined by the effectiveness of those efforts. For those efforts to succeed, educators need more consistent definitions, conceptual frameworks or models, and measures of school climate, grounded in research and theory, to guide the implementation of practical and effective interventions. This chapter offered a definition and conceptual framework of school climate, grounded in research and theory, for that purpose. Measures that align with the definition and conceptual framework and are designed to help schools identify their school climate strengths and needs are the focus of Chapter 10.

The conceptual framework focuses on malleable characteristics of schools, including mechanisms and practices for change, that have been shown to lead to greater academic achievement and social-emotional competencies, including fewer behavior problems and the mental health of students. School characteristics are subsumed under four domains of school climate: social-emotional support, structure, engagement, and safety. Throughout the remaining chapters, evidence-based strategies and interventions within each of those domains are presented for improving school climate. The chapters align roughly with the four domains, although the strategies and interventions focus on improvements within the given domain (e.g., improving teacher-student relations). It should be understood that those improvements help achieve the longer-term aims of academic achievement and social-emotional competencies. Chapters 2, 3, and 4 address the domain of social-emotional support, with Chapter 2 presenting recommendations for improving teacher-student relationships, Chapter 3 for improving student-student relationships, and Chapter 4 for developing social, emotional, and moral competencies that underlie self-discipline.

Aligning with the domain of structure, teacher-centered strategies and interventions of classroom management and schoolwide discipline are presented in Chapter 5 and 6. Whereas Chapter 5 focuses on preventing behavior problems, Chapter 6 focuses on correcting behavior problems (while simultaneously helping develop self-discipline). As emphasized in those chapters, and consistent with the authoritative approach to classroom management and school discipline, the strategies and interventions recommended in those chapters should always be used in combination with those presented for the domain of social-emotional support. The domain of engagement is the subject of Chapter 7, where additional evidence-based strategies and interventions are recommended for improving students' emotional, cognitive, and behavioral engagement. They are in addition to the recommendations presented in the previous chapters that also certainly improve engagement (e.g., supportive teacher-student relationships, teaching social and emotional skills, and effective classroom management). The domain of safety is the subject of Chapter 9, in which issues of safety are discussed (e.g., how safe are schools, what are the advantages and limitations of such safety measures as suspensions, cameras, and school resource officers) and recommendations for improving school safety are presented. A particular aspect of safety, bullying, is the focus of Chapter 8, in which recommendations for preventing and responding to bullying (beyond those presented in previous chapters) are presented. Finally, as noted earlier, Chapter 10 presents measures of school climate, with a focus on the Delaware School Surveys, that align with each of the four domains of school climate and dimensions. In that chapter, guidance is provided on how to use school climate data to guide efforts to improve school climate.

CHAPTER 2

PROMOTING POSITIVE TEACHER-STUDENT RELATIONSHIPS

> One cannot influence anybody unless one has first established a friendly relationship. This fundamental premise is often neglected. Most difficulties with children are the logical outgrowth of disturbed relationships between child and adult. The same child who seems unmanageable to one teacher may be, and often is, cooperative with another. If a good relationship exists, serious disturbances of cooperation hardly ever arise.
>
> (Dreikurs, 1968, p. 59)

One might well argue that from the perspective of teachers and students, what best defines school climate is how teachers relate to their students, and students to their teachers. This is likely true for several reasons. First, one way or another almost every minute of a students' school day, including time spent in the classroom and often outside of the classroom, is determined by the student's teacher(s). This includes where they are to be, how they are to behave, the lessons taught and how they are taught, and whether their lives in school are miserable or joyous. Second, the teacher-student relationship impacts every other dimension of school climate. For example, how teachers relate to their students, including not just their caring and emotional support but also their instruction and classroom management, greatly influences how students relate to one another (Verschueren, Doumen, & Buyse, 2012). This includes friendships that students develop and bullies they might encounter. For more obvious reasons, teacher-student relationships also greatly influence student engagement and school safety. It is difficult to learn, or teach, in the context of conflictual and negative relationships. Likewise, students feel less safe in schools in which teachers and students do not trust and like one another. For example, students are more inclined to report bullying to teachers who they view as supportive and likely to help (Cortes & Kochenderfer-Ladd, 2014).

It is no wonder then that the teacher-student relationship is widely recognized as critical to a teacher's effectiveness in the classroom and is viewed as a central aspect of school climate. In a survey of students aged 15–19, teachers, principals, education researchers, education policymakers, and parents of school-aged children in 23 countries, McKnight, Graybeal, Yarbro, and Graybeal (2016) asked them to identify the most important qualities, or dispositions, of an effective (or good) teacher. Across countries, including both wealthy and poor ones, across all categories of respondents, and at both primary and secondary grade levels, the most valued quality was the ability to relate or connect with students. Respondents viewed the ability to develop strong teacher-student relationships as requiring such qualities as compassion, trust, patience, caring, and kindness. Although knowledge and skills in teaching were also viewed as important, they were not valued as highly as caring and supportive relationships.

The teacher-student relationship has two broad dimensions: social-emotional support and instructional support (Hamre & Pianta, 2005). In this chapter, however, the focus is on social-emotional support. Instructional support is covered in other chapters, particularly the chapter on student engagement, but also the chapter on preventing behavior problems. This is consistent with the authoritative approach to classroom management, school discipline, and school climate, as presented in the previous chapter, which views social-emotional support as one of its two primary dimensions and structure as the other. In the context of the teacher-student relationship, social-emotional support refers to teachers caring about their students, but also to being attuned to and responding to their needs and treating *all* students with respect.

Although the focus of this chapter is on the *teacher*-student relationship, teachers are not the only adults in a school whose interactions with students are critical to school climate and the welfare of students. For the sake of brevity, the term teacher-student relationships is used throughout this chapter, but in most cases when used it should be viewed as including all members of the school staff who relate with students, including school administrators and support staff.

The Importance of Teacher-Student Relationships

Of the theories discussed in Chapter 1 that support the framework for school climate in this book, two are most relevant to teacher-student relationships: attachment theory (Ainsworth, 1989) and self-determination theory (Ryan & Deci, 2017). As follows from attachment theory, the positive effects of teacher-student relationships can be attributed largely to students having greater feelings of security when they know that their teachers care and support them (e.g., Pianta, 1999). In turn, they experience less stress and greater self-confidence, self-efficacy, and engagement in learning (Ahnert et al., 2012). When a sense of security, closeness, and support is lacking, students are reticent to explore and take advantage of learning opportunities on their own, and are less able to cope with academic, social, and emotional challenges in school. Self-determination theory offers a similar, yet slightly different, perspective. It emphasizes the importance of the basic psychological needs of relatedness, autonomy, and competence being met for children to be motivated and engaged in learning and to be socially and emotionally adjusted. In the context of the classroom, the positive teacher-student relationship is instrumental in meeting each of those needs.

As also noted in Chapter 1, warm and supportive relationships between teachers and students are associated with a number of positive student outcomes. They include greater academic engagement and valuing of school (Cheung, 2019; Danielsen, Wiium, Wilhelmsen, & Wold et al., 2010; Huang, Lewis, Cohen, Prewett, & Herman, 2018) and academic achievement (Roorda, Jak, Zee, Oort, & Koomen, 2017; Roorda, Koomen, Spilt, & Oort, 2011). They also include students exhibiting greater prosocial behaviors (NICHD Early Child Care Research

Network, 2006; Pianta & Stuhlman, 2004), fewer antisocial behaviors (Buyse, Verschueren, Verachtert, & Van Damme, 2009; Gregory et al., 2010; O'Connor, Dearing, & Collins, 2011), and fewer internalizing problems such as depression and low self-esteem (Brand, Felner, Shim, Seitsinger, & Dumas, 2003; Spilt, van Lier, Leflot, Onghena, & Colpin, 2014). These effects have been shown to be both short- and long-term. For example, in a longitudinal study that followed a large and diverse sample of students from elementary school into secondary school, positive teacher-student relations, as reported by both teachers and students, were found to be related to fewer behavior problems and greater prosocial behavior, both concurrently and up to four years later (Obsuth et al., 2017). In another recent study, a more favorable teacher-student relationship was found to moderate the association between bullying victimization and depression (Huang et al., 2018). That is, the depression among victims of bullying, including among students who were both bullies and victims, was much less when the teacher-student relationship was viewed favorably.

Another important outcome of positive teacher-student relationships, and one that is related to each of the other positive outcomes noted above, is that students often internalize the positive values their teachers hold and communicate in the classroom and throughout school (Hughes, 2002; Wentzel, 2002)—such as respect, hard work, and kindness. Thus, when the teacher-student relationship is positive, students are more motivated to comply with their teachers out of respect, rather than out of fear of punishment or the promise of rewards (Wentzel, 1997, 2006). A final important outcome, and one reflecting mental health, is that when the teacher-student relationship is positive, students and teachers tend to be happier and more satisfied with school (Baker, 1999; Croninger & Lee, 2001; Osterman, 2000). Relatedly, they perceive themselves more favorably, as seen in higher self-esteem and self-confidence (Ryan & Grolnick, 1986).

Research suggests that the positive effects of a warm and supportive teacher-student relationship is strongest for those students at greater risk for negative academic and social-emotional outcomes. This would include students with either externalizing problems, such as acting-out and noncompliance (Decker, Dona, & Christenson, 2007; Hamre & Pianta, 2005; Wang, Brinkworth, & Eccles, 2013), or students with internalizing problems, such as depression and anxiety (Wang et al., 2013; Yu, Li, Wang, & Zhang, 2016). For those students, and others who often experience various life stressors, including economic disadvantage, peer rejection, and bullying, a positive teacher-student relationship serves as a buffer, protecting them from multiple negative outcomes associated with externalizing and internalizing problems and life stressors (Hamre & Pianta, 2005; National Research Council and Institute of Medicine, 2009; Spilt et al., 2014). Social-emotional support, with emphases on supportive teacher-student relationships, compassion, and responsiveness to psychological needs, is widely recognized as a key element of trauma-informed practices and trauma-sensitive schools (SAMHSA's Trauma and Justice Strategic Initiative, 2014).

Negative Teacher-Student Relationships

A healthy teacher-student relationship refers not only to positive characteristics of a teacher, but also to the absence of a negative relationship. A negative relationship is one that is overly-dependent or conflictual, with the latter being more common (Hamre & Pianta, 2009). In overly-dependent relationships, students, who are typically lacking in self-confidence and autonomy or ridden with anxiety, cling to the teacher and fail to explore and accept challenges on their own. Conflictual relationships are most common with students who exhibit behavior problems, especially frequent antisocial or aggressive behaviors (Birch & Ladd, 1998; O'Connor, 2010). At greatest risk are males and students in middle school and high school (Hamre & Pianta, 2007; Jerome, Hamre, & Pianta, 2009; O'Connor, 2010). Also at increased risk of conflictual relationships are students with histories of poor attachment with their mothers (Verschueren et al., 2012) and students with internalizing problems, such as depression and anxiety (Pianta & Stuhlman, 2004). Interestingly, not only are students with internalizing problems at greater risk for conflictual teacher-student relationships, but so too are *teachers* with internalizing problems. That is, teachers who have higher levels of stress, more depressive symptoms, and lower self-efficacy tend to have more negative relationships with their students (Hamre & Pianta, 2004; Mashburn, Hamre, Downer, & Pianta, 2006; Yoon, 2002).

Longitudinal studies have found that a negative teacher-student relationship, as early as kindergarten, predicts a number of negative academic and social-emotional outcomes in later elementary school and beyond (Hamre & Pianta, 2001; Hughes, Luo, Kwok, & Loyd, 2008). For example, in a large-scale longitudinal study of a diverse population of students, Hamre and Pianta (2001) found that a negative teacher-student relationship in kindergarten predicted poor grades and academic achievement test scores throughout elementary school and into the eighth grade. Fortunately, students having positive relationships with their teachers can compensate for also having negative ones. In a recent longitudinal study of high school students, Martin and Collie (2019) found that a greater number of positive relationships than negative relationships with teachers outweighed the harmful impact of negative relationships on student engagement.

A conflictual relationship does not necessarily mean that the teacher-student relationship, per se, *causes* negative outcomes or that it is the only cause or the primary factor involved. To be sure, the teacher-student relationship is only one small piece of the puzzle as to why children behave as they do, both in and out of school, and why the negative outcomes above are found (Baker, Grant, & Morlock, 2008). It is clear that a large number of risk factors contribute to those negative outcomes, including the student's behaviors (and factors associated with those behaviors) that lead to the negative relationship. In most cases a conflictual teacher-student relationship should not be interpreted as a one-way relationship—a relationship determined solely by the behavior of either the student or the teacher. The relationship is typically bidirectional (Doumen et al., 2008; Houts, Caspi, Pianta, Arseneault, & Moffitt, 2010).

Qualities of Teachers that Strengthen the Teacher-Student Relationship

In addition to research demonstrating the importance of a supportive teacher-student relationship, research has identified behaviors, or actions, of teachers that help explain why students like them and perceive them as caring, warm, respectful, and supportive. Students prefer teachers who demonstrate the following qualities.

- *They convey warmth, caring, and respect.* These qualities are shown in listening to individual students and learning about their interests and opinions, and by offering guidance, help, and support, for academic and other school-related problems (Driscoll & Pianta, 2010; Weinstein, 2006; Weinstein & Romano, 2014). In interviews of a diverse group of high school students in urban high schools, Ozer, Wolf, and Kong (2008) found that among the qualities of teachers that students respected the most was demonstrating an interest in students not just as learners but also as *persons*. In the previously mentioned survey of students (aged 15–19), teachers, principals, education researchers, education policymakers, and parents of school-aged children, results found, across each of those groups, the following teacher personality characteristics were associated with positive teacher-student relationships: caring, kindness, patience, understanding, compassion, fairness, trustworthiness, humor, and friendliness (McKnight et al., 2016).
- *They have good classroom management skills.* This is the structure dimension in the authoritative approach. Effective teachers manage student behavior using primarily proactive and positive techniques, including building positive teacher-student relationships, while using punitive techniques sparingly (Mitchell & Bradshaw, 2013). Expectations are high and encouragement is frequent (Ozer et al., 2008). Students do not respect teachers who fail to manage their classrooms effectively (McKnight et al., 2016).
- *They do not embarrass or humiliate students.* Students feel singled out, and often embarrassed or belittled, when their failures are pointed out before the class and their successes are overlooked—good teachers avoid this (Ozer et al., 2008). Especially during adolescence, the correction of misbehavior should be done privately more so than publicly, when feasible, as preferred by adolescents.
- *They do not punish students harshly, especially for minor offenses.* Not only do the most effective teachers prefer positive over punitive techniques, but they recognize the importance of students perceiving rules and consequences as fair (Weinstein, 2006; Weinstein & Romano, 2014).
- *They demonstrate good teaching skills.* They know their subject matter and show it. They are well organized, have high expectations, and motivate and engage students by making learning fun and interesting, which includes using humor and demonstrating enthusiasm in teaching (McKnight et al., 2016; Weinstein, 2006; Weinstein & Romano, 2014).
- *They are sensitive and responsive to the psychological and developmental needs of their students.* This includes the three basic needs of all students (Ryan & Deci, 2017): competence (e.g., "I'm good at what is important to me."), relatedness ("Others care about me."), and autonomy ("Others don't control me; I have choices."). It also includes knowledge and understanding of learners, and being sensitive and responsive to other cognitive, emotional, and social needs and differences that often vary as a function of age and development (McKnight et al., 2016; Montuoro & Lewis, 2015).
- *They communicate often with the families of their students.* Students exhibit fewer behavior problems and greater academic achievement when their parents are actively involved in their education (Reinke, Smith, & Herman, 2019). A positive teacher-student relationship fosters parental involvement (Cheung, 2019). Supportive teachers recognize the importance of

communicating and collaborating with the families of their students. The communications are supportive—to help solve any school-related problems students may have, but also to provide positive feedback about their students and promote collaboration in meeting their needs.

The relation of the above qualities and characteristics of warm and caring teachers to teacher effectiveness is not culturally-specific. Multiple studies have highlighted that certain racial or ethnic groups, including African-American and Hispanic, benefit greatly from close and supportive relationships with their teachers (e.g., Decker et al., 2007; Meehan, Hughes, & Cavell, 2003) as do students who feel alienated or those living in poverty (Weinstein, 2006). Thus, teachers need not worry that with respect to building and maintaining supportive teacher-student relationships that any of those groups require unique qualities of teachers.

Recommended Strategies and Interventions for Improving Teacher-Student Relationships

Based on school climate surveys completed by students, teachers/staff, and parents, most schools are likely to find that teacher-student relationships are favorable. Indeed, over the past 15 years of assessing school climate in Delaware schools, we have found the highest scores on the teacher-student relationships' subscale of the student and teacher versions of the Delaware School Climate Survey (see Chapter 10 for the survey). Few schools, and especially elementary schools, received scores that warranted the need for intensive and ongoing schoolwide professional development in this area. Regardless of need, however, we found that most schools welcomed recommendations for helping teachers and staff to build and maintain positive teacher-teacher relationships. Such recommendations follow.

1. *At the school level, consider adopting an evidence-based program that focuses on building and maintaining positive teacher-student relationships.* This is especially important if evidence exists, such as from surveys, that relationships are poor. Interestingly, in a comprehensive review of programs for improving classroom management, including those targeting social-emotional development, Korpershoek and colleagues (Korpershoek, Harms, de Boer, van Kuijk, & Doolaard, 2016) concluded that although all programs recognized the importance of positive teacher-student relationships "in none of the programs is this component explicitly integrated in the intervention or at least not in the descriptions of the interventions." (p. 652). A noteworthy exception is the Responsive Classroom Approach, which is designed for elementary and middle schools (see www.responsiveclassroom.org).

   The Responsive Classroom Approach is supported by research showing that it improves school climate (including teacher-student interactions), instruction, and academic achievement (e.g., Brock, Nishida, Chiong, Grimm, & Rimm-Kaufman, 2008; Rimm-Kaufman et al., 2014). The approach focuses on four major components: *positive community*, *effective management*, *engaging academics*, and *developmental awareness*. Strategies for improving teacher-student relationships are linked to each of those components. The beliefs of teachers and their interactions with students are viewed as mediating the effectiveness of each component. Key features of this comprehensive approach include morning meetings, student choice and autonomy, developmental appropriateness in instruction and elsewhere in the learning environment, effective classroom management strategies (e.g., including 4–5 clear rules with logical consequences, and student-student conflict resolution), and home-school communication. The Responsive Classroom Approach offers workshops and on-site professional development to schools, as well as on-going consultation.

2. *Participate in an evidenced-based professional development program for improving teacher-student relationships.* The Responsive Classroom Approach offers intensive professional development for improving teacher-student relationships and social and emotional learning. Another evidence-based program for professional development that focuses on teacher-student relationships is My Teacher Partner (see https://curry.virginia.edu/myteachingpartner). In addition to completing online curriculum materials, participating teachers receive web-mediated individualized coaching from a trained consultant who views classroom videos recorded by the teacher about every two weeks throughout the school year. The coach and teacher review and evaluate the teacher's actions on the recordings separately, note their observations, and then discuss them. Of particular focus are teacher-student interactions related to emotional support and instructional support and the teacher's classroom organization skills. Results of the video observations are summarized and an action plan is developed to improve teaching skills, but especially skills related to teacher-student relationships. For purposes of improvement, teachers have access to an extensive video library with examples of best practice. They also have the option of completing a three-credit online college course (via University of Virginia's Curry School of Education). Research among preschool, primary, and secondary school teachers has shown participants to be more effective in their interactions with students, and students tend to improve both academically and socially (e.g., Mikami, Gregory, Allen, Pianta, & Lun, 2011).

3. *Demonstrate the general qualities of effective teaching and instruction.* This applies not only to classroom teachers, but to all instructional and support staff. Among the qualities that students value most highly in teachers are those that simply characterize good teaching. Effective teachers convey that they know the content or subject area(s) well; present material clearly; provide assistance to individual students when needed; teach at a good pace; keep students on-task; show enthusiasm; use a variety of instructional methods, and generally engage students in learning (McKnight et al., 2016; Wentzel, 1997). Those and other strategies and recommendations for promoting student engagement and motivation are presented in Chapter 7.

4. *Follow the authoritative approach to classroom management, school discipline, and school climate by balancing social support and structure.* Students not only recognize and appreciate the importance of good teaching and instruction, but also effective classroom management. Students appreciate teachers who combine support, or responsiveness, with structure—the two key dimensions of the authoritative approach. Support is best seen in

warmth, caring, and responding to students' psychological needs, whereas structure is best seen in high expectations, clear rules, and fair consequences. Teachers who focus solely on the first part of this equation and ignore the second part by trying to become the students' best friend are likely to garner little respect. Although students might view the class or teacher as "fun," they also recognize that fun does not always foster learning and especially order and safety. Whereas this chapter focuses more on the first part, support, the importance of the second part, structure, must not be overlooked. Structure is the focus of Chapters 5 and 6, on preventive and corrective techniques of classroom management.

5. *Model qualities that help build and maintain positive relationships, especially those related to liking of others.* The same general qualities that characterize the most likeable individuals in nearly all professions apply to teachers, administrators, and other staff. That is, students like teachers who are caring, kind, compassionate, understanding, respectful, patient, fair, trustworthy, humorous, friendly, and convey a sense of professionalism (McKnight et al., 2016). The following are ways that teachers and staff might exhibit those qualities:
    - Greeting students when they enter the school and classrooms.
    - Joining students for lunch, even if only occasionally.
    - Using humor: sharing funny stories and jokes.
    - Making positive comments on students' papers, journals, and other work, or placing positive notes (or "stickems") on students' desks, work folders, or lockers.
    - Being attuned to students' academic, social, and emotional problems or concerns by listening, showing empathy, and providing support and help when needed.
    - Modeling professional behaviors that educators expect of their students, including being at school or class on time, remaining calm when angry or frustrated, and respecting and caring about others.
    - Being in the classroom or school building before and after class for students to talk to.

6. *Use praise often to help build and strengthen teacher-student relationships.* Praise and rewards serve to reinforce desired behaviors, including skills that foster positive relationships, but they also are invaluable in helping students view their teachers favorably. This is especially true when the use of positive techniques, such as praise and rewards, exceeds the use of punitive techniques and is viewed as being delivered in a sincere manner. A few tips on the wise and strategic use of praise, rewards, and other recognitions follow (see Bear, 2010; Bear, Homan, & Morales, 2019, for a more thorough list of recommendations on the wise and strategic use of praise and rewards):
    - *Use praise, rewards, and other recognitions in a variety of forms.* This includes verbal and nonverbal praise (smile, a "fist bump" or high five), privileges (e.g., free time), tangible rewards, and so forth.
    - *Be creative.* Students enjoy novelty and surprise, and the aim here is not so much as to motivate student engagement and achievement as it is to create a positive relationship and climate.
    - *Be sure that praise is presented in a sincere manner.* Faint praise can do more harm than good to a relationship.

- *Avoid presenting rewards in a manner that the student views as controlling ("If you do this, you'll get this.").* Such use can be damning to a student's sense of autonomy, as well as intrinsic motivation (Ryan & Deci, 2017).
7. **Directly teach students the skills that foster positive relationships.** This recommendation encompasses modeling exemplary interpersonal behaviors (Recommendation 5) and praising and rewarding desired interpersonal skills (Recommendation 6). However, it also includes much more, especially when needed. Some students, especially in the earlier grades, and those, irrespective of age, who lack interpersonal skills, need to be taught those skills more deliberately and in a more planned and systematic fashion. This includes teaching relationship skills as part of the SEL curriculum. As reviewed in Chapter 4 on social and emotional learning, most SEL programs include the teaching of relationship skills. They aim to develop interpersonal skills in general, but also more specific skills that teachers desire, such as listening, working hard, helping others, and being trustworthy.
8. **Make sure rules and consequences are fair and equitable, and check to see if students perceive them as such.** Students are more likely to view teachers (and school) unfavorably if they view their rules as unfair (Free, 2014). See Chapter 5 on preventive classroom management for specific recommendations on developing and implementing clear behavioral expectations and fair rules and consequences.
9. **When correcting misbehavior, strive to protect a positive teacher-student relationship.** Preventing the reoccurrence of misbehavior should be the primary aim when correcting misbehavior. Maintaining a positive teacher-student relationship is invaluable in helping achieve that aim. The following strategies might help:
   - *Where feasible, correct the misbehavior privately instead of publicly.* For example, teachers and administrators should discuss the misbehavior with the offending students privately after class or school or in the hallway.
   - *Emphasize students' strengths, including those that might help prevent misbehavior.* For example, in correcting misbehavior the adult might say: "I know you're a kind person, and probably didn't mean to do that. I haven't seen you do it before. I trust you'll think more about Alissa's feelings the next time you think about saying something unkind." Or, student might be asked to identify skills and qualities they possess that will help them from repeating the misbehavior.
   - *Focus on the specific behavior, not the student per se.* To help protect the student's self-esteem, teachers should communicate that it is the misbehavior that is unacceptable—*not* the student. Students of all ages are quick to interpret corrections as implying dislike ("My teacher doesn't like me. She's always yelling at me."). This can be avoided by making it clear that it is the student's behavior that is a problem and not the student.
   - *Communicate that adults in school are there to help, but that the student shares responsibility to improve behavior.* The responsibility for improvement should be shared by the adult correcting the misbehavior and the offending student (and in many cases also classmates and

family). This does not mean that the teacher, or the student, is necessarily to *blame* for the misbehavior. When correcting misbehavior, less time should be spent discussing the "cause" than discussing together how the problem might be solved, or fixed. Help might come in the form of adults providing guidance, reminders, and other support, or altering what occurs in school that contributes to the problem behavior, including actions of the teacher or others. The key here, however, is communicating that school officials (and perhaps the student's peers) want to help the student and that they care. This requires remaining calm, yet firm; avoiding raising one's voice, or doing so very sparingly; and especially listening, guiding, and supporting.

- *Point out why the misbehavior might harm relationships, especially the teacher-student relationship.* This should be done briefly, without belaboring the point. The student might be asked to put himself or herself in another person's shoes, such as that of a victim or of the classroom teacher.
- *Communicate optimism; that with effort and by working together, the student's behavior will improve.* It should be made clear what improvement looks like (e.g., what behaviors must replace those of current concern) and that the student has the ability to exhibit the expected replacement behaviors. If the student does not know what is expected or lacks the expected skills, plans should be made to teach them. Most students know the school rules and that what they did was wrong. Regardless, it is important that adults communicate that they believe the student can and will improve. This does not mean, however, that they refrain from communicating that punitive consequences will be imposed if the behavior does not improve. It does mean that the focus should not be on punitive consequences and threats thereof. Students (and adults) do not like others who threaten them. It is okay for adults to communicate that their *jobs require* that they maintain an orderly, safe, and respectful environment that promotes learning, and that imposing fair consequences for misbehavior is often required. However, in doing so they should strive to make sure to balance this message with one of care and support.

10. **Get to know every student individually.** Teachers should take time to learn each student's interests, preferences, talents, skills, and cultural values and about the student's family (as much as the student feels comfortable revealing). For example, at the beginning of the school year, a teacher might have students complete a survey that asks about their interests or strengths, or have students interview one another and share their findings with the class. Students might also write about themselves in journals. Teachers should highlight similarities and differences across students, including cultural ones, while devoting special attention to positive and interesting characteristics of individual students who might benefit the most from extra attention.

11. **Get students to know teachers (and staff) better.** For example, teachers might complete the above activities themselves (i.e., having a student interview them, or completing the same survey students complete). Teachers and staff might share their childhood experiences, family background, interests, hobbies, and favorite books and movies. People like others more when they learn that they share similarities and interests.

12. ***Devote attention to each individual student.*** The time can be brief, but teachers should try to make at least one positive interaction daily, or as frequently as feasible. For example, they might simply ask about, or comment on, an aspect of the student's life (e.g., "How was the game Saturday?" "I like your sweatshirt, where did you get it?" etc.), or place a brief sticky note on the student's desk, or in the student's notebook, commenting positively about something the student did.

    Where feasible, teachers, and other staff, attend after-school events in which students participate, such as sports and extracurricular activities, while making sure students know they were there. The author recalls one of his sons noting how much it meant to him when his teachers (in both elementary school and high school) came out to watch one of his soccer games. Since then, they have always been referred to as his "favorite teachers." Indeed, the interest shown by these teachers largely led him to becoming a high school teacher.

    Caring teachers notice students who are having academic or personal difficulties. They listen, express concern, and respond with care and support. Banking Time (Driscoll & Pianta, 2010) is an evidence-based intervention that has been shown to improve teacher-student relationships and thus help prevent behavior problems and reduce teacher-student conflict. At the core of the intervention is that the classroom teacher simply plans to spend time with a student individually and in a positive manner. Although Banking Time was designed for children in preschool and early elementary grades, and it would be difficult to implement beyond elementary school, aspects of the intervention apply to all grades, especially demonstrating interest and caring.

    It is much more difficult for teachers to devote individual attention to students when they have large or multiple classes. Regardless, efforts should be made to devote some attention to each individual student. For a small class size this could mean almost every day, whereas for five different classes it would mean less often.

13. ***Treat students equally; do not indicate "favorites" (or "non-favorites") in the classroom.*** Teachers should reflect upon the time and attention they give to each student: Are there students who tend to be neglected (and who feel that way)? Are there ones who receive more attention than others, positive or negative? Do teachers, counselors, and the staff communicate to students that they have "favorites" (or "non-favorites") in the classroom? Conflict and neglect affect not only individual students, but may well harm adults' relationships with other students who perceive the teacher as having favorites and as being selective in caring about others.

14. ***Foster students' sense of autonomy and self-esteem.*** As discussed in Chapter 1, autonomy is one of the three basic psychological needs of students, with relatedness and competence being the other two. Autonomy is important in teacher-student relationships for several reasons. First, students, especially adolescents, prefer teachers who are not overly controlling—who adopt a more student-centered, rather than teacher-centered, approach to classroom management (McKnight et al., 2016). This would include giving students choices and actively involving them in decision-making. Second, as with relatedness and competence, a sense of autonomy is important to one's self-concept and self-esteem (Ryan & Deci, 2017). Highlighting a student's strengths, demonstrating social support, and fostering a sense of autonomy

help develop and maintain positive teacher-student relationships, but those strategies also are good for promoting the student's self-esteem or overall sense of self-worth (Manning, Bear, & Minke, 2006). Specific recommendations on fostering autonomy, as well as overall self-esteem, are presented in Chapter 7 on student engagement.

15. *Provide schoolwide and classroom activities that promote positive teacher-student interactions.* At the schoolwide level this would include sports, clubs, extracurricular activities, and activities in which staff and students participate together, such as service learning, pep rallies, fundraisers by students and faculty, and mentoring programs. At the classroom level this would include such activities as playing fun learning games and projects that require teacher-student collaboration, field trips, and class or morning meetings.

16. *Hold class or morning meetings that promote positive relationships.* Nearly half a century ago, Rudolph Dreikurs' (1968) popular model of classroom management emphasized the importance of a weekly class meeting, lasting about 30 minutes, as a way to help students understand themselves and their classmates and to encourage teacher and student sharing of responsibility and democratic decision-making. Class meetings are now popular in more modern models of classroom management, including the research-supported Responsive Classroom Approach, and are viewed as a way to develop both student-student relationships and teacher-student relationships. In this approach a morning meeting is held every day (grades K-6), during which students gather in a circle at beginning of the class to greet one another, share what is happening in their lives, participate in a group activity that fosters social skills and positive interactions (e.g., a game, dancing, singing), and hear the teacher's morning message that addresses plans for their day. A similar classroom meeting, the "Responsive Advisory Meeting," is part of the Responsive Classroom Approach in middle school. As with the morning meeting, its purpose is to teach and reinforce social and emotional skills associated with positive teacher-student and student-student relationships, such as caring, trust, social perspective-taking, empathy, respect, and cooperation.

17. *Establish and maintain positive relationships with the families of students.* If a student's parent dislikes a teacher, it is very likely that the student will too. Likewise, teachers have a much better chance of convincing a student who dislikes them that they are caring if the student's parents view the teacher that way. To help establish positive teacher-home relations, it's important that *positive* messages about each student are communicated to the student's home. Teachers and staff should not wait for problems to occur before communicating with parents. When problems do occur, however, teachers should communicate care and support and share in the responsibility for addressing the problems (see Chapter 6 on corrective techniques).

18. *For students with poor relationships with teachers, do the above and more.* At times none of the above will work, and more is needed. The teacher is only one part of the teacher-student relationship. The student is the other part. Despite the best efforts, qualities, and skills of teachers and other staff, not all students respond favorably to their efforts to build and maintain positive relationships. Students who fail to respond favorably require greater effort in implementing the above recommendations, with them needing to be implemented with greater frequency and intensity. They also often warrant

more intensive supports that go beyond what the typical classroom teacher, and the school, might reasonably provide. Guided by a comprehensive assessment of the student's needs that identifies factors contributing to poor relationships with others, supports might include social skills training, family therapy, parent management training, or individual counseling/therapy. Another evidence-based intervention which has been shown to improve student engagement, including relationships with others in school, is the Check and Connect, as discussed in Chapter 7. A key element of this school-based intervention is a mentor who routinely checks in with the student and helps build connectedness with a mentor.

19. *Keep care of yourself.* Education is a stressful profession; emotional stress is one of the primary reasons for teacher burnout and for teachers leaving the profession (Provasnik & Dorfman, 2005). And stress can be contagious: the more stressed a teacher is, the more likely students also will be stressed, and vice versa (Jennings & Greenberg, 2009; Oberle & Schonert-Reichl, 2016). Teachers who are able to manage stress and their emotions effectively are not only happier and more emotionally adjusted, but also are more effective in their teaching, including in building and maintaining positive teacher-student relationships (Jennings & Greenberg, 2009). Thus, it is important that teachers, and other staff, are attuned not only to the emotional health of their students, but also to their own emotional, and physical, health. When stressors cannot be alleviated, stress needs to be managed, which may require training in relaxation and stress management techniques, such as mindfulness and other meditation and relaxation techniques, yoga, and physical exercise.

Summary

As the saying goes, "it takes two to tango." This applies to teacher-student relationships, as either the teacher or the student can make life in a classroom enjoyable or miserable. Teaching differs from dancing, however, in that one person, the teacher, is both dance instructor and dancer. Thus, although responsibility for the teacher-student relationship is shared by the teacher and student, it falls most greatly on the teacher. That responsibility applies to each and every student—a responsibility that greatly impacts student engagement, academic achievement, and social and emotional development. This responsibility applies to all adults in schools with whom students relate. Just as a teacher can make a student's life happy or miserable, so too can an administrator, paraprofessional, bus driver, school resource officer, cafeteria worker, school counselor, and others.

Ample research has documented the critical importance of teacher-student relationships to school climate and its association with all other aspects of school climate and other valued educational outcomes. Those outcomes include students' academic achievement and social-emotional well-being. Consistent with an authoritative approach to classroom management, the qualities of teachers that help build and maintain positive teacher-student relationships consist of a combination of *social-emotional support* (i.e., caring and responsiveness to students' psychological needs, including teaching self-discipline) and *structure* (i.e., teacher-centered strategies for preventing and correcting misbehavior).

CHAPTER 3

PROMOTING POSITIVE STUDENT-STUDENT RELATIONSHIPS

Importance of Student-Student Relationships

Positive student-student relationships are critical not only to a positive school climate but also to students' social, emotional, and academic development. Students who perceive their relations with peers favorably and who have one or more friends tend to have a more positive self-concept and higher self-esteem (Demaray & Malecki, 2002; Spilt et al., 2014). Relatedly, they also are more likely to be engaged in school (De Laet et al., 2015; Li, Lynch, Kalvin, Liu, & Lerner, 2011; Wang & Eccles, 2012b), to have positive relations with their teachers (Kiuru et al., 2015), and to experience higher academic achievement (Danielsen et al., 2010; Wentzel et al., 2004). Overall, they are more satisfied with school (Jiang et al., 2013). It is no wonder, then, that for many students, especially those in secondary school, positive student-student relationships, particularly close friendships, is the one aspect of school climate they value most highly (National Research Council and Institute of Medicine, 2009).

In contrast to favorable outcomes associated with positive student-student relationships, students who lack peer acceptance and support have fewer opportunities to learn and practice social skills and to develop healthy friendships and relationships with others, including friendships that serve as a valuable resource during times of stress (Kupersmidt & DeRosier, 2004). They also are at greater risk of being victims of bullying (Jenkins & Demaray, 2012; Wang et al., 2009). Peer support and friendships help prevent stress and bullying victimization and buffer associated internalizing and externalizing problems. Internalizing problems include low self-esteem and self-concept, loneliness, depression, and suicide (Carney, 2000; Demaray & Malecki, 2002; Spilt et al., 2014). Externalizing problems include acting out, aggression, and delinquent behaviors (Brand et al., 2003; Demaray & Malecki, 2002; Sturaro et al., 2011). Poor student-student relationships and their negative effects are widely recognized as playing a major role in the trajectory of student disengagement from school (Estell & Perdue, 2013). That is, students with a history of poor peer relationships are at great risk for greater school avoidance (Buhs et al., 2006), poor academic achievement (Buhs et al., 2006; Perdue et al., 2009; Stewart, 2008), and eventually dropping out of school (French & Conrad, 2003). For many students the negative outcomes associated with poor peer relationships are lasting, following them into adulthood (Parker & Asher, 1987).

Factors Influencing Student-Student Relationships

Student-student relationships entail individual and group behavior in social context, and thus are influenced by multiple individual and environmental factors. There is little, if anything, that teachers and schools can do about many of those factors, such as genetics, poverty, poor role models, and the many stressors that students experience at home and in the community. However, many other factors *are* malleable—factors that teachers and schools can, and should, target to improve student-student relationships. This section focuses on two sets of such factors: (1) characteristics of individual students; and (2) characteristics of teachers, classrooms, and schools. That both sets of factors play a major role in student-student relationships, and interact with one another, is supported by several lines of research. With respect to the influence of individual differences, research shows that problems developing positive peer relationships typically begin as early as preschool, especially among students who are aggressive and noncompliant, and that the problems are fairly stable across time and different contexts (Ostrov, Perry, & Blakely-McClure, 2018). Research also shows, however, that school climate matters, as indicated in studies finding that about one half to two-thirds of children who are socially rejected during a school year are *not* socially rejected the following school year (Coie & Dodge, 1983; Vitaro, Gagnon, & Tremblay, 1990).

Individual Student Characteristics. Of great value in preventing poor student-student relationships and developing interventions is knowledge of the characteristics of students who are accepted by their peers and who have close friendships, as well as knowledge of the characteristics of those who are neglected or rejected. Such knowledge helps educators identify and target the behaviors, thoughts, and emotions that need to be developed or strengthened and ones that need to be confronted, remediated, or otherwise reduced. What are the characteristics associated with peer acceptance, peer support, and close friendships? As one might guess, students tend to like peers who exhibit prosocial behaviors such as friendliness, kindness, helpfulness, and cooperation (Asher & Mcdonald, 2009; Torrente, Cappella, & Neal, 2014; Wentzel et al., 2004). In general, students are more accepting and less rejecting of peers who are engaged in school: Those who complete their work, do not disrupt the learning of others, and do well academically. However, this relationship between peer acceptance and engagement declines with increasing grade level (Lubbers, Van, Snijders, Creemers, & Kuyer, 2006; Torrente et al., 2014). Interestingly, the positive relationship has been shown to be as true among African-American students as it is among Caucasian students, which is a finding contrary to the view that the African-American students are less accepting of their peers who "act white" (Torrente et al., 2014). Possessing valued nonacademic skills and talents, such as athletic ability applied in team sports, also is associated with positive relations with peers (see Kupersmidt & DeRosier, 2004).

As one also might guess, in general, students are much less likely to accept or befriend classmates who are lacking in the above areas. Students are especially prone to socially reject classmates who are aggressive, disruptive, noncompliant, impulsive, lacking in communicative skills, social withdrawn or overly shy, and those who exhibit social-cognitive deficits (e.g., social understanding, social problem-solving skills, moral reasoning) (see Asher & Mcdonald, 2009; Hay, Payne, & Chadwick, 2004; Rose-Krasnor & Denham, 2009 for reviews). The relations between many of those characteristics and social rejection often are reciprocal. For example, externalizing problems increase the likelihood that students will be socially rejected, and being socially rejected increases the likelihood that a student will exhibit externalizing problems such as aggression toward peers (Sturaro et al., 2011). The relation between social acceptance and academic engagement also is likely reciprocal (Juvonen, Espinoza, & Knifsend, 2012). These reciprocal relations have important implications for intervention: Both the social rejection by peers *and* the behaviors of rejected students that are associated with social acceptance and rejection should be targeted in prevention and intervention efforts. This requires coordinated efforts by teachers and students, and often by parents and support staff.

Box 3.1 lists behaviors, values, and social tasks, drawn from both research and their inclusion in evidence-based curriculum programs for social and emotional learning or social skills training, that are commonly associated with peer acceptance and friendship. The absence of those behaviors, or their opposites (e.g., blaming others instead of apologizing), should be expected to be associated with peer rejection and lack of friendships.

Box 3.1 Social Skills and Tasks Related to Positive Student-Student Relationships

- apologizing
- accepting an apology
- accepting responsibility for one's actions
- asserting oneself
- advocating for self and others
- caring
- comforting others
- complementing others
- cooperation
- conversational skills, including beginning and closing a conversation, not monopolizing discussion, listening, and respecting differences of opinion
- coping skills, including coping with frustration, failure, social rejection, and stressors
- delay of gratification
- emotion regulation, especially regulation of anger
- emotional expression, such as expressing appropriately when upset, sad, or angry
- empathy
- engagement
- fairness
- gratitude/appreciation

(continued)

(continued)

- helping others
- honesty
- impulse control
- integrity
- keeping a secret
- listening skills
- loyalty
- managing conflict
- negotiating
- perseverance
- refraining from bragging
- respecting others, including individual and cultural differences
- resolving conflicts and disagreements with peers and others
- responding appropriately to winning and losing
- requesting assistance
- resisting peer pressure
- restraint (e.g., refraining from alcohol and drug use)
- responsible decision-making, including moral and ethical responsibility
- sharing with others
- social perspective-taking
- social problem-solving
- trustworthiness

Teacher, Classroom, and School Characteristics. In the contexts of classrooms and schools, perhaps the strongest determinant of student-student relationships is the approach, and corresponding strategies, that teachers and other school staff use to teach and develop prosocial behavior and prevent and manage antisocial behavior. As discussed in multiple chapters of this book, ample research shows that an authoritative approach is best for preventing and correcting behavior problems and developing self-discipline. Recall from Chapter 1 that there are two key dimensions of the authoritative approach. The first is social-emotional support, which includes responsiveness to students' psychological needs. The second dimension is demandingness, or structure. With respect to fostering positive student-student relationships, responsiveness may be of greater importance than demandingness (Gest & Rodkin, 2011; Kiuru et al., 2015; Mikami, Reuland, Griggs, & Jia, 2013). This is particularly true if one's aim is to promote skills and assets, such as those in Table 3.1, that are associated with prosocial interactions. Research shows that peer acceptance increases in classrooms (Donohue, Perry, & Weinstein, 2003; Mikami et al., 2013) and schools (Solomon, Watson, Delucchi, Schaps, & Battistich, 1988) when student-centered, or responsiveness-focused, practices (as opposed to teacher-centered and structure-oriented behavioral practices) are implemented.

This does not mean that structure is not important in promoting prosocial interactions and peer acceptance. Without clear behavioral expectations, fair rules and consequences, routines, procedures, supervision, and monitoring, it is very difficult for teachers to be responsive to students' developmental needs and for students to interact in a positive manner. Without adequate structure, teachers are much more likely to spend time correcting behavior problems than fostering positive student-student relationships and developing the social and emotional competencies that underlie them. Structure is important for all students, but especially those who are lacking in peer relationship skills and assets. For example, when teachers provide increased structure for students who exhibit antisocial behavior and who are not well accepted by their peers, their on-task behavior and social acceptance improve (De Laet et al., 2015).

Student-student relationships are more positive in classrooms and schools where teacher-student relationships are positive (Donohue et al., 2003; Kiuru et al., 2015; Mikami et al., 2013)—where teachers demonstrate social-emotional support, including responsiveness to student's psychological needs, and especially the need for belongingness. This can largely be explained by social learning theory, and particularly principles of modeling and positive reinforcement, but also by attachment theory. That is, consistent with social learning theory, children are more inclined to exhibit prosocial behaviors toward others when they observe their teachers modeling those behaviors and positively reinforcing their peers when they demonstrate the same behaviors (Howes, Hamilton, & Matheson, 1994). Likewise, consistent with attachment theory, students are more likely to emulate the behaviors of teachers whom they like and respect (Hughes, Cavell, & Willson, 2001; Pianta, Hamre, & Stuhlman, 2003). More specific to student-student relationships, students also are more socially accepting of classmates toward whom teachers demonstrate positive affect (Nesdale & Pickering, 2006).

The strategies that educators use to prevent and correct behavior problems influence student-student relationships both directly and indirectly. The influence occurs directly via deliberate efforts to teach and reinforce behaviors associated with positive relationships and to prevent and correct behaviors associated with negative relationships. The influence also occurs indirectly by establishing norms that promote and maintain prosocial interactions among students, oppose antisocial behavior, and lead students to believe that others care about them (Thomas & Bierman, & the Conduct Problems Prevention Research Group, 2006; Wentzel, 2014). Such norms increase peer acceptance, including acceptance of peers of different races and ethnicities (Nesdale, Griffith, Durkin, & Maass, 2005; Nesdale, Maass, Durkin, & Griffiths, 2005).

Classroom and school norms are determined by values, attitudes, and behaviors of students but also by the related actions of teachers and staff. In classrooms and schools with norms that promote prosocial behavior and help prevent antisocial behavior, teachers and staff are accurately attuned and responsive to the peer group affiliations and social dynamics of students. That is, they know which students are leaders and good role models and which ones are aggressive or dominating of others, victims of bullying, socially neglected, disliked, rejected, or lacking friendships (Gest et al., 2014; Hamm, Farmer, Dadisman, Gravelle, & Murray, 2011; Norwalk, Hamm, Farmer, & Barnes, 2016). This knowledge helps guide classroom management and intervention efforts, as might be seen in seating arrangements of students, the close monitoring of student behavior, and providing academic and social activities that prevent behavior problems and foster positive student-student interactions.

Research shows that curriculum lessons also help determine norms that promote positive student-student relationships. For example, lessons and class discussions about racism and prejudice can reduce attitudes of racism and prejudice among students, helping create a norm of respect and acceptance (Aboud & Doyle, 1996; Hughes, Bigler, & Levy, 2007). Hughes and colleagues (2007) found that when students were taught lessons about African-American racism occurring throughout history, Caucasian students decreased their prejudiced attitudes toward African-Americans.

Recommended Strategies and Interventions for Improving Student-Student Relationships

In this section, specific strategies and interventions of social-emotional support are presented for building and improving student-student relationships. As discussed previously, structure also is critical in building and improving positive student-student relationships. Structure-based recommendations are not included here because they are the focus of chapters on preventing and correcting behavior problems (Chapters 5 and 6), student engagement (Chapter 7), and safety (Chapter 9).

1. *Adopt an evidence-based program or curriculum of improving student-student relationships.* Numerous programs exist for improving student-student relationships and particularly for developing specific behaviors associated with positive student-student relationships, including those behaviors listed in Table 3.1. Few programs, however, have been subject to rigorous empirical research as to their effectiveness. Before adopting a program, it is wise to examine program reviews and evaluation results. As discussed in Chapter 4 on SEL, an excellent resource for reviewing SEL programs, including those for improving student-student relationships, is the website for Collaborative Academic, Social, and Emotional Learning (see CASEL.org). Of the SEL programs reviewed by CASEL, it is the author's opinion that the following have the strongest evidence of improving student-student relationships: PATHS (Promoting Alternative Thinking Strategies; Kusche & Greenberg, 2012), Second Step Social-Emotional Learning (Committee for Children, 2019), and the Responsive Classroom Approach (Center for Responsive Schools, 2019). Each of these programs is described in Chapter 4.

    If a school is looking to adopt an evidenced-based program for improving student-student relationships then consideration also should be given to evidence-based programs for preventing bullying, such as the Olweus Bullying Prevention Program (www.violencepreventionworks.org) and KiVa Anti-Bully Program (www.kivaprogram.net/). These programs are described in Chapter 8 on bullying.

2. *Highlight the importance of positive student-student relationships in behavioral expectations, classroom and school rules, and in the teaching of SEL skills.* This applies to both the school and classroom levels. At the school level, the school should review its mission statement to make sure it emphasizes the importance of positive student-student relationships (as well as teacher-student relationships) not only in behavioral expectations and

rules but also in developing specific social and emotional skills. At least one major schoolwide behavioral expectation should center on student-student relationships, such as "respect others" or "be kind to others." Additional behavioral expectations should be linked to student-student relationships, where appropriate, such as "Be responsible."

The importance of student-student relationships and related skills should be communicated in morning announcements, posters, pep rallies, school newsletters, the school's website, the school's handbook, parent conferences and meetings, and in the context of professional staff development. During disciplinary encounters, especially when peer conflicts exist, the primary focus should be on fostering empathy and social perspective taking and restoring or building positive peer relationships. Consistent with restorative justice and inductive discipline practices, and as discussed in Chapter 6 on correcting misbehavior, why student-student relationships are important and how to develop and maintain them should receive greater attention than the direct teaching of rules and consequences that govern negative student-student relationships, particularly after the early grades.

At the classroom level, SEL lessons and activities, either embedded throughout the regular curriculum, especially in literacy and history, or taught in an SEL curriculum, should highlight the critical importance of positive student-student relationships. Classic books about peer relationships abound, such as *Lord of the Flies* (Golding, 1954) and *The Chocolate War* (Cormier, 1974). Likewise, lessons on getting along with others can easily be found in social studies, especially when covering government, civics, and communities. Class discussions of such books and lessons serve as excellent means of addressing current classroom- and school-centered issues related to peer acceptance, respect, and friendship.

At the beginning of the school year teachers should consider developing a class vision statement jointly with students that centers not only on student engagement and learning but also on student-student relationships (and how they relate to learning). Throughout the school year, lessons and activities should be explicitly linked to the class's vision statement, and students should be reminded to monitor their success in fulfilling that vision.

3. **Provide activities throughout the curriculum that foster social interactions and help students get to know one another better.** Students tend to establish friendships with others who are close in physical space and who share similar demographic characteristics (e.g., socioeconomic status, gender, race) and behavioral characteristics (e.g., shared interests, values, sports, hobbies, etc.) (Neal, Neal, & Cappella, 2014). Some suggestions for facilitating interactions between students follow:
    - *Use lessons and activities that ask students to identify and share their interests, skills, and talents.* For example, have students write and share their autobiographies or interview one another and share their findings with the class. Be sure to highlight similarities and differences between students, while emphasizing that differences are to be respected. The website for Education World (www.educationworld.com/) offers a large number of "Icebreakers," developed by teachers, to be used, particularly early in the school year, to help students get to know one another.

- *Play fun games that promote positive social interactions.* This would include a full variety of academic games in the classroom, team sports in physical education classes, and supervised games during recess. Such games are often used to promote positive student-student relationships (thus enhancing social acceptance) and foster emotional engagement in school.
- *Strategically arrange, and periodically alter, classroom seating.* This should be done to facilitate students getting to know one another and to help establish new friendships. Seating arrangements often influence students' attitudes toward one another. For example, Aboud and Doyle (1996) found that when students were paired with a classmate who exhibited a different level of prejudice and together they were asked to discuss positive and negative racial stereotypes, students with initially higher prejudice reduced their prejudice attitudes. Seating arrangements are especially important for students who are lacking friendships or are socially rejected by their peers, and benefit from increased opportunities for positive social interactions.

  Where feasible, seat students in clusters instead of rows that mix groups based on (a) seating preferred by students (e.g., next to a reciprocated friend), and (b) the need to include those at risk of peer rejection/isolation. For example, during one marking period a grouping of four students might include two friends interspersed with two classmates without friends. The seating would be changed the next marking period or sooner if the seating disrupts learning or is harmful to others.

4. **Offer a wide range of extracurricular activities and encourage all students to participate in at least one.** This recommendation applies mainly to high schools and middle schools. Students of all grades, and especially those who do not participate in extracurricular activities, should be encouraged to participate in other adult-supervised clubs and group activities outside of school to help develop peer relationship skills. They could include the YMCA, YWCA, 4-H Club, scouts, church groups, sports teams, Boys Club, Girls Club, and so forth.

   Extracurricular activities include sports at all levels (e.g., competitive and extramural); student government; and student school clubs, such as business and vocational, service, game, academic, culture, religious, foreign language clubs, and clubs for the arts. Participation in extracurricular activities, including sports, has been shown to be associated with greater academic achievement and emotional adjustment, and with having more friends who are prosocial and exhibit fewer behavior problems (Fredricks & Eccles, 2006, 2008). The positive outcomes for extracurricular activities and sports likely occur via increased opportunities to interact with others, and especially in areas of shared interests and skills, but also via positive role models, expectations of self-discipline, and a shared sense of community and interdependence. Interestingly, research shows that the greatest positive social effects of participation in extracurricular activities and sports tend be with those students who were previously rejected by peers or who exhibited behavior problems. That is, over time the rejected students become more socially accepted (Sandstrom, 1999) and those with behavior problems exhibit fewer ones (Mahoney, 2000; Mahoney & Cairns, 1997).

5. ***Require and encourage participation in service learning activities.*** Similar to participating in extracurricular activities and sports, participating in service learning has been found to be associated with positive outcomes, including fewer behavior problems, increased prosocial skills and social acceptance, and with greater empathy, dependability, trustworthiness, and self-efficacy in helping others (Hart, Matsuba, & Atkins, 2008). Service learning activities can be provided in multiple ways, such as service clubs, class projects, schoolwide initiatives, and required courses/credits in high school. Several states require service learning for graduation or give credit toward graduation for completion of service learning, and many private schools also require it.
6. ***Use peer-assisted learning.*** Peer-assisted learning (PAL) activities, which include cooperative learning and peer tutoring and mentoring, increase opportunities for social interactions. Compared to traditional instruction, and specific to student-student relationships, students in PAL programs have been shown to have greater class cohesion, empathy, friendships, and peer acceptance (including greater acceptance of minority students and students with disabilities); fewer behavior problems; and better social and academic skills (Ginsburg-Block, Rohrbeck, & Fantuzzo, 2006; Ginsburg-Block, Rohrbeck, Fantuzzo, & Lavigne, 2006).

    When using PAL it is wise to consider students' developmental stage. For example, elementary students may work best in pairs with students of a similar skill level, whereas older students may be able to work in larger groups with students of varying skill levels. It is also important to consider which students work well with one another. For cooperative learning activities, it helps to arrange for each group, or dyad, to include at least one student who is a skilled leader and who is effective at helping others understand and complete the assigned tasks (Doll, Brehm, & Zucker, 2014).
7. ***Be attuned to social dynamics.*** Classroom and school climates are more positive when teachers and staff are accurately attuned to the social dynamics of the classroom and peer group affiliations and respond accordingly. This entails knowing which students are aggressive or dominating of others, victims of bullying, socially neglected, disliked or rejected, and lacking friendships (Gest & Rodkin, 2011; Norwalk et al., 2016). It also entails knowing *where* and *when* undesired behaviors are likely to occur (e.g., hallways, cafeteria, recess, gym), and planning and responding accordingly. Teaching teachers to be more attuned and responsive has been shown to improve school climate (Hamm et al., 2011).

    The following are sources of information that teachers might use to help them to learn about student-student relationships and social dynamics.
    - *Observations.* Observing student interactions during structured and unstructured activities, both inside and outside of the classroom, is a valuable way to discover which students are more or less accepted, neglected, and rejected (and bullied).
    - *School records and reports.* Written reports from previous teachers and current teachers in other classes about students' behavior and peer relations often offer useful information.
    - *Teachers and staff.* For example, discussions at grade-level staff meetings is an excellent source of information on group dynamics and is often valuable in revealing if the same dynamics occur across settings.

- *Office disciplinary referrals.* When behavior problems occur, especially those reflecting poor student-student relationships, track *where, when, and who.* In the cafeteria? During lunch? In hallways between classes? On the playground during recess? Are certain students the primary offenders of actions that harm others? Systems for tracking office disciplinary referrals, such as the SWIS Suite (www.pbisapps.org/Applications/Pages/SWIS-Suite.aspx), help serve this purpose.
- *Parents.* A good source of information is from conversations and conferences with parents, particularly when parents express concerns about their child's relations with other students.
- *Students.* In addition to school climate surveys, information directly from students might come from disciplinary encounters, private conversations, class discussions, individual or small group interviews, private journals, and messages in a private suggestion or class problem-solving box. A simple sociometric tool is asking students to write down the names of five students in the class that they like to work with. A matrix is created and completed, which is used to identify those students who are lacking in social acceptance and friendships (for specific instructions, see http://wh1.oet.udel.edu/pbs/wp-content/uploads/2016/10/Instructions-for-Sociometric-Seating-Tool.docx). Results help guide seating arrangements, PAL, and other recommendations in this section.

Based on information gathered from those sources, steps should be taken to influence social dynamics, with the primary aim of promoting positive peer relations. Knowing which students are accepted or rejected, and which ones tend to be more accepting or rejecting of others, should guide seating arrangements. Where feasible (e.g., elementary schools with multiple classes at each grade), it also should be used to assign students to classes at the beginning of the school year. Research shows that the impact of classroom composition is greatest for children with significant behavior problems: Students with behavior problems are affected most negatively when they are placed in classrooms composed of a high number of other students with behavior problems (Barth, Dunlap, Dane, Lochman, & Wells, 2004). Thus, grouping students with behavior problems together should be avoided.

8. **Provide ample models of acceptance, respect, caring, and other behaviors associated with peer acceptance and liking.** Teachers and staff should reflect upon the extent to which they model the same behaviors they desire in students, including the behaviors in Table 3.1. If teachers and staff are respectful and caring, they should expect students to learn to act the same. If teachers relate poorly to students, it would be hypocritical not to expect the same from students in their interactions with peers and others, including teachers. Thus, many of the recommendations in Chapter 2 on teacher-student relationships apply to improving student-student relationships.

Teachers should point out and discuss role models of prosocial behaviors that appear throughout the curriculum (e.g., literacy, history) in sports, entertainment, government, and community. In providing role models for students, recognize that students are more likely to emulate models that they view as sharing similar characteristics, such as gender, race, age, and who possess skills that they find attractive and desire, such as friendliness, caring, and a sense of humor. In presenting models, effectiveness of modeling also is enhanced when both specific skills (e.g., entering a group, or resisting peer pressure) and general dispositions (e.g., caring, friendliness) are highlighted in the models, the modeling is of real-life or realistic situations, and students are reinforced for expressing an interest in the models and especially for exhibiting the behaviors modeled (Bear, 2010).

9. *Use praise and other recognitions wisely and strategically to highlight and reinforce positive student-student relationships.* When prosocial emotions, thoughts, and actions occur that are associated with positive relationships with others, such as those in Table 3.1, they should be recognized. Typically, this should be accompanied with praise; praising either the specific behavior (e.g., "I appreciate how you helped Maureen with the assignment.") or the disposition or character trait reflected in the behavior (e.g., "Thanks for being a helpful and caring person."), or praising both ("e.g., Thanks for helping Maureen, and for being a caring person.").

With respect to student-student relationships and the use of praise and rewards, it is important for teachers not to communicate that they like or dislike some students more so than other students. Studies, especially those conducted in elementary schools, show that students' liking of classmates is influenced by their teacher's affect toward and preference for particular students (Nesdale & Pickering, 2006). That is, students tend to have greatest liking toward classmates whom teachers show greatest preference. The opposite also is true: Students are likely to dislike and socially reject classmates that teachers publicly show little preference. Communicating liking of certain students and disliking of others fosters a hierarchical social network, as opposed to an egalitarian one, in which social rejection is more likely to occur (Brock et al., 2008; Cappella, Kim, Neal, & Jackson, 2013; Gest & Rodkin, 2011).

Thus, teachers need to be cautious when using praise and other recognitions in the context of social comparisons that might be interpreted by students as indicating the liking of certain students and not others. This is often a great challenge: How might teachers praise and recognize desired behaviors in some students without other students perceiving the students who are frequently praised as the teacher's favorites, and themselves as less liked? Obviously, one way is to be sensitive to communicating favoritism in one's actions by monitoring if certain students receive frequent praise and recognition while others receive none or little, or worse only negative recognition. A few additional tips follow:

- For students who exhibit greater behavior problems than others, and thus are more likely to have greater conflict with teachers and be corrected more frequently (and especially in front of peers), extra efforts should be made to recognize and praise, both privately and publicly, their positive behaviors.
- Students should be encouraged to praise and reinforce one another for prosocial behavior. This would include encouraging students to express gratitude toward the prosocial behavior of others and catching others being good. In the lower grades this would include "tootling," reporting only the good behavior of classmates instead of tattling to the teacher

about their bad behavior (Skinner, Cashwell, & Skinner, 2000). At other grade levels it might consist of students posting praise notes on the desks of students or on the wall (Morrison & Jones, 2007; Nelson, Caldarella, Young, & Webb, 2008).

Chapters 4 and 5 present additional recommendations on the strategic and wise use of praise and rewards to teach prosocial behavior and develop social and emotional skills, including peer relationship skills.

10. *Hold class or morning meetings that promote positive relationships.* Nearly half a century ago, Rudolph Dreikurs' model of classroom management was among the most popular models, and many current models, or parts thereof, are derived from Dreikurs' classical writings (e.g., Dreikurs, 1968). Among the more enduring aspects of the model, Dreikurs placed great emphases on both teacher-student and student-student relationships, and the importance of weekly class meetings in fostering those relationships. Class meetings, lasting about 30 minutes, were recommended to help students understand themselves and their classmates and to encourage teacher and student sharing of responsibility and democratic decision-making. Class meetings are now found widely in current models of classroom management, including the research-supported Responsive Classroom Approach (Center for Responsive Schools, 2019; see www.responsiveclassroom.org/) and the Caring School Community (Center for the Collaborative Classroom, 2018; see www.collaborativeclassroom.org/programs/caring-school-community/) (see both websites for books and support materials for conducting class meetings). Class meetings provide an excellent context to develop positive student-student and teacher-student relationships as well as the full range of social and emotional learning skills.

In the Responsive Classroom Approach a morning meeting is held every day (grades K-6), during which time students gather in a circle at beginning of the class to greet one another, share what is happening in their lives, participate in a group activity that fosters social skills and positive interactions (e.g., a game, dance, song), and hear the teacher's "morning message" which addresses plans for their day. The meeting's primary purpose is to foster a positive classroom climate characterized by trust, support, and collaboration, and to help develop social, emotional, and academic learning. A similar classroom meeting, the responsive advisory meeting, is part of the Responsive Classroom Approach in middle school. As with the morning meeting, its purpose is to build positive relationships and foster social and emotional learning.

Holding a daily classroom meeting is likely to be more feasible in elementary than in middle school and high school, where students have multiple teachers and classes. After the early elementary grades, some teachers may also prefer not meeting daily. In those contexts, however, it would still be wise to hold class meetings to discuss academic or social issues, including classroom concerns, whenever feasible. Consistent with an authoritative approach to classroom management, class meetings encourage teacher and student sharing of responsibility and democratic decision-making and promote autonomy. In doing so, they also are likely to foster positive perceptions of teachers among students, especially compared to a more authoritarian approach.

Summary

When students get along with one another and demonstrate such interpersonal prosocial qualities as caring, friendliness, and respect toward one another, safety is seldom a problem, students are more inclined to view school rules as clear and fair, teacher-relationships are likely more favorable, less bullying occurs, and students are more likely to be engaged emotionally, cognitively, and behaviorally. In turn, students experience greater academic achievement and social and emotional competence. This is unlikely to be the case, however, when student-student relationships are poor, and especially when they are characterized not only by the lack of interpersonal prosocial qualities but by non-acceptance, rejection, and aggression toward peers.

Multiple factors influence how students relate to one another in school, and primary among those reasons are (a) characteristics of students and (b) characteristics of teachers, classroom, and the school. Each set of characteristics influence student-student relationships in a reciprocal and ongoing fashion. Just as peer acceptance or rejection is largely influenced by a student's social and emotional skills, so too are student-student interactions and relationships, including peer acceptance or rejection, influenced by the teacher's approach to classroom management, the class composition, and what occurs in hallways, the cafeteria, and throughout the building. Each of those factors operate to establish norms that either promote or hinder positive student-student relationships.

A number of evidence-based packaged programs for improving student-student relationships, which include lessons and staff development, are available for schools to adopt, with some having much stronger evidence of effectiveness than others. A shared characteristic of the most effective programs is consistency with the authoritative approach, as espoused throughout this book, which emphasizes a balance of responsiveness and demandingness. Whether a school adopts a program or not, however, it is strongly recommended that strategies for building and maintaining positive student-student relationships, such as those presented in this chapter, are infused throughout the school curriculum and everyday life of the classroom and school.

CHAPTER 4

DEVELOPING SOCIAL AND EMOTIONAL COMPETENCIES AND SELF-DISCIPLINE

Co-authored with Angela Soltys

> "Evidence confirms that supporting students' social, emotional, and academic development benefits all children and relates positively to the traditional measures we care about: attendance, grades, test scores, graduation rates, college and career success, engaged citizenship, and overall well-being."
> (Aspen Institute National Commission on Social, Emotional, and Academic Development, 2019, p.18).

Social and emotional competence is defined as "acquiring and effectively applying the knowledge, attitudes, and skills necessary to recognize and manage emotions; developing caring and concern for others; making responsible decisions; establishing positive relationships and handling challenging situations capably" (Zins & Elias, 2006, p. 1). Consistent with this definition, and drawing from decades of research on social and emotional development, and multiple theories guiding them, the CASEL has identified five core social and emotional learning (SEL) competencies that constitute general social and emotional competence: *responsible decision-making, self-management, relationship skills, social awareness, and self-awareness*. As discussed in Chapter 1, the teaching and developing of social and emotional competencies is a major dimension of the social-emotional support domain in school climate. To be sure, positive teacher-student relationships and student-student relationships are critical aspects of social-emotional support, but social-emotional support also includes responsiveness to students' social and emotional needs. This requires both social support and deliberate efforts to develop within students the social and emotional competencies that foster student engagement, safety, academic achievement, and mental health.

In this chapter, CASEL's five core social and emotional competencies and research demonstrating their importance are first described, followed by a brief summary of theories supporting the SEL approach and research supporting the effectiveness of SEL programs. Next, the relations between CASEL's five core social and emotional competencies and self-discipline are discussed, followed by mechanisms of moral disengagement that often explain why students who are socially and emotionally competent fail to demonstrate self-discipline and act morally. The chapter ends with recommendations for developing social and emotional competencies, especially those that underlie self-discipline.

CASEL's Core Social and Emotional Competencies

Before describing and discussing CASEL's social and emotional competencies, it should be emphasized that they are closely interrelated, influencing and influenced by one another. For example, responsible decision-making influences relationships just as relationships often influence responsible decision-making. This is seen in students choosing which peers they associate with and peer pressure influencing student's responsible decision-making. It also is important to recognize that to one extent or another, the same or similar skills underlie multiple social and emotional competencies. For example, social perspective-taking and empathy are major aspects of social awareness, but they also are critical to responsible decision-making, especially when caring and rights of others are to be considered. Likewise, social perspective-taking and empathy are important to self-management and relationships, particularly when those competencies involve respecting, caring, and not harming others. Thus, although it helps heuristically to conceptualize social and emotional competencies as comprising five different competencies, educators should recognize that they are interrelated and overlapping. In practice this means that students' weaknesses and strengths in one area of social and emotional competence are likely to influence other areas. It also means that when teaching skills such as social perspective-taking and empathy to strengthen one core social and emotional competency, teachers are also likely strengthening other competencies.

Supporting Research

In this section, each of CASEL's five core social and emotional competencies is described. Research linking each competency to valued educational outcomes, especially to student behavior, academic achievement, and social-emotional well-being is also discussed.

Responsible Decision-Making. Responsible decision-making refers to the ability to make decisions at school, home, and in the community that are socially and morally responsible. It requires skills in identifying, analyzing, and solving social and moral problems and evaluating and reflecting on consequences of one's choices and actions, including their impact on oneself and others. At the core of responsible decision-making is social problem-solving and moral reasoning that reflects an understanding of and valuing issues of justice, caring, and acceptance of responsibility.

Ample research with children and adolescents shows that good social problem-solving skills are associated with less aggression, delinquency, and frequency of bullying others and of being bullied (Cassidy, 2009; Cook, Williams, Guerra, Kim, & Sadek, 2010; Swearer, Wang, Berry, & Myers, 2014). Social problem-solving skills also have been shown to be related to greater peer acceptance (Lansford, Malone, Dodge, Pettit, & Bates, 2010; Newcomb, Bukowski, & Pattee, 1993; Pakaslahti, Karjalainen, & Keltikangas-Järvinen, 2002), more friendships (Schonert-Reichl, 1999), and greater behavioral, academic, and emotional adjustment in general (Dubow, Tisak, Causey, Hryshko, & Reid, 1991; Siu & Shek, 2010). Likewise, a large body of research finds moral reasoning, which is a critical aspect of responsible decision-making, to be related to student behavior, both prosocial behavior (Eisenberg, Zhou, & Koller, 2003; Malti & Krettenauer, 2013; Ongley, Nola, & Malti, 2014) and antisocial behavior (Malti & Krettenauer, 2013; Wyatt & Carlo, 2002). Such research finds that self-centered, hedonistic reasoning (i.e., focusing on gaining external rewards and avoiding punitive consequences) is associated with greater antisocial behavior and less prosocial behavior, whereas moral reasoning that is oriented more toward others and grounded in empathy and anticipated guilt is associated with less antisocial behavior and greater prosocial behavior (Carlo, Mestre, Samper, Tur, & Armenta, 2010; Manning & Bear, 2011; Stams et al., 2006).

Self-management. Self-management refers to effectively regulating one's thoughts, emotions, and behaviors. Proficiency in this competency requires impulse control, delay of gratification, anger management, setting goals and striving to achieve them, coping skills, and the ability to persevere when faced with set-backs and obstacles. Students with greater self-control, which includes managing thoughts, emotions, impulses, and performance, tend to have more positive interpersonal skills and relationships with others (Boman, Krohn, Gibson, & Stogner, 2012; Tangney, Baumeister, & Boone, 2004); fewer internalizing and externalizing behavior problems (Eisenberg, Spinrad, & Eggum, 2010); higher self-esteem, less psychopathology, and better health (e.g., physical health; sleep quality; less cigarette, alcohol, and drug abuse) (Bub, Robinson, & Curtis, 2016; Moffitt et al., 2011; Romer, Duckworth, Sznitman, & Park, 2010); and greater academic achievement and competence (Allan, Hume, Allan, Farrington, & Lonigan, 2014; Duckworth, Tsukayama, & Kirby, 2013; Hernández et al., 2018). Research suggests a causal connection between self-control and academic achievement (Duckworth, Tsukayama, & May, 2010), with self-control predicting academic achievement better than talent and IQ (Duckworth & Seligman, 2005, 2017). Not surprisingly, students lacking in self-management skills, or self-control, tend to be at risk for multiple negative outcomes in addition to poor school achievement, including greater involvement in crime and bullying, poorer physical and mental health, lower income, and greater substance abuse later in life (Griffin, Lowe, Acevedo, & Botvin, 2015; Kwak & Oh, 2017; Moffitt et al., 2011).

Closely related to self-control is the ability to delay gratification. Students who are able to delay gratification, or resist an immediate reward for a larger or more lasting later reward, tend to have greater social competence and academic achievement; are better able to manage stress and frustration; engage in fewer risk behaviors; and have better planning skills (Duckworth et al., 2013; Herndon, Bembenutty, & Gill, 2015).

Relationship Skills. Relationship skills refer to the ability to form and maintain positive relationships with others. They include listening to others, working cooperatively, handling conflict constructively, seeking and providing help when needed, and resisting peer pressure. As reviewed in Chapter 3 on student-student relationships, a large body of research has shown the importance of peer relationship skills in social and emotional well-being. For example, students lacking peer relationship skills are at greater risk for a number of negative outcomes, such as peer rejection, bullying victimization, and loneliness (Boulton, Trueman, Chau, Whitehand, & Amatya, 1999; Kwak & Oh, 2017). In contrast, those with strong relationship skills tend to be more popular, socially accepted, and have more reciprocated friendships (Kwon, Kim, & Sheridan, 2012; Newcomb et al., 1993); exhibit greater prosocial and fewer antisocial behaviors (Newcomb & Bagwell, 1995; Wentzel, 2005); be more engaged in school (Jimerson, Egeland, Sroufe, & Carlson, 2000; Kwon et al., 2012); and have more positive emotional well-being (Wentzel, 2005; Wentzel & Muenks, 2016), Finally, supportive relationships with others, especially peers, parents, and teachers, also serve as protective factors for students against the effects of negative experiences such as bullying and abuse (Adams & Bukowski, 2007; Flaspohler, Elfstrom, Vanderzee, Sink, & Birchmeier, 2009).

Social Awareness. Social awareness refers to the ability to recognize and understand the needs and perspectives of others. It is grounded in the moral emotions of empathy, empathy-based guilt, and shame. Those abilities and emotions are associated with respecting and not harming others, appreciating diversity and individual differences, and responding to the needs of others (i.e., helping directly or seeking help from others). Students lacking in social perspective-taking demonstrate fewer prosocial behaviors (Cigala, Mori, & Fangareggi, 2015; Fitzgerald & White, 2003; Tamnes et al., 2018) and greater aggression (Berger, Batanova, & Cance, 2015; Fitzgerald & White, 2003; Li et al., 2015). Likewise, students lacking in empathy exhibit fewer prosocial behaviors (Findlay, Girardi, & Coplan, 2006; Masten, Morelli, & Eisenberger, 2011; Taylor, Eisenberg, Spinrad, Eggum, & Sulik, 2013), and greater antisocial and externalizing behaviors (Batanova & Loukas, 2016; Berger et al., 2015; Eisenberg, Eggum, & Di Giunta, 2010). Empathy and subsequent prosocial behavior has also been linked to greater academic achievement, engagement, and overall school success (Caprara, Barbaranelli, Pastorelli, Bandura, & Zimbardo, 2000; Spinrad & Eisenberg, 2014). The lack of social awareness, as seen in the absence of the moral emotions of empathy-based guilt and shame, is a defining characteristic of "cold and callous" individuals (Frick & White, 2008).

Self-awareness. Self-awareness refers to skills in recognizing and understanding one's own emotions, interests, values, strengths, and weaknesses and how one's thoughts and emotions impact behavior. This incorporates self-concept, self-confidence, and self-efficacy. Research on self-concept shows that most children view moral behavior as central to their overall sense of self (Harter, 2006). Similarly, research in moral development shows that for many individuals, a "moral identity" is critical to their overall sense of self and happiness (Hardy & Carlo, 2005; Hart, Atkins, & Donnelly, 2006).

Greater self-awareness is associated with additional positive outcomes. Students with stronger self-efficacy and confidence tend to have greater school engagement and academic achievement (Multon, Brown, & Lent, 1991; Olivier, Archambault, De Clercq, & Galand, 2019; Stankov, Lee, Luo, & Hogan, 2012). They also experience less bullying victimization and are less likely to be perpetrators of bullying and cyberbullying (Cheng & Furnham, 2002; Kokkinos &

Kipritsi, 2012; Navarro, Yubero, & Larrañaga, 2015). Self-awareness also is related to students' peer relationships and status. Popular students tend to think of themselves in more positive ways compared to students of average peer status (Boivin & Bégin, 1989). Finally, research shows that self-efficacy beliefs related to friendships, or friendship self-efficacy, ameliorates the negative effects of social victimization and reduces internalizing problems (Fitzpatrick & Bussey, 2014).

Supporting Theories

As seen above, research links each of CASEL's social and emotional competencies to multiple valued outcomes, including academic achievement and social and emotional well-being. Their significance also is firmly grounded in multiple theories supported by research in psychology, particularly those with historical roots in the works of John Dewey (1938) and constructivist theories on the development of learning (Piaget, 1965; Vygotsky, 1987). Those theories view students as active rather than passive learners. As such, the aim of education, and the SEL approach, is not the direct transmission of knowledge and social skills and the adult management of student behavior, as commonly found in behavioral models in psychology or classroom management (including Positive Behavioral Interventions and Supports [PBIS]). Instead, the aim is to develop within students the SEL skills required of self-governing and responsible citizens in a democratic society. Modern day theories and frameworks sharing this perspective, and upon which the SEL approach is based, include those reviewed in Chapter 1 (i.e., bioecological theory, attachment theory, self-determination theory, social control theory, social cognitive theory) but also social information processing theory (Crick & Dodge, 1994), moral development theory (Kohlberg, 1984), prosocial development theory (Eisenberg, Fabes, & Spinrad, 2006), emotions theory (Goleman, 1995; Izard, 1991), self-concept theory (Harter, 2006), attribution theory (Weiner, 2006), social-ecological theory (Bronfenbrenner, 1979), and positive psychology (Gilman, Huebner, & Furlong, 2009).

Effectiveness of SEL Programs

Additional support for the SEL approach also comes from research demonstrating that school-based SEL intervention programs produce important valued outcomes in education. In a comprehensive, and often cited, meta-analysis of 213 studies that implemented SEL programs, Durlak, Weissberg, Dymnicki, Taylor, and Schellinger (2011) found significant improvements among students in multiple areas related directly or indirectly to school climate, including student engagement and academic achievement, attitudes (i.e., about the self, the school, and school safety), social and emotional skills (e.g., identifying emotions, perspective-taking, social problem-solving), and externalizing and internalizing behaviors (e.g., positive social behavior, conduct problems, emotional distress). Three other meta-analyses have supported and extended the findings of Durlak and colleagues. Wigelsworth et al. (2016) reviewed 89 SEL program studies conducted internationally and found significant positive effects on social-emotional competence, prosocial behavior, conduct problems, emotional distress, and academic achievement. Sklad, Diekstra, De Ritter, Ben, and Gravesteijn

(2012) investigated both the short-term and follow-up (i.e., at least seven months post-intervention) effects of school-based universal SEL programs. Their synthesis of 75 studies revealed positive immediate effects on social-emotional skills, prosocial behavior, antisocial behavior, self-image, mental disorders, substance abuse, and academic achievement. Follow-up positive effects also were found for all outcomes, although some of the effects decreased over time.

A recent meta-analysis by Taylor, Oberle, Durlak, and Weissberg (2017) of 82 SEL intervention studies conducted internationally, which included over 97,000 students of all grade levels, replicated earlier findings of long-term effects. Positive outcomes lasting from 6 months to 18 years post-intervention were found for SEL skills, attitudes, positive social behavior, conduct problems, emotional distress, drug use, and academic performance. These effects were found across demographic groups (i.e., race, socioeconomic status, country of implementation). Positive and lasting effects also were found on outcomes less frequently assessed in SEL research, including peer and family relationships, school attendance, graduation rates, college attendance, and arrests. The study also showed that higher social-emotional competence at the end of the initial intervention was the best predictor of positive long-term outcomes.

Another aspect of effectiveness is cost effectiveness: Do the benefits of the SEL program justify their costs? In addressing this question, Belfield et al. (2015) conducted a thorough cost analysis of six SEL programs of demonstrated effectiveness in improving social-emotional adjustment and academic achievement. Those programs included the Responsive Classroom Approach, as described previously in Chapter 2, and the Second Step program which is described later in this chapter. The research concluded that "SEL interventions can easily pass a benefit-cost test. In fact, the weighted average benefit-cost ratio across all six interventions with prior evidence of effectiveness indicates that identified benefits outweigh the costs by a factor of 11:1" (p. 46).

SEL and Self-Discipline

As emphasized in Chapter 1, a primary aim of education has always been to develop social and emotional competencies that underlie *self-discipline*. Self-discipline refers to students regulating their own behavior, exhibiting prosocial behavior, and inhibiting antisocial behavior while requiring minimal external governance. In Baumrind's model of authoritative parenting, the development of social and emotional competencies that underlie self-discipline and autonomy is a major part of responsiveness to children's psychological needs. Self-discipline requires skills in each of CASEL's areas of social-emotional competence. It requires awareness that a social or moral problem exists (i.e., social awareness); skills in solving social and moral problems (i.e., responsible decision-making), self-management of one's emotions and inhibiting impulsive behavior; and self-confidence or self-efficacy to act upon one's decision (self-awareness). Finally, at the core of self-discipline is building and maintaining relationships with others, which call for demonstrating prosocial behavior and inhibiting anti-social behavior.

Although each SEL competency is related to self-discipline, perhaps most important is responsible decision-making *and* acting upon one's decisions. Clearly, self-awareness, social awareness, self-management, and relationship skills are important, but they do not ensure socially and morally responsible behavior. Indeed, skills in the other four domains of competency may be used to support irresponsible and harmful behaviors. That is, many individuals have keen social awareness and self-awareness, excellent interpersonal skills, and manage their emotions and behavior quite well, but nevertheless act in socially and morally irresponsible ways. Examples abound, and often in the popular press, of individuals who are socially aware of the needs of others but ignore them or have no empathy or sympathy; individuals who manage their behavior well, and intend to harm others, and do so effectively; and individuals establishing relationships for self-serving, if not harmful, purposes. Hence, CASEL's five social and emotional competencies are necessary but not sufficient for moral behavior.

Moral behavior requires the ability to experience moral emotions, such as empathy, empathy-based guilt, and shame. It also requires the ability to engage in higher levels of moral reasoning based on the needs of others, social justice, and appreciation of laws and ethical principles. Other-oriented moral reasoning and moral emotions that spark moral action, such as empathy and anticipated guilt and shame, *must first be activated* before they can direct moral behavior (Bandura, 2016; Hoffman, 2000). By deactivating, or disengaging, self-regulatory mechanisms, students (and adults) are able to absolve themselves of any responsibility for failing to act morally or for acting immorally, and in turn, avoid feelings of guilt and shame. Thus, a great challenge to educators aiming to promote social and emotional learning, and especially responsible decision-making and self-discipline, is to identify and confront the mechanisms that students employ to avoid responsibility for their actions and acting in a moral and socially responsible manner.

Mechanisms of Moral Disengagement

Bandura and colleagues (Bandura, 2016; Bandura, Caprara, Barbaranelli, Pastorelli, & Regalia, 2001) have identified eight social cognitive mechanisms, called *mechanisms of moral disengagement*, that individuals employ to deactivate self-regulatory mechanisms such as empathy and anticipated guilt and shame. A large body of research has shown that mechanisms of moral disengagement are associated with multiple forms of anti-social and aggressive behavior, including bullying (for a meta-analytic review, see Gini, Pozzoli, & Hymel, 2014), as well as the absence of prosocial actions, such as bystanders failing to intervene (Doramajian & Bukowski, 2015; Gini, 2006; Thornberg, Pozzoli, Gini, & Jungert, 2015). Bandura's eight mechanisms of moral disengagement, and examples of each, follow:

- *Attribution of blame.* Blame is attributed to the victim (e.g., "She started it." "She deserved it.").
- *Displacement of responsibility.* Responsibility is displaced upon someone else in a position of authority, control, or authority (e.g., "I was made to it." "Jessica told me to.").
- *Diffusion of responsibility.* Blame is shared with the group (e.g., "Others did it too." "I wasn't the only one.").

- *Moral or social justification.* Reasons are given to justify the behavior (e.g., "I had a good reason for it." "I didn't mean to hurt him.").
- *Euphemistic and convoluted language.* Language is used to sanitize one's behavior and to convince others, and oneself, that the behavior was either not bad or intentional (e.g., "I was joking and teasing, not bullying." "I was just kidding.").
- *Exonerative or advantageous comparison.* Assumption of responsibility is deflected by comparing one's behavior with the (worse) behavior of others (e.g., "But others were worse." "Did you see what others did?").
- *Disregard, distortion, and denial of harmful effects.* Harmful effects are disputed, minimized, or denied (e.g., "It was no big deal; he's not hurt.").
- *Dehumanization.* The victim is presented as lacking positive qualities, not worthy of respect, or deserving of harm (e.g., "He's a wimp, and no one likes a wimp." "He's so stupid." "His kind don't belong here.").

Mechanisms of moral disengagement are used alone or in combination. If one fails to work, another one is tried. When they go unchallenged and are effective in avoiding punishment or wrongdoing, they are negatively reinforced, and thus become repeated over time. This serves to further hamper prosocial actions and promote antisocial ones by absolving oneself of a sense of social and moral responsibility. Given the important role of mechanisms of moral disengagement in moral behavior, it behooves educators to not only develop SEL skills, but also to confront the mechanisms of moral disengagement that students commonly use to avoid applying SEL skills (see Recommendation #7 below).

Recommended Strategies for Promoting SEL and Self-Discipline

Curriculum lessons are the core of most SEL programs; however, when implemented correctly there is much more to developing social and emotional competencies in the SEL approach than the teaching of lessons from a curriculum. The SEL approach recognizes the importance of all domains of school climate and the dimensions within them, including the domains of social-emotional support, structure, engagement, and safety. It is understood that educational strategies within each domain help establish the necessary conditions for teaching SEL lessons, but also for students to apply and hone the SEL skills they are taught. For example, self-management, responsible decision-making, relationship skills, and social awareness are observed, practiced, and reinforced in social interactions with teachers and peers. Likewise, to one extent or another, each SEL competency concerns student engagement and school safety. Either directly or indirectly, most, if not all, of the strategies recommended in other chapters help develop SEL competencies. Thus, the first recommendation refers to strategies presented in other chapters, followed by additional recommendations for promoting SEL, with a particular emphasis on developing skills that underlie self-discipline.

1. *Implement strategies for improving those areas of school climate that facilitate the development of social and emotional competencies, particularly teacher-student relationships, student-student relationships, and student engagement.* Although strategies presented in all other chapters help develop

social and emotional competencies, those in three domains of school climate tend to receive greatest emphasis in most SEL programs: teacher-student relationships, student-student relationships, and student engagement. Considered as key features of the SEL approach, their importance is emphasized in nearly all schoolwide SEL programs.

Teacher-student relationships. Other than SEL curriculum lessons, perhaps no other feature of SEL receives greater attention than the quality of teacher-student relationships (Bear, Whitcomb, Elias, & Blank, 2015). This is perhaps best seen in the research-based Responsive Classroom Approach, as reviewed in Chapter 2 on teacher-student relationships, wherein teachers' responsiveness to students' psychological needs of competence, relatedness, and autonomy is the foremost feature.

Student-student relationships. Skills related to student-student relationships are targeted in nearly all SEL curricula. Those skills include listening, respect, social perspective-taking, empathy, conflict resolution, and resisting peer pressure. In addition to curriculum-based activities, many SEL programs implement strategies in which students learn *and* apply peer relationship skills. For example, both the Responsive Classroom Approach (Center for Responsive Schools, 2019) and the Caring School Community program (Center for the Collaborative Classroom, 2018) use peer-assisted and cooperative learning activities to promote both academic achievement and social and emotional learning. Others, such as the Teaching Students to Be Peacemakers Program (Johnson & Johnson, 2006), focus on peer mediation, in which students are trained to be actively involved in preventing and resolving peer conflicts. Finally, most SEL programs strongly recommend that students actively participate in extracurricular activities, such as student government, sports, and clubs, especially those that provide models of SEL skills and opportunities to practice them.

Student engagement. Finally, the SEL approach recognizes that student engagement—cognitive, behavioral, and emotional engagement—influences, and is influenced by, each of the five SEL competencies. Indeed, many skills targeted in SEL programs are engagement skills, such as exerting one's best effort, completing assignments, and having a positive mastery-oriented mindset (cognitive engagement), paying attention and following rules (behavioral engagement), and viewing oneself and peers positively (emotional engagement). Thus, the strategies recommended in Chapter 7 for student engagement apply to developing multiple social and emotional learning skills.

2. **Adopt an evidence-based commercially-produced SEL curriculum.** The advantages of a packaged curriculum are that teachers are provided lessons that are already developed, field-tested, and typically scripted. The lessons also incorporate a variety of methods of teaching, with supporting materials such as entertaining videos, songs, and dances that capture students' attention. Such materials are difficult and expensive for teachers to self-produce.

Although there are multiple advantages to adopting a commercially produced SEL program, there also are disadvantages. Fortunately, many of the disadvantages can largely be avoided with careful planning, a wise selection of programs, and the provision of adequate resources and professional development. Among the disadvantages are that teachers and students often perceive SEL as something taught and practiced only during "SEL time," or "social skills training time." This is particularly likely to occur when the lessons are not taught by the classroom teacher, but by support staff such as the school counselor. When SEL skills are taught at a set time of day, generalization and maintenance of skills are likely to be problematic, especially if deliberate efforts for generalization and maintenance are not planned and implemented. Efforts to foster generalization and maintenance should include teaching SEL skills throughout the day by embedding them into the general curriculum (see Recommendation #3 below), prompting students to apply the skills taught, and reinforcing them when they do so.

Another disadvantage of packaged programs is that too often the lessons go untaught or are otherwise lacking in fidelity of implementation (Durlak & DuPre, 2008). There are many reasons why this might occur. Among the reasons are that teachers perceive a program and its lessons as not needed, ineffective, conflicting with their philosophy, too demanding on their time, a low educational priority, or requiring teaching skills for which they lack training or that they are not adequately trained to teach (Bear, 2013; Fullan, 2007). When such reasons for resisting implementation are apparent or anticipated, efforts should be made to address them through discussion, program modifications, and staff development.

Finally, another disadvantage of adopting a packaged SEL program is that the effectiveness of many of the programs is unknown. Although many SEL programs have been shown to be effective, very few have undergone the scrutiny of randomized controlled studies. Randomized controlled studies are considered the gold standard among researchers. Even fewer have undergone randomized control trials *and* were found to improve behaviors commonly associated with self-discipline, especially reduced antisocial behavior and increased prosocial behavior. Two popular curriculum-based SEL programs with extensive research supporting their effectiveness are PATHS and Second Step Social-Emotional Learning, as described below.

PATHS (Promoting Alternative Thinking Strategies) (Preschool–Grade 6) (https://pathsprogram.com)

Lessons in PATHS target self-control, emotional awareness, empathy, relationship and social skills, and social problem-solving. Separate sets of scripted lessons and support materials (e.g., family handouts, ways to link lessons to the general curriculum) are provided for preschool/kindergarten, grades 1–4, and grades 5–6. Lessons are 20–30 minutes long and designed to be taught two to three times weekly. PATHS is designed to be integrated within academic subjects, particularly language arts and social studies. Professional development training is offered.

Numerous research studies support the efficacy of PATHS in improving student behavior. Specifically, studies have shown increases in students' prosocial behaviors, compliance, social competence, social acceptance, social problem-solving, and academic achievement, and decreases in aggression, conduct problems, and negative emotional symptoms (Conduct Problems Prevention Research Group, 2010; Crean & Johnson, 2013; Domitrovich, Cortes, & Greenberg, 2007; Humphrey et al., 2016; Schonfeld, Adams, Fredstrom, Tomlin & Voyce, 2012). Not all studies, however, have reported reduced behavior problems. Several studies found no effects on students' problem and antisocial behavior, although significant effects were found for prosocial behavior (e.g., Hamre, Pianta, Mashburn, & Downer, 2012).

Second Step Social-Emotional Learning (Preschool–Grade 8) (www.secondstep.org/)

Separate kits exist for preschool (ages 4 & 5), elementary (grades K-5), and middle school (grades 6–8). The preschool lessons and support materials (e.g., puppets, recordings of songs, home activities, posters, feeling cards) cover units on empathy (6 lessons), skills for learning (6 lessons), emotion management (6 lessons), friendship skills and problem-solving (7 lessons), and transitioning to kindergarten (3 lessons). The elementary school curriculum has 3–4 units per grade level, targeting empathy (6–9 lessons), skills for learning (4–9 lessons), emotion management (5–7 lessons), and social problem-solving (6–7 lessons). At the elementary school level, separate kits also are provided for bullying prevention and child protection units. A "Principal Toolkit" also is offered, which consists of recommendations and support materials to reinforce social-emotional skills schoolwide, such as in assemblies, morning announcements, staff agenda items, and information sent home. The middle school curriculum consists of four units: mindsets and goals (7 lessons); values and friendships (5 lessons); thoughts, emotions, and decisions (5 lessons); and serious peer conflicts (9 lessons). Lessons and activities take less than 10 minutes at the preschool level, and approximately 20–30 minutes at the elementary and middle school levels. The elementary and middle school curricula include engaging music and video lessons, rarely found in other programs, several of which have won awards. Professional development training is offered for all grade levels.

Studies of the effectiveness of Second Step programs have reported improvements in students' social-emotional skills, engagement, and prosocial behaviors, and reductions in externalizing and internalizing behaviors, including aggression, non-compliance, bullying, and anxiety (Espelage, Low, Polanin, & Brown, 2015; Espelage, Low, Van Ryzin, & Polanin, 2015; Holsen, Smith, & Frey, 2008; Low, Cook, Smolkowski, & Buntain-Ricklefs, 2015). However, results of a recent meta-analysis (Moy & Hazen, 2018) of 24 studies on Second Step casts doubt on its effectiveness in improving student behavior. The researchers examined three types of outcomes: content knowledge, prosocial behavior, and antisocial behavior. They grouped and examined studies by their design: independent group design studies (i.e., randomized controlled trials and quasi-experiments) and single-group designs (i.e., pre-test and post-test design) separately. The analyses revealed that for both study designs there were statistically significant increases in program content knowledge, but only single-group designs showed a statistically significant effect on prosocial behavior. Neither study design found statistically significant impacts on antisocial behavior. A notable limitation of the meta-analysis, however, was that a number of frequently cited research studies on Second Step were not included. This was because those studies failed to report necessary data for reviewers to produce an effect size or because the studies had outcome variables that were not included in the meta-analysis.

Excellent resources for selecting among SEL programs are provided by CASEL (see www.casel.org/guide/) and by the RAND Corporation (Grant et al., 2017). In addition to looking for programs shown to be effective, it is important to examine the scope of each program and its components. As noted in the program reviews by CASEL, some programs are primarily, if not exclusively, lesson-based, whereas others include additional guidance and training on integrating or infusing the teaching and practice of student-student relationships skills throughout the everyday life of the classroom and school.

CASEL also provides schools with resources and guidance to assist them in selecting, implementing, and evaluating evidence-based instructional practices and curricula for social and emotional learning. CASEL also works with states and school districts in developing and promoting standards to advance social and emotional learning (see https://casel.org/state-standards-to-advance-social-and-emotional-learning/).

3. ***Embed SEL lessons into the general curriculum and everyday life of the school.*** Embedding SEL lessons into the school's existing general curriculum, such as in literacy, social studies, or health, should be considered as an alternative, or as an addition, to adopting a packaged program (Bear, 2005, 2010; Jones & Bouffard, 2012). Indeed, many teachers already teach SEL lessons as part of their school's "hidden curriculum," wherein lessons are taught in the context of core subject areas and often without the teacher's awareness that they are developing SEL competencies. That is, the lessons are not identified or viewed as SEL lessons per se. Examples are teaching SEL competencies when reading and discussing children's literature (e.g., *Pinocchio, Lord of the Flies, Diary of Anne Frank, To Kill a Mockingbird, Charlotte's Web*) and topics in social studies such as slavery, the Holocaust, the Vietnam War, civil rights, constitutional rights, and the influence of media. In so doing, teachers often use many of the SEL instructional strategies recommended and used in packaged programs. Strategies for teaching SEL lessons embedded in the existing curriculum include creative writing assignments, journal writing, poetry, debates, role-plays, video productions, drama, art, music, and research surveys and interviews.

   To foster additional skill development, and while enhancing generalization and maintenance of skills learned, SEL lessons should not only be infused throughout the general curriculum but also embedded into other instructional practices and classroom management practices. These would include morning announcements, assemblies, class meetings and disciplinary encounters. This approach to embedding lessons into the general curriculum and infusing additional SEL activities throughout the everyday life of the school is taken by the Caring School Community program (Center for the Collaborative Classroom, 2018) and Responsive Classroom Approach (Center for Responsive Schools, 2019).

   As with a packaged curriculum, an SEL program that embeds lessons throughout the general curriculum has its advantages and disadvantages. One advantage is that teacher resistance is less likely to occur since teachers view the lessons as already part of the general curriculum, and not as another thing added to their plates. To prevent this reaction, SEL lessons that are currently being taught in the hidden curriculum should be made visible, such that teachers recognize they are already teaching SEL skills while simultaneously covering standards in the general curriculum. For example, when teaching a lesson on slavery (and the perspective of slaves and issues of justice and civil rights), both social studies and SEL standards are addressed. Another advantage to embedding SEL lessons throughout the curriculum is that it encourages teachers to capitalize on "teachable moments," such as in the context of class meetings and discussions about topics related to SEL competencies. Such lessons often entail real-life and real-time issues, not hypothetical ones.

There also are disadvantages, however, to relying on lessons infused throughout the curriculum and on teachable moments when developing SEL skills. Foremost among them is that existing lessons and teachable moments may not cover all social and emotional competencies desired or might do so in a fragmented fashion. It is largely for these reasons that many schools adopt a packaged program, with sequenced lessons for teaching SEL skills and guidance to teachers on how best to teach them. Such programs are typically used together with lessons already in the existing curriculum. Another disadvantage is that aligning lessons in the general curriculum with SEL competencies requires considerable time and staff development.

4. *Use praise and rewards in a wise and strategic manner that promotes intrinsic motivation and autonomy.* Praise and rewards are commonly used to teach and reinforce desired behavior, with decades of research demonstrating their effectiveness in managing student behavior (Landrum & Kauffman, 2006). Much less research has examined the impact of the frequent and systematic use of praise and rewards on students' perceptions of school climate.

In a recent study of 30,071 students in grades 3–12, Bear, Yang, Mantz, and Harris (2017) found that whereas the use of frequent praise and rewards was related to students' positive perceptions of school climate, the teaching of social and emotional competencies was a stronger predictor of a positive school climate than were either the use of praise and rewards or the use of punishment. Use of praise and rewards for good behavior related significantly and positively with students' perceptions of school climate, and use of punishment related significantly and negatively. However, the effects of teaching social and emotional competencies were nearly twice that of the use of praise and rewards and the use of punishment.

The use of praise and rewards, and particularly the use of tangible rewards, has not been without criticism. Primary among the criticisms has been that too often rewards are overused and used in ways that actually harm intrinsic motivation and stifle the development of moral development and autonomy (Bear, 2010). Indeed, studies suggest that under certain conditions tangible rewards may harm intrinsic motivation and promote extrinsic motivation (Ryan & Deci, 2017). Intrinsic motivation is observed in students helping and not harming others because they value kindness and understand how their behavior affects others, and students following rules out of respect of adults and an understanding of their purpose. In contrast, extrinsic motivation is seen in students behaving to avoid punishment or to gain external rewards, which is the self-centered and hedonistic motivation that characterizes the lowest levels of moral development (Kohlberg, 1984) and is commonly found among the most aggressive and antisocial individuals (Stams et al., 2006). When schools rely solely or primarily on rewards and punishment to manage student behavior and fail to develop intrinsic and other-oriented reasons for helping and not harming others, they run the risk of encouraging extrinsic motivation and hedonistic moral reasoning.

Research on intrinsic and extrinsic motivation has identified several conditions under which rewards, especially tangible rewards (e.g., a prize, candy) are likely to be ineffective and harm intrinsic motivation (Ryan & Deci, 2017). One is when tangible rewards are used by adults in a manner that is perceived by students as controlling or manipulating. For example, the adult communicates the message "You need to do this in order for me to reward you, and not punish you." Another condition is that of social comparison, which is when adults compare students to one another, and especially publicly (e.g., "Angela earned five points and a reward, but you didn't."). Not only might those conditions promote self-centered moral reasoning and extrinsic motivation, but they also are likely to be met with resistance, especially among adolescents who resent adult control and social comparisons.

Most of the research demonstrating harmful effects of rewards on intrinsic motivation has been conducted in controlled laboratory settings, and thus the extent to which the same conditions normally occur in classrooms is questionable (Akin-Little & Little, 2009). A recent study (Bear, Slaughter, Mantz, & Farley-Ripple, 2017) of over 10,000 students in grades 5–12 addressed this issue. The study examined the impact of the everyday use of praise and rewards on extrinsic and intrinsic motivation as reported by students. Extrinsic motivation was assessed with such self-report items as "I help others because I might get a reward" and "I help because teachers might praise me," whereas intrinsic motivation was assessed with items such as "I help because I care about others" and "I would feel bad about myself if I didn't help." The researchers found that greater use of praise and rewards was associated with higher extrinsic prosocial motivation but was *not* associated with lower intrinsic prosocial motivation. Interestingly, punitive consequences seemed to have the most harmful effects, as they were associated with greater extrinsic and lower intrinsic prosocial motivation. Another interesting finding was that regardless of the frequency of the use of praise and rewards, students were much more likely to give intrinsic reasons for their prosocial behavior than extrinsic reasons.

Together, those results led the researchers to conclude that most schools do not need to worry about the frequent and common use of praise and rewards being associated with less intrinsic prosocial motivation at least not in the short-term. Long-term effects were not examined, however. In interpreting their findings, the researchers also surmised that the socially controlling and social comparative use of rewards, as used in laboratory settings, might be much less common in classrooms, and that when they do occur their effects might be buffered by positive teacher-student relationships. Nevertheless, they recommended that praise and rewards be used wisely and strategically in ways that promote intrinsic prosocial motivation rather than extrinsic prosocial motivation and self-centered moral reasoning.

Thus, the recommendations that follow focus on the use of praise and rewards for promoting intrinsic prosocial motivation, autonomy, and self-discipline, while discouraging extrinsic motivation and self-centered moral reasoning. They are supported by research in the areas of classroom management (Brophy, 1981, 2004; Reeve, 2009, 2015), autonomy and locus of control (Weiner, 2006), effective feedback (Brophy, 1981, 2004; Henderlong & Lepper, 2002), and the effects of rewards on intrinsic and extrinsic motivation (Deci, Koestner, & Ryan, 1999, 2001; Ryan & Deci, 2017). These recommendations should be implemented together with general recommendations presented in Chapter 4 on the use of praise and rewards for teaching and reinforcing behavior and managing student behavior.

- *Use tangible rewards as little as necessary to teach and maintain the desired behavior.* Tangible rewards should primarily be used to reinforce desired behavior or effort when teaching a behavior that is new, difficult, or of little interest to a student, and intrinsic motivation is lacking. It makes little sense to use rewards more than needed. Frequent and systematic use of tangible rewards (including point cards and tokens), especially when not needed to motivate prosocial behavior, increases the risk of potential harm to intrinsic motivation. Thus, they should be used only occasionally for behavior that is motivated intrinsically—when sincere praise is typically sufficient for recognizing and reinforcing desired behaviors. This recommendation is consistent with the *principle of minimal sufficiency* in developmental psychology and the *least restrictive alternative* in behavioral psychology. The principle of minimal sufficiency states that an adult is more likely to foster students' intrinsic motivation for behavior change and sense of autonomy when using *just enough* external pressure to bring about compliance without making students feel that they are being coerced (Lepper, 1983). Similarly, the principle of the least restrictive alternative in behaviorism states that preference should always be given to interventions that are least likely to limit or restrict the student's freedom while still achieving the desired objective (Barton, Brulle, & Repp, 1983). When tangible rewards are used frequently and systematically, such as when intrinsic motivation is lacking, planned efforts should always be made to fade their use as students demonstrate the desired behaviors and learn that there are reasons other than extrinsic ones to act prosocially.
- *When rewards are used be sure to recognize the efforts and autonomous choices of students.* Administering rewards in this manner is likely to lessen perceptions of external control and foster self-perceptions of autonomy and an internal locus of control. It also avoids the mindset that the primary reasons why one should comply with rules and obey authority is to obtain rewards and avoid punishment.
- *Administer rewards spontaneously and unexpectedly.* Rewards are less likely to be perceived as controlling and to harm intrinsic motivation when they are provided in a surprise or unexpected manner. The key to this method is *not* informing students that they will receive a reward if certain expectations are met but providing the reward unexpectedly when the expectations are met. For example, a teacher surprises the class with 20 minutes of free time on Friday for all or most students completing their homework during the week.
- *Reward (and praise) not only students' prosocial behavior but also the thoughts, emotions, and dispositions that underlie the behavior.* Social and emotional competencies demonstrated by students should always be highlighted, but so too should the thoughts and emotions that drive them. For example, when rewarding the class for acts of kindness and no bullying behaviors, the thoughts and emotions for being kind should

be highlighted. This should include recognizing and praising general dispositions (e.g., "You're a kind person." "You're someone who really cares about others."). Research shows that praising general dispositions is more effective than praise alone (Eisenberg et al., 1996).

- *Make a deliberate effort to communicate that rewards are used to give informative feedback.* Feedback serves the valuable purpose of informing students what they are doing well and in what areas they might need to improve (and how to do so). By focusing on the informative function of rewards (and praise), teachers help avoid students perceiving the rewards as controlling. It also helps to emphasize that rewards are determined by the students, and not the person disseminating them.

5. *Provide ample models of the use of social and emotional learning skills.* Modeling promotes learning SEL skills in multiple ways. It informs students of appropriate ways of thinking, feeling, and acting; motivates them to think, feel, and act the same as the model; promotes values and standards that underlie the thoughts, feelings, and behaviors observed; and elicits cognitions (e.g., problem-solving) and emotions (e.g., empathy, sorrow) that motivate prosocial behavior or inhibit harmful behavior (Bandura, 1986).

In previous chapters, modeling of behavior was a recommended strategy for promoting positive teacher-student relationships and student-student relationships. That recommendation is repeated here, but with increased emphasis on modeling SEL skills and the thoughts and feelings that underlie them. That is, students should be presented with multiple models of the thought processes and feelings that guide self-discipline and prosocial behavior. Examples include modeling steps to social problem-solving (e.g., "What is the problem I'm facing? What are some solutions? Which solution might be best?"), calming oneself down (e.g., "I first need to take a few deep breaths."), and taking the perspective of others (e.g., "I wonder how others will feel if I do this?"). Such modeling should be presented *live* for students to observe, as seen in teachers thinking aloud when solving real-life social and moral problems in the classroom, and, where appropriate, having students to do the same (e.g., "Shelby, will you please share with the class what you were thinking and feeling when you helped Lizzy?").

Modeling cognitions and emotions also should be considered when discussing current events in the media (e.g., "I wonder if this is what he was thinking when he solved that problem?"), and in the context of curriculum lessons, such when discussing and role-playing what characters in literature and history were thinking and feeling. Several SEL packaged programs include videos and songs to help guide students' thinking when faced with social and emotional challenges. An excellent example are the award-winning videos and songs in Second Step Social-Emotional Learning.

To enhance the effectiveness of modeling, research shows that it helps if the models of the desired behaviors are viewed by students as being competent in the skills modeled and as having interpersonal qualities that they find appealing, such as friendliness, sense of humor, and other qualities of interest or desired by students (e.g., athletic, musical, or artistic abilities, financial success). Other features that enhance the effectiveness of modeling include

(a) providing diversity in the role models provided (i.e., the models vary in gender, race, socioeconomic status, cultural backgrounds), which increases the likelihood that more students will view the model as sharing similar characteristics; (b) highlighting both specific skills (e.g., problem-solving, calming oneself) and generalized dispositions (e.g., kindness, caring) displayed by the model; (c) demonstrating a variety of skills or solutions to a problem; (d) applying modeling to real-life problems that students encounter, or might encounter in the future (as opposed to only hypothetical ones); and (e) having teachers and others in school (including classmates, where appropriate and feasible) recognize and reinforce students when they exhibit the behavior, thoughts, and emotions desired and modeled.

6. *Hold class or morning meetings that promote SEL.* As discussed in the previous chapter on student-student relationships (see Recommendation #10), class meetings provide an excellent context to foster positive peer relations. This also applies to fostering other SEL skills. Class meetings are particularly invaluable for including students in the decision-making process, which often increases their commitment to decisions made.

7. *Develop SEL skills during disciplinary encounters.* Disciplinary encounters provide an excellent educational opportunity for developing social and emotional competencies, and especially those that underlie self-discipline. Recommended steps for correcting misbehavior are presented in Chapter 6. As discussed in that chapter, distributing punishment, ranging from a verbal warning to suspension, is often appropriate (and required in most schools' codes of conduct), but the primary goal when correcting misbehavior should be to help prevent the misbehavior from reoccurring and to repair any harm that has been done, including harm to relationships. This calls for the teaching of SEL skills, and disciplinary encounters provide an excellent opportunity to do so. During disciplinary encounters, it behooves educators to focus not only on the misbehavior itself, and why it is wrong, but also on the thoughts and feelings, or the absence thereof, that might have contributed to the misbehavior. Following what is referred to as *inductive discipline* (Baumrind, 2013), or *induction* (Hoffman, 2000), students should be challenged to consider the impact of their behavior on others—how it makes others feel (including not only a victim, but classmates, the teacher, parents, etc.). The aim is to induce perspective-taking and empathy. Greater attention is directed to the impact of the behavior on others and how to repair any harm done rather than on the consequences of behavior to oneself. Inductive discipline is found in the Responsive Classroom Approach (Responisve Classroom, 2018) and the Caring School Community program as well as in the more recently popular restorative practices (Restorative Practices Work Group, 2014).

Questions that might be asked during disciplinary encounters to help develop CASEL's five social emotional competencies follow. As emphasized in Chapter 6, when these and similar questions are used, it is important that it is in the context of a supportive and noncoercive teacher-student relationship, and that efforts are made to maintain a positive relationship.

Responsible decision-making. What are some other choices you could have made that would have avoided this problem? What can you do to fix the problem?

Self-management. What will you do to avoid repeating the same problem behavior and to manage your behavior the next time a similar situation occurs? Show me, while telling me what you should be thinking and feeling.

Social awareness. How do your choices and actions (past, present, and future) impact others, including other students involved, classmates, teachers, and your parents? How do you think they feel?

Relationships. How does the behavior influence how others view you and your relationships with them? What might you do to repair any relationships that have been harmed?

Self-awareness. What might you think next time before you exhibit the same behavior that might help you stop (assuming the student possesses the skills)? How do your choices and actions make you feel?

As discussed in Chapter 6, and supported by research on authoritative parenting, a calm, yet confrontative, style should be used to challenge the student's (faulty) reasoning behind the misbehavior. This might call for confronting mechanisms of moral disengagement, as recommended next.

8. ***Tactfully confront mechanisms of moral disengagement.*** This strategy is recommended in Chapter 6 on the correction of misbehavior, and applies beyond disciplinary encounters. It applies whenever students deny or avoid responsibility for their actions or voice that others should do the same. This often occurs during SEL lessons and other classroom activities such as during class meetings and discussions. Examples are when students voice self-centered moral reasoning that neglects or dismisses the perspectives, intentions, feelings, and rights of others. Regardless of whether the perspectives and intentions of others were wrongful or rightful (e.g., harm was or was not intended), students should be challenged to consider and judge them, while reflecting upon and applying such SEL skills as responsible decision-making, social awareness, and relationship skills to support prosocial behavior and denounce antisocial behavior. Students should be encouraged to challenge the self-centered moral reasoning of classmates.

    Regardless of the context in which mechanisms of moral disengagement are observed, they should be confronted tactfully and not in a manner that is coercive (e.g., "You're wrong." "That makes no sense."). Instead, the manner should be more Socratic, or questioning, conveying puzzlement about why the needs, feelings, and rights of others are not considered, challenging them to take the perspective of others, and otherwise providing adult and peer models of responsible decision-making to help guide their future behavior.

9. ***Communicate and collaborate with the families of students.*** The goal of SEL is for students to apply SEL skills at school but also at home and elsewhere in society. For skills to be applied at home, it behooves schools to provide parents with guidance as to what SEL skills are being taught in school and how they might help guide and reinforce their children in applying them at home and elsewhere. Many SEL programs include strategies for doing so, such as newsletters, websites, and parent meetings. Two good sources of information on SEL and the home are the websites for CASEL (https://casel.org/in-the-home/) and Edutopia (www.edutopia.org/SEL-parents-resources).

10. *Arrange and encourage service learning.* Service learning activities entail helping others in a community such as through service clubs, class projects, schoolwide initiatives, and required courses in high school. Several states require service learning for graduation from public high school or give credit toward graduation for completion of service learning. Many private high schools also require service learning. Participating in service learning has been found to be associated with a wide range of positive student outcomes, including fewer behavior problems, greater academic achievement, increased social acceptance, and greater social and emotional skills (e.g., empathy, dependability, trustworthiness, and self-efficacy in helping others) (Hart, Matsuba, & Atkins, 2008).

Research shows that the most effective K-12 service learning programs have the following features (RMC Research Corporation, 2009): (a) sufficient duration and intensity (e.g., not just working a few hours or one day in a soup kitchen, but for a more extended period); (b) one or more activities that entail a collaborative partnership that is mutually beneficial in meeting both community and student/school needs; (c) active (not passive) student engagement in activities that the students find meaningful and of personal interest, which include active involvement, with adult guidance, in planning, implementing, and evaluating their service experiences; (d) an emphasis on understanding and perspective-taking, diversity, and mutual respect; and (e) students engaging in meaningful and ongoing reflection about the service learning experiences—reflecting upon how the experiences relate to one's self-concept and relationship to society.

11. *Combine strategies for developing social-emotional competencies with strategies that focus more on structure.* As seen in this chapter, the major strength of the SEL approach is its emphasis on the social-emotional domain of school climate, which includes both social support and responsiveness to students' psychological needs. A common weakness of SEL programs, especially compared to behaviorally oriented programs, is a general lack of evidence-based strategies that provide the necessary structure for preventing and correcting behavior problems. An emphasis on such evidenced-based and teacher-directed strategies is a recognized strength of the SWPBIS approach to school discipline (Bear, 2010). That approach places much greater emphasis than the SEL approach on behavioral techniques for managing student behavior, and especially the importance of clear behavioral expectations and the systematic use of antecedents and consequences, including frequent use of praise and rewards. In light of research on authoritative parenting, classroom management, school discipline, and school climate, as discussed in Chapter 1, showing that a balance of social-emotional support and structure is needed for greatest effectiveness, it makes sense that schools integrate strategies commonly found in the SEL and SWPBIS approaches to school discipline and preventing behavior problems (Bear, 2010; Osher, Bear, Sprague, & Doyle, 2010; Sprague, Whitcomb, & Bear, 2018). Integrating the two approaches entails combining recommended strategies in this chapter with more structure-based strategies presented in Chapters 5 and 6 on preventing and correcting behavior problems and in Chapter 7 on student engagement.

Summary

Positive teacher-student and student-student relationships are critical aspects of school climate, and students' social and emotional competencies underlie the quality of those relationships. Of the five general social and emotional competencies highlighted by CASEL, relationship skills are certainly most relevant to positive teacher-student and student-student relationships. However, it is difficult to imagine students relating well with others without the social and emotional competencies of self-management, social awareness, responsible decision-making, and self-awareness. Developing skills and competence in each of those areas is essential to positive relationships with others, as well as to school climate in general. It also is critical to meeting the psychological needs of students, beyond the need of relatedness, for students to be optimally engaged in school and experience emotional well-being. Thus, in this chapter and throughout the book social-emotional support entails not only supportive relationships but also additional mechanisms of responsiveness to students' psychological needs, as found in the SEL approach.

CHAPTER 5

TEACHER-CENTERED STRATEGIES FOR PREVENTING BEHAVIOR PROBLEMS

As discussed in Chapter 1, the primary aims of classroom management and school discipline are twofold, with the first aim being more short-term and the second more long-term: (1) maintaining an orderly environment that is conducive to learning and (2) developing social and emotional competencies that underlie self-discipline. Both share a combination of strategies for preventing and correcting behavior problems. However, strategies for maintaining an orderly environment tend to be more teacher- or adult-centered than those for developing social and emotional competencies. They largely constitute what was presented in Chapter 1 as the structure domain in an authoritative approach to classroom management, school discipline, and school climate.

With respect to classroom management, and especially effectiveness in minimizing behavior problems, research has consistently shown that the best teachers are authoritative, focusing much more on preventing than correcting behavior problems (Brophy, 1996; Brophy & McCaslin, 1992). To be sure, the most effective teachers use corrective strategies, which at times are the same punitive consequences for misbehavior that are commonly used by less effective teachers, such as taking away privileges, contacting parents, and even removing a student from the classroom (as a last resort). However, because the most effective teachers are more skilled in strategies for preventing behavior problems, and use them more frequently, they have much less need for corrective strategies.

This chapter focuses on teacher-centered strategies for preventing behavior problems, whereas the next chapter focuses on those for correcting behavior problems. Many, and some of the best, strategies for preventing behavior problems were already presented in previous chapters and thus are not covered in any depth here. Of particular relevance to preventing behavior problems were strategies presented in Chapter 2 on teacher-student relationships, Chapter 3 on student-student relationships, and Chapter 4 on social and emotional competencies, and ones on student engagement that will be presented later in Chapter 7. As emphasized in those chapters, teachers prevent behavior problems by building and maintaining warm and supportive relationships with their students; promoting peer acceptance, respect, and support; developing social and emotional competencies that underlie students' self-discipline; and employing teaching and instructional strategies that motivate and engage students in learning.

Before presenting strategies for preventing behavior problems, the chapter reviews theories and research that has guided much of the literature on effective classroom management and school discipline, with particular emphases on the ecological, behavioral, and social and emotional learning approaches. Research based on those three approaches has led to the identification and explanation of multiple factors that characterize the most, and least, effective teachers and schools in the prevention of behavior problems. The strengths and weaknesses of each approach are discussed. The strategies and interventions recommended for preventing behavior problems draw from the strengths of the approaches while also addressing their weaknesses.

Guiding Theories and Research

Since the 1960s, three evidence-based approaches have dominated the literature on classroom management and school discipline: the ecological approach, the behavioral approach, and the SEL approach (Bear, 2015; Osher et al., 2010). Because the SEL approach was covered in Chapter 4, it is not covered in this chapter. As will be seen in the current chapter, with respect to preventive strategies, the SEL, ecological, and behavioral approaches share many of the same teacher-centered strategies. That is, they have much more in common than differences. However, the SEL approach differs from the other two approaches in its greater emphases on *student-centered* strategies and interventions for developing social and emotional competencies and for building and maintaining supportive teacher-student relationships. Those strategies were presented in chapters 2 and 4, respectively.

Ecological Approach

Most preventive strategies found in today's textbooks on classroom management originated from research in the 1960s, 70s, and 80s that was driven by the ecological approach. To be sure, those strategies, as well as all other preventive strategies in this chapter, existed before then, but it was the ecological approach that first documented their effectiveness via research in the school. The ecological approach is grounded in the understanding that the ecology of the classroom, and particularly how teachers teach and structure their classrooms, largely determines student engagement and the presence or absence of behavior problems (Brophy, 2010; Doyle, 2006). The ecological approach has its early roots in classic studies of classroom management conducted by Jacob Kounin and colleagues in the 1960s and 1970s (Kounin, 1970; Kounin & Gump, 1974).

Characteristics of Effective Teachers. While observing classrooms, Kounin and colleagues identified certain qualities of the most effective teachers, especially for engaging students and preventing behavior problems. Foremost among them were:

- *Withitness*—teachers closely monitoring student behavior and intervening early when misbehavior was anticipated or first observed; thus, preventing misbehavior from interfering with learning and becoming contagious.
- *Overlapping*—teachers handling multiple events or demands simultaneously.

- *Momentum*—teachers presenting lessons at a quick pace, while soliciting frequent responding from students. This also refers to teachers minimizing interruptions and helping ensure brief and efficient transitions between lessons and activities.
- *Smoothness*—teachers presenting lessons at an even flow, free from interruptions.
- *Group alerting*—teachers using verbal and nonverbal cues, prompts, and similar techniques to effectively establish and maintain the attention of all students.

The ecological approach drove much of the *school effectiveness* research popular in the 1980s (e.g., Doyle, 2006; Gettinger, 1988). That research was invaluable in identifying characteristics of teachers and schools that were most effective in preventing behavior problems and fostering student engagement and achievement. Not surprisingly, many of the characteristics identified were the same as those found by Kounin and his colleagues. They have continued to be supported by research and thus are found today in nearly all major textbooks on classroom management (e.g., Emmer & Evertson, 2017; Evertson & Emmer, 2017; Weinstein & Novodvorsky, 2015; Weinstein & Romano, 2019). Chief among the characteristics of the most effective teachers are:

- *They monitor student behavior closely and respond quickly to signs of misbehavior.* They demonstrate a combination of what Kounin called "withitness" and "overlapping." Whether moving about the classroom or sitting behind their desks, and more commonly the former, they constantly scan the classroom, and respond quickly to the earliest signs of potential or actual behavior problems or of students otherwise needing attention. They do so while performing multiple tasks simultaneously and in a seamless fashion.
- *They provide academic instruction and activities that motivate and engage students.* This refers to Kounin's concepts of momentum and smoothness. The most effective teachers engage students in learning with a variety of instructional strategies—strategies to be discussed in Chapter 7 on engagement.
- *They capitalize on efficient procedures and routines.* As with motivating instructions, efficient procedures and routines help ensure momentum smoothness. Procedures inform students what course of action is required to execute or complete an activity or task. Procedures become routines when repeated over time and performed habitually by students with little or no teacher supervision. Recognizing that unstructured activities invite misbehavior, effective teachers make sure that procedures and routines provide the structure needed to guide students in performing general tasks (e.g., turning in work completed, using supplies and materials, getting a drink or going to the restroom) and making transitions from activity to activity.
- *They establish and maintain high behavioral expectations.* Beginning with the first day of school, effective classroom managers set and maintain high expectations, or standards, and apply them to *all* students. Expectations are communicated in established procedures and routines, but also in rules and consequences for violating them. Expectations are explained clearly and discussed with the class. Where needed, such as in early grades and when skills

are lacking, they are taught directly, modeled, and retaught to either individuals or the class as a whole. Behaviors consistent with the expectations are practiced and reinforced. Expectations are responsive to individual, developmental, and cultural differences.
- *They arrange their classrooms in ways that are conducive to teaching and learning.* Desks, chairs, supplies, and materials are arranged in a manner that facilitates teaching and learning, fosters the smooth flow of student traffic, and enhances monitoring and supervision.
- *They use praise and rewards wisely and strategically.* They recognize that praise and rewards serve multiple functions, such as fostering student attention and engagement, providing feedback, helping to strengthen positive teacher-student relationships, and reinforcing desired behaviors.

Strengths and Weaknesses of the Ecological Approach. The foremost strength of the ecological approach is that it has identified observable and malleable characteristics of teachers and schools that prevent behavior problems and foster learning. Decades of research have confirmed the importance of the characteristics that Kounin and other school effectiveness researchers first documented. For example, clear expectations, fair rules, close monitoring of student behavior, and use of positive and punitive consequences (and especially positive consequences) have been shown to be associated with greater prosocial behavior (Bradshaw et al., 2012); fewer behavior problems and disruptive behaviors (Gottfredson, 2001; Way, 2011, Welsh, 2000; 2003), including bullying and school violence (Gregory et al., 2010; Johnson, 2009); and greater student engagement and academic achievement (Benner et al., 2008; Welsh, 2000, 2003).

The primary shortcoming of the ecological approach was that by focusing on the actions of teachers and other observable features of classrooms and schools it largely ignored the influence of individual characteristics of students and the influence of factors other than the teacher on student behavior and learning, such as the influence of peers, the home, and community. How children think and feel and how to best develop social and emotional competencies was not a focus (as it is in the SEL approach). The focus on teacher behavior, however, was consistent with the ecological approach's aim of identifying teacher-directed strategies for managing student behavior (rather than for developing self-discipline).

Behavioral Approach

Grounded in behaviorism and behavior modification techniques of B.F. Skinner, especially techniques of positive reinforcement, punishment, and extinction, behavior modification applied to classroom management first became popular in American schools in the 1960s and 1970s. Among popular books of behavior modification applied to classroom management was *Assertive Discipline* (Canter, 1976), which sold over a million copies. Teachers were attracted to behaviorism's focus on the environment being the primary cause of student behavior and the theoretical understanding that teachers can, and should, control the classroom environment, and thus student behavior. It was believed that teachers could effectively manage student behavior by asserting their authority and using behavior modification techniques that Skinner and other behaviorists had found effective in their laboratories with rats and pigeons.

Whereas the first editions of *Assertive Discipline* emphasized assertiveness in the use of techniques of punishment in correcting misbehavior (Canter, 1976), beginning in the 2001 edition (Canter & Canter, 2001) emphasis shifted to the use of more positive techniques, especially the systematic use of positive reinforcement for both preventing and correcting misbehavior (Bear, 2005). This shift from an emphasis on use of punishment, including school suspensions, to greater use of positive techniques for preventing behavior problems and teaching desired behavior was seen not only in *Assertive Discipline*, but in the use of behavioral techniques in general. Primary among positive techniques was the systematic use of positive reinforcers, ranging from praise to tokens and tangible rewards.

Positive Techniques and Antecedents for Preventing Behavior Problems. In addition to the systematic use of positive reinforcers in preventing misbehavior, more recently behaviorists have emphasized the importance of the role of observable antecedents in behavior, and particularly antecedents that teachers control. Using positive reinforcement and controlling antecedents are viewed as positive alternatives to the use of punitive practices to manage student behavior. To be sure, many of the antecedents that behaviorists have identified are the same as those identified by researchers who have adhered to the ecological approach. That is, in preventing behavior problems the following positive practices and techniques are emphasized by behaviorists, including advocates of School-Wide Positive Behavioral Interventions and Support (SWPBIS) (e.g., Kern & Clemens, 2007; Sugai & Horner, 2008):

- Frequent and systematic use of positive reinforcement of desired behaviors;
- Clear behavioral expectations and rules; procedures, routines, and similar practices that increase predictability (e.g., schedules, visual displays);
- Instruction that is quickly paced, elicits frequent responses from students, and is matched with the skills and interests of individual students; seating arrangements that prevent behavior problems and foster learning; and
- Frequent monitoring of student behavior (including proximity control—teachers being near students, especially when the first signs of behavior problems appear).

For the most part, the ecological and behavioral approaches have identified the same preventive techniques of classroom management. However, the behavioral approach places greater emphases on the frequent and systematic use of praise and rewards. This includes the appropriate schedule of reinforcement (e.g., continuous versus intermittent) and the use of multiple types of reinforcers (e.g., praise, tangible and social rewards, privileges, tokens).

The two approaches also have differed in the type of research used. Whereas the ecological approach has depended mainly on correlational research (e.g., showing that the techniques correlate with positive outcomes), the behavioral approach has typically used experimental research, especially single-subject designs, that demonstrate causal relations. Another difference between the two approaches is that whereas the ecological approach has identified *general* techniques of effective classroom management, the behavioral approach has identified much more specific and observable aspects of those techniques. Often those identified aspects are translated into specific steps to guide teachers in the implementation of the respective techniques. For example, behaviorists have identified *precorrection*, *precision requests*, and *high probability requests* as antecedent-based techniques that help prevent behavior problems by increasing the likelihood that a student will follow or comply with a request.

Precorrection simply refers to the teacher providing verbal or nonverbal prompts, such as reminders and demonstrations, for a student to begin a task or otherwise engage in the desired behavior and then reinforcing the student immediately for doing so. Teachers are advised to do so privately, where feasible, and before any sign of noncompliance is seen, but is anticipated.

A *precision request* is simply a verbal statement that communicates precisely what the teacher expects from the student. It can serve as a precorrection, such as "Anthony, I need you to begin the worksheet now, and I appreciate you doing so" (before any signs of noncompliance), but more often serves as correction (i.e., when noncompliance is first seen), such as "Anthony, please return to your seat." If the student fails to respond favorably within a few seconds, a second precision request, as appropriate (i.e., depending on the severity of the behavior), is made, such as "Anthony, I need you to return to your seat now." This may be accompanied with a warning of the consequences of noncompliance. If the student responds favorably to either request, the student is praised; but if noncompliance continues, consequences for noncompliance are invoked (see next chapter on correction for recommendations).

A *high probability request* is similar to a precision request but includes consideration of the likelihood that the request will be met with compliance. That is, a high probability request is one that is likely to produce a compliant or favorable response. For example, "Anthony, I need you to complete ten pages of math problems" is precise, but unlikely to be met with compliance. However, requesting that Anthony complete "the first three items in the next two minutes" greatly increases the odds that Anthony will comply.

Precision and high probability requests are most valuable when noncompliance is anticipated and before it is observed, such as for Anthony who has a history of not starting his work when others do. Before requesting a behavior for which noncompliance is anticipated (i.e., making a low-probability request), the teacher would first make a couple of precise requests that are likely to elicit compliance (e.g., asking Anthony to do something that he has done before, or likes to do). Completing a high-probability request helps establish what is called *behavioral momentum*. That is, with Anthony having now complied with several requests, the odds are greater that he will comply with the next request. This strategy is often effective in obtaining a student's compliance but also motivating academic engagement (e.g., a student who dislikes math is given a few easy math problems before being given more difficult ones).

School-Wide Positive Behavioral Interventions and Supports. At the school-wide level, the behavioral approach to classroom management and school discipline, with its roots in behavior modification, is best seen today in SWPBIS, and particularly the model associated with Dr. Rob Horner at the University of Oregon and Dr. George Sugai at the University of Connecticut (Sugai & Horner, 2009). There are other models of SWPBIS, but their model is by far the most popular. Unfortunately, definitions and conceptualizations of SWPBIS vary, and thus SWPBIS schools differ greatly in the programs and strategies they implement. For example, during the early years of SWPBIS Horner stated that "There is no difference in theory or science between positive behavior support and behavior modification. These are the same approach with different names" (Horner, 2000, p. 99). SWPBIS was simply the schoolwide application of PBS, or PBIS.[1] Consistent with this early definition, techniques of behavior modification, and especially the systematic use of positive reinforcement, became the most common feature of SWPBIS schools—a feature still found in many schools today.

More recently (i.e., 2020), SWPBIS has been described as a "multi-tiered framework to make schools more effective places. It establishes a social culture and the behavior supports needed to improve social, emotional, behavioral, and academic outcomes for all students" (www.pbis.org/topics/school-wide). Although the definitions of SWPBIS have changed, behavioral interventions have always been at its core.

Most advocates of SWPBIS, including Horner, now argue that the basis of SWPBIS is not behavior modification per se, but *applied behavior analysis* (Sugai & Horner, 2009, 2010). The major difference between behavior modification and applied behavior analysis is that the latter emphasizes the importance of assessing, or analyzing, the functional relationship(s) between a targeted behavior and what is occurring in the environment that causes observed changes in the behavior (e.g., Does the student exhibit the behavior to gain attention or to avoid aversive consequences?). The approach recommends that all interventions, both preventive and corrective, be guided by functional behavioral assessment regardless of whether they are implemented at the individual, classroom, or schoolwide levels (O'Neill, Albin, Storey, Horner, & Sprague, 2014).

Whether guided by an assessment of functional relationships or not, the behavioral techniques that teachers actually use to change, or modify, behavior tend to be one and the same. Whereas positive reinforcement (e.g., praise, privileges, preferred activities, tangible rewards, tokens) has been the technique most commonly recommended for increasing desired behavior, punishment, extinction, and response cost (e.g., taking away privileges) have been most commonly used for decreasing targeted behaviors (Landrum & Kauffman, 2006). Supported by decades of research demonstrating their effectiveness in increasing or decreasing behavior (and without use of functional behavioral assessments), use of each of those techniques can be seen in nearly every classroom today (Alberto & Troutman, 2013; Landrum & Kauffman, 2006).

Key Features of SWPBIS. In addition to being grounded in behaviorism and its application of evidence-based techniques of behavior modification or applied behavior analysis, four key features are commonly cited as characterizing SWPBIS (e.g., Bear, 2010; Horner, Sugai, Todd, & Lewis-Palmer, 2005; Sprague et al., 2018; Sugai & Horner, 2009, 2010): (1) a multi-tiered system of prevention, interventions, and supports; (2) ongoing collection and use of data for decision-making; (3) supportive systems; and (4) direct teaching of behavioral expectations and social skills using behavioral techniques.

Multi-tiered System of Prevention, Interventions, and Supports

SWPBIS targets three levels of prevention, interventions, and supports, commonly referred to simply as Tier 1, Tier 2, and Tier 3. Traditionally, in mental health and medical models of prevention (which includes intervention) these three tiers have been referred to as primary, secondary, and tertiary levels or universal, selected, and indicated levels (Adelman & Taylor, 2006). In this chapter, the three tiers refer to students with behavior problems, but the tiers can apply to preventing a number of academic and mental health concerns, such as poor reading skills, drug abuse, and depression/suicide. Tier 1 targets the whole classroom and school, focusing on teacher-centered strategies and schoolwide supports designed to prevent future behavior problems for all students. This would include both antecedent-based strategies, as presented earlier, but also consequence-based strategies used in response to the most common behavior problems found to be generally effective. Tier 2 focuses on subgroups of the general school population deemed to have higher than average risk for exhibiting behavior problems, as determined by the presence of risk factors, such as Attention Deficit/Hyperactivity Disorder (ADHD) or early signs of behavior problems that are resistant to common interventions in the classroom. It is assumed that those students would benefit from small group social skills training and other supports and early interventions. Tier 3 targets those individual students with the greatest needs—students who are exhibiting chronic or serious behavior problems that have resisted common Tier 1 and 2 interventions and supports in the classroom. Those students typically require intensive, comprehensive, and individualized interventions and services provided both inside and outside of school.

Ongoing Collection and Use of Data to Guide Decision-Making

Although multiple sources of data exist, the most common source of data to guide decision-making and assess outcomes in SWPBIS schools has been office disciplinary referrals. As recommended by Horner et al. (2005), SWPBIS schools are to organize and analyze disciplinary data "(1) per day and per month, (2) per type of problem behavior, (3) per location in the school, (4) per time of day, and (5) per child" (p. 374). Only recently has SWPBIS added school climate data as a recommended source (Sprague et al., 2018). In analyzing data, schools are to use the applied behavior analysis framework to conduct a functional behavioral assessment, similar to ones most commonly conducted at the individual student level but with the group being the unit of analysis. For example, if a large number of referrals come from the cafeteria, the SWPBIS team might hypothesize that the students are seeking attention of peers or are avoiding eating because they do not like what is served.

Supportive Systems

Supportive systems refer to (1) team-based implementation, which includes developing and implementing an action plan based on a needs assessment;

(2) ongoing administrative leadership; (3) commitment and active participation of support staff in SWPBIS practices; (4) adequate personnel, time, and training; (5) budgeted support; (6) an adequate information system (e.g., website, newsletters, meetings); and (7) clear guides and tools for implementation (see the National Center on Positive Behavioral Interventions and Supports website, www.pbis.org, for practice guides and tools).

Direct Teaching of Behavioral Expectations and Social Skills Using Behavioral Techniques

Expected behaviors and social skills are taught directly to students, with the aim of "systematically teaching rule-following behaviors within each school routine and setting" (Simonsen & Sugai, 2009, p. 136). Consistent with behaviorism, they are to be observable, measurable, and clearly defined. Schoolwide behavioral expectations of teachers and staff are to be posted in classrooms and schoolwide. The most common behavioral expectations refer to respect, responsibility, and safety (e.g., Respect Others, Be Responsible, Be Safe) and "emphasize student compliance" (Lynass, Tsai, Richman, & Cheney, 2012, p. 159).

Specific social skills consistent with the behavioral expectations are to be taught directly. For example, Gresham and Elliott (2008) give the following guidance for the teaching of social skills: (a) tell students what the social skill is and why they are to exhibit it; (b) model the social skill, including necessary steps it entails; have the students demonstrate the skill (e.g., using role plays and feedback from teacher and peers); (c) have students practice the skill in the classroom: (d) positively reinforce students for exhibiting the skill; (e) monitor student progress, which includes encouraging students to self-evaluate and self-reinforce the skills taught; and (f) plan for generalization (students are asked to apply the skill in multiple contexts, via homework and other opportunities).

In positively reinforcing students for exhibiting social skills taught and expected, many SWPBIS schools use tokens (e.g., coupons, tickets), exchangeable for tangible rewards or privileges. Many also use behavioral matrices (posted throughout the school) to inform students of the specific skills subsumed by the more general behavioral expectations (Lynass et al., 2012; Simonsen et al., 2012). For example, Horner, Sugai, Todd and Lewis-Palmer (2005, p. 369) give the following recommended example for teaching responsibility (as seen in obedience to expectations, rules, and adult authority):

In the classroom: Bring books and pencils to class. Do homework.

In gym: Participate. Wear appropriate shoes.

In the hallway: Keep books, belongings, litter off floor.

On the playground: Stay within the recess area.

In the bus area: Keep your books and belongings with you.

Although positive reinforcement is clearly preferred, and emphasized, SWPBIS clearly recognizes that fair punitive consequences for inappropriate behavior are also employed.

Strengths and Weaknesses of the Behavioral Approach. As is true with the ecological approach, the behavioral approach has been invaluable in identifying practices that characterize the most effective teachers and schools. Additional major strengths shared by both approaches (as well as with the SEL approach) are their emphases on (a) evidence-based practices; (b) prevention rather than correction; (c) greater use of positive than punitive techniques; and (d) the aim of creating a positive school climate. The SWPBIS approach has three additional strengths seen in the key features discussed previously (Bear, 2010): (a) a multi-tiered system of prevention, interventions, and supports; (b) an ongoing collection and use of data to guide decision-making; and (c) supportive systems.

The fourth key feature of the SWPBS approach that was listed previously, *the direct teaching of behavioral expectations and social skills using behavioral techniques*, is the one feature of SWPBIS that is more unique to the behavioral approach than other approaches. This feature might be viewed more as a limitation than a strength, especially when applied at Tier 1 and not in combination with more student-centered techniques for developing social and emotional competencies. That is, research supporting the direct teaching of social skills, which is typically done in small groups, has produced mixed results, with effect sizes generally ranging from small to moderate (Elliott, Frey, & DiPerna, 2014; Wilson & Lipsey, 2007). Effects tend to be less when studies examine if they are lasting or generalize beyond the setting in which they are taught (Bullis, Walker, & Sprague, 2001; Landrum & Kauffman, 2006; Maag, 2005, 2006).

Moreover, there is a lack of studies and evidence demonstrating the effectiveness of social skills training, especially at Tier 1, in preventing behavior problems and developing social and emotional competencies associated with self-discipline. Studies claiming its effectiveness tend to be limited to those that use office disciplinary referrals (ODRs) or suspensions as the measured outcome—as a proxy for reduced behavior problems and improved social skills. There are many limitations of DROs as an outcome measure, and chief among them is that they assess how *adults* respond to students' noncompliance and not necessarily how often students exhibit antisocial or prosocial behavior or the quality of the school climate (Bear, 2013).

In a meta-analysis of the effects of classroom management programs and strategies used in elementary school classrooms, the SWPBIS approach was found to have no significant impact on academic, behavior, social-emotional, and motivational outcomes (Korpershoek et al., 2016). Other programs and interventions (including The Good Behavior Game, Second Step Social-Emotional Learning, and PATHS) were found to have small to moderate effects, with those targeting social-emotional skills being slightly more effective than others. This finding relates to several additional major shortcomings of the behavioral approach (Bear, 2010).

First, as largely true with the ecological approach, and noted previously, the behavioral approach focuses almost exclusively on the use of teacher-centered techniques to manage or control student behavior (i.e., bring about compliance) rather than the use of a combination of teacher-centered and student-centered techniques for developing social and emotional competencies associated with prosocial behavior and the inhibition of antisocial behavior (see Chapter 4). Although those techniques are often invaluable for managing student behavior, when needed, most educators do not agree that a primary aim of education is to control or manage students, but instead is to develop self-discipline. Parents also agree (Rose & Gallup, 2000).

Second, there is little emphasis in the behavioral approach on the importance of the quality of the teacher-student relationship, especially as perceived by students, in preventing behavior problems. Too often the quality of the teacher-student relationship is equated with teachers simply using more positive than punitive techniques, and techniques that must be observable and yield data.

Third, the behavioral approach has a very limited perspective on the determinants of human behavior. The immediate environment, and especially the teacher, is seen as determining student behavior. When students misbehave, it is assumed that the teacher is at fault. There is little recognition of the role of students' thoughts, emotions, educational history, peer influences, home factors, and so forth as major determinants of behavior. Moreover, nearly all behavior is viewed as simply serving one of two functions—students seeking attention or avoiding what they dislike. This perspective translates into the simplistic assumption that the direct teaching of rules and appropriate behavior, using principles of behaviorism and particularly the systematic use of praise and rewards, is sufficient for desired behavior. As discussed in Chapter 4, an emphasis on the use of praise and rewards has been a subject of much controversy, with critics arguing that it may be harmful to intrinsic motivation and encourage a self-centered, hedonistic mindset that one should act prosocially only when it results in recognition, reward, or other benefits to oneself (with no empathy or appreciation of the impact of one's actions on others).

Recommended Teacher-Centered Strategies and Interventions for Preventing Behavior Problems

In this section, general strategies and more specific interventions for preventing behavior problems are presented. As discussed in the first recommendation that follows, of primary focus are structure-based and teacher-centered strategies and interventions not presented in other chapters, and especially those that the ecological and behavioral approaches have identified as characterizing the most effective teachers and schools. This is done to reduce redundancy in recommendations across chapters, while also highlighting the role of structure via use of teacher-directed strategies and interventions in improving school climate.

1. *Implement strategies for improvement in domains of school climate that are directly related to classroom management and preventing behavior problems, particularly strategies for fostering positive teacher-student and student-student relationships, developing social and emotional competencies, and promoting student engagement.* As discussed in Chapter 1, and emphasized throughout this book, techniques for improving structure, or demandingness, also help foster social-emotional support and vice versa. It is difficult to teach and develop social and emotional competencies in environments that are chaotic and not conducive to teaching and learning. Furthermore, both structure and social-emotional support prevent behavior problems and do so in multiple ways. This is perhaps best seen in

structure-oriented strategies, such as those practices highlighted in the ecological and behavioral approaches, fostering student engagement. But it also is seen in social support-oriented strategies fostering student engagement and preventing behavior problems. For example, as discussed in the chapters on teacher-student and student-student relationships, fewer behavior problems are seen in classes and schools where positive social relationships prevail. Where poor relationships are not prevalent, preventive techniques presented in this chapter are much less likely to be effective (Way, 2011). This also holds true for strategies that focus on developing social and emotional learning: In schools where students possess social and emotional competencies and are actively engaged, there are fewer behavior problems and thus less need for teacher-centered techniques of prevention. Thus, for preventing behavior problems, it behooves schools to target not only teacher-centered strategies and interventions presented in this chapter, but also more student-centered ones presented in other chapters.

To one extent or another, and either indirectly or directly, recommendations presented in other chapters, and especially those on teacher-student relationships, student-student relationships, social and emotional learning, and student engagement help prevent behavior problems. However, recommendations on student engagement are most directly related to the prevention of behavior problems in the classroom. Those actions are listed briefly below and are described more thoroughly in Chapter 7.

- *Use a style of teaching that fosters student engagement.* This recommendation encompasses many of the strategies mentioned previously in this chapter and Chapter 7 that help prevent behavior problems by keeping students actively engaged in learning. Those strategies include presenting lessons that are novel and fun, using a variety of instructional methods (e.g., peer-assisted learning, simulations and role-plays, educational games); showing enthusiasm toward the subject matter; teaching at a quick pace that calls for frequent responses from students; and ensuring high rates of success, especially when new concepts are first introduced.
- *Directly teach skills related to engagement, as needed.* For basic skills of engagement (e.g., listening, attending, not bothering others), direct teaching is generally required only in the early grades when those skills are first expected. Thereafter, reminding students of the commonly expected behaviors, and rules pertaining to them, is typically sufficient for most students.
- *Praise or otherwise recognize desired behaviors, while providing feedback that is substantive and constructive.* Desired behaviors should not go unrecognized. Praise and other recognitions (including rewards) serve multiple functions. Not only do they often reinforce the desired behavior, but they foster positive teacher-student relationships and provide valuable feedback. (Specific recommendations on the use of praise and rewards are presented in Recommendation 5.)
- *Highlight models of cognitive, behavioral, and emotional engagement.* This refers to adults in school serving as models of engagement-related behaviors. It also refers to highlighting models of engagement-related behaviors throughout the general curriculum.

- *Offer choices.* Choice fosters a sense of autonomy, which, in turn, fosters cooperation.
- *Give movement and relaxation breaks.* Giving students breaks from sitting and listening increase concentration and engagement (and often physical health). Breaks might consist of time to stretch, exercise, or engage in yoga, mindfulness, guided imagery, progressive muscle relaxation, and other relaxation techniques.
- *Align instructional methods and activities with the individual abilities and interests of students.* Work that is too difficult or of little challenge and interest to students is a common trigger for behavior problems.
- *Focus on mastery.* As reviewed in Chapter 7 on student engagement, a focus on mastery is a common characteristic of the most effective teachers, including those in schools with a high percentage of at-risk students.
- *In general, encourage a growth mindset instead of a fixed ability mindset.* In Chapter 7 on engagement, this recommendation is specific to academic learning, but students also should be encouraged to apply a growth mindset toward behavior in general, not just academic learning. That is, students should understand that not just academic abilities, but also how they act or behave, is not fixed (e.g., "That's how I am." or "I can't help it, I have ADHD."), and that effort is critical for change.
- *Challenge students to set goals.* Students should be encouraged to set not only academic goals, but also behavioral goals—both short-term and long-term. Goals might not only be set by individual students but also by the class. For example, the class as a whole might be challenged to set goals related to behavioral expectations, or class rules: "Our goal is to have 90% homework completion (which earns 15 minutes free time)." "Our goal is to work one hour with not having to be reminded of any classroom rule."
- *Encourage self-evaluation.* After setting goals, students need to evaluate the extent to which they are achieved. Achieving a goal might earn a reward (e.g., a no homework pass). Goal setting, self-evaluation, and self-reinforcement are aspects of self-management, which is a social and emotional competency targeted in nearly all schoolwide and classroom programs for social and emotional learning (see Chapter 7 on engagement). Self-management is important in its own right, but also invaluable in developing a sense of autonomy. Self-management also is a highly recommended strategy for correcting misbehavior of individual students, and thus is covered in more detail for that purpose in Chapter 6.
- *Seek support from the home.* Support from the home helps prevent both academic and behavioral problems for all students. It is especially important when problems continue despite the implementation of common techniques of prevention and correction.

2. ***Establish clear schoolwide behavioral expectations and rules at both the schoolwide and classroom levels.*** Schoolwide behavioral expectations and rules communicate to students what behaviors are expected. Behavioral expectations differ from school rules in that they are more general, referring to broad positively-stated schoolwide goals for student behavior. As noted previously, schoolwide behavioral expectations are a major feature of SWPBIS schools, with the most common behavioral expectations referring

to respect, responsibility, and safety (e.g., Respect Others, Be Responsible, Be Safe). Other behavioral expectations often found in SWPBIS schools refer to motivation to learn, caring, kindness, working together, attitude, and self-control (Lynass et al., 2012).

Rules are much more specific than schoolwide behavioral expectations. Rules consist of statements designed to govern or regulate student behavior, including behaviors that fall under a school's broad behavioral expectations. Whereas schoolwide behavioral expectations are almost always worded positively, rules can be worded positively or negatively (e.g., "Keep your hands and feet to yourself." "No use of cell phones."). Nearly all schools have a Code of Conduct that presents students, parents, and school staff with schoolwide rules and a range of punitive consequences that are invoked when they are not followed. Typically, schoolwide behavioral expectations and rules are established by a committee consisting of teachers, administrators, and support staff (and preferably with parents and students).

In addition to schoolwide behavioral expectations and rules, most teachers have additional expectations and rules that are more specific to their classrooms, such as those targeting homework, use of cellphones, and other desired and undesired behaviors. Some teachers prefer adopting schoolwide expectations as their classroom rules while giving specific examples of how each schoolwide behavioral expectation translates into specific classroom behaviors. For example, being responsible would include turning in homework on time, showing respect would entail listening to others when they are speaking.

At both the schoolwide and classroom levels it is recommended that behavioral expectations and classroom rules are:

- *Aligned with the school's mission statement and goals.* Such alignment should be communicated clearly to students, parents, and teachers, making it clear that the school's mission and goals go beyond academic achievement.
- *Linked to more specific classroom and school rules.* Although classroom rules may be in addition to schoolwide rules, they should always be consistent with and never in conflict with them.
- *Applied and practiced in efficient procedures and routines.* Like rules, procedures and routines communicate behavioral expectations. For example, students demonstrate responsibility when following classroom procedures and routines pertaining to turning homework assignments and use of materials and supplies. Likewise, at the schoolwide level students demonstrate responsibility and respect when transitioning safely and smoothly from one location to another (e.g., to bathroom, bus, other classes).
- *Few in number.* It is generally recommended that schoolwide behavioral expectations and classroom rules not exceed four or five (Gable, Hester, Rock, & Hughes, 2009). It is difficult for students to remember more, and a longer list often contributes to students' perceptions of an overly controlling negative school climate.
- *Clear and precise.* Whether presented verbally or visually (i.e., posted in classrooms and hallways), behavioral expectations and rules should be clear and precise. Major stakeholders (e.g., teachers, parents,

students) should agree to the specific behaviors that are included in each one. Agreement is found in schools with fewer behavior problems (Duke, 1989).
- *Taught to all students and retaught as needed.* Behavioral expectations and rules should be presented during the first day or week of school. The class should discuss what the rules entail, what behaviors are consistent and inconsistent with the rules, and why the rules are important (including positive outcomes for exhibiting the expected behaviors and negative consequences for not doing so). As developmentally appropriate, behaviors consistent with the behavioral expectations should be modeled. Throughout the school year students need to be reminded of the behavioral expectations. Rules should be retaught, as needed, which should be more often for younger rather than older students.
- *Highlighted in models presented throughout the general curriculum and the everyday life of the school.* This includes being highlighted and discussed during lessons (e.g., a lesson in literacy that refers to responsibility) but also modeled by all adults in the school. If students are expected to be on time for class, teachers should not be late for school and class.
- *Positively reinforced.* At all grade levels students should be recognized and reinforced for meeting behavioral expectations and following the rules. As noted in Recommendation 5, however, the frequency and type of recognition should vary based on grade level and student needs.
- *Shared with parents.* Parents should not only be aware of the expectations and rules, but also encouraged to reinforce behaviors consistent with them.
- *Linked with supports when they are not met.* When resistance to common techniques of prevention and correction is seen, additional interventions and supports are needed, as discussed in the next chapter.

3. **Strive to make rules and their consequences fair, which includes students perceiving them as fair.** Clarity of behavioral expectations, rules, and consequences is of utmost importance, but so too is their fairness. Because behavioral expectations are typically worded positively and not linked to punitive consequences, fairness is generally of less concern with respect to expectations than rules. When students perceive rules to be unfair, they are less inclined to follow them (Arum, 2003; Brand et al., 2003; Gottfredson et al., 2005; Welsh, 2000, 2003). This harms school climate not only by fostering behavior problems, but also by harming the teacher-student relationship. That is, students view teachers (and school) less favorably when they perceive rules as unfair. In a national study of over 30,000 students, Arum (2003) found that students' perceptions of fairness correlated positively and significantly with their willingness to obey the rules, and also with their academic achievement (i.e., grades were higher in schools where students perceived rules to be fair). As one might predict, if students viewed rules as overly-harsh they also judged them to be unfair. However, they also viewed rules to be unfair if they were thought to be too lenient. Students supported moderately strict rules, viewing them as fair and effective, but especially when they perceived them as being imposed by adults with legitimate moral authority—by adults they respected and believed to be fair, supportive, and not overly controlling. Arum's findings are consistent with research in social

psychology on procedural justice (Tyler, 2006; Tyler & Degoey, 1995). That research has demonstrated that adults are more likely to comply with police and judges when they believe them to be fair (Gregory & Weinstein, 2008).

In reviewing research and recommended best practices presented in popular textbooks on classroom management (e.g., Curwin, Mendler, & Mendler, 2008; Evertson & Emmer, 2017; Jones & Jones, 2010; Weinstein, 2006), Bear (2010) found the following two characteristics of classroom rules to be critical to their effectiveness:

- *Rules are clear to students, their parents, and teachers/staff.* Presented at the very beginning of the school year, all stakeholders understand what each rule means and why it is needed. This requires that the rule is presented, both orally in writing and in language that everyone understands (e.g., at the appropriate reading level when written, and in the language spoken by parents). Specific examples of the rule, and behaviors to which it applies, are given. Efforts should be made to word rules positively, denoting the behaviors that students are to exhibit (e.g., "Raise your hand to speak"). Examples should be given of both rule-abiding and rule-violating behaviors pertaining to the rule. To ensure that parents have read the rules (classroom or schoolwide), it is often recommended that they sign that they have done so.

- *Rules are fair and reasonable.* As discussed earlier, students are much less likely to accept and comply with rules that they view as overly harsh, trivial, or otherwise unfair and unreasonable. They also dislike rules that are too lenient. To help avoid rules being perceived as too harsh or too lenient, it behooves teachers to include students in their development. Including students is likely to foster a greater sense of ownership and more willing compliance, as opposed to grudging compliance. If not feasible or preferred by the teacher, the teacher should at least explain and discuss why each rule is important, fair, and reasonable. Unlike classroom rules, schoolwide rules (and behavioral expectations) are not normally developed each year but continue from year to year. Schoolwide rules are typically set at the district level by a committee representing teachers, administrators, other school personnel, parents, and the community. Nevertheless, student participation at the schoolwide level is recommended for the same reasons as the classroom level.

In justifying each rule, and increasing the likelihood that students (and parents) find it reasonable, it also is recommended that the fairness of rules be grounded in constitutional rights, such as safety, property rights, respect for the rights and needs of others, and personal and social responsibility (Duke, 2002; Gathercoal, 2001). Weinstein (2006) also recommends that when establishing rules teachers ask themselves: (1) Is there a compelling reason for the rule? (2) Will the rule enhance classroom climate and learning? and (3) Can a clear rationale for the rule be given to students, parents, and administrators?

4. *Monitor student behavior frequently, while recognizing desired behaviors and responding quickly to early signs of misbehavior.* This has consistently been shown to be a major characteristic of teachers who are effective in preventing behavior problems (Brophy, 2004; Brophy & McCaslin, 1992).

It refers to what Kounin (1970, 1974)) called *withitness*, and it also incorporates the concept of *overlapping*. These two qualities are seen in teachers being hypervigilant, constantly scanning the classroom, moving about (and especially near those who are off-task); praising those students who are on-task and others exhibiting desired behavior reflecting self-discipline, while giving verbal or nonverbal prompts and warnings to those who are off-task; and simultaneously providing assistance and support to students who appear frustrated with an assignment. Most teachers demonstrate these qualities and most students are well aware that their behavior is monitored. A close eye, and the actions above, are especially needed for students lacking self-discipline and thus who are at greatest risk of misbehavior.

This recommendation applies not only to teachers and classrooms, but to all staff throughout the school building. Close monitoring and quick response to early signs of behavior problems is especially important in places where behaviors most commonly occur, such as hallways, the cafeteria, the playground, where buses load and unload, and other congested areas. As such, all staff should be trained in preventing and responding to early signs of misbehavior, including bus drivers, cafeteria workers, paraprofessionals, and other support staff.

5. *Create and maintain a physical environment that is conducive to teaching and learning and helps prevent behavior problems.* Unfortunately, too often there is not a lot that teachers and staff can do to improve the physical environment of the classroom and school. It is well established that congested areas foster behavior problems in school (Astor, Benbenishty, Marachi, & Meyer, 2006), and that acts of violence in society are more likely to occur when people are crowded and uncomfortable (e.g., in buildings with no air conditioning, poor heating, poor seating, etc.) (Berkowitz, 1989a, 1989b). However, decreasing the teacher-student ratio, adding new and spacious classrooms, and increasing the comfort of the classroom are usually beyond the control of most teachers. When crowding and poor environmental conditions exist, the best that many educators can do is to increase supervision.

Despite limitations to the extent to which teachers and staff can improve the physical structure of their school or classroom, there are other ways to change the physical environment to help prevent behavior problems and foster learning. For example, teachers should minimize distractions, presenting a classroom that is attractive, yet not overly stimulating. Chairs, desks, and other furniture should be arranged to reduce congestion as much as possible, to allow for the smooth flow of students, and for the teacher to circulate easily and quickly about the room. Materials and supplies are well organized, such that students (and the teacher) can readily access them in an efficient manner, without disrupting others. The classroom is made attractive, with decorative walls, posters, plants, workstations, and so forth. Finally, safety should always be of concern; thus, the school campus should have appropriate lighting, locks, two-way communications systems, alarm systems, and additional safety equipment as appropriate and needed, such as surveillance cameras (see Chapter 9).

6. *Use praise and rewards wisely and strategically.* One of the most common techniques used by educators to manage student behavior is the use of

praise and rewards. One survey found that over 90% of classroom teachers reported using rewards on a daily or weekly basis (Social and Character Development Research Consortium, 2010). Teachers were not asked about their use of praise, but it is very likely that an even higher percentage used praise more frequently than rewards. Praise and rewards are used to recognize and express approval of desired behaviors, and to reinforce, or increase the frequency, of those behaviors. Praise is given either verbally (e.g., "Great job!") or nonverbally (e.g., a warm smile or fist bump). Rewards also come in different forms, with the most common being tangible rewards (e.g., a sticker, snack), a preferred activity or privilege (e.g., screen time, extra recess, time to listen to music), and points, tokens, or tickets that can be exchanged for rewards.

Although both praise and rewards should be used in the classroom and throughout the school, praise should be used much more frequently. Praise has many practical advantages over rewards: it requires no planning (such as with point systems and tangible rewards) or cost and it's easy to administer. Praise also is likely to be perceived as less controlling, especially among adolescents (see Chapter 4 for discussion of the negative effects when rewards are perceived by students to be controlling).

Unquestionably, praise and rewards are effective in teaching new skills and increasing the strength of existing ones. Not only do they often reinforce behavior, but they also provide valuable feedback (Brophy, 1981). Praise and rewards are particularly valuable when working with students lacking motivation. Finally, the use of praise and rewards is strongly associated with positive teacher-student relationships (McIntosh, Filter, Bennett, Ryan, & Sugai, 2010) and an overall positive school climate (Bear, Yang, Mantz, & Harris, 2017).

Despite the frequent use of praise and rewards, such use is not without criticism, and especially toward the use of tangible rewards. The primary criticism is that tangible rewards can harm intrinsic motivation and encourage self-centered moral reasoning (e.g., "You should follow rules to get a reward."). That criticism, and related research, is discussed in Chapter 4 on social and emotional learning. As discussed in that chapter, there is little research showing that tangible rewards, as commonly used in the schools, harms intrinsic motivation and stifles moral development. This is particularly true if rewards are used in combination with other strategies for developing social and emotional competencies, and those strategies receive greater emphasis. Nevertheless, to increase the effectiveness of rewards while also avoiding any potential harm, educators are advised to use praise and rewards strategically and wisely. This includes avoiding using rewards in a manner that is perceived by students as manipulative or overly controlling, and especially in a manner that teaches students that the primary reason to act prosocially is to gain rewards and avoid punishment.

Two sets of recommendations are given below. Whereas the first set refers to the general use of praise and rewards, the second set applies to how to use rewards in a strategic and wise manner to avoid harm to intrinsic motivation and self-centered moral reasoning based on earning rewards.

General Recommendations on Use of Praise and Rewards[2]

- *Praise and reward specific behaviors, skills, and achievements.* Specific behaviors include those that demonstrate effort, such as working hard to achieve a goal. Often, it is more important to reinforce the small steps, reflecting effort made toward a final goal than achievement of the goal itself. Without doing so, the final might never be achieved.
- *Communicate sincerity when praising and rewarding student behavior.* Most students recognize *faint* praise, such as when praise is not given in the context of warmth or enthusiasm or otherwise is communicated in a manner that is lacking in sincerity. The same holds for how rewards are administered. When praise and rewards are perceived to be insincere, or not deserved, the effects can be more negative than positive.
- *Praise and reward immediately and more frequently when the targeted behavior is first seen or seldom occurs.* Once the behavior becomes more established and is seen more often, use praise and rewards more intermittently.
- *Provide variety and novelty.* Students often tire of the same reward used over and over. This also applies to praise—there are many, many ways to praise and reward students, and teachers should use them to gain students' attention and interest, but also to reinforce the desired behavior.
- *Include students in choosing rewards.* Allowing students to help determine rewards and the behaviors to be rewarded fosters a sense of autonomy and helps avoid students, especially older students, from perceiving rewards as being used in a controlling manner. Perhaps more importantly, allowing students to choose among options increases the likelihood that the reward is found to be effective. Students' voices in selecting and choosing rewards should be encouraged at the individual, classroom, and schoolwide levels. However, it is particularly important when working with individual students, as they vary greatly in what they like and dislike. Thus, a reinforcement menu, consisting of a list of reward options, is highly recommended, especially with younger students.
- *Recognize developmental and cultural differences in preferences for praise and rewards.* Rarely should the same rewards be used for all ages. Although it might seem obvious that kindergarteners should not be treated the same as high school students, the author has heard numerous complaints from high school teachers who are asked by administrators to disseminate tokens to students for good behavior, with a typical comment: "They might get tickets for being good in kindergarten, but they won't get them next year in college or at work!"). Also often overlooked as a developmental difference is that most adolescents prefer to be praised privately rather than publicly (Burnett, 2002). Cultural differences also are found in preferences for public or private recognition: Public recognition, either with praise or tangible rewards, is often frowned upon in many Asian cultures (de Luque & Sommer, 2000).
- *Encourage peers to praise one another.* Encouraging students to praise classmates for exhibiting prosocial behaviors serves to highlight and reinforce those behaviors, but also teaches students to practice good interpersonal skills (i.e., praising others).

- *Encourage self-reinforcement.* Students should learn that at times others will not praise or reward their prosocial actions, but the behavior is still quite praiseworthy and perhaps worthy of self-reward. A sense of pride in acting prosocially should not be contingent upon external praise and rewards.
- *Plan for maintenance and generalization of the desired behavior.* Maintenance refers to the extent to which the student continues to display the behavior after the intervention, or praise and reward, has been removed. Generalization refers to the extent to which the student performs the behavior in a variety of settings and situations. Ways to promote maintenance and generalization include having multiple people (e.g., peers, teachers and staff, parents) reinforce desired behaviors throughout the school setting (e.g., hallway, cafeteria, playground) and wherever else they are exhibited, highlighting real-world applications of the social-emotional skills when they are taught, and providing opportunities for students to practice learned skills in a variety of settings.

Recommendations for Avoiding Harm to Intrinsic Motivation and Self-Centered Moral Reasoning

- *Use tangible rewards as little as necessary to teach and maintain the desired behavior.* Rewards should be administered contingent upon the desired behavior (or effort made) when teaching a behavior that is new, difficult, or of little interest to a student, and especially when intrinsic motivation is lacking. It makes little sense to use them more than needed. Frequent and systematic use of tangible rewards (including point cards and tokens), especially when not needed to motivate prosocial behavior, increases the risk of potential harm to intrinsic motivation. Thus, they should be used only occasionally for behavior that is motivated intrinsically. This recommendation is consistent with the *principle of minimal sufficiency* in developmental psychology and the *least restrictive alternative* in behavioral psychology. The principle of minimal sufficiency states that an adult is more likely to foster students' intrinsic motivation for behavior change and sense of autonomy when using *just enough* external pressure to bring about compliance without making students feel that they are being coerced (Lepper, 1983). Similarly, the principle of the least restrictive alternative in behaviorism states that preference should always be given to interventions that are least likely to limit or restrict the student's freedom while still achieving the desired objective (Barton, Brulle, & Repp, 1983). When used frequently and systematically, such as when intrinsic motivation is lacking, planned efforts should always be made to fade their use as students demonstrate the desired behaviors and learn that there are reasons other than extrinsic ones to act prosocially.
- *When rewards are used, be sure to recognize the students' effort and autonomous choice.* Administering rewards in this manner is likely to lessen perceptions of external control and foster self-perceptions of autonomy and an internal locus of control. It also avoids the mindset that the primary reasons why one should comply with rules is to obtain rewards and avoid punishment.

- *Administer rewards spontaneously and unexpectedly.* Rewards are less likely to be perceived as controlling and to harm intrinsic motivation when they are provided in a surprising or unexpected manner. The key to this method is *not* informing students that they will receive a reward if certain expectations are met but providing the reward unexpectedly when they do meet the expectation (e.g., the whole class completed all homework throughout the week, so the teacher surprises them with 20 minutes of free time on Friday).
- *Reward (and praise) not only students' prosocial behavior, but also the thoughts, emotions, and dispositions that underlie the behavior.* Social and emotional competencies demonstrated by students should always be highlighted, including responsible decision-making, empathy, autonomy, social awareness, relationship skills, and self-management of emotions and behavior. Praising both observed behaviors and general dispositions (e.g., "You're a kind person." "You're someone who really cares about others.").
- *Communicate that rewards are used primarily for informative feedback.* Feedback serves the valuable purpose of informing students what they are doing well and in what areas they might need to improve (and how to do so). By focusing on the informative function of rewards (and praise), one helps avoid students perceiving the rewards as controlling. Informative feedback should highlight the importance, value, and usefulness of the desired behavior, both presently and in the future. This helps communicate that there are good reasons to exhibit the behavior other than simply to earn rewards.
- *In general, avoid communicating that students should follow rules, or act prosocially, simply to get a reward and to avoid punishment.* Students need to learn that there are many other good reasons for good behavior, especially reasons that focus on needs of others and the impact of one's behavior on others (see Chapter 4 on SEL for related strategies).

Summary

The prevention of behavior problems is key to effective classroom management and school discipline. The most effective teachers and schools prevent behavior problems in multiple ways. They include building and maintaining positive teacher-student and student-student relationships and developing students' social and emotional competencies—strategies in the social-emotional support domain of school climate. Positive and supportive relationships and social and emotional competencies are rarely sufficient, however, in preventing behavior problems and for ensuring that students are engaged and safe in school. As emphasized in the authoritative approach to classroom management, school discipline, and school climate, effective prevention requires both social-emotional support *and* structure. Structure consists of strategies that are more teacher- or adult-centered and used to manage student behavior, which consists of preventing and correcting behavior problems.

As seen in this chapter, three theoretical approaches to classroom management and the prevention of behavior problems have guided much of the research: the ecological, behavioral, and SEL approaches. Research generated by those approaches has identified and provided a greater understanding of the characteristics of teachers and the techniques they employ to effectively manage student behavior and prevent behavior problems. Recommendations presented in this chapter followed from such research, with an emphasis on those that are teacher-centered and not covered in other chapters.

Notes

1. Positive behavior support, or PBS, became positive behavior support and intervention, or PBIS, after the Public Broadcasting System warned of lawsuits for infringing on their use of the acronym PBS).
2. These recommendations are adapted from Bear, 2010 and Bear et al., 2019, and are elaborated on in those sources.

CHAPTER 6

CORRECTING BEHAVIOR PROBLEMS

Most behavior problems can be prevented, and educators who are most effective in preventing behavior problems use a combination of strategies and interventions, as presented throughout this book, and especially those in the school climate domains of social-emotional support, structure, student engagement, and safety. Nevertheless, even the best teachers cannot prevent all behavior problems, as at one time or another all students misbehave, with such misbehavior ranging from very minor and occasional acts of noncompliance that interfere with teaching or learning (e.g., talking without permission, not completing homework) to more serious and chronic acts that threaten the safety of others (e.g., bullying, fighting, possession of illegal substances or weapons). Thus, all teachers must be prepared to correct behavior problems when preventive techniques fail. In doing so they should have two goals in mind: (1) to stop or decrease the current misbehavior and (2) reduce the likelihood of future occurrence.

Achieving both goals typically calls for the continuation of preventive techniques but also some form of *punishment*, referred to in this chapter as *punitive consequences*. In psychology, particularly in the fields of behaviorism and applied behavior analysis, punishment refers to any action or outcome that serves to decrease the frequency of a behavior (Alberto & Troutman, 2013). Thus, by definition, punishment "works." That is, if it fails to decrease the targeted behavior, it is not punishment. This is why the term *punitive consequences* is used in this chapter, as there are times when what is intended to be punishment is *not* effective in decreasing behavior problems; thus, by definition, it is not really punishment. Punitive consequences are *intended* to decrease behavior problems but might not always do so. Punitive consequences include responses to undesired behavior ranging from a verbal reminder or "evil eye" to suspension from school. They also include *response cost*—taking something away as a consequence of the misbehavior. To a lesser extent than punitive consequences, *extinction* is used to decrease a behavior. Extinction consists of removing what reinforces the behavior. An example is ignoring misbehavior that functions to gain attention. Extinction is used much less often than punitive consequences because many misbehaviors disrupt learning and thus are difficult to ignore, and because it is often unclear if it is attention alone that is reinforcing the behavior.

As discussed next in this chapter, there are both advantages and limitations to the use of punitive consequences. Well aware of their limitations, the most effective teachers and schools use punitive consequences but do so in a manner that addresses the limitations, such as using them in a fair, just, and caring manner and only in combination with more positive techniques for teaching and reinforcing replacement, or more desired, behaviors. Combining positive techniques with punitive techniques in the correction of misbehavior, and especially positive techniques that provide social-emotional support and help develop social and emotional competencies, is the approach emphasized in this chapter. This is not only because it is the most effective approach for decreasing behavior problems, as seen in ample research on authoritative discipline, but also because it is critical to a positive school climate. That is, the frequent use social and emotional techniques and infrequent use of punitive techniques are strong predictors of a positive school climate (Bear et al., 2017). After discussing the advantages and limitations of the use of punitive consequences, general guidance is provided on the effective use of corrective techniques. This is followed by research-supported interventions for responding to mild to serious behavior problems.

Advantages of the Wise and Strategic Use of Punitive Consequences

There *are* good reasons why punishment, or punitive consequences, is widely used to correct misbehavior. Nevertheless, ample research shows that punitive consequences are generally effective for modifying human behavior, including for purposes of classroom management and school discipline (Landrum & Kauffman, 2006). That research clearly shows that nearly all forms of behavior problems in the classroom decrease, at least in the short term, in response to punitive consequences. Two additional advantages to the use of punitive consequences, when used wisely and strategically are: they deter behavior problems and they help develop self-discipline.

Punitive Consequences as Effective Deterrents.

Punitive consequences serve as effective *deterrents* of problem behavior (Bandura, 1986). In reviewing the research literature on punishment as a deterrent for criminal behavior, Bandura explained three types of negative deterrents: *self-sanction, social sanction, and legal sanction*. Self-sanction is the most effective deterrent: Individuals refrain from violating laws when they have internalized moral standards supporting them and when they anticipate experiencing empathy-based guilt and shame for violating them. As stated by Bandura (1986), self-sanction "is the most effective form of deterrence because antisocial behavior is renounced, even in situations in which there is little or no risk of getting caught" (p. 274). Unfortunately, many students, and adults, lack self-sanctions, or what is referred to in this book as self-discipline. Moreover, too often they use various mechanisms of moral disengagement that negate self-sanctions, such as denying responsibility, blaming others, and making excuses (Bandura, 2016; Gini, Pozzoli, & Hymel, 2014). Thus, society requires social and legal sanctions to deter illegal behavior, and schools require the same to deter behavior problems that interfere with learning. Many punitive consequences used in schools, especially those for moderate to serious behavior problems, serve as legal sanctions, but they also can serve as powerful social sanctions when students view them as fair and reasonable (Arum, 2003). Suspension is a good example of a legal sanction, and also often as a social sanction.

Bandura (1986) argues that while social and legal sanctions are most critical in governing the behavior of those lacking self-sanctions, they also are in the best interest for everyone. This is because too few individuals are guided solely by self-sanctions and thus require social and legal sanctions to deter harmful behavior. It should be emphasized that Bandura concludes that although negative consequences are effective in deterring illegal behavior, *so too are positive deterrents.* Thus, he endorses a combination of the two, which is a position well supported by research in social psychology on the effectiveness of punishment and rewards in promoting cooperation (Balliet, Mulder, Van Lange, & Paul, 2011), as well as research in school discipline and classroom management on the importance of a comprehensive and authoritative approach that balances social-emotional support and structure (Bear, 2015; Gottfredson et al., 2005; Gregory et al., 2010; Gregory & Weinstein, 2008).

Punitive Consequences and Self-discipline. In both deterring behavior problems and responding to behavior problems, punitive consequences help develop self-discipline. As discussed previously in Chapter 1, authoritative parents and teachers, those who are most effective in developing student's self-discipline, are demanding and use punitive consequences. Students learn that certain behaviors are wrong by the nature of those behaviors resulting in punitive consequences. But, in contrast to authoritarian educators, authoritative educators do not use punitive consequences as their primary means of developing self-discipline. Instead, they teach students other reasons not to exhibit those behaviors, such as the impact of the behavior on others. They also emphasize autonomy as opposed to external control, and ensure that when punitive consequences are used, which is sparingly, it is combined with warmth and support (Baumrind, 1996).

Punitive consequences are also frequently used to help achieve the second goal of correction—preventing misbehavior from recurring. However, due to their many limitations, as discussed next, punitive consequences are often insufficient in achieving this goal. That is, the misbehavior might cease immediately, or short-term, but it returns later at the same or increased rate, and especially when punitive consequences are no longer salient. For example, a student is verbally reprimanded for getting out of her seat, returns to her seat, but continues to get out of her seat later when the teacher is not looking.

Limitations of Punitive Consequences

Primary among the limitations of punitive consequences are the following (Bear, 2005, 2010):

- *They are likely to produce undesirable side effects.* When punished, students often experience the negative emotions of frustration, anger, anxiety, fear, guilt, and shame. Not only might these emotions negatively impact general emotional and social well-being, but when unregulated they also are likely to impact learning, as seen in poor attention, concentration, and memory. This is especially true when students perceive the consequences as unfair or overly harsh. When this occurs, the negative emotions often lead to retaliation (verbal or physical), revenge (e.g., deliberate attempts to undermine authority), avoidance or withdrawal (e.g., refusal to complete work, skipping classes, truancy, or dropping out), or dislike of those perceived to be the source of the negative emotions (e.g., teacher, principal, peers, or school in general). For example, research shows suspension to be associated with poor teacher-student relationships and a general lack of connectedness with school (Anyon, Zhang, & Hazel, 2016; Balfanz, Herzog, & Mac Iver, 2007).

- *They teach students what not to do, rather than what they should do.* As astutely noted almost half a century ago by Winett and Winkler (1972), punitive consequences teach *deadman* behaviors—behaviors that can be performed by a dead person. Unless combined with other positive techniques, which too often is not the case, punitive consequences fail to teach prosocial behaviors or thoughts and emotions that should replace those that led to being punished. This would include repairing any harm that might have been done, either physical (e.g., damaged property) or social-emotional (e.g., harm to relationships and feelings of others).
- *Students simply learn "not to get caught."* Not engaging in misbehavior simply because you will or *might* get caught constitutes the lowest level of moral reasoning—self-centered, based on fear of consequences to oneself, without any consideration of why else the behavior is wrong (Kohlberg, 1984). When this mindset governs student behavior, the constant presence of adults or constant monitoring of behavior is necessary for students not to misbehave.
- *Students learn to punish others.* They learn that punitive consequences, and threats thereof, are effective in controlling others and gaining compliance. Students also observe, and often emulate, additional undesired behaviors, thoughts, and emotions that coincide with the use of punitive consequences, such as anger and manipulating or threatening others.
- *The effects are often non-lasting and dependent on the presence of adults.* When there is little or no fear of getting caught (i.e., no adults or camera are present), or when the punitive consequences are ineffective (e.g., the student perceives that the misbehavior is worth the risk of getting caught or worth the anticipated punitive consequences), the misbehavior is likely to continue.
- *They fail to address the multiple factors that likely contributed to the misbehavior.* Multiple individual and environmental factors determine behavior, and punitive consequences seldom change them. For example, punishing a student does little if anything to address poor peer relations, a negative teacher-student relationship, ineffective classroom management practices, the student's lack of motivation or academic skills, or students' attitudes and beliefs supporting the misbehavior.
- *Their use is often reinforcing to those who use them, as well as to the students who are on the receiving end.* Three types of reinforcement are often seen when punitive consequences are invoked: negative reinforcement, positive reinforcement, and self-reinforcement. First, *negative reinforcement* is likely to occur via the cessation of the misbehavior that the teacher/administrator finds aversive, or what the student finds aversive (e.g., completing work, a nagging teacher, or school in general). The immediate removal of the student, such as with suspension, eliminates, at least short-term, what is viewed as aversive by either the adult or student, or both. Thus, the noncompliance is likely to be repeated by the student, and so too is the act of removal by the teacher, because both behaviors are negatively reinforced.

Second, *positive reinforcement* is likely to occur. For example, the teacher who refers a student to the office for noncompliance is praised by an administrator or other teachers for not tolerating misbehavior. Likewise, both the teacher and administrator might be positively reinforced with praise from others, including the school board and the community, for running a "tight ship" that doesn't tolerate misbehavior. With respect to student behavior, the misbehavior leading to suspension is positively reinforced when students find that it is more enjoyable to be at home than at school while suspended. This happens when students are allowed to play video games, watch television, or otherwise engage in fun activities instead of doing schoolwork. Finally, the use of punitive consequences also can be *self-reinforcing*. This is seen when teachers or administrators experience a sense of control and power when punishing others.

- *Too often they are imposed in a racially biased manner.* This is too often seen in the greater use of suspensions with African-American students than other students, and particularly for relatively minor behavior problems, such as noncompliance, as opposed to more serious transgression such as criminal acts. Researchers attribute disproportionality in suspension rate to an implicit bias among many educators (Gregory & Mosely, 2004; Gregory et al., 2010).
- *In general, the frequent use of punitive consequences creates a negative school climate.* Classrooms and schools are not pleasant places for either students or teachers when punitive consequences are ever-present.

When Punitive Consequences are Needed: Using Them Wisely and Strategically

Because punitive consequences are often effective in stopping or decreasing behavior problems, serve as deterrents of future behavior problems, and help develop self-discipline, to one extent or another they are found in every school and classroom. They also are found, however, because educators often have no choice in their use. That is, codes of conduct in nearly all schools, as well as state and federal laws, *require* that punitive consequences, including harsh ones (e.g., suspension and expulsion) be invoked for certain rule infractions. With respect to the use of punitive consequences in school discipline and classroom management, what differentiates the most effective and ineffective schools and teachers is not *whether or not* they use punitive consequences, but *how often* and *in what manner* they do so. As noted in the previous chapter, the most effective teachers—those characterized by the authoritative approach—have to correct misbehavior much less often than other teachers because they are successful in executing a broad range of preventive strategies, especially those that engage students and build and maintain positive teacher-student relationships. When misbehavior does occur, the most effective teachers also tend to view disciplinary encounters differently, and thus *respond* differently than their less effective counterparts (Brophy, 2004; Brophy & McCaslin, 1992). This not only is observed in the techniques that teachers employ to prevent and correct misbehavior, but perhaps more importantly in the following mindsets and dispositions that characterize educators who follow an authoritative approach to correcting misbehavior.

- *They understand that most misbehavior is developmentally normal and view disciplinary encounters as educational opportunities.* As noted in Chapter 4 on SEL, disciplinary encounters provide excellent opportunities for developing social and emotional competencies of self-management, social awareness, relationship skills, responsible decision-making, and self-awareness. The most effective classroom managers and schools understand this. To be sure, they hold high behavioral expectations, but they also recognize that students will not always meet them. Perfect behavior is not expected, although effort toward it is. Effective teachers recognize that minor misbehavior (e.g., not completing homework, talking without permission, conflicts with peers) is developmentally normal, and that even occasional instances of more serious acts (e.g., fighting, lying, cheating) are to be expected.

  When misbehavior first occurs, the more effective (i.e., authoritative) teachers tend to view this as an educational opportunity to help develop social and emotional competencies that underlie self-discipline. In contrast to authoritarian teachers, their initial response is not one of meting out punitive consequences. To be sure, they use punitive consequences, but do so much more sparingly. Authoritative teachers recognize that invoking punitive consequences might be appropriate (and a simple, easy, and immediate response), but that it is insufficient for developing social and emotional competencies. Disciplinary encounters require strategies of teaching, not law enforcement—an authoritative, not authoritarian approach to discipline and classroom management. Failing to demonstrate expected social skills is viewed similarly to failing to demonstrate an expected math skill—as an error or deficiency that requires the correction of mistakes, which likely includes a need for additional teaching and support.

- *They handle disciplinary encounters in a calm, patient, respectful, yet firm and timely, manner.* They communicate disappointment, but they do not argue with the student. Rarely, if ever, do they demonstrate anger, recognizing that doing so would model the lack of managing emotions and likely interfere with problem-solving. Perhaps most importantly, they recognize that there is a right and wrong time for correcting misbehavior. Generally, the right time for correcting misbehavior is immediately after the misbehavior occurs. However, an exception is when emotions interfere with effective communication. That is, emotion either interferes with the student's listening and understanding of the corrective message, or emotion interferes with the teacher adequately expressing the intended and preferred message. Anger is a common example of an interfering emotion. When angry, before discussing the misbehavior and its correction, teachers should wait until after they (both the adult and the student) have calmed down or they have someone else attend to the problem behavior.

  Effective teachers also are patient and understand that behaviors rarely improve immediately and that the development of self-discipline takes a long time. Finally, they recognize and respect not only individual differences, but also cultural and racial differences. They respect the feelings, thoughts, and dignity of *all* students.

- *They are fair and strive to be perceived as such by their students.* In being fair, they are not too harsh or too lenient. They are just and impartial. They are consistently fair in their actions, treating all students equally while allowing for different consequences when the circumstances surrounding the behavior are not the same. For example, they might not impose the same consequences for a first-time offender versus a repeated offender; for a student who is remorseful versus one who is defiantly unforgiving; for a student provoked by peers versus one who clearly instigated the behavior problem, and so forth. They act like judges who act judiciously, fairly, wisely, and with discretion.

They are concerned not only about *being* fair, but also recognize the importance of *being perceived* by others as fair. As emphasized in multiple chapters throughout this book, students' perceptions of the fairness of rules and their consequences is a strong determinant of student behavior, school climate, and school safety (Arum, 2003; Benner et al., 2008; Brand et al., 2003; Gottfredson et al., 2005; Mayer & Leone, 1999; Welsh, 2000, 2003). To be sure, being viewed as fair is often a great challenge when the consequences for misbehavior are inconsistent across cases, including for good reasons, such as those noted above. Nevertheless, the most effective educators reflect upon, and respond to, any indications of unfairness or bias, either real or perceived, toward individuals and groups.

With respect to cultural differences in the effectiveness of techniques for preventing and correcting misbehavior in school, research has not shown any technique to be uniquely effective for a particular cultural or racial group (Gregory et al., 2010; Kauffman, Conroy, Gardner, & Oswald, 2008). Instead, research shows that techniques consistent with the authoritative approach, characterized by demandingness and support, are best for everyone (Gorman-Smith, Tolan, & Henry, 2000; Gregory et al., 2010; Mandara & Murray, 2002; Shumow, Vandell, & Posner, 1999; Taylor, Hinton, & Wilson, 1995). This includes applying each of the dispositions and mindsets in this section to *all* students.

- *They strive to protect the student's sense of self-worth, dignity, autonomy, and the student's rights.* They avoid harming a student's sense of self-worth, dignity, and autonomy by focusing on the specific behavior, not the person. They communicate that what the student did was wrong, but that it does not make the student a bad person. They avoid using sarcasm, and especially humiliating students. They listen to the student's perspective. They make sure that the student is actually responsible for the misbehavior (e.g., the student is not falsely accused), especially when correction entails punitive consequences. This includes protecting the student's right of due process, especially where required by law (e.g., in cases of suspension and expulsion). Where feasible, they handle the disciplinary encounter privately, and not before peers. They emphasize the student's strengths, especially those that might be used to help correct the misbehavior and stop it from recurring. They voice optimism that the behavior will improve. In helping to maintain a sense of autonomy, they provide choices, where appropriate (e.g., choice of punitive consequences and choice of strategies to take to improve behavior).

- *They work to maintain a positive teacher-student relationship, and to reestablish it when broken.* They understand that social-emotional support and structure characterize the authoritative approach, and the best teachers. If a positive relationship is harmed, they work to reestablish it. Maintaining and reestablishing a positive relationship is largely achieved by demonstrating the qualities above, especially patience, fairness, respect, and not harming the student's sense of self-worth, dignity, and autonomy, but it also is achieved by communicating warmth, caring, and support. As such, the strategies recommended in Chapter 2 on teacher-student relationships are valued highly and practiced consistently.

Recommended Strategies and Interventions for Correcting Behavior Problems

In this section, eight general recommended strategies for correcting behavior problems in the classroom and school are presented. Whereas the first seven apply to nearly all behavior problems, the last one is specific to students with serious and chronic behavior problems. More specific interventions for correcting behavior problems are presented in Box 6.1 and are discussed in the second recommendation below. The strategies and interventions presented in this section are in addition to those presented in other chapters that also should be used to help correct behavior problems, especially those for building and maintaining positive teacher-student and student-student relationships (Chapters 2 & 3), developing social and emotional competencies (Chapter 4), preventing behavior problems with effective classroom management (Chapter 5), engaging students (Chapter 7), preventing bullying (Chapter 8), and promoting school safety (Chapter 9). Recommendations presented in those chapters should always be used in combination with those presented here.

Multiple factors should determine the extent to which the eight strategies and each of the interventions in the box should be implemented. Primary among them are: (a) the severity and frequency of the behavior and its impact on learning; (b) the age developmental level of the student; (c) the teacher's professional training, competence, and acceptance of the strategy or intervention; and (d) practical and situational factors, such as the immediacy of addressing the problem and the feasibility of its implementation (e.g., the time and resources required, the impact of the intervention on others).

1. *Identify factors within students and their environments that contribute to the problem.* Where feasible, the identified factors should be targeted in interventions. Behavior is influenced by multiple factors, which includes those within the student, the classroom, the school, the home, and the community. Typically, a combination and interaction of factors determine behavior. For example, how a student responds to teasing or bullying is determined not only by the student's social and emotional competencies, such as anger management and responsible decision-making, but also by various environmental factors, both proximal (e.g., peers supporting the bully or the victim; the student anticipating teacher support) and distal (history of being bullied, home stressors and support). Identifying factors that determine or contribute to the misbehavior provides greater understanding of the misbehavior. Perhaps more importantly, it often helps guide interventions by pinpointing factors that are most malleable and best targeted for modification.

The informal process of identifying contributing factors and reflecting upon how they might best be addressed has existed since educators first dealt with behavior problems. Recently, however, it has become more formalized, commonly referred to as *functional behavioral assessment* (FBA). Calling the process a FBA gained considerable popularity with the inclusion of the term in the Individuals with Disabilities Education Act (IDEA). That law requires that a formal FBA be conducted "as appropriate" under certain circumstances for students with disabilities who might be suspended from school or otherwise removed from their current placement because of their behavior. Such formal FBAs are typically conducted and documented by school psychologists and other members of a student's Individual Educational Program (IEP) team. When done well, FBAs include multiple methods of assessment, with the most common being behavioral observations, interviews with the student and teacher(s), and standardized rating scales completed by the teacher, parent, and student.

Unfortunately, far too often formal FBAs are not done well and thus provide classroom teachers and parents with little useful information that they did not already know. This is especially true when they are guided by a narrow, yet popular, ABC behavioral approach. This approach focuses on Antecedents to the behavior, the Behavior, and the Consequences of the behavior—antecedents, behavior, and consequences that are observable in the environment. The conclusion, or hypothesis, commonly reached from this type of assessment is that the behavior is caused, or triggered, by what is observed in the environment and that the student's response to that trigger serves one of two functions: positive reinforcement (i.e., gaining attention or a desired object or activity) or negative reinforcement (avoiding demands, people, and undesired activities) (Crone & Horner, 2003; Crone, Horner, & Hawken, 2010). Less common functions determined by the ABC approach are communication and self-stimulation (Crone & Horner, 2003).

This narrow ABC approach to FBA has several limitations. First, it is very simplistic, yielding information that most teachers (and others) would likely guess without conducting a formal FBA. That is, training is not required for most teachers (and laymen) to guess that students misbehave to get attention or what they want, and to avoid doing what they don't want to do. Second, it fails to identify multiple, and often critical, factors contributing to the behavior problem that are not observable or easy to observe in the school, such as home factors, peer relationships, and a student's thoughts and feelings. Third, for the most common behavior problems, the information obtained from this type of FBA seldom leads to interventions that are more effective than those *not* guided by the FBA (Bruni et al., 2017; Vance, Gresham, & Dart, 2012).

In light of those limitations, the majority of behavior problems do not need a formal FBA. A formal FBA should be saved for those students who are found to be resistant to common techniques of prevention and correction. These students would consist primarily of the 1-5% of students, mostly at Tier 3 in a multi-tiered system, who require a behavioral intervention plan consisting of intensive and comprehensive interventions and supports (Gresham, 2004). If a formal FBA is needed, it is recommended that it covers much more than that covered in the simplistic ABC approach.

That is, it should include all factors—cognitive, emotional, behavioral, and environmental (proximal and distal)—that contribute to the problem behavior. This would require not only classroom observations, but also other assessment techniques such as interviews with the student, teacher(s), parents, and possibly peers; a thorough review of the student's educational and behavioral history and response to interventions; and the completion of student, teacher, and parent rating forms and checklists of behavior and contributing factors.

In sum, it certainly makes sense to identify and reflect upon factors that contribute to a student's behavior, and most teachers do so (Brophy & McCaslin, 1992). Whether called an FBA or not, when conducted either informally or formally this process provides insight as to what factors might be influencing the behavior and is often helpful for selecting interventions, especially for students who are shown to resist common interventions. For example, it is useful to know that increased off-task behavior is influenced not only by the neighboring peer (thus, one might change seating) and the difficulty of the work assigned (thus, one might adapt the material), but also by recent stressors at home (thus, one should collaborate with parents, or recommend counseling). However, in the majority of cases of misbehavior in the classroom, a formal FBA is not needed, necessary, nor helpful for many teachers. Time might be better spent helping develop and implementing effective interventions.

2. ***Implement evidence-based interventions that best match the nature and severity of the misbehavior.*** Interventions implemented to correct misbehavior should be evidence-based, supported by research as to their effectiveness in reducing the targeted undesired behavior and increasing desired behavior. That an intervention is effective, or "works," in stopping the misbehavior is not sufficient. The intervention also should teach or increase desired behavior and the social and emotional competencies that underlie self-discipline. Of equal importance in the effectiveness of the intervention is that it is fair and ethical. That is, its harshness should always be proportional to the severity of the offense and the circumstances involved.

Box 6.1 lists evidence-based interventions for correcting misbehavior that are commonly found in textbooks and research reviews on classroom management and school discipline (e.g., Bear, 2010; Brophy, 1996; Emmer & Evertson, 2017; Evertson & Emmer, 2017; Jones & Jones, 2016; Kauffman & Landrum, 2018; Marzano, 2003). The interventions are listed in a hierarchical fashion of increasing intensity and power assertion on the part of the teacher or other adult who implements the intervention. There are two sets of interventions. The first set consists of interventions commonly used in response to the most frequent behavior problems in classrooms, such as students not attending to tasks, getting out of their seats, and other relatively minor rule violations and acts of noncompliance. They include interventions that are used for both preventing and correcting behavior problems. That is, they are implemented before misbehavior occurs but also afterwards, such as prompting a student and praising desired behavior.

The second set, presented in the second section of the box, builds upon the first. They are best implemented when the first set of interventions are not effective in correcting common and relatively minor behavior problems.

Interventions in this section address more serious violations of school rules that cause a great deal of classroom disruption and/or harm to the student or others. As discussed in Recommendation 8, most students exhibiting serious and chronic behavior problems typically require services, resources, and supports beyond those found in most classrooms.

Deciding what combination of interventions are to be implemented should be guided by the principle of minimal sufficiency where feasible (i.e., where code of conduct does not require otherwise). This is particularly important when the misbehaving student views the punitive consequence as unfair and is not persuaded about its fairness after explanation and reasoning (Grusec, 2012). Recall from Chapter 5 on prevention, and in the context of the use of external rewards, the principle of minimal sufficiency calls for the use of the least amount of external pressure necessary to change behavior. Thus, whereas a simple redirection or reasoning might first be used to gain compliance, techniques of increasing greater power assertion would be employed only after those techniques fail. Using punitive consequences that are less harsh, yet fair, has several advantages. First, the student is more likely to perceive the consequences as not overly controlling and coercive. This is likely to result in greater acceptance, as it is less likely to harm intrinsic motivation and moral development. Second, regardless of perceptions of fairness, at times harsher interventions often are no more effective or are less effective than milder ones. Two good examples are time-out and suspension. Removing a young student for 100 minutes instead of 10 minutes, or suspending a student for 10 days instead of 1, is likely to be less rather than more effective. Not only does the student lose more academic time, but the harsher intervention is more likely to provoke negative emotions that interfere with learning, teacher-student and student-student relationships, and attachment to school.

When implementing the interventions in Box 6.1, their effectiveness should be closely monitored. This might entail formally recording the frequency and intensity of the behavior to gauge progress toward decreasing the undesired and increasing the desired behaviors. If the first interventions in the hierarchy are found to be ineffective, consideration should be given to altering them (e.g., increasing frequency and making sure they are implemented with fidelity), and adding additional interventions that are next in the hierarchy. To increase fidelity of implementation, especially with more complex interventions (e.g., implementing the Good Behavior Game), it helps to follow a checklist of specific implementation steps and to seek consultation, as needed, from others who have implemented the intervention successfully.

3. *Whether or not punitive consequences are invoked, include positive interventions for teaching or increasing the desired behavior.* This recommendation addresses perhaps the foremost limitation of punitive consequences: The failure to teach and support desired behaviors, unless one views the absence of undesired behaviors as constituting desired behaviors. The recommendation applies when responding to behavior problems, regardless of whether or not punitive consequences are invoked. For many misbehaviors, punitive consequences are unnecessary and replacement techniques, or competency building techniques, *are* sufficient for decreasing the misbehavior and increasing the desired behavior. Examples include ignoring a student

who calls out in class or talks to a peer while simultaneously praising others for raising their hands.

In choosing interventions for teaching and increasing replacement behaviors, attention should be given to the same factors listed earlier when considering the use of punitive consequences, such as the type and severity of the problem behavior and the developmental level of the student. Another key consideration, however, should be whether the problem behavior reflects a *"can't do"* problem, which is a skill-based deficiency, or a *"won't do,"* which is a motivation-based deficiency (Gresham, 1981). That is: "Is the student lacking the desired skill, or is the skill in the student's repertoire but not exhibited?" For example, some students may lack social problem-solving skills that are needed to resolve social conflicts or they may lack academic skills required to complete an assignment. Others possess those skills but simply fail to apply them. However, for "can't-do" problems, desired skills first need to be taught, followed by techniques of motivation. For "won't-do" problems, the choice of replacement techniques should be motivation-centered (including use of positive reinforcement). Regardless of whether it is a "can't do" or "won't do" problem, one's aim when correcting misbehavior should always be to teach and reinforce replacement behaviors, which requires techniques other than punitive ones.

4. ***In addition to replacement behaviors, focus on the impact of the student's behavior on others and, where applicable, the need to restore any harm done.*** Not all misbehavior causes harm to others, but when it does the student needs to "fix" the problem. The student needs to demonstrate what will be done differently in similar situations in the future, but also needs to repair or restore any harm the misbehavior may have inflicted upon others. As noted previously, the primary message in a disciplinary encounter should not be "If you do that again, you'll be punished." When this is the message, students simply learn that you should not get caught. Instead, the message should focus on other reasons *why* the behavior is wrong. Those reasons should focus on the impact of the misbehavior *on others*, and particularly those harmed by the behavior, with the goal of inducing perspective-taking, empathy, and a reasonable amount of empathy-based guilt. For example, one might ask: "How do you think Angela felt about what you said to her?" "How might you feel if someone did the same to you?"

The process of inducing empathy and empathy-based guilt when correcting misbehavior is called *induction*, or *inductive discipline*. Inductive discipline is supported by research showing that it is a common technique used by authoritative parents to foster internalization of the values of caring and concern about others and a sense of responsibility for one's own actions (Eisenberg, Fabes, & Spinrad, 2006; Hoffman, 2000). Inductive discipline is found in several research-supported SEL programs, especially the Responsive Classroom Approach (Responsive Classroom, 2018) and the Caring Schools Community (Watson & Battistich, 2006). In more recent years, focusing on the impact of one's behavior on others, and restoring any harm done during disciplinary encounters has often been referred to as a *restorative practice*, or *restorative justice* (e.g., Advancement Project, 2014).

In addition to the impact of the behavior on others, and depending on the nature of the behavior (and time available), additional reasons also should be discussed—reasons other than "bad behavior is punished if you get caught." They include the impact of one's behavior not only on the victim(s) but also on those less directly involved and those likely to be concerned ("How might your parents feel if they learn about what you did? How do you think it makes *me* feel? How about other classmates?"), and the impact on one's future, reputation, self-concept, and moral identity. Depending on the context, this might consist of repairing or replacing damaged property or apologizing (or otherwise showing remorse) in order to try to repair any emotional harm done to another person as well as to regain that person's trust and respect.

5. *Encourage acceptance of responsibility for one's actions and for improving behavior.* Perceptions of autonomy, self-control, and choice are core aspects of self-discipline. As true with adults, students are more likely to act in a manner consistent with their values and beliefs when they attribute responsibility for their behavior to themselves rather than to others (Glasser, 1969; Weiner, 2006). As discussed in Chapter 4 on SEL, disciplinary encounters present excellent opportunities for students to learn that their own decision-making and choices determine their behavior. As with teachers, students should recognize that multiple factors determine human behavior, but they also need to understand that *they are ultimately responsible for their own behavior*, with this understanding increasing with age (e.g., adolescents should be more responsible than preschoolers). Assuming responsibility applies to both present and future behavior. During disciplinary encounters, this should entail a commitment to changing behavior.

Although students should be responsible for their own behavior, it is important to emphasize that the responsibility also is to be shared by the school, as schools have a moral and social responsibility to help students develop social and emotional competencies that will lead them to make the right choices. Strategies throughout this book for improving all aspects of school climate help share responsibility, especially strategies for developing social and emotional competencies. Of particular relevance would be strategies for promoting social and emotional competencies that underlie the acceptance of responsibility for one's behavior. Within the context of correcting misbehavior, this would include strategies that help develop empathy-based guilt (i.e., feeling badly and responsible about one's behavior because of its harmful effects on others). Guilt is the primary emotion that underlies a sense of responsibility for one's misbehavior ("What I did was wrong, and I feel badly that I did it as it hurt someone"). Unlike shame, which is a more pervasive and negative emotion than guilt, characterized by feeling worthless as a person, it is easy to relieve the feeling of guilt by "fixing" the harm done to others. A challenge during disciplinary encounters is to induce empathy-based guilt and not shame.

In addition to inducing empathy-based guilt and acceptance of responsibility for one's actions, which are aims of inductive discipline and restorative practices, another strategy that is often appropriate during many disciplinary encounters, especially when students deny responsibility or excuse their misbehavior, is confronting mechanisms of moral disengagement. As discussed in Chapter 4 on SEL, mechanisms of moral disengagement often explain why individuals experience no empathy, guilt, or sense of responsibility after committing a harmful act. Denials, excuses, and other mechanisms of moral disengagement should be tactfully challenged in an authoritative manner (i.e., not in an interrogative or authoritarian manner) that holds the student accountable, yet strives to maintain a positive adult-student relationship.

6. *Follow a social problem-solving framework.* Each of the recommended interventions and practices presented so far should be applied within a problem-solving framework consisting of problem-solving steps that the student can use to avoid repeating the misbehavior. Such steps are taught in most curriculum based SEL curriculum programs, and students should be encouraged to apply them, including during disciplinary encounters. For example, Second Step Social-Emotional Learning (Committee for Children, 2019) teaches students to STEP: (1) Say the problem (without blame); (2) Think of solutions (safe and respectful); (3) Explore consequences (what could happen if ... .); and (4) Pick the best solution (make your plan). Other programs use similar social problem-solving steps. The first step almost always focuses on identifying the problem behavior and *why* it is a problem that needs a solution. Exactly why the student is being corrected should be clear. This should include presenting evidence, where needed, that the student indeed committed the misbehavior (and the opportunity for the student to appropriately challenge the accusation and evidence). Upon identifying the behavior, discussion should center on why the behavior is wrong with an emphasis on the negative impact on others (Recommendation 4), and what might be done to fix the problem and avoid it being repeated in the future (Recommendations 3 & 4 above).

After identifying and discussing the problem behavior, solutions are brainstormed and each one is evaluated. Solutions from the student should certainly be solicited by asking such questions as: "What might you do in the future to avoid this problem? What have you done in the past that worked? What do others do?" However, teachers should not hesitate to prompt or offer solutions when students fail to come up with good solutions on their own nor should they hesitate to challenge ones given by students that are inappropriate or likely to fail. Whether or not each solution is a "good" one, and why, should be discussed by asking such questions as: Is it fair? Is it the right thing to do? How will it impact others? Will it be effective?

In the final step, the student chooses the best solution(s) and commits to trying it. Where appropriate, such as when the solution entails new skills or the student otherwise is not confident in implementing the solution, role-playing should be used to help teach and practice the skills needed to implement the solution effectively. The problem-solving process should lead to an action plan, either oral or written. If written, the action plan might be framed as a traditional contract that specifies the targeted behavior and its consequences—both punitive consequences for the undesired behavior and positive ones for the replacement behavior.

Of course, meeting individually with the student, and following problem-solving steps, is neither feasible nor appropriate for all problem behaviors. This is especially true for common and minor problem behaviors, such as getting out of one's seat and talking without permission, that are responsive to less time-consuming techniques (e.g., proximity control, verbal prompts) and when the student clearly knows what the problem is and how to exhibit the desired behavior.

7. *Share responsibility for helping improve the student's behavior.* Although students should accept responsibility for their behavior in school, so too should teachers and staff share that responsibility. This is consistent with the understanding that human behavior is reciprocally determined by the individual and the individual's environment, which includes not only the behavior of the student and others, but also their thoughts and emotions. Sharing responsibility applies to both preventing and correcting misbehavior. In the context of disciplinary encounters, the teacher's and school's sharing of responsibility should be communicated in demandingness and structure as seen in high behavioral expectations, fair consequences, and confronting denials and excuses, but also should be communicated in social-emotional support. Such social-emotional support is observed in teachers providing guidance to help students solve problems, restore any broken or harmed relationships, and choose and exhibit appropriate behavior. It also is seen in the mindsets and dispositions of teachers, discussed earlier in this chapter, in which teachers (a) view most behavior problems as normal and view disciplinary encounters as educational opportunities; (b) handle disciplinary encounters in a calm, patient, respectful, yet firm and timely, manner; (c) are fair, and try to be perceived the same by students; (d) strive to protect students' sense of self-worth, dignity, and autonomy; and (e) work to maintain positive teacher-student relationships.

Social-emotional support also should be communicated by the adult handling the discipline encounter, conveying optimism that the student's behavior will improve. This does not mean that the teacher refrains from expressing disappointment in the student's behavior, but that the teacher conveys that the student's behavior is not fixed and thus can be altered. In conveying optimism, the teacher might remind the student of instances in which appropriate behavior was not exhibited under the same circumstance, and also highlight any strengths of the student that might help prevent the misbehavior from reoccurring. Finally, with respect to communicating shared responsibility, educators also should emphasize that adults are largely responsible for student behavior. It is their moral and legal duty, and their job to (a) maintain an environment that is orderly, safe, and conducive to learning and (b) to develop social and emotional competencies, including self-discipline.

8. *Seek assistance in helping students with chronic and serious behavior problems.* Most mild to moderate problem behaviors are responsive to common interventions, both punitive and positive ones. This is particularly true when they are used in combination, in a planned and systematic fashion, and with fidelity. However, more intensive interventions are needed when mild to moderate problem behaviors are resistant to those interventions. Other behaviors, whether frequent or not, also warrant more intensive interventions by the nature of their severity and present or potential impact on the well-being and safety of the student or others. Examples are threats of suicide, severe anxiety or depression, and violent and other behaviors governed by a school's code of conduct and that call for out-of-school suspension, expulsion, or additional services and supports. Such interventions, services, and supports commonly characterize the third tier of the multitiered model of interventions and supports (called the tertiary or indicated level in

preventive mental health models). Some are listed in the second section of Box 6.1. However, many of the same interventions also are often found at Tier 2 (called secondary or selective level in mental health prevention). Tier 2 targets those students who are not necessarily exhibiting behavior problems that are resistant to interventions but who are *at great risk* of doing so due to their previous history and other risk factors (e.g., poor anger management, poor school achievement, lack of peer acceptance and friendships).

In addition to behavior problems that are resistant to intervention, the following are common indicators of the need for more intensive interventions, services, and supports (Bear, 2010): (a) an Individualized Educational Program, or Behavioral Intervention Plan, for the student exists and refers to the presence of emotional and behavioral problems; (b) a psychiatric diagnosis indicating behavior problems (especially conduct disorder or oppositional defiant disorder); (c) the student has a history of referrals to the office, intervention teams, or support staff; and (d) the results of a comprehensive screening system, such as with teacher ratings of problem behaviors, indicating the seriousness of the behavior(s). When the need for more intensive interventions is indicated, teachers should not hesitate to seek assistance and support from others, including administrators, mental health specialists (e.g., school psychologist or counselor), and fellow teachers.

As seen in Box 6.1, many of the interventions for students at Tiers 2 and 3 are the same as at Tier 1. They differ, however, in how they are delivered. That is, they should be delivered in a more frequent and systematic fashion. For example, students with serious or chronic behavior problems are likely to need more frequent monitoring, praise for desired behavior, and on-going communication and collaboration with the home. Additional and different interventions also are often needed, which typically require special training and need to be implemented by those qualified to do so. This would include qualified mental health specialists within or outside of the school, such as school psychologists, school counselors, clinical psychologists, and social workers.

The most effective interventions and supports for students with serious or chronic conduct problems tend to have the following characteristics (Bear, Webster-Stratton, Furlong, & Rhee, 2000; Epstein, Atkins, Cullinan, Kutash, & Weaver, 2008; Epstein, Fonnesbeck, Potter, Rizzone, & McPheeters, 2015; Kauffman & Landrum, 2018).

- *They are individualized.* They are tailored to the specific strengths and needs of the individual student. An individualized program should be guided by a comprehensive assessment of the student's social, emotional, and cognitive functioning at school and home.
- *They are intensive and comprehensive.* They target not only the primary behavior of concern, but also any additional risk and protective factors. This also refers to being broad-based, adhering to a system or wraparound framework in which a network of mental health specialists, educators, and others in the community work together with the student, the school, and the student's family.
- *They include a parent component.* This ranges from close, ongoing communication (e.g., daily report card) to parent management training, with the latter typically needed for more serious and chronic conduct problems.

- *They are supported by research.* They are supported by empirical research as to their effectiveness and utility for the targeted behaviors. Cognitive-behavioral therapy, behavior management, and parenting interventions tend to be most effective.
- *They are implemented with fidelity.* This requires that those implementing the interventions be well qualified, having received special training and professional development. It also requires adequate resources and funding.
- *They begin early and are sustained over time.* They are not one-shot interventions but are lasting. This includes beginning intervention early (i.e., early age, or as soon as risk factors or problem behaviors are evident). It also includes providing on-going follow-up after the interventions are ended or decreased.

Box 6.1 Interventions for Correcting Behavior Problems

Section I: Mild to Moderate Behavior Problems

These interventions are most appropriate for minor acts of misbehavior, such as students not attending to directions, talking on or using cellphones without permission, getting out of their seats, being tardy for class, and engaging in mild conflicts with other students (including fights in which no serious harm is inflicted, and it occurs for the first time). Interventions appearing later in this section and in the following section should be used when (a) the misbehavior continues despite the use of the interventions earlier on the list and (b) when the misbehavior is deemed more serious, such as causing or potentially causing harm to others and thus warranting more intensive interventions.

Ignore the Misbehavior (i.e., Extinction).

- This works best when the teacher's attention is reinforcing the target behavior.
- When used, combine with reinforcement of appropriate behavior.
- Expect the target behavior to become worse before it gets better and to quickly return to its previous state when not reinforced in the future.
- Ignoring is generally inappropriate for behaviors that disrupt learning or are harmful to the student or others.

Use Physical Proximity

- Simply move toward the student or stand/sit nearby.

Redirect Nonverbally

- Establish eye contact and give a facial expression, hand signal, or other nonverbal cue (e.g., snap fingers, clap hands) that expresses that you are aware of the behavior and it is to stop.

(continued)

(continued)

Redirect Verbally

- Simply state the student's name or incorporate it into the lesson.
- Direct the student to participate in the lesson.
- Tell the student what the student should be doing and/or remind the student of the respective rules.
- Praise around the misbehavior (praise another student for modeling the desired behavior).
- Remind the student of previous good behavior.
- Use "I" messages ("It bothers me when you talk at the same time that I'm trying to teach the class.")
- Where appropriate (e.g., several redirections are given), also warn the student of the negative consequences of the behavior.

Increase Praise, Recognition, and Positive Reinforcers of Desired Behaviors

Outside of the disciplinary encounter make deliberate efforts to reinforce appropriate behavior and enhance the teacher-student relationship. This serves not only to prevent future misbehavior, but also to correct misbehavior by increasing the frequency of replacement behaviors.

- Catch the student being good: As a rule of thumb, try to reinforce the student at least three times for every one negative correction. Follow recommendations on the use of praise and rewards presented in Chapter 4.
- In general, increase the time spent in positive interactions with the student. Use positive reinforcement techniques in a more deliberate, planned, and systematic fashion. This might include various forms of differential reinforcement (e.g., differential reinforcement of omission of behavior, differential reinforcement of incompatible behavior, and differential reinforcement of lower rates of behavior).
- Use the Premack principle (reward the student with the activity the student prefers to engage in).
- Provide opportunities for the desirable behaviors to be exhibited and reinforced in a variety of realistic settings. Reinforce with a variety of reinforcers.
- Involve parents in the reinforcement, where feasible. For example, call or email the parents or send progress reports home reporting good behavior. Use of a daily report card should be considered.

Hold a Class Meeting

- This is most appropriate when the problem behavior is shown by multiple students.
- Guide students through social problem-solving steps during which they discuss why the targeted behavior is indeed a problem (including

its impact on self and others), review classroom and school rules concerning the behavior, brainstorm solutions, and decide upon a class plan to help prevent the behavior's reoccurrence.

Require Self-reflection about the Misbehavior and How to Improve

This would take the form of spending time in a time-out or calming area (including quietly at the student's desk), a written self-reflective report, or a private meeting with the teacher. The nature and extent of the self-reflection would obviously depend on such considerations as the teacher's time and preferences, the student's age and abilities, and the severity of the problem behavior.

- This should occur when the student is calm, not angry. If meeting with the student, the teacher should avoid arguing, remain firm and supportive, and convey optimism that the behavior will improve.
- Focus should be on how the behavior is to improve.
- Use a social problem-solving approach in which the student (a) identifies the problem and its consequences (including its impact on others); (b) generates and evaluates alternative solutions, and chooses the best one(s); and (c) commits to improving behavior, with a plan that sets goals and actions for achieving them.
- Use scaffolding or dialoguing, applying as much guidance and assistance as is developmentally needed to help the student through the problem-solving process.

Implement Behavioral Self-management

This would consist of one or more of the following techniques:

- Self-recording, in which the student records the frequency of specific identified behaviors in a behavioral diary or on a data recording sheet.
- Self-evaluation, in which the student self-records the behavior, but also evaluates the behavior against a specific criterion.
- Self-reinforcement, in which the student self-records, self-evaluates, and self-reinforces.
- Use a recording system (e.g., point card, homework log) to monitor changes in behavior and earning of rewards.

Use Response Cost

This refers to taking away previously earned or given rewards and privileges, such as recess, free time, or allowing students to sit where they prefer.

- Always use in combination with interventions above, and particularly positive reinforcement.
- Remove privilege or reward immediately and without argument after the misbehavior occurs.

(continued)

(continued)

- Make sure that the rules are clear; that is, that the student understands what responses, or behavior, cost a loss of rewards or privileges.

Develop and Implement an Individual Behavioral Contingency Contract

- Define the behavior in clear and concise terms. Behaviors should be easy to monitor and record.
- Make sure that the contract is fair, clear, and positive.
- Include an easy way to record the behavior.
- Start small with respect to goals.
- Include the student in planning the contract. Allow for negotiation.
- The written contract should include a statement of the goals of the contract, clearly specified responsibilities of the student (and the teacher), the times/days the contract is in effect, the consequences for successful completion, the consequences if the student fails to fulfill his or her responsibilities, starting and renegotiation dates, and signatures of all parties concerned (student, teacher, and parent).
- Be sure to follow up on the student's progress on both a short and long term basis.
- Modify and change the contract when needed.
- Work together with the student's parents, informing them of the student's progress.
- For additional guidelines and a sample contract, see: www.interventioncentral.org/behavioral-interventions/challenging-students/behavior-contracts

Implement a Group Contingency

There are three types of group contingency interventions, with research supporting each one (Maggin, Pustejovsky, & Johnson, 2017).

- *Dependent group contingency*. If one or a small number of students are targeted for intervention, consider a dependent group contingency in which a reward, to be shared with the class, is contingent upon the behavior of the student(s) targeted.
- *Independent group contingency*. If every student in the class is individually targeted for the intervention (e.g., on-task behavior), consider an independent group contingency, in which each student earns a reward contingent upon that individual's behavior.
- *Interdependent group contingency*. If a number of students might benefit from the contingent use of rewards, consider an interdependent group contingency system. One or more groups, which might be the entire class or subgroups within it, share a reward contingent upon that group's behavior. Common examples are the class earning extra recess for the good behavior of the class or earning a no-homework pass for the weekend as a reward for 90% of the class completing their homework during the week.

The *Good Behavior Game* (GBG) (Barrish, Saunders, & Wolf, 1969) is a popular interdependent group contingency supported by a wealth of research demonstrating both short-term and long-term effectiveness (Flower, McKenna, Bunuan, Muething, & Vega, 2014). Two or more teams of students in a class compete to earn rewards contingent upon the behavior of their team (all teams can win, however). Its success has been attributed not only to earning rewards and a gaming atmosphere, but also the fun and motivational manner in which the game is played, students learning and practicing social skills, positive peer pressure and cooperation, greater engagement in academics while the game is being played, and teachers spending more time teaching and less time correcting misbehavior (Kellam et al., 2008; van Lier, Vuijk, & Crijnen, 2005).

For examples and steps for implementing each of the above group contingency interventions see www.interventioncentral.org/behavioral-intervention-modification. For steps for implementing the GBG while also fostering self-discipline, see Bear, Biondi, & Morales, 2019.

Use Restitutional Overcorrection

- Have the student fix the problem (often called restitutional overcorrection; e.g., the student replaces a broken pencil).
- Have the student repeatedly practice the correct behavior (often called positive practice overcorrection). For example, as a consequence of writing on his or her desk, the student has to wash all desks in the classroom.

Use Time-out from Reinforcement

This refers to time-out from reinforcement as a punitive consequence, in which the student is removed from his or her current setting in the class to another place in the classroom or is removed from the classroom and sent to the office or another setting in the school. Although called various names (e.g., Attitude Adjustment Room; Intervention Room), removal to another setting is most commonly referred to as in-school suspension or detention.

- Recognize that time-out is not effective for students who want to be removed from the classroom (i.e., an environment that presents a negative climate, with few reinforcers of appropriate behavior), resulting in negative reinforcement (however, also recognize that student removal for disruptive behavior may serve the purpose of helping *others* learn).
- Use after the above techniques have failed (unless otherwise required by code of conduct).
- Make clear when and why the procedure will be used.
- Use an appropriate setting (safe, monitored by an adult, no reinforcers).
- Be firm and calm and simply state the problem and the related rule.
- Do not argue or lecture before, during, or after time-out.

(continued)

(continued)

- Be consistent and keep time-out short (e.g., use a timer). Add time if the student is noncompliant during time-out.
- During the time of removal, have the student complete academic work that the student is missing.
- Combine with techniques presented previously, as appropriate, especially application of a problem-solving approach that addresses the behavior that led to the removal.

Record and Show the Student a Video of the Behavior

This technique has been shown to be effective in increasing on-task behavior among students with and without ADHD (Bray & Root, 2016). For this purpose, the targeted student is recorded, and is aware of the recording, while demonstrating exemplary attending skills (with cues and prompting, when needed). The student then watches the video throughout the week. Video recording also would be useful when a student either denies exhibiting a given misbehavior (e.g., talking to peers without permission) or argues that the behavior is not a problem requiring correction. In this case, the video might be recorded without the student's knowledge and shown to the student to facilitate an action plan. If the behavior continues, the teacher might consider showing the video to the student's parents. Regardless of the purpose of the recording, parent consent should first be obtained.

Garner Support from the Home

- Connect with the student's parents or guardians and communicate that the student's behavior has recently been resistant to the above interventions and that you would appreciate their support.
- If misbehavior continues, use a daily report card (DRC) to inform the home of the student's misbehavior. For steps on designing and implementing a DRC, and sample forms, see: www.healthyinfo.com/consumers/ho/ADD.daily.report.card.pdf.
- Another useful system for informing parents daily of the student's behavior is Class Dojo (https://www.classdojo.com), which is a popular App-supported online system for communicating with parents. It includes a behavior management component in which students earn "Dojo Points" based on their positive behavior.
- Hold a teacher-parent-student conference that addresses the student's behavior and focuses on what the student, school, and home might do to improve it.
- Develop a formalized behavior intervention plan that specifies interventions to be implemented and the responsibilities of the school, home, and student.

Section II. Serious or Chronic Behavior Problems

The following strategies and interventions are for more serious violations of school rules that cause a great deal of classroom disruption, such as continual noncompliance or defiance or physical or verbal aggression toward peers or teachers. Note that a school's code of conduct and many state laws dictate the consequences for many serious misbehaviors.

Use a Combination of the Interventions in Section 1

- Do so in a more intensive, planned, systematic, and sustained fashion. For example, implement a contingency contract, with student input, that delineates both positive and punitive consequences, implement the Good Behavior Game, and work closely with the student's home using a daily report card.

Arrange for Individual Mentoring

As discussed in Chapter 7 on engagement, mentoring has been shown to increase student engagement and thus prevent dropping out of school. The Check and Connect mentoring program has a strong research base, having been shown to not only improve engagement, but also to reduce behavior problems (Christenson & Havsy, 2004). In this program, a school staff member, the mentor, meets at least weekly with the student, and is responsible for developing a supportive relationship with the student and communicating frequently with the student's family. The staff member monitors the student's engagement-related behaviors, such as attendance, grades, and behavioral referrals, and works with the student and the family in implementing interventions. Although most commonly implemented in secondary school, the program can be implemented at all grade levels. For more information, see: http://checkandconnect.umn.edu/.

Refer the Student to Mental Health Specialists or Others with Expertise in Areas of Need

- Refer to the staff and/or team for consultative assistance and support services.
- Depending on school policies and procedures and the needs of the student, this might entail a referral to the school's intervention team or directly to a mental health specialist in the school such as a school psychologist or school counselor. Those individuals would decide if a further referral is warranted, including for services outside of the school.

(continued)

(continued)

- Where needed and appropriate, a comprehensive individual intervention plan should be developed, guided by a comprehensive assessment that examines both proximal and distal factors (including environmental, cognitive, emotional, and medical) that influence the student's behavior and can be targeted in interventions.
- Mental health specialists may be inside or outside of the school setting, such as school psychologists, school counselors, social workers, and clinical psychologists, as needed. The services should include an assessment of the individual student's needs linked to individualized and evidence-based interventions such as:
  - cognitive behavioral therapies (including those that focus on teaching social problem-solving and social skills)
  - behavioral interventions guided by applied behavioral analysis
  - anger management training (including teaching coping and relaxation skills; e.g., Coping Power Program, see www.coping-power.com/)
  - parent management training (e.g., Incredible Years Program, see www.incredibleyears.com/programs/)
  - family therapy (e.g., multisystemic therapy, functional family therapy);
  - medication, particularly when ADHD is diagnosed

Remove the Student from the Class or School

- Prefer in-school suspension or detention (during school hours, after school, or Saturday detention) over out-of-school suspension. Recognize the many limitations to suspension, and particularly out-of-school suspension (see limitations of punitive techniques discussed earlier in this chapter, and the additional limitations to suspension as discussed in Chapter 9 on school safety).
- Suspend the student out-of-school only when necessary and as a last resort (or as required by the code of conduct).
- If the student is removed from the classroom or school, ample opportunities and supports should be provided to allow the student to progress in the academic curriculum and help remediate behaviors that led to removal. This is easier to do with in-school rather than out-of-school suspension.
- But be aware of special provisions in the Individuals with Disabilities Education Act governing the removal of students with disabilities for more than 10 school days.

(continued)

Expel from School

- Expel students as required in the code of conduct for serious offenses such as the possession of weapons or drugs or causing or threatening serious acts of violence.
- Where feasible, place the student into an alternative education program or other restricted educational and/or mental health setting in which student's needs are addressed.

Copyright 2008 by the National Association of School Psychologists, Bethesda, MD. Adapted and reprinted with permission from the publisher. www.nasponline.org. Bear, G. G. (2008). Best practices in classroom discipline. In A. Thomas & J. Grimes (Eds.), *Best Practices in School Psychology V* (pp. 1403–1420). Bethesda, MD: National Association of School Psychologists.

Summary

Most behavior problems can be prevented. However, because schools cannot control all factors that determine student behavior, teachers and staff need to be skilled in correcting a wide range of behavior problems. What interventions are used and the manner in which they are implemented determines their effectiveness in stopping the immediate misbehavior and reducing the likelihood of its recurrence. This also largely determines students' perceptions of school climate. Whereas practices that are harsh and viewed as unfair by students often stop a given misbehavior and might reduce the likelihood of its recurrence, they almost always have a negative impact on students' perceptions of teacher-student relationships and the fairness of rules and consequences.

Multiple evidence-based interventions for correcting behavior problems were presented in this chapter, while highlighting that their effectiveness, including their impact on school climate, hinges on how they are implemented. In general, the effectiveness of corrective interventions, including punitive consequences, is enhanced when they are combined with positive practices for teaching replacement behavior and developing the social and emotional competencies that underlie self-discipline. As discussed in the chapter, those practices entail not only specific evidence-based interventions but also the mindsets and dispositions that characterize the authoritative and SEL approaches to school discipline.

CHAPTER 7

FOSTERING STUDENT ENGAGEMENT

Student engagement refers to the extent to which students value and are involved in academic and social activities in school (Li & Lerner, 2013; Reeve, 2013). Engagement is closely related to motivation but differs in that engagement is the outward manifestation of motivation—students are actively involved in learning (Skinner, Pitzer, & Steele, 2013). Typically, when students are motivated to learn engagement is observed. Motivation, whether intrinsic or extrinsic, is necessary but not sufficient for engagement (Reschly & Christenson, 2013). For example, a student might be motivated to engage in learning or school activities but fail to do so because of the lack of skills, interfering emotions, or various classroom and school factors such as peer influences or a mismatch between the curriculum and the student's skill level. Generally, however, when students are motivated, they also are engaged.

Three types of student engagement are commonly recognized by researchers: emotional, behavioral, and cognitive (Fredricks et al., 2004; Lee & Shute, 2010; Reschly & Christenson, 2013; Wang & Eccles, 2012a). *Emotional engagement* refers to students' positive and negative affective reactions and feelings toward school. They include liking or disliking teachers, classmates, and school in general; being interested or bored at school; and experiencing a sense of belonging/connectedness or feeling isolated and rejected. *Behavioral engagement* refers to behaviors that indicate that students are interested and involved in academic and other school-related activities. It is seen in students attending to tasks, following school rules and norms, and participating in school activities. *Cognitive engagement* refers to the desire and willingness among students to exert their best effort toward learning, to apply the best learning strategies, accept challenges, and persist when tasks are difficult. Of the three types of engagement, cognitive engagement is most similar to motivation, particularly intrinsic motivation. As one might notice, behavioral and cognitive engagement are closely related and not easy to distinguish from one another. Indeed, some researchers view them as one construct (Reschly & Christenson, 2012).

As discussed in Chapter 1, in one form or another student engagement is commonly recognized by researchers as one of the primary domains of school climate. In research on school climate, engagement also is often treated as an outcome of school climate, or as an outcome of a domain and dimension of school climate, such as teacher-student relationship and bullying. In the theoretical model of school climate presented in Chapter 1, student engagement is viewed as a separate domain of school climate, but one that is highly influenced by social-emotional support and structure. In this chapter the importance of student engagement to school climate, academic achievement, and social-emotional well-being is first discussed. Next, the chapter looks at characteristics of students, classrooms, and schools that help explain why some students are more or less engaged than others. Because the critical roles of teacher-student and student-student relationships were discussed in previous chapters, they receive little attention in this chapter. The chapter ends with recommendations for improving school climate by promoting student engagement.

Importance of Student Engagement

A wealth of research shows that student engagement promotes positive outcomes and protects students from negative outcomes. As one might expect, student engagement is strongly associated with academic achievement: Students who are engaged in school have higher academic achievement (Baroody et al., 2016; Catalano, Haggerty, Oesterle, Fleming, & Hawkins, 2004; Lei, Cui, & Zhou, 2018). Relatedly, they exhibit greater attendance (Klem & Connell, 2004) and are more likely to complete school (Catalano et al., 2004; Fredricks et al., 2004). Indeed, the least engaged students are five times more likely than other students to drop out (Rumberger & Rotermund, 2012).

Engagement promotes academic achievement, which in turn promotes further engagement and achievement. It is well established that prior academic achievement is positively related with later engagement and school bonding (Voelkl, 2012). This relation is seen as early as kindergarten, with research showing that academic readiness skills upon school entry predict engagement and later academic achievement (Bodovski & Farkas, 2007). The same applies to values, goals, aspirations, and emotions that support achievement (Wang & Peck, 2013): They support achievement, but so too does achievement foster those qualities.

When students are engaged, they exhibit fewer behavior problems (Hirschfield & Gasper, 2011), including aggression and bullying (Yang, Sharkey, Reed, Chen, & Dowdy, 2018). Engagement also influences behavior outside of school. Students who are engaged in school are less likely to belong to a gang and engage in delinquent and violent acts (Catalano et al., 2004; Li & Lerner, 2011). They also exhibit fewer health-risk behaviors, including cigarette smoking, alcohol and substance use, and sexual activity (including teenage pregnancy) (Bond et al., 2007; Catalano et al., 2004; Manlove, 1998). Finally, compared to students who are disengaged from school, engaged students are more likely to be accepted and liked by their peers (Hughes & Kwok, 2006); are more inclined to like themselves, as seen in greater positive self-esteem and self-efficacy (Booth & Gerard, 2014; Osterman, 2000); are less at risk of depression (Carter, McGee, Taylor, & Williams, 2007); and are more likely to attend college (Wang & Peck, 2013) and obtain higher status occupations, irrespective of college attendance (Abbott-Chapman et al., 2013).

Student engagement is not only associated with multiple outcomes for students, but also for teachers and staff. In schools in which students are engaged, teachers devote more time to teaching, and teachers and students spend less time with problems of discipline. For example, there are fewer suspensions, especially among African-American students, in schools with greater student engagement (Gregory et al., 2016). There also is less teacher burnout (Covell, McNeil, & Howe, 2009).

Factors Influencing Student Engagement

As emphasized in Chapter 1 and noted in other chapters, multiple factors, operating at multiple system levels and often in a bidirectional or multidirectional fashion, influence human behavior. This certainly applies to student engagement. For example, just as teacher-student and student-student relationships impact student engagement, so too does the engagement of students in learning, and school activities influence relationships with others. With a primary focus on malleable factors, two sets of factors that greatly influence student engagement are discussed in this section: (1) individual student characteristics and (2) classroom and school characteristics.

Individual Student Characteristics. Cognitive, behavioral, and emotional engagement capture a wide range of characteristics of students, both individually and collectively. Four categories of student characteristics that greatly influence engagement are discussed: (1) social and emotional learning (SEL); (2) interfering emotions and behaviors; (3) basic psychological needs; and (4) age, gender, race/ethnicity, and socioeconomic status (SES).

Social and Emotional Learning

Each of the five social, emotional, and learning competencies highlighted in the SEL approach, as discussed in Chapter 4, greatly influence student engagement. Those competencies are responsible decision-making, relationship skills, social awareness, self-management, and self-awareness. For example, relationship skills and social awareness are central to emotional engagement; students lacking in empathy, social perspective-taking, and conflict resolution skills are at risk of conflictual teacher-student relationships and for not being socially accepted by peers. In turn, they are at risk for not experiencing a sense of belonging or connectedness in school (i.e., low emotional engagement). Likewise, students lacking skills of responsible decision-making and self-management are at risk of low behavioral engagement. This is seen in students who fail to complete assignments and to follow class rules.

Support for the enduring impact of SEL competencies on engagement comes from a recent longitudinal study of children from preschool into middle school (Buhs, Koziol, Rudasill, & Crockett, 2018). The study focused on aspects of temperament, which refers to "biologically-based dimensions of individuality that influence developmental outcomes by shaping how persons engage with their surroundings" (Teglasi, 2006, p. 391). The researchers found that higher levels of negative affect and lower levels of effortful control (an aspect of self-regulation) in preschool predicted less emotional engagement in middle school. Negative affect and effortful control were assessed by mothers rating their children's temperament at age 54 months. Items on the negative affect scale assessed anger, frustration, fear, and sadness, whereas those on the effortful control scale assessed inhibition of impulsive behavior. Children with low effortful control in preschool were found to have poorer peer and teacher relationships in elementary school (third and fifth grades). Children with high negative emotions (i.e., anger, frustration, fear, sadness) in preschool reported worse peer relationships in elementary school and, in turn, less emotional engagement in middle school. Thus, the study demonstrated that certain temperament or personality characteristics that reflect SEL skills impact relationships with others in elementary school, influencing engagement in school. The researchers concluded that the findings highlight the need for educators to target social experiences and relationships to help prevent disengagement among students with social and emotional deficits.

Interfering Emotions and Behaviors

Just as the lack of social emotional competencies greatly determine engagement, so too does the presence of emotions and behaviors that interfere with engagement and learning. These would include internalizing problems such as depression (Wang & Peck, 2013), anxiety (Hughes & Coplan, 2018), and fear of failure (Caraway, Tucker, Reinke, & Hall, 2003), and externalizing problems such as anger, defiance, noncompliance, overt aggression, and delinquency (Cillessen & Mayeux, 2007; Perdue et al., 2009). Research indicates that the relationship between engagement and problem behaviors are reciprocal (Wang & Fredricks, 2014). Engagement is especially low when interfering emotions and behaviors are intense or lasting, and when peers share the same behaviors (Oelsner, Lippold, & Greenberg, 2011).

Relatedly, environments that foster those interfering emotions and behaviors also foster low student engagement, such as students being exposed to high levels of stress (Raufelder et al., 2014) or community violence (Barofsky, Kellerman, Baucom, Oliver, & Margolin, 2013), or attending a school in which they feel unsafe (Côté-Lussier & Fitzpatrick, 2016). Individual trauma often results from an event, series of events, or set of circumstances experienced by an individual as emotionally or physically harmful or life threatening, with the effects negatively impacting the individual's present and future functioning and well-being (Finkelhor, Turner, Shattuck, & Hamby, 2015; SAMHSA's Trauma and Justice Strategic Initiative, 2014).

Basic Psychological Needs

Students are more likely to be academically motivated and engaged when their basic psychological needs of belongingness, competence, and autonomy are met (Raufelder et al., 2014; Ryan & Deci, 2017). A sense of belongingness, or connectedness, is part of emotional engagement. As discussed in previous chapters on teacher-student relationships and student-student relationships, students are more engaged academically when they feel supported by their teachers and peers. Perceptions of support from teachers and peers are not only instrumental in meeting the psychological need of belongingness but also the needs of competence and autonomy (Ryan & Deci, 2017)—feeling that one is capable, worthwhile, and self-governing.

Support from the home also is important. Engagement, especially behavioral engagement, is seen in higher academic achievement among students whose parents provide ample support by being directly involved (e.g., helping with homework, volunteering at school) in their child's education (Bryce, Bradley, Abry, Swanson, & Thompson, 2018; Wang & Sheikh-Khalil, 2014). The influence of direct parent involvement is stronger in early elementary school than in later grades (Bryce et al., 2018). However, at all grade levels both direct and indirect parent support influences student engagement by fostering feelings of competence and autonomy and a strong desire among students to meet their parents' expectations in school and to maintain their overall approval (Cheung & Pomerantz, 2012).

Age, Gender, Race/Ethnicity, and SES

The individual student characteristics above are ones that are malleable and often targeted in interventions to promote student engagement. Other student characteristics, however, are not malleable (at least not by schools), but nevertheless provide insight into what factors place students at risk for low engagement and should be kept in mind when planning for prevention and intervention. Primary among those factors are age, gender, race/ethnicity, and SES. As students progress from elementary to middle to high school, they tend to become less engaged and school bonding decreases (Balfanz et al., 2007; Burns, Martin, & Collie, 2018; Hughes & Cao, 2018). However, the vast majority of high school students (i.e., over 85%), irrespective of race/ethnicity, have high emotional engagement, as seen in their reporting that they like school (Ackert, 2018).

In general, boys are less engaged and connected to school than girls (Booth & Gerard, 2014; Oelsner et al., 2011). With respect to socioeconomic status (SES), students attending lower SES schools and who are from lower SES homes tend to be less behaviorally and cognitively engaged (Ackert, 2018; Lee & Burkam, 2002). The effects of home SES on behavioral and cognitive engagement is seen as early as kindergarten (Lee & Burkam, 2002). The SES of individual students and schools often explains differences in engagement that are commonly reported between racial and ethnic groups. However, in a national sample of white, African American, and Mexican-origin Latino 10th graders in American schools, Ackert (2018) recently found that regardless of a student's or school's SES status, all racial/ethnic groups had less emotional engagement (i.e., liking of school) in schools with high concentrations of white students compared to schools with fewer white students. *Greater* behavioral engagement (i.e., participation in school activities and involvement/completion of coursework) also was found: Regardless of a student's or school's SES status, all racial/ethnic groups had greater behavioral engagement in schools with high concentrations of white students.

In sum, individual student characteristics often explain why two students differ in their behavioral, cognitive, and emotional engagement when their classroom environments are largely the same, such as when their teacher presents them with the same instructional tasks, uses the same methods of instruction and classroom management, and all other aspects of the classroom environment are basically the same (e.g., same peer support). Individual student characteristics often account for differences in student behavior over time and across settings. For example, a student might simply hate math but enjoy all other subjects, and thus is disengaged when math is taught.

Classroom and School Characteristics. Just as individual characteristics of students often account for differences in engagement between and within students, so too do multiple classroom and school factors. For example, teachers vary in the quality and effectiveness of their teaching and classroom management, with differences seen both between and within teachers. Some teachers are more or less effective than others, and individual teachers are more or less effective from day to day, as well as within a given day and relate better to some students than others. Likewise, the quality of peer relations is seldom the same for all students within the same classroom, or even for the same student from day to day and within a given day. As discussed in Chapter 1, all major theories of human development recognize that it is the interaction of the individual and the environment that determines behavior, with influences being dynamic and bidirectional. To be sure, nearly all environmental factors that influence human behavior, in general, also influence student engagement. These include both proximal and distal factors. These factors are not only in the immediate environment, including the classroom and elsewhere in schools, but also events happening at home or in the world, ranging from stress and trauma-inducing events at home to natural disasters such as tornadoes and earthquakes.

Many of the characteristics of classrooms and schools associated with greater student engagement are one and the same, and primary among them is an authoritative approach to classroom management and school discipline. That approach was described in Chapter 1. With respect to student engagement, research shows that a combination of social-emotional support and structure, as found in the authoritative approach, promotes behavioral, emotional, and cognitive engagement (Cornell et al., 2016; Gettinger & Walter, 2012; Weyns, Colpin, DeLaet, Engels, & Verschueren, 2018; Yang et al., 2018). The lack of social-emotional support from teachers and peers is a major factor associated with indicators of disengagement, including high absences, poor participation in class and school activities, and dropping out of school (Archambault, Janosz, Fallu, & Pagani, 2009; Croninger & Lee, 2001; Wang & Fredricks, 2014). Social-emotional support and structure are among the foremost factors at both the classroom and school levels that influence student engagement. Additional factors that are more specific to classroom and school characteristics are discussed next.

Classroom Characteristics

At the classroom level, a number of teaching practices characterize teachers who are most effective in promoting student engagement and achievement (Davis & McPartland, 2012; Fredricks et al., 2004; Gettinger & Walter, 2012; Griffiths, Lilles, Furlong, & Sidhwa, 2012; Hafen et al., 2012; Johnson, Perez, & Uline, 2013; Katz, 2013; National Research Council, 2005). Those practices are listed below:

- focus on mastery of material taught
- challenging tasks (not too difficult nor too easy)
- students set their own learning goals and monitor progress toward them;
- teaching enthusiastically

- stimulating activities, including novelty and fun lessons that help achieve educational objectives
- quick pacing with minimal "down time"
- ensuring high rates of success, especially when new concepts are first introduced
- clarity, including frequent use of visual representations
- frequent monitoring and evaluation, including understanding of directions and material presented
- student choice and decision-making (supporting autonomy)
- student ownership of the activity's conception, execution, and evaluation
- collaboration with peers (e.g., peer-assisted instruction and small group activities)
- emphasis on higher order thinking skills and teaching strategies for students to use to solve problems, rather than the memorizing discrete facts
- high expectations for every student
- instructions are matched, or aligned, with the abilities, interests, talents, culture, and goals of students. this requires knowing every student well
- assistance, guidance, and support provided as needed, and especially during independent work
- authenticity—tasks emphasize real-life applications
- modeling that highlights behaviors associated with emotional, behavioral, and cognitive engagement (models might be the teacher, peers, or others outside of school)
- frequent acknowledgement or reinforcement of students for their effort and achievements

The first practice listed above, a focus on mastery of material taught, deserves special attention. Researchers have identified two general types of achievement goal orientations related to student engagement in academic tasks: a *performance goal orientation* and a *mastery goal orientation.* A performance goal orientation is seen in student engagement being motivated by receiving good grades or other recognitions and by outperforming others. It also is seen in students avoiding poor grades, negative evaluations by others, and other negative consequences of poor performance (e.g., being grounded at home). In contrast, a mastery goal orientation is grounded much more in intrinsic motivation, as seen in students engaging in academic tasks because they enjoy them, wanting to learn and improve their skills, and a desire to master the material. A large body of research has demonstrated that a mastery goal orientation, rather than a performance goal orientation, is associated with greater academic achievement and understanding (see Wigfield, Eccles, Schiefele, Roeser, & Davis-Kean, 2006 for a review).

In a comprehensive study of teaching practices found in America's best urban schools, Johnson et al. (2013) concluded that an emphasis on the mastery of material was the foremost factor that characterized the highest performing teachers and schools. The study was limited to those schools, both elementary and secondary, that won the National Excellence in Urban Education Award, with many of them also recognized as National Blue Ribbon Schools, National Title I Distinguished Schools, and schools on the *U.S. News & World Report's*

List of Best High Schools in America. Multiple indicators of student engagement were used in selecting these schools: high academic achievement for every demographic group they served (including all racial/ethnic groups, English learners, and students with disabilities), attendance rates, graduation rates, and suspension/expulsion rates. The researchers found that:

> Teachers focused persistently and doggedly on leading all children to master explicit academic objectives. While many urban schools sabotage their improvement efforts by rigidly trying to "cover" all of the standards or by insisting that they "keep pace" with a pacing guide, these more successful schools chose to focus on getting their students to master key academic content (sometimes at the expense of ignoring some standards).
>
> (pp. 4–5)

These teachers had clear, well-planned and organized, objective-driven lessons that helped ensure that *all* students achieved mastery, or a "deep understanding and/or skill" (p. 8) related to the concept or content taught. Having students simply recall what was taught was viewed as insufficient.

School Characteristics

In addition to the multiple factors discussed previously that occur at both the classroom and school levels, decades of research on school effectiveness and student engagement (e.g., Bingham & Okagaki, 2012; Côté-Lussier & Fitzpatrick, 2016; Davis & McPartland, 2012; Voelkl, 2012) have identified the following school characteristics to be associated with greater student engagement and school effectiveness.:

- smaller schools (this would include establishing learning academies at the secondary level) and smaller class sizes
- frequent and appropriate monitoring of student academic progress
- an environment that is physically attractive, safe and orderly, and conducive to learning
- an environment viewed by students as one that treats students fairly and equally regardless of their gender, race, socioeconomic status, and culture (school equity)
- positive home-school relations
- norms that value education
- instructional leadership

More specific to student engagement, greater emotional engagement is found in schools that provide multiple extracurricular activities, including clubs and sports (Davis & McPartland, 2012). This is likely because those schools provide greater opportunities for students to interact with peers and faculty and to participate in activities that they most enjoy. Likewise, research suggests that student engagement is greater in schools with teachers of similar race/ethnicity as the students, particularly in schools with large numbers of racial and ethnic minority students of low socioeconomic status (Bingham & Okagaki, 2012).

Recommended Strategies and Interventions for Promoting Student Engagement

As discussed in Chapter 1 and emphasized throughout this book, the domains of school climate are closely interrelated, with deficits or strengths in one domain influencing other domains. This is certainly true for student engagement. To one extent or another student engagement influences, and is influenced by, all other domains and dimensions of school climate, including teacher-student relationships, student-student relationships, social and emotional learning, school safety, bullying, and techniques of classroom management and school discipline. Addressing any weaknesses in those areas is likely to improve student engagement. Thus, it is important that teachers and schools with poor student engagement first closely examine all other domains of school climate, and dimensions within them, to determine weaknesses that might be contributing to poor student engagement. Identified areas should then be targeted for intervention. Tools for assessing weaknesses in school climate are the focus of Chapter 10, whereas ways to address them are covered in chapters throughout the book on the respective domain or dimension.

Because specific recommendations for improving other domains and dimensions of school climate, while also improving student engagement, are highlighted in other chapters, the recommendations in this section focus primarily on additional ways to foster student engagement, with emphases on instructional methods and activities.

1. *In general, implement a wide range of strategies that are consistent with the authoritative approach.* If the school's goal is to improve student engagement, of primary attention for assessment and likely intervention should be the domains that define the authoritative approach: social-emotional support and structure. Within those two domains are the dimensions of teacher-student relationships, student-student relationships, responsiveness to students' psychological needs (i.e., social and emotional learning), classroom management strategies for preventing behavior problems, and the correction of misbehavior. As reviewed in chapters aligned with each of those domains, improvements in each domain have been shown to increase student engagement. For example, with respect to the social-emotional support domain, even brief interventions that improve teacher-student relationships have been shown to increase student engagement (Cook et al., 2018; Duong et al., 2019) and reduce aggressive behavior (Miller et al., 2017). Interventions for improving student-student relationships also foster student engagement, especially emotional engagement, such as peer assisted learning, extracurricular activities, and teachers being attuned and responsive to the social interactions among students. Likewise, a large number of programs that teach social and emotional skills have been shown to improve student engagement and achievement (Durlak et al., 2011).

    With respect to the domain of structure, multiple structure-oriented classroom management strategies, as presented in Chapter 5 on preventing behavior problems, foster student engagement. They include clear behavioral expectations, routines, and procedures; fair rules and consequences; quick pacing; and frequent monitoring of behavior and acknowledgement of desired behavior. In light of the wealth of research and theory linking social-emotional support and structure to student engagement, it behooves schools to target those two domains of school climate in their efforts to improve student engagement.

2. *Use of a variety of instructional methods and activities for motivating and engaging students.* For both preventing behavior problems and fostering academic achievement, the most effective teachers motivate and engage students by employing a variety of evidence-based instructional methods and activities that keep students on-task, interested, and actively engaged. Whereas such methods and activities are generally directed more toward promoting cognitive and behavioral engagement than emotional engagement, they are often effective in promoting all three. That is, students typically enjoy school more, or are more emotionally engaged, when presented with teaching and activities they find interesting, challenging, and fun.

Drawing from research on teacher effectiveness in promoting learning and achievement, as listed previously in this chapter, the following types of activities are recommended for keeping students on-task and actively engaged:
- instruction that is enthusiastic, quickly paced, and calls for frequent responding from students
- project-based learning
- inquiry based learning
- peer-assisted learning
- class discussions and debates
- simulations and role-plays
- computer and other technology-based activities
- educational games

3. *Communicate clearly that high expectations apply to every student.* This applies to teaching and instruction in general, as well as to specific assignments and grading criteria. Expectations should be clear and fair. Educators throughout the school should communicate the belief that every student is capable of meeting high expectations. Such communication has been shown to be of particular value when working with African American students who are mistrusting of school (Yeager, Trzesniewski, & Dweck, 2013).

4. *Directly teach, as needed, skills related to engagement.* This applies to behavioral, cognitive, and emotional engagement. It also applies much more so in early elementary school than later grades and to students whose lack of engagement is more skill based than motivation based. For example, behavioral engagement requires attending and organizational skills as well as following rules. Those skills are typically taught directly in the early grades but also to many older students who continue to lack or exhibit them, such as students with Attention Deficit/Hyperactivity Disorder (ADHD) and other disabilities. Likewise, cognitive engagement requires metacognitive strategies for learning, which often need to be taught directly. Finally, emotional engagement requires social and emotional skills, such as empathy, perspective-taking, and conflict resolution.

In teaching engagement skills, consideration should be given to implementing an evidenced-based SEL program shown to be effective in improving engagement. On average, SEL programs increase academic achievement by approximately 11% (Durlak et al., 2011). Among those programs with a strong research base are those described in Chapter 4 on SEL: Responsive Classroom Approach (Kindergarten–Grade 6), Second Step Social and Emotional Learning (Preschool–Grade 8), and PATHS (Promoting Alternative Thinking Strategies).

5. ***Provide frequent praise and recognition of desired behaviors and feedback that is substantive and constructive.*** This includes using praise and rewards wisely and strategically: Recognizing and reinforcing engagement behaviors and providing constructive feedback, while striving to promote intrinsic motivation rather than extrinsic motivation. Feedback should include clear and specific guidance as to how to improve (Siegle & McCoach, 2007; Thayer, Cook, Fiat, Bartlett-Chase, & Kember, 2018). Additional and more specific recommendations on the wise and strategic use of praise and rewards that increase student engagement are presented in Chapter 4 on SEL and Chapter 5 on preventive classroom management.

6. ***Highlight models of cognitive, behavioral, and emotional engagement.*** This can be done by highlighting individuals throughout the curriculum and in current news who exhibit exemplary engagement, such as in government, science, sports, and the arts (see Chapter 4, Recommendation 5, for characteristics of effective models). Students should discuss what motivates and engages those and other individuals, and what behaviors and supports are associated with their engagement. Perhaps more importantly, all teachers and staff should model engagement, as observed in their work, attitudes, and relationships with others.

7. ***Align instructional methods and activities with the individual abilities and interests of students.*** This is not always feasible, but where viable and appropriate, efforts should be made to match instructional methods and activities with the interests, values, goals, and preferences of individual students. This is especially important when working with students who are lacking in engagement. Student surveys and interviews can help identify the interests of students.

8. ***Provide instructional methods and activities that present authentic and challenging tasks.*** Authentic refers to tasks that center on the real-life application of skills that are learned. An example is applying math and science skills to solve real-life problems that students might actually encounter, especially those that are of high interest to students. At all age levels, and increasing with age, tasks should call for higher order thinking skills to solve challenging, complex, and multidimensional problems. Students should be encouraged to explore different solutions, think critically, and discuss their problems and solutions. Challenging authentic tasks are often commonly presented in the context of project-based learning and inquiry-based learning activities.

9. ***Offer choices.*** Effective teachers offer students multiple activities and assignments to choose from to demonstrate learning and mastery (where feasible and appropriate). Allowing choice promotes intrinsic motivation and helps meet the basic psychological need for autonomy (Ryan & Deci, 2017). When students experience a sense of autonomy, they are more inclined to be engaged and perform better. Obviously, students should not be allowed to choose not to do the work, to do less work than their peers, or perform

below expectations. Good examples of using choice to foster engagement and learning are allowing students to choose between several similar homework assignments, between different ways to apply or demonstrate a skill, and to select among books to read or topics to research.

10. *Focus on mastery.* A focus on mastery means valuing depth of student understanding over the superficial recall of facts. It calls for incorporating all of the other recommendations in this chapter for promoting engagement and helping students achieve mastery. It also requires reteaching, as needed. As noted earlier, Johnson et al. (2013) found that a focus on mastery is the primary characteristic of the most effective teachers in the highest performing urban schools. Those teachers plan for mastery and develop clear and explicit objective-driven lessons to help achieve their goal of all students demonstrating mastery of the material taught, as opposed to simply covering a set standard or what is presented in the curriculum.

11. *Challenge students to set goals.* Research has shown that goal setting is an effective motivational strategy for improving engagement, including mastery learning. Goals should be both short-term and long-term, with long-term goals becoming increasingly important in adolescence. Goals, especially long-term goals, should reflect values, interest, talents, and skills. A short-term goal might be learning or mastery of new material in a given subject area (i.e., a mastery goal) or performing well on test of knowledge of the subject (i.e., a performance goal). A long-term goal might be going to college to become a nurse, going to trade school to become a carpenter, or entering the military. Long-term goals should always subsume short-term goals, and often short-term goals should include shorter-term goals, or subgoals (e.g., performing well in practices, doing well at a game, concert, or other event). Whereas most motivation theorists and researchers place greater emphasis on the importance of mastery goals over performance goals, they also recognize the value of both (Vansteenkiste et al., 2004; Vansteenkiste, Timmermans, Lens, Soenens, & Van den Broeck, 2008). For example, learning or mastering subject material is more important than students' grades, but the importance of good grades and valuing them should not be dismissed, as good grades often help students achieve their goals and provide valuable feedback on their progress.

    To help students set goals, especially long-term goals, activities should be given that challenge students to reflect upon their values, interests, strengths, and weaknesses and how and why they should link them to their goals. This includes thinking about why a goal is important, what must be done to best achieve that goal, what obstacles might lie ahead and how to avoid or deal with them, and how one might evaluate progress toward meeting a goal. These steps would apply to both short-term and long-term goals, as well as any subgoals. For example, for homework completion, which is a common indicator of behavioral engagement, students might be asked to reflect upon why homework is important. When reflecting they would be prompted to relate the importance of homework for learning the material and receiving good grades, to describe the steps they should follow to best complete homework (e.g., recording assignments, establishing a homework routine, working where distractions are minimal, etc.), and to think about, and plan for, potential obstacles (e.g., a cell phone, friends, siblings, etc.).

A variation of goal setting is personal best (PB) goal setting in which students set personally challenging and self-referenced goals that they strive to meet. This approach to goal setting is grounded in a growth mindset framework (Dweck, 2012). In PB goal setting students are challenged to outperform their past personal performances or efforts, which means doing their personal best (Burns et al., 2018). Students who employ this motivational strategy exhibit greater self-improvement and behavioral engagement, including better planning, monitoring, persistence, and task management (Burns et al., 2018).

The primary roles of teachers in BP goal setting are to help students set their goals and to self-monitor progress toward them, but also to provide constructive feedback throughout the process. Success, or goal attainment, should be based on evaluating one's performance not in comparison to that of others, but in comparison to one's own past performance (Martin, 2015). Students are challenged to identify areas needing personal improvement and to set PB goals to motivate their actual engagement. This should include four key components (Burns et al., 2018): (1) helping students accurately identify goals that align with what constitutes their personal best—goals that are not too difficult or too easy to meet; (2) helping students monitor and evaluate progress in achieving their goals (e.g., self-recording); (3) helping students set specific shorter-term goals, or subgoals; and (4) helping students to garner support, as needed, from others to achieve their set goals.

12. *In general, encourage a growth mindset instead of a fixed ability mindset.* A focus on mastery and goal setting, as recommended above, helps encourage a growth mindset. This is best done by communicating the value of effort, persistence, and challenge, and not communicating (implicitly or explicitly) that ability is fixed (particularly that the student is lacking in ability). Students should learn that people can change, including intellectually, and that a growth mindset can help make one smarter (Paunesku et al., 2015; Yeager et al., 2014).

13. *Encourage self-evaluation.* Teachers should encourage students to monitor and evaluate their own progress, whether it is toward meeting individual goals or evaluating products or assignments completed. For example, in evaluating goals, teachers might have students record daily, or weekly, something new they have learned or something at which they have excelled (Siegle & McCoach, 2007). Self-evaluation should be incorporated into daily tasks and assignments to allow students to identify and learn from their mistakes, and to reflect upon achieving their goals and mastery of material (Kitsantas, Reiser, & Doster, 2004). For self-evaluations, as well as external evaluations (e.g., grades), teachers should encourage students to focus on their personal progress toward learning new skills. They might have students reflect upon what they have learned since the beginning of the school year and when graded on a test or project, to focus more on the information conveyed in the grade than on the grade per se or how their skills compare to those of others.

14. *Seek support from the home.* Support from the home is important for the engagement of all students, but especially those who are disengaged or at risk of disengagement. Parental support requires on-going communication and collaboration between teachers and parents. This is particularly important in homework completion, but it also helps to keep parents abreast of

their student's behavior and academic progress, and more so for some students than others. Whereas a standard report card, parent conferences, and posting homework assignments and their completion on the class website are sufficient for many students and their parents, others require more frequent communication and collaboration between the school and home.

15. *For students who are disengaged from school, or at great risk of disengagement, implement more intensive support and interventions.* This includes implementing each of the recommendations above, but doing so with greater intensity and frequency, such as increased reinforcement of desired behaviors, allowing for choice more often, matching instruction with student interests, and increasing contact and collaboration with the home. Efforts should be more individualized and comprehensive, which are likely to require additional resources and often mental health specialists. In cases of chronic or marked disengagement, such as frequent refusal to complete work or a sudden drop in engagement, a formal assessment by a school psychologist should be conducted. The assessment should include identifying individual, classroom, school, and home factors contributing to disengagement, as well as the student's specific strengths and weaknesses. Recommended interventions should align with the assessment results, which should range from those recommended in this section to more intensive ones that are provided outside of the regular classroom. The latter would include individual counseling, social-skills training, family therapy or parent management training, and individual tutoring or mentoring,

If problems of disengagement are schoolwide, consideration should be given to the need for system-wide changes at the school level, as well as to the need of adopting an evidence-based program that targets students who already exhibit disengagement. Such a program would be more intensive than the more prevention-focused SEL programs listed previously. One of the most popular and effective programs is Check and Connect (Christenson & Havsy, 2004). In the context of individual mentoring, the program places great emphasis on building and maintaining a supportive mentor-student relationship and developing students' problem-solving skills. A school staff member, the mentor, meets at least weekly with the student, and is responsible for developing a supportive relationship while communicating frequently with the student's family. The staff member monitors the student's engagement-related behaviors, such as attendance, grades, and behavioral referrals, and works with the student and his or her family in implementing interventions for improving student engagement. Although most commonly implemented in secondary school, the program can be implemented at all grade levels. For more information, visit: http://checkandconnect.umn.edu/

Summary

When students are highly engaged they demonstrate greater academic achievement and exhibit fewer behavior problems. It is no surprise then that student engagement is commonly targeted in efforts to improve school climate. Those efforts tend to focus on the characteristics of students, teachers, schools, and classrooms that either foster or hamper student engagement. Primary among the student characteristics are social and emotional competencies, the presence or absence of interfering emotions and behaviors, and students' basic psychological needs of competence, belonginess, and autonomy. Primary among characteristics of classrooms and schools are supportive relationships (teacher-student, student-student, and school-home), effective classroom management and school discipline, and the use of various instructional practices shown to motivate and engage students. Because recommendations for building and maintaining supportive relationships and for effective classroom management and school discipline are the focus of other chapters, recommended strategies in this chapter focus primarily on instructional practices that teachers should use to foster the cognitive, behavioral, and emotional engagement of all students.

CHAPTER 8

PREVENTING AND REDUCING BULLYING

For over a decade now bullying has received widespread attention in the mass media, with a major focus on the physical and psychological harm it afflicts victims of bullying and others. At its worst, the negative impact of bullying is seen in suicides and homicides among students, occurring inside and outside of school. Whereas feelings of helplessness, shame, and depression as a result of being bullied have led victims to take their own lives, feelings of shame, anger, and revenge also have led victims to take the lives of others, as seen in multiple school shootings. Fortunately, such extreme cases of violence as a result of bullying are rare. Much more common is the less violent, but often equally disconcerting, psychological and social harm experienced by victims of bullying. Bullying not only harms victims but also nearly all aspects of school climate, including student-student relationships, teacher-student relationships, student engagement, and school safety.

This chapter first examines how bullying is defined, why prevalence rates vary greatly, the different types of bullying, and warning signs of bullying. Next, the negative outcomes of bullying and why some students are more likely than others to experience bullying and its negative outcomes are examined. Finally, exemplary bullying prevention programs are discussed followed by more specific recommended strategies and interventions for preventing and responding to bullying.

Definition and Prevalence

As defined by the United States Department of Education (2019), bullying is "unwanted, aggressive behavior among school aged children that involves a real or perceived power imbalance. The behavior is repeated, or has the potential to be repeated, over time." This definition emphasizes two aspects of bullying that differentiate bullying from other forms of peer aggression. First, a power imbalance, or power differential, exists: The bully is in a position of strength relative to victim and thus it is difficult for the victim to defend himself or herself. For example, the bully may be physically stronger or more popular than the victim or have access to embarrassing information about the victim and uses, or threatens to use, those sources of power to cause the victim physical, psychological, or social harm. Second, the aggressive act is not a one-time occurrence, but is repeated over time or is likely to be repeated. The Department of Education's definition lacks a third differentiating aspect of bullying that typically appears in the research literature and other definitions of bullying: *intentionality*. This refers to the bully's behavior not being accidental or impulsive, but meant to inflict physical, psychological, or social harm.

In sum, to be considered bullying, aggressive and harmful actions must entail an imbalance of power, be repeated over time, and be intentional. As such, many common acts of teasing, arguing, peer rejection, and fighting among peers should not necessarily be considered bullying, even if they are harmful, because they lack one or more of those three criteria.

Although power differential, repetition, and intentionality are included in most definitions of bullying, educators should be aware they are not included in many measures of bullying (Jia & Mikami, 2018). This should cause educators to question if bullying is truly being assessed in the instruments they are using. Measures of bullying also differ in other ways. For example, whereas some measures simply use one sentence to ask students if they have been bullied (e.g., Blake, Lund, Zhou, Kwok, & Benz, 2012; Nansel et al., 2001), others first present students with a definition of bullying. Still other measures ask students to respond to the extent to which they have experienced a list of specific bullying behaviors (e.g., Kokkinos & Panayiotou, 2007; Ttofi & Farrington, 2011), with the behaviors often differing across measures. For example, the measure may or may not include teasing or cyberbullying. Finally, some use a combination of methods (e.g., Bear, Mantz, Glutting, Yang, & Boyer, 2015; Swearer, Wang, Maag, Siebecker, & Frerichs, 2012). Measures also differ in how frequently the behavior(s) must occur to be considered bullying (e.g., "once a week" versus "at least once a month").

Such differences in definitions and measures of bullying make it difficult to compare research results across studies, but it also has led to prevalence rates for bullying victimization that vary greatly. National studies indicate that about 20% of students ages 12 to 18 report having been bullied at least once during the school year and 12% report having been bullied at least once a week; 15% of students, grades 9–12, report having been victims of cyberbullying (Musu et al., 2019). However, prevalence rates vary greatly in the literature from 0 to 100 depending on measures and criteria used and the populations sampled (Bear et al., 2015; Rose et al., 2015). For example, in their study of over 12,000 parents of students in kindergarten through fifth grade, Bear et al. (2015) found that the prevalence rate depended largely on whether a response of "sometimes" or "once or twice a month" constituted bullying. Parents responded to a single global item asking how often their child experienced bullying in school. When *sometimes* served as the cut-off criterion for bullying, the prevalence rate was 22.3% for children without disabilities and 29.8% for children with disabilities. For children with disabilities, the prevalence rate ranged from 0% to 66.7%, depending on the disability (highest was for children with emotional disabilities). However, when *once or twice a month* was instead used as the lower-bound cut-off point, prevalence rates dropped markedly: Prevalence rates were 5.2% for children without disabilities, 7.3% for children with disabilities, and 0% to 41.7% for the ten different types of disabilities.

Bear et al. (2015) also found that prevalence rates varied markedly depending on whether bullying was assessed with the single bullying item asking if the student was bullied or with multiple items assessing specific bullying behaviors, such as being hit or threatened, teased, or excluded by peers. For those items the word bullying was never used. Response rates often doubled when bullying was based on responses to one or more of the specific bullying behaviors compared to responses to the global bullying item. This finding is consistent with research showing that students often do not view specific bullying behaviors as constituting bullying (Jia & Mikami, 2018). This might be because they understand that a power imbalance, repetition, and intentionality must exist, or that they view reporting of bullying as stigmatizing and reflecting a weakness on their part.

Types of Bullying

Most researchers view bullying as existing in three different forms (Card & Hodges, 2008): physical, verbal, and social/relational. A fourth form of bullying, cyberbullying, also is recognized by most educators.

- *Physical bullying* refers to physical attacks on a victim and includes such behaviors as hitting, kicking, pushing, tripping, making rude hand gestures, spitting, stealing or breaking others' belongings, and threatening any of those behaviors (note, however, on some measures this is included as verbal bullying).
- *Verbal bullying* refers to attacks by words or vocalizations. It includes teasing, name-calling, saying hurtful or mean things, threatening, taunting, and inappropriate sexual comments.
- *Social/relational bullying* (also often called either social or relational bullying rather than social/relational bullying) refers to behaviors that cause, or threaten to cause, damage to peer relationships, and particularly to friendship and acceptance. Such behaviors are excluding others, spreading rumors about others, embarrassing someone publicly, telling others not to be friends with someone, and getting students to say mean things about others.
- *Cyberbullying* refers to acts of aggression that occur through electronic means, such as sending mean or hurtful messages via text message, instant messaging, or email and posting mean or hurtful things about others on social media.

Some researchers, including several leading researchers in the field (e.g., Olweus & Limber, 2018), do not view cyberbullying as a form of bullying, but instead as the means of engaging in one of the other three types of bullying, such as using a cell phone for name calling, making physical threats, and embarrassing others. Others question if cyberbullying meets all of the same criteria as the other three forms of bullying, such as having a power differential or having to be repeated over time (Antoniadou & Kokkinos, 2015).

Warning Signs of Bullying. Teachers, students, and parents should be aware of how bullying is defined and its different types, but also should recognize the warning signs that bullying may be happening. This is especially important because victims and witnesses are often reluctant to report bullying, with victims feeling embarrassed or ashamed, and both victims and witnesses fearing retaliation or thinking that nothing will or can be done to stop it (Baly, Cornell, & Lovegrove, 2014; Cortes & Kochenderfer-Ladd, 2014). The federal website www.stopbullying.gov gives the following warning signs:

Signs that a child is being bullied:

- has unexplainable injuries or destroyed, stolen, or "lost" clothing, electronics, books, and other items
- feels sick or fakes illness to avoid school (e.g., has frequent headaches or stomachaches)
- loses interest in school or schoolwork or has declining grades
- exhibits changes in eating habits (e.g., skipping meals at school or home, binge eating)
- has frequent nightmares or trouble sleeping
- avoids social situations or has a sudden loss of friends
- displays feelings of helplessness or decreased self-esteem
- exhibits self-destructive (e.g., running away), self-harming, or suicidal behaviors

Signs that a child is bullying others:

- is increasingly aggressive and gets into verbal or physical fights
- receives frequent punitive consequences at school (e.g., detention, office visits)
- has extra money or new belongings without explanation
- blames others for his or her problems and doesn't accept responsibility for his or her actions
- is competitive and worries about reputation or popularity
- has friends who bully others

Negative Outcomes of Bullying

The effects of bullying in school are often pervasive, having a negative impact not only on the victims of bullying but also on the bullies themselves, as well as on bystanders.

Effects on Victims of Bullying. Primary among negative effects of bullying on victims are various internalizing problems, including: psychosomatic problems such as headaches, stomach pain, and sleeping problems (Gini, 2008; Gini & Pozzoli, 2009); lower self-esteem (Tsaousis, 2016; van Geel, Goemans, Zwaanswijk, Gini, & Vedder, 2018); depression and loneliness (Gini, 2008; Reijntjes, Kamphuis, Prinzie, & Telch, 2010; Rueger & Jenkins, 2014); suicide ideation, suicide attempt, and self-injury (Bannink, Broeren, van de Looij-Jansen, de Waart, & Raat, 2014; Claes, Luyckx, Baetens, Van de Ven, & Witteman, 2015); greater fear and anxiety toward school, and feeling less connected, attached, and safe (Boulton et al., 2009; Faris & Felmlee, 2014; Hutzell & Payne, 2012). Victims of bullying also are at increased risk of externalizing academic problems, including delinquent and problem behaviors such as substance use, stealing, physical fighting, vandalism (Lester, Cross, & Shaw, 2012), and bringing a weapon to school (Valdebenito, Ttofi, Eisner, & Gaffney, 2017); peer rejection and isolation (Nansel et al., 2001; Nation, Vieno, Perkins, & Santinello, 2008); and lower academic engagement and achievement (Buhs, Ladd, & Herald-Brown, 2010; Rueger & Jenkins, 2014).

Internalizing and externalizing problems are both outcomes *and* predictors of bullying victimization (Reijntjes et al., 2010, 2011). That is, the influence is bidirectional. For example, students who are bullied are at greater risk of low self-esteem, but so too are those with low self-esteem at greater risk of being bullied (van Geel et al., 2018). There is some evidence that the effects are stronger for internalizing problems predicting bullying victimization than vice versa. A recent longitudinal study of adolescents in grades 7 and 8 (Chu, Fan, Lian, & Zhou, 2019) found that whereas internalizing problems, and especially depression and general anxiety, predicted bullying victimization, bullying victimization did not predict internalizing problems.

Effects on Perpetrators of Bullying. Bullies, or perpetrators of bullying, also are at greater risk for many of the same negative outcomes experienced by their victims. Those outcomes include anxiety and depression (Seals & Young, 2003); psychosomatic symptoms (Gini, 2008); suicide ideation and attempts (Klomek, Marrocco, Kleinman, Schonfeld, & Gould, 2007); delinquency, substance abuse, and criminality (Bradshaw, Waasdorp, Goldweber, & Johnson, 2013; Ttofi, Farrington, Losel, & Loeber, 2011); less school bonding, or connectedness (Haynie et al., 2001); and poorer academic engagement and achievement (Huang et al., 2018; Smokowski & Kopasz, 2005).

Effects on Bystanders and Others. Students who witness bullying, but are neither perpetrators nor victims, are at increased risks for many of the same internalizing and externalizing problems experienced by perpetrators and victims. For example, Rivers, Poteat, Noret, and Ashurst (2009) found that witnessing bullying was associated with a range of a number of mental health risks, including anxiety, depression, psychosomatic symptoms, hostility, paranoid ideation, and substance use.

The climate of a classroom or school is unlikely to be positive when bullying is pervasive. Indeed, as discussed in Chapter 1, bullying is often viewed as a separate domain or dimension of school climate or as part of student-student relationships or safety. Regardless how it is viewed, it is clear that it impacts each individual domain and dimension of school climate. For example, in addition to influencing student-student relationships, bullying influences teacher-student relationships (Elledge, Elledge, Newgen, & Cavell, 2016), with bullying often creating conflictual relations. The same applies to home-school relationships: Parents are unlikely to view a school favorably when their children are victims of bullying. Bullying also affects disciplinary practices (Cornell et al., 2015; Klein, Cornell, & Konold, 2012), diverting time from instruction and causing teachers and staff to devote greater efforts to preventing and correcting bullying and related behaviors. Finally, bullying influences student engagement and safety. As noted earlier, victims and witnesses are less engaged academically and feel less safe (Boulton et al., 2009). Moreover, compared to their peers, both victims and perpetrators are more likely to bring weapons to school (Valdebenito et al., 2017).

Why Some Students and Schools Experience Greater Bullying than Others

Whereas bullying can negatively impact students, especially victims, most students do not experience bullying and many who do so have few, if any, negative side effects, especially lasting ones. This is seen in meta-analytic reviews of the research literature finding small to moderate effect sizes for bullying victimization in predicting internalizing problems (Reijntjes et al., 2010) and externalizing problems (Reijntjes et al., 2011). For example, Hoover, Oliver, and Hazler (1992) found that more than 75% of middle to high school students reported being bullied at some point during their school life but fewer than 15% indicated that they felt they had been severely affected in any particular domain of adjustment (e.g., academic, emotional, or social).

In this section, risk and protective factors are examined that largely account for why some students experience greater bullying than others and why the effects are not always negative or lasting. Of particular focus are factors, or characteristics, of students, classrooms, and schools that research has shown to be associated with bullying. The influence of those factors on bullying are best understood within the context of a social-ecological systems model of human behavior, which views bullying as a complex phenomenon influenced by multiple interacting factors that may foster, prevent, or suppress its various forms (Espelage & Swearer, 2004; Swearer & Hymel, 2015). According to this model, factors operate at various levels, including the individual level (e.g., factors characterizing individual bullies, victims, bystanders, teachers, parents, and others involved), relationship level (e.g., relationship between bullies, victims, bystanders; teacher-student relationships; home-school relationships), classroom and school levels (e.g., classroom management, school discipline, school climate) and home, community, and societal levels (e.g., support from parents, role models in the community, state laws). Factors influence one another in an ongoing, dynamic, bidirectional or multidirectional, and contextual-specific fashion. For example, just as an individual bully can impact the behavior of teachers and peers and the climate of a classroom and school, so too can the behavior of teachers and peers and the climate of a classroom and school impact bullying. The social-ecological model emphasizes that many of the multiple factors influencing bullying are alterable, or malleable, and thus should be targeted in school efforts to prevent bullying and lessen its negative impact.

Not all factors that influence bullying are malleable. Other factors are malleable but altering them is generally beyond the scope of schools or very difficult for schools to do so. Examples are physical appearance and health of students. Nevertheless, an awareness of those factors often helps explain differences between students in bullying victimization and perpetration. Knowledge of those factors also can guide intervention efforts by making schools more aware of which students are at greatest risk. Most common among the factors related to bullying victimization that are largely non-alterable are gender, sexual orientation, having a disability, physical health and appearance, age, and grade level.

Studies have yielded mixed findings with respect to gender and bullying, with results often varying depending on age of students and the type of bullying. The one consistent finding, however, is that males are more likely to be perpetrators of bullying (Álvarez-García, García, & Núñez, 2015; Smith, López-Castro,

Robinson, & Görzig, 2018), and especially physical bullying (Kljakovic & Hunt, 2016). Most studies also report that boys are more likely to be victims. The gender gap in bullying decreases in mid-adolescence, when physical bullying declines and cyberbullying increases (Smith et al., 2018).

Students are more likely to be bullied based on sexual orientation than on gender: Those who identify as lesbian, gay, bisexual, transgender or questioning are at greater risk (Birkett, Espelage, & Koenig, 2009). Another population of students at greater risk are students with disabilities, especially when the disability entails behaviors that disrupt the learning of others, which is common with emotional disturbance, autism, and Attention Deficit Hyperactivity Disorder (ADHD; Bear et al., 2015; Blake et al., 2012).

Physical health also is related to the risk of being bullied. For example, students are at increased risk if they are obese or have other physical conditions (Ma, 2002). Age and grade level also make a difference, with most studies, but not all, showing that the least amount of bullying occurs in high school and the greatest in middle school (Álvarez-García et al., 2015; Nansel et al., 2001). Within the same grade, younger students in a class are at greater risk of being bullied than older ones (Kljakovic & Hunt, 2016). Finally, having been bullied previously predicts being bullied in the future (Kljakovic & Hunt, 2016).

Each of the above factors are associated with a greater risk of being bullied. However, *it is important to note that none of these factors, or their combination, dictates that an individual student will be bullied*. They simply increase the risk. The risk increases as the number of risk factors increases.

Protective Factors. A number of protective factors influence bullying—malleable ones that schools should target for prevention and intervention—and explain why many, if not most, students with the risk factors discussed above are *not* bullied or experience no lasting negative effects. Those factors are discussed next. For heuristic purposes they are grouped into two general categories: (1) individual student factors, including the student's friends and family and (2) classroom and school factors. Note that in discussing each of these two sets of factors, and consistent with a social-ecological framework, it is well recognized that the factors do not operate in a vacuum and that many of the factors, both within and across categories, influence not only bullying victimization, but also influence the other factors in a multidirectional and dynamic fashion. For example, a student's social and emotional functioning influences friendships, peer relations, and classroom climate, just as friendships, peer relations, and classroom climate influence a student's social and emotional functioning. And, each of these factors, often operating together, influence bullying victimization and its impact on other factors.

Individual Student Characteristics

Certain characteristics of students, and ones that are more malleable than the characteristics discussed earlier, have been shown to be associated with bullying victimization and its negative effects. They include characteristics that lie within a student, particularly social and emotional skills, or lack thereof, and characteristics that are more external yet specific to the individual student, such as support from close friends and the home. In a systematic review of meta-analytic studies of bullying, including cyberbullying, Zych et al. (2018) found that personal student competencies were the strongest protectors against victimization. Results showed that students who are least likely to be bullied are those who are socially and emotionally competent. Socially, they exhibit few, if any, behavior problems (Analitis et al., 2009; Haynie et al., 2001; Saarento et al., 2013) and have good social skills, including social decision-making and the ability to avoid and negotiate situations of potential conflict and disagreement with peers (Hong, Espelage, Grogan-Kaylor, Allen-Meares, 2012). They possess and employ effective coping strategies when faced with bullying behaviors, such as social problem-solving skills and seeking support from others (Kochenderfer-Ladd & Skinner, 2002). They also tend to view themselves positively, having high self-esteem and self-confidence and an absence of internalizing problems (Chu et al., 2019; van Geel et al., 2018).

Students who experience no or little bullying tend to be in control of their emotions: They recognize, understand, and regulate their emotions (Hong et al., 2012; Ma, 2002). In contrast to students who are prone to being bullied, they tend not to be submissive, socially anxious, or overly angry when teased, excluded, or threatened (Hodges & Perry, 1999; Saarento et al., 2013). They also do not blame themselves for being bullied (Graham & Juvonen, 1998; Visconti, Sechler, & Kochenderfer-Ladd, 2013).

Finally, students who are seldom bullied tend to have friends who are not victims of bullying and who are likely to support norms against bullying, including standing up against bullies (Duffy & Nesdale, 2009; Faris & Felmlee, 2014). Having close friends not only helps prevent bullying victimization, but also provides emotional and social support that buffers victims from the negative outcomes of bullying when bullying does occur (Boulton et al., 1999; Wang et al., 2009).

Much less research exists on the risk and protective factors associated with bullying perpetration than with bullying victimization. However, reviews of the existing literature find that conduct problems, social problems, school problems, and age (i.e., greater bullying by younger students) are predictors of bullying perpetration (Kljakovic & Hunt, 2016; Zych et al., 2018). Often found to be associated with conduct problems are a lack of empathy (Álvarez-García et al., 2015) and moral disengagement (Hymel & Bonanno, 2014). Zych et al. reported that among protective factors against bullying perpetration, good academic performance and other-oriented social competencies, especially empathy, were the strongest.

Parenting and parent support also are related to bullying victimization and perpetration (Zych et al., 2018). The influence is both indirect and direct. Indirectly, good parenting, especially an authoritative style of parenting, provides students with the social and emotional skills, as listed above, that help protect students against being perpetrators and victims of bullying (Lereya, Samara, & Wolke, 2013). That style includes the absence of harsh and abusive practices and neglect; parenting characteristics associated with increased risk of being a bully and/or victim (Lereya et al., 2013). Parents also play more direct roles in bullying, as seen in the advice they give to their children (e.g., "fight back") and how they respond when they see their children bullying others or when their children are victims. When parental support is high, victims are much less likely to experience internalizing problems such as depression (Conners-Burrow, Johnson, Whiteside-Mansell, McKelvey, & Gargus, 2009; Morin, Bradshaw, & Berg, 2015).

School and Classroom Characteristics

Just as individual characteristics of a student largely determine if a student will be a victim or perpetrator of bullying in school, so do characteristics of schools and classrooms. A consistent finding in the research is that less bullying occurs in schools and classrooms characterized by a positive school or classroom climate (Espelage & Hong, 2019; Zych et al., 2018), and especially a climate characterized by connectedness, as seen in positive teacher-student and student-student relationships (Huang et al., 2018; Low & Van Ryzin, 2014; Plank, Bradshaw, & Young, 2009) and by norms against bullying (Duffy & Nesdale, 2009; Elsaesser, Gorman-Smith, & Henry, 2013; Sentse, Veenstra, Kiuru, & Salmivalli, 2015). Positive teacher-student and student-student relationships not only serve to prevent bullying but also to buffer victims from its negative effects (Huang et al., 2018). Norms against bullying are part of a positive school climate. They are established in multiple ways and at multiple levels, including in district policies and the actions of parents. Likewise, they are closely related to teacher-student and student-student relationships: It is the actions of teachers and students that most directly convey in a classroom that bullying is not acceptable and that prosocial behaviors, including support of victims, are highly valued.

As emphasized throughout this book, an authoritative approach, with a balance of social-emotional support and structure, characterizes effective classroom management and school discipline, and a positive school climate. It also has been shown to characterize classrooms and schools in which bullying is less likely to occur (Gregory et al., 2010). Research has firmly established that social-emotional support, as seen in positive teacher-student relationships, is particularly important in preventing bullying and minimizing its negative impact (Barboza et al., 2009; Boulton et al., 2012). Positive teacher-student relationships entail teachers demonstrating a combination of social-emotional support and structure. Teachers who are most effective in preventing bullying convey to students, through their thoughts and actions, that they disapprove of bullying, are attuned to peer interactions that foster bullying, and will respond immediately and effectively to all forms of bullying (Elledge et al., 2016; Veenstra. Lindenberg, Huitsing, Sainio, & Salmivalli, 2014).

Effective teachers not only prevent and stop bullying quickly when they first see signs of it, but also provide help and support to victims of bullying (Eliot et al., 2010). Students are much more likely to seek their help when such actions of teachers are present and students believe that their teachers (and peers) will support and not punish them when they speak out against or assert themselves against bullies (Eliot et al., 2010; Nation et al., 2008; Saarento et al., 2013).

Positive student-student relationships in the classroom and school are equally important to teacher-student relationships in preventing bullying and its negative impact. Ample research shows that less bullying occurs in classes and schools where students experience acceptance, respect, trust, and support from their peers (Elsaesser et al., 2013; Gage, Prykanowski, & Larson, 2014; Henry, Farrell, Schoeny, Tolan, & Dymnicki, 2011). As is true with positive teacher-student relationships, when student-student relationships are perceived favorably and students understand that their peers support them, they are more likely to stand up against bullies, and bystanders are more likely to intervene (Rigby & Johnson, 2006; Saarento et al., 2013). The protective value of teacher-student relationships and student-student relationships can be attributed to several interrelated mechanisms discussed previously: (a) norms and sanctions against bullying; (b) greater self-confidence among students when their basic psychological need of belongingness is met; and (c) awareness that others will support them when bullying occurs.

Bullying Prevention Programs

Reviews of research on the effectiveness of bullying prevention programs have yielded mixed results. Whereas some programs have been shown to be effective, others have not (Evans, Fraser, & Cotter, 2014; Ferguson, San Miguel, Kilburn, & Sanchez, 2007; Merrell, Gueldner, Ross, & Isava, 2008; Ttofi & Farrington, 2011). The more recent reviews have tended to yield more favorable results than earlier reviews, suggesting that efforts in schools to prevent bullying have improved. Yet, overall, the effects of bullying prevention programs tend to be small. Evans et al. (2014) found that only half of the studies they reviewed reported a reduction in bullying perpetration. The effects were better, however, in reducing bullying victimization, with 67% of the studies finding significant effects. Two other comprehensive reviews (Gaffney, Ttofi, & Farrington, 2019; Ttofi & Farrington, 2011) reported that, on average, programs reduced bullying perpetration about 18% to 20% and bullying victimization about 15% to 16%. These reviews did not include cyberbullying. In a review of anti-cyberbullying programs, Gaffney, Farrington, Espelage, and Ttofi (2019) reported decreases of about 9% to 15% in perpetration and about 14% to 15% in victimization.

Based on the results of these studies, one can conclude that although school-based bullying prevention programs, in general, reduce bullying, the effects tend to be small, and a large number of programs are ineffective. As with most other types of prevention and intervention programs, the effectiveness of bullying programs depends largely on the fidelity of implementation (e.g., Haataja et al., 2014). Quite simply, programs are more effective when implemented as intended and not haphazardly. In addition to the importance of implementing programs with fidelity, bullying prevention programs are more effective when implemented over a longer period of time (e.g., multiple years), with greater intensity (e.g., teachers receive more extensive professional development), and when they consist of multiple components (Gaffney et al., 2019; Ttofi & Farrington, 2011).

Components of Effective Programs. In their comprehensive meta-analytic review of studies of school-based bullying programs, Ttofi and Farrington (2011) examined program components that were associated with effectiveness. Consistent with research on classroom management and school discipline (Bear, 2015), the authoritative approach received substantial support in preventing bullying. Indeed, two popular international programs included in this review, and most other recent reviews, that were found to be most effective are grounded in the authoritative approach: The Olweus program (and similar ones inspired by the work of Olweus) and the KiVa program. These two programs are described briefly in the next section as exemplary programs. Both emphasize establishing norms against bullying by building and maintaining positive teacher-student and student-student relationships and holding clear expectations and firm sanctions against bullying. For example, in the Olweus programs, in addition to talking to the student (and victim), consequences of bullying include taking away privileges, closer supervision (e.g., at recess staying near a student who bullied a peer), and sending the student to the office. The effectiveness of these and other programs was attributed largely to being implemented with intensity and fidelity over an adequate period of time. The following components were found to be associated with their effectiveness in reducing bullying, as measured by either perpetration (bullying) or victimization (being bullied):

Found to reduce bullying:

- parent training and meetings (parent information also was effective, but not as much as training and meetings)
- playground supervision
- disciplinary methods for preventing and responding to bullying (i.e., those consistent with an authoritative, and not authoritarian/zero tolerance, approach)
- classroom management practices, including clear expectations/rules
- teacher training (interestingly, this was found to be related to bullying but not victimization)
- whole-school policy against bullying
- school conferences
- cooperative group work

Found to reduce bullying victimization:

- disciplinary methods for preventing and responding to bullying (i.e., those consistent with an authoritative, and not authoritarian/zero tolerance, approach)
- parent training and meetings (parent information also was effective, but not as much as training and meetings)
- use of videos in lessons
- cooperative group work

Interestingly, "work with peers" was found to be associated with *increases* in bullying and victimization, although only the latter was statistically significant. This referred to programs in which students were formally engaged to work with their peers in preventing and responding to bullying, such as via peer mediation, peer mentoring, and encouraging bystander intervention.

Another interesting finding was that programs tended to be more successful when implemented in European countries, especially Scandinavian countries, than in the United States. This is a common finding in evaluations of the popular Olweus programs (Ttofi & Farrington, 2011), and one that is often attributed to student populations in Scandinavian countries being more homogeneous, having fewer behavior problems and less poverty (Evans et al., 2014). In support of this position, bullying intervention studies in the United States have reported greater program success in schools where students are more engaged and a lower proportion are of low socioeconomic status (Low & Van Ryzin, 2014).

Three Exemplary Programs. Among bullying prevention programs found to effective in reducing bullying, three popular programs have received perhaps the greatest research support with respect to both quantity and quality of the research: (1) the Olweus Bullying Prevention Program (www.violencepreventionworks.org); (2) the KiVa program (www.kivaprogram.net/program); and (3) Second Step Social-Emotional Learning (www.secondstep.org/). Both the Olweus and KiVa programs are comprehensive whole-school programs for children and adolescents that include classroom, individual student, schoolwide, and community components. The Olweus program has been shown to reduce bullying perpetration and victimization (Limber, 2011; Olweus & Limber, 2010a, 2010b), as has the KiVa program (Kärnä et al., 2013; Salmivalli, Kärnä, & Poskiparta, 2011). The general aim of both programs is to develop norms against bullying. Sequenced curriculum lessons, which include videos on bullying, are only one part of both programs. Other research-supported components are a schoolwide policy against bullying, extensive teacher/staff training, and information provided to or meetings held with parents. Both programs train teachers and staff to provide interventions and supports for victims and bullies, but KiVa places relatively greater emphasis on this component. In KiVa, school teams are trained to intervene at the individual and group levels and to encourage prosocial peers of the victim to provide support to the victim.

Second Step Social-Emotional Learning (grades K-8) is a curriculum-based program, consisting primarily of lessons, many with engaging musical videos, that teach students such social-emotional skills as managing emotions, resisting peer pressure, social problem-solving, respecting others, and coping with frustration and stressors. Studies have reported that the program improves students' social skills, prosocial goals, and behavior, and reduces physical aggression, sexual violence perpetration, and homophobic name-calling victimization (Espelage, Low, Polanin, & Brown, 2013b; Espelage, Low, Polanin, & Brown, 2015; Frey, Nolen, Edstrom, & Hirschstein, 2005; Grossman et al., 1997). Second Step Bullying Prevention Unit (K-5) is similar to Second Step Social-Emotional Learning, with an emphasis on curriculum lessons for preventing aggression and bullying but also includes lessons on teaching students how to recognize, report, and refuse bullying. It also consists of staff development about bullying, including how to recognize it and how to intervene and work with bullies, victims, and bystanders. Materials for the homes of students also are included. Although this new version of Second Step has not been evaluated, its effectiveness should be similar or better to that of Second Step Social-Emotional Learning since they have similar lessons and the newer program includes much greater training and material for teachers and parents. Randomized control-group studies are currently underway.

Recommended Strategies and Interventions for Preventing and Responding to Bullying

In this section, recommended evidence-based strategies are given for preventing and responding to bullying. They are drawn from much of the research presented above on program effectiveness, but also from additional sources authored by experts on bullying, as cited. To avoid redundancy in recommendations presented in other chapters, those recommendations receive little attention here.

Preventing and Reducing Bullying 141

However, because of their critical importance in preventing and responding to bullying, readers should be reminded of them, as highlighted below in the first four brief recommendations.

1. *Build and maintain positive teacher-student relationships.* As discussed earlier, a wealth of research has shown that social-emotional support, which includes responsiveness to students' needs, is associated with less bullying and less negative outcomes when bullying occurs. Research also shows that teacher-student relationships are a critical part of classroom management and disciplinary practices (Bear, 2015), which Ttofi and Farrington (2011) found to characterize effective bullying prevention programs. Specific recommendations for improving teacher-student relationships are presented in Chapter 2.
2. *Build and maintain positive student-student relationships.* This includes peers working to create prosocial norms against bullying and also providing support to victims of bullying. It also would include strategies that foster cooperative learning, which Ttofi and Farrington (2011) found to be important in reducing both bullying perpetration and victimization. Specific recommendations for improving student-student relationships are presented in Chapter 3.
3. *Ensure that additional classroom management and disciplinary practices are in place that prevent behavior problems, including bullying, and that develop social and emotional competencies.* Consistent with an authoritative approach to classroom management, school discipline, and school climate, this would include implementing multiple strategies that combine and balance social-emotional support and structure. In addition to strategies for promoting positive teacher-student and student-student relationships and developing SEL competencies, this would include more structure-oriented strategies such as having clear behavioral and academic expectations, routines, and procedures; fair rules and consequences; and close monitoring and supervision of student behavior. It also would include strategies that foster student engagement. When students are actively engaged in learning they are less likely to be engaged in bullying or other misbehavior. As noted earlier, academic engagement and achievement is among the strongest protectors against bullying perpetration (Zych et al., 2018). See Chapters 4, 5, 6, and 7 for specific recommendations for improving developing social and emotional competencies, preventing behavior problems with effective classroom management, correcting behavior problems, and promoting student engagement.
4. *Collect and analyze data related to bullying and bullying victimization.* This should include surveys of students, teachers/staff, and the home, and of the different types of bullying (physical, verbal, social-relational, and cyber). It also should include data on when and where bullying most often occurs. Data should be used to guide the need for interventions and supports, and to evaluate their effectiveness (see Chapter 10).
5. *Establish a schoolwide policy against bullying.* Every school should have a definition of bullying that is consistent with that of the school district and state law, where applicable, and that is embedded in a schoolwide policy against bullying. The definition also should be consistent with modern theory and research on bullying that emphasizes intentional harm (physical

or psychological), an imbalance of power, and that the behavior continues over time. Bullying should be differentiated from other forms of aggression, which may be equally or more harmful, such as fighting, as well as from behaviors that might be misinterpreted as bullying, such as playful teasing. Students and teachers/staff should understand that teasing may or may not constitute bullying. Teasing is not bullying when it is not intended to be hurtful; does not result in hurt feelings; does not continue over time (when it is hurtful); and when it is generally reciprocated (i.e., the teaser and person being teased tease one another).

The schoolwide policy, including a definition of bullying, should be taught to all students. It also should be communicated to students, teachers, staff, and families in multiple ways, such as via the school's website, newsletters, assemblies, the student handbook, posters, class meetings, meetings with parents, in professional development activities for teachers and staff, and so forth. Some schools include signed contracts, in which students (and parents) sign that they understand what bullying is and agree to work against it. The contract often includes the use of school computers, cellphones, and other electronic devices in school. Whether in a contract or elsewhere in policy, students and parents should be informed of the scope of the school's authority, which includes not only campus grounds but also bus stops and activities conducted off-campus via digital devices (e.g., cyberbullying) if such use creates "substantial disorder and disruption" at the school or "substantially interferes with requirements of appropriate discipline in the operation of the school" (Paget, 2013).

The policy should include a range of likely consequences, depending on the circumstances, for students who bully others, and include additional interventions and supports for bullies and victims. Imposing punitive consequences is viewed by students as critical to preventing further bullying (Cunningham et al., 2016). Developing and disseminating a schoolwide policy helps ensure that the school community has a common understanding of bullying, its effects on victims, bullies, the classroom, and the school, and that the school stands firmly against bullying. To be effective, especially during adolescence, such communication activities must be viewed by students as credible and engaging, and not consist primarily of repetitive negative messages (e.g., rules and laws about bullying); otherwise they might trigger increased bullying (Cunningham et al., 2016). The schoolwide policy should identify what is being done to prevent bullying, which should include practices that follow.

6. *Directly teach lessons about bullying.* This might be done using lessons from an evidence-based packaged program, such as the Oleweus, KiVa, or Second Step Social-Emotional Learning programs. As discussed in Chapter 4 on SEL, teaching about bullying should occur by infusing lessons into the general curriculum, such as in literacy, language arts, social studies, and health, as well as in the context of lessons and messages presented in school assemblies, morning announcements, posters, and other forms of media. Lessons should include what bullying is, its negative impact, how to prevent it, and how to respond when bullying is seen or experienced.

Unfortunately, research is lacking as to the most effective student responses to being bullied. However, the U.S. Department of Health and

Preventing and Reducing Bullying 143

Human Services (www.stopbullying.gov) provides several tips and strategies for preventing and responding to bullying, which are often found in bullying prevention programs. They include:
- Using a calm and assertive voice, telling the bully to stop.
- Walking away.
- Avoiding places where bullying most likely occurs, while preferring places where it is least likely to occur (e.g., where adults or supportive peers are present).
- Acting as if the bully is joking and try to laugh it off. Humor might also be used.
- Seeking support from a friend.
- Informing a teacher, parent, or other adult who may be able to help.

Students should learn that these strategies might or might not work since their effectiveness hinges on multiple factors (e.g., the type of bullying, the characteristics of the bully, the actions of bystanders). Students also should be taught that certain practices are generally ineffective, such as retaliating or threatening retaliation, ignoring the bullying, rumination, distancing from the bullying situation, and other forms of passive and reactive coping (e.g. crying and aggressive behavior; Flanagan et al., 2013).

7. ***Develop and implement an anonymous process by which students can report all forms of bullying.*** The process should be anonymous to reduce the fear of retribution for reporting. Reporting should include the name of the bully and the victim, a description of the behavior, and where it occurred. The process, which might entail the use of a website or mailbox in the school, should be explained to all students, school staff, and parents.

8. ***Closely monitor and supervise student behavior in settings where bullying is most likely to occur.*** Bullying and other behavior problems are most likely to occur where adult supervision and monitoring of student behavior is lacking or absent, such as the playground (at grades with recess), bathrooms, hallways, and on the school bus (Craig, Pepler, & Atlas, 2000; Migliaccio, Raskauskas, & Schmidtlein, 2017). Knowledge of where bullying occurs most often should be gleaned from recorded incidents (e.g., office referrals and student reports) and student surveys.

9. ***When bullying occurs, respond immediately.*** The response should be consistent with best practices for correcting misbehavior, as presented in Chapter 6. The response should depend on such factors as the seriousness of the behavior, the age of the student, the circumstances involved, and whether or not the behavior constitutes bullying. This should include the following (Bear, Homan, & Harris, 2019):
- *Responding in a calm, caring, yet firm manner, while communicating the situation is being taken seriously and that the behavior will not be tolerated.*
- *Attending to any immediate needs, such as physical harm or emotional distress.*
- *In general, and where feasible, addressing the behavior privately.* Confronting the bully in front of peers can be humiliating, especially to the victim, and might aggravate the situation, provoking retaliation. Likewise, confronting the bully in the presence of the victim might embarrass the victim. Thus, the perpetrator and victim should be handled

separately. However, in determining what happened it would be appropriate to meet with both the bully and victim (and possibly bystanders), but only when retaliation or humiliation is not anticipated.
- *Determining what happened.* Adults should listen to the perpetrator and the aggressor, and to bystanders where appropriate. It is important to determine (a) if the behavior constitutes bullying and (b) the circumstances involved.
- *Communicating that the adult will help stop the behavior.* As noted earlier, students are more likely to report bullying when they feel teachers or others will actively intervene. In responding to bullying, it is important that adults focus on preventing the bullying from reoccurring and what will help achieve that aim. This includes communicating that specific actions will be taken to stop bullying and help the victim. Where appropriate, the actions (and who is responsible for implementing them) should be incorporated into an intervention and support plan.
- *Having the aggressor reflect upon the negative impact of the behavior.* Punitive consequences, as appropriate for the situation, are to be made clear. However, it is important to communicate to the aggressor that the behavior is wrong regardless of any forthcoming punishment. Adults should communicate that what makes bullying wrong is its negative impact on others, especially the victim, and not whether or not one gets caught and punished. The student should be challenged to take the perspective of others and think about how the behavior impacts the victim and others (e.g., the aggressor's future, the perceptions of others, the classroom and school climate). This helps develop empathy and a sense of responsibility. This might be done verbally during the disciplinary encounter, and preferably via role playing (asking the aggressor to assume the perspective of the victim and perhaps others, such as non-supporting bystanders, parent, and teacher).
- *Do not give messages and advice that is likely to make the situation worse.* This would include:
    o Communicating that the victim is to blame.
    o Advising the victim to simply ignore the bullying (especially when this is the only strategy to be used).
    o Encouraging the victim to resolve the problem on his or her own. This works for many conflicts between friends and equal peers but not when imbalance of power exists.
    o Encouraging the victim to retaliate.
    o Communicating that the bully is a bad person. It is fine to communicate that the behavior is bad, but not that the student is bad. Changing one's actions is much easier than changing one's self.
10. **Where needed, develop an individual intervention and support plan.** This goes beyond the immediate response to the bullying and disciplinary encounter. It involves implementing new interventions and supports that will be needed to stop the bullying and help the victim, and ones that are not currently in place. As discussed in Chapter 6 on correction, when negative consequences are imposed for the aggressor (e.g., removing privileges, parent

conference, in-school or out-of-school suspension) they always should be combined with positive strategies for preventing further incidents, including teaching replacement behaviors as needed (e.g., assertiveness, friendship skills, and coping skills for the victim; empathy, perspective-taking, and anger management for the aggressor), and for reinforcing desired behaviors at school. The plan for the aggressor also should include reparative actions to be taken (e.g., apologize, repair or replace anything damaged or stolen). It might also include educational actions, where appropriate, such as reading a book or watching a video on bullying or writing a paper about bullying. A separate plan should be developed for the aggressor and victim. Both plans include actions to be taken by the given student *and* by the school (e.g., increased monitoring, change in seating, arranging for peer support, providing additional lessons on bullying).

Where feasible, there should be a separate meeting with the parents of both students to share the school-based plan and solicit their input and suggestions for change in the plan. If a formal meeting is not possible, the plan should be shared in writing, including information on what the home might do to help. A meeting with parents, and their active input, is particularly important if supports outside of the regular classroom are needed, including outside of school, such as social skills training, counseling, and parent management training.

11. *Provide information about bullying to all homes of students.* Information about bullying should be prepared and shared with parents and caregivers, and include:
    - What constitutes bullying and its different forms.
    - Warning signs that bullying is occurring.
    - The impact of bullying.
    - Factors that influence bullying and establishing those that the home can influence;
    - The school's policy on bullying.
    - What the school is doing to prevent and respond to bullying.
    - What the home can do to help.

    Preferably, the information should be presented at meetings with parents, such as at open-houses and parent-teacher conferences. However, the information should also be distributed by other means, such as in printed materials sent home and websites. When bullying incidents occur, a parent-school conference should be held to discuss the incident and discuss ways to help at home. Where appropriate, parent trainings also should be offered, especially for parents of bullies and victims (but held separately).

12. *Provide teachers and staff with professional development on bullying.* As noted earlier, bullying programs are most effective when they are implemented with fidelity, over multiple years, and include staff training. Staff development should be ongoing, and not be a one-shot occurrence. It is recommended that all topics presented in this chapter should be included in the training sessions:
    - What bullying is and its different forms.
    - Warning signs that bullying is occurring.
    - The impact of bullying.

- Factors that influence bullying, establishing those that teachers and staff influence.
- Strategies for preventing and responding to bullying.

Note that the three evidence-based programs presented earlier (Oleweus, KiVa, and Second Step Social-Emotional Learning) offer training to schools.

Summary

Bullying is a form of peer aggression that entails intentionality, repetition, and a power differential. It can have a profound and lasting negative impact on victims, as well as on classrooms and schools. The extent to which bullying occurs and its harmful effects vary greatly across students, classrooms, and schools. This can be explained by multiple influencing factors, including malleable ones that are subject to change and thus should be targeted in bullying prevention programs. Those factors include individual student characteristics, particularly the social and emotional competencies of students, and various characteristics of teachers, classrooms, and schools. Although evidence is mixed with respect to the overall effectiveness of bullying prevention programs, many have been shown to be effective. Moreover, there is ample evidence supporting the use of authoritative strategies of responsiveness and structure, as commonly found in the most effective programs, for preventing behavior problems, including bullying. Those strategies were highlighted in this chapter.

CHAPTER 9

SCHOOL SAFETY
What Works and What Doesn't

Of all the domains of school climate covered in this book, one may well argue that safety is the most fundamental and important. As seen in previous chapters, students' learning and mental health are likely to suffer in schools with poor teacher-student and student-student relationships, bullying, unclear behavioral expectations and rules, and a general lack of student engagement. Not only do students achieve less academically in those schools, but they also are at greater risk for a variety of social and emotional problems, including acting out and general unhappiness (Macmillan & Hagan, 2004; Wei & Williams, 2004). When students are not safe, the outcomes can be much worse, and often tragic, including death, as seen in school shootings and suicides of students who have been bullied. Non-victims also suffer: Students who experience, either directly or indirectly, violent traumatic events often have lasting anxiety, depression, sadness, anger, fear, and avoidance of school (Kim & Leventhal, 2008; La Greca et al., 2008).

Feeling unsafe in school does not hinge on the occurrence of shootings and suicides; it entails other acts of aggression that are less violent and tragic. This includes bullying, as discussed in the previous chapter, and physical fighting. Approximately 6% of students ages 12–18 report that they avoid at least one school activity or class or one or more places in school because they think someone might attack or harm them (Musu, Zhang, Wang, Zhang, & Oudekerk, 2019). Obviously, it is difficult for students to achieve academically when they are not in a class, but it also is difficult for students to develop social and emotional competencies and experience general well-being and happiness when they live in fear. It is no wonder then that safety is commonly viewed as a basic psychological need (Maslow, 1943), and is at the forefront of most federal and state efforts to improve school climate. Unquestionably, our nation's schools should be safe havens for teaching and learning, and ideally free of all crime and violence.

This chapter begins by examining the construct of school safety, especially how it is defined and assessed. Estimates of schools being viewed as safe or unsafe vary greatly depending on how safety is defined and assessed, but especially which indicators are used when reporting on school safety. Next, characteristics of schools that are more or less safer than others are reviewed. As in other chapters, the focus is on malleable factors that schools might target to improve safety while recognizing that many other factors that influence school safety are largely beyond the control of schools. Those other factors include violence at home, in the community, and portrayed in media; poor parental monitoring and supervision; and lack of school funding and resources. The chapter ends with recommended strategies and interventions for improving school safety.

Instead of focusing exclusively in this chapter on best practices, a popular approach to school discipline that is *not* best for safety is first examined: the zero tolerance approach. This approach is characterized by the pervasive use of exclusionary practices, particularly suspension and expulsion from school, and omnipresent security measures. This might be the best approach for schools that share the same aim as prisons, which is to maximize safety and security, with little or no regard for social and emotional learning. However, it is not a wise choice among schools that value a positive school climate that promotes the development of social and emotional competences. Unfortunately, with its aim of social control using punishment and constant surveillance, the zero tolerance approach to school discipline is found in many schools, and too often in the name of safety.

Aspects of school safety covered thoroughly elsewhere in this book are not covered here, including bullying. As discussed in Chapter 8, bullying is perhaps the primary reason why many students feel unsafe in school. To be sure, bullying *is* a major indicator of school safety, but it is not covered in this chapter simply because it is covered thoroughly in the previous chapter. If bullying is the only indicator of the lack of safety in a school, then the interventions and strategies in that chapter should suffice.

As with bullying, other aspects of school climate and recommendations related to school safety covered in other chapters are not covered here. This includes the critical importance of building teacher-student and student-student relationships, teaching social and emotional competencies, engaging students in school, and using additional strategies and techniques for preventing and correcting behavior problems. Unquestionably, those aspects of school climate influence school safety and are equal to or more important than the strategies highlighted in this chapter in preventing acts of violence and ensuring that students feel safe and are safe.

Are Children Safe in School?

The answer to this question depends largely on how one defines being safe and addresses "Safe from what? School shootings? Physical assault and physical aggression? Rape or sexual assault? Exposure to drugs? Theft? All crimes? Disorder in a school? Bullying?" With respect to school shootings and other serious acts of violence that result in death or serious bodily injury, there are few places in society in which children are safer than in school (Cornell, 2015). Children and adolescents are much more likely to be killed or seriously injured in their homes or community, riding a bicycle, and especially riding in vehicles. As reported in the 2019 national report, "Indicators of School Crime and Safety: 2018," published by the National Center for Education Statistics (NCES), U.S. Department of Education and Bureau of Justice Statistics (Musu et al., 2019), 18 students, ages 5–18, were victims of homicides and 3 of suicides at school during the 2015–2016 school year. This compares to 1,478 homicides and 1,941 suicides of youth of the same age occurring outside of school during the same time period. Thus, approximately 99% of student homicides occur outside of school.

Although more common than homicides, serious violent incidents also occur rarely at school. In the NCES report, serious violent crimes were one of the multiple indicators of school climate and safety. Serious violent incidents include rape or attempted rape, sexual assault, robbery (with or without a weapon), physical attack or fight with a weapon, and threat of a physical attack with a weapon. In American schools, the rate of occurrence for each of those incidents is less than 1 crime per 1,000 students, with about 15% of public schools recording one or more serious violent incidents. Those rates suggest that schools *are* safe, at least from serious violent incidents. However, when fights or physical attacks (without a weapon) and threats of physical attack with or without a weapon are added to the above crimes as "violent incidents" recorded by schools, the percentage of schools recording one or more violent incidents increases dramatically, with 69% of public schools recording one or more incidents of violent and seriously violent crime (about 18 crimes per 1,000 students). Those percentages were lower for reporting the incidents to police, as opposed to the school recording the incidents but not reporting them to the police. Fighting and physical attacks without a weapon were the most commonly recorded incidents, with 65% of public schools reporting such. About 9% of students, grades 9–12, reported having been in a physical fight on school property during the previous 12 months.

Far fewer schools are safe when all types of crime, both violent and nonviolent, are added as indicators of school safety. Those include theft; vandalism; distribution, possession, or use of illegal drugs; possession or use of alcohol; possession of a firearm or explosive device (ranging from a firecracker to a bomb); possession of a knife or sharp object; and inappropriate distribution, possession, or use of prescription drugs. Approximately 79% of public schools report one or more of those crimes.

Included in the government report is a potpourri of additional indicators of safety based on behaviors of students that greatly increases the number of schools that would be deemed unsafe. Indeed, if one adds the following indicators to those above, it is unlikely that any school is safe.

- Percentage of students, ages 12–18, reporting they have been bullied at least once during the school year (20%; 15% for cyberbullying in grades 9–12).
- Percentage of schools in which students, ages 12–18, reporting gangs in their school (9%).
- Percentage of students reporting being the target of hate-related words at school (6%) and seeing hate-related graffiti at school (23%).
- Percentage of public school teachers reporting that student tardiness and class cutting interfered with their teaching (38%).
- Percentage of public school teachers reporting being threatened with injury (10%) and having been physically attacked (5.8%). The percentage of physical attacks was 9.2% for elementary teachers and 2.4% for secondary teachers.
- Percentage of schools reporting disciplinary problems and serious disciplinary actions, as discussed next.

What does the NCES report include as disciplinary problems and serious disciplinary actions? *Disciplinary problems* include student bullying, student racial or ethnic tensions, student sexual harassment of other students, student harassment of other students based on sexual orientation or gender identity, student verbal abuse of teachers, student acts of disrespect for teachers other than verbal abuse, and widespread disorder in classrooms (fortunately, the latter was reported by only 2.3% of public schools.) Among those problems, bullying was most common, with 12% of schools reporting it as a problem that occurred at least weekly.

What are called *serious disciplinary actions* in the report differs markedly from all other indicators of safety. This indicator focuses not necessarily on the specific behavior of students, but on actions *taken* by schools in response to what is viewed as unsafe behaviors. In the 2019 report, those actions are out-of-school suspensions lasting five days are more, removals with no services for the remainder of the school year, and transfers to specialized schools. As with the 2018 report, serious disciplinary actions in the 2019 report differ greatly than previous reports. In the 2017 report (Musu, Zhang, Wang, Zhang, & Oudekerk, 2017), serious disciplinary actions included both in-school and out-of-school suspensions, regardless of length of time; expulsions; referrals to law enforcement; school related arrests; and corporal punishment. No explanation was given for this major change. Using the new 2019 indicators for serious disciplinary actions, 37% of schools take at least one serious disciplinary action.

No data were given in the 2018 and 2019 reports on suspensions of fewer than five days, nor on racial/ethnic group differences in the use of suspensions. Suspensions received considerable attention in the 2017 report. In that report approximately three million students had received in-school and out-of-school suspension each annually. About 7% of all students were suspended in-school and 6% out-of-school. The highest percentage of students suspended were black, with 20% of those suspended being black males and 11% being black females. Those percentages compare with 6% and 2%, respectively, for white males and females, and 2% and 1%, respectively, for Asian males and females.

Unlike the multiple indicators above which tap unsafe behaviors of students or a school's response to those behaviors, the NCES report also includes safety and security measures taken by public schools as an indicator of school safety. The NCES reports that the vast majority of public schools (99%) implemented one or more security measures to help ensure safety. Those measures consist of controlled access to the building, security cameras, ID badges, an enforced strict dress code or student uniforms, random dog sniff checks for drugs, random metal detector checks, written codes of conduct, visitors' requirement to sign in, hallway supervision by school staff, security guards and/or assigned police officers, and locker checks. Whether or not the presence of those measures indicates that a school is safe or unsafe, or makes much difference with respect to safety, is subject to debate, as will be discussed later.

The last indicator included in the NCES report, although discussed in a limited manner, is perceptions of school safety. The report found that 4% of students, ages 12–18, were afraid of attack or harm at school during the school year and 6% avoided at least one school activity or class in one or more place in school during the school year because they thought someone might attack or harm them. Interestingly, in light of results of all of the previous indicators of safety in the NCES report these percentages are surprisingly low. That is, despite data showing schools are unsafe, about 95% of students do *not* avoid a school activity or place in school out of fear. Indeed, in our research in Delaware schools we consistently find that over 90% of teachers and parents and about 85% of students report that they (or their children) feel safe in school. Of course, one might rightfully argue that about 15% of students or teachers feel unsafe, which is very important. Yet, those data provide weak support for the conclusion that most students, or schools, are not safe.

So, are schools safe? As seen above, the answer depends on what one uses as an indicator of safety. Depending on which indicator is chosen, one might argue that schools are the safest places in our society, or that nearly every school is unsafe.

Factors Contributing to School Safety

What makes some schools safer than others? As found in the NCES reports, school demographics play a large role. A school is more likely to be safe from most crimes if it is an elementary school rather than a middle school or high school and has a small rather than large student enrollment. For example, 57% of elementary schools reported violent crimes, compared to 88% of middle schools and 90% of high schools (Musu et al., 2019). Likewise, 54.6% of schools with enrollments under 300 reported a violent crime, compared to 86.4% of schools with enrollments of 1,000 or more (Musu-Gillette, Zhang, Wang, Zhang, & Oudekerk, 2017). Violent crimes also are much higher among schools in which students live in communities with high rates of poverty and crime. In schools in which 76–100% of students were eligible for free or reduced-price lunch, 71.2% of those schools reported incidents of violent crime, compared to 50.8% of schools in which only 0–25% of the students were eligible for free or reduced-price lunch (Musu-Gillette, Zhang, Wang, Zhang, & Oudekerk, 2017).

Most schools have little, if any, control over student enrollments, poverty, or location. However, there are a host of other factors that are much more malleable that influence school safety. Many of them have already been covered in previous chapters. As argued in those chapters, schools are safer when they have a positive school climate (Booren, Handy, & Power, 2011; Bosworth, Ford, & Hernandez, 2011), where teacher-student, student-student relationships, and home-school relationships are positive, promoting both a sense of connectedness with school and others, as well as prosocial norms. Students also are safer in schools characterized by additional elements of effective classroom management and school discipline, including behavioral expectations and rules that are clear, fair, and enforced consistently (Bosworth et al., 2011; Fisher, Viano, Curran, Pearman, & Gardella, 2018; Kitsantas, Ware, & Martinez-Arias, 2004), and teachers and staff who are highly visible and frequently monitor student behavior, especially in areas where violence and other crimes are most likely to happen, such as in hallways and stairwells (Bosworth et al., 2011). Likewise, students are safer in schools where they are cognitively, behaviorally, and emotionally engaged (Catalano, Haggerty, Oesterle, Fleming, & Hawkins, 2004; Skiba et al., 2004), and in schools that make concerted efforts to develop social and emotional competencies (Espelage, Low, Polanin, & Brown, 2013b; Jones, Brown, & Aber, 2011). Finally, students tend to feel safer in schools with physical safety features, especially security cameras, secure entrances, and locked doors (Bosworth et al., 2011; Wilcox, Augustine, & Clayton, 2006). However, as discussed next, not all physical safety features, including the presence of school resource officers and use of metal detectors, have been shown to increase feelings of safety. Indeed, safety features can have the opposite effect, creating a negative school climate (Devlin & Gottfredson, 2018; Hirschfield, 2018).

Zero Tolerance Approach: Increasing Safety with School Suspensions and Maximum Security Measures

If one's sole aim is to create an environment that is safe from violence, weapons, drugs, and crime, a school might simply remove students who are violent, who bring weapons and drugs into school, and otherwise commit crimes. Indeed, if that's one's aim, it is extremely difficult for one to challenge the argument that students are less likely to commit crimes *in* school when they are *not in* school. In support of that aim, few would argue that crimes *should* be tolerated, especially crimes that harm others, and that students who commit them should go unpunished, including their removal from school, in order to protect the safety of others. As discussed later, a major problem with this aim, and particularly removing students to achieve it, is that it conflicts with the traditional aims of education, which are to promote academic achievement and social-emotional development.

Zero tolerance policies, which require student removal from school via suspension or expulsion for certain crimes that harm others or threaten harm to others, gained popularity in the mid- and late-1990s. They were largely in response to the rapidly increasing presence of weapons, drugs, and other crimes in schools, including school shootings such as at Columbine High School in 1999. Zero tolerance policies soon became enacted into state and federal laws, as seen in the 1994 Gun-Free Schools Act, which required the expulsion of students for possession of guns. At that time, most schools also developed school codes of conduct, or "sentencing manuals" (Curtis, Batsche, & Mesmer, 2000), that listed behaviors resulting in removal from school or other harsh punitive consequences. Many teacher associations and unions supported zero tolerance policies, especially when faced with an increasing number of their members reporting student behavior that greatly interfered with their teaching, including verbal and physical assaults on teachers. Such student behavior became a common reason for leaving the profession (Karcher, 2002; Smith & Smith, 2006). The general public, teacher associations and unions, and educational leaders often demanded, and the majority of voters supported, such zero tolerance policies (Rose & Gallup, 2000). As a result, most public schools now have no option in suspending or expelling students for crimes and certain other offenses, as school codes of conduct and state laws demand it (Curran, 2016).

Supporters of zero tolerance policies believe that they make schools safer and more orderly by punishing offenders, reducing the likelihood that the behavior will reoccur; deterring others from engaging in the same behavior; and simply removing students who threaten safety, interfere with teaching and learning, or otherwise have a harmful impact on peers and learning. Those policies were never intended to help educate or rehabilitate the offenders, although some incorrectly believe that punishment serves that purpose. Instead, their primary aim has been to make schools safe by simply removing students who threaten school safety and order.

Unfortunately, it was not long until zero tolerance policies, including some policies that were reasonable ones, proliferated into what became known as the *zero tolerance approach* to school discipline, or what Kauffman and Brigham (2000, p. 278) referred to as "something stupid—getting tough on little things without allowing discretion in what to do about them." Instead of *reasonable* zero tolerance policies being one part of a comprehensive approach to school discipline—ones targeting only serious and harmful behaviors, and administered fairly and judiciously (e.g., in consideration of the circumstance involved)—a zero tolerance mentality was applied to nearly all types of rule violations. What emerged was a pervasive authoritarian approach to school discipline in which school removal was seen as the solution to improving school safety.

In a pervasive zero-tolerance approach, all acts of noncompliance and misbehavior, as identified in the school's code of conduct, are to be caught and punished quickly, irrespective of the circumstances involved and the offending student's previous history of behavior. Expediency in removing offending students, and not a fair and judicious process, often is the primary aim. Typically, suspensions are combined with an additional emphasis on pervasive security measures, including surveillance cameras, school police or resource officers, metal detectors, and random searches of students' possessions (e.g., locker and book bag searches, dogs sniffing for drugs). While relying primarily on catching students misbehaving and punishing them, the approach's aim is the management of student behavior, albeit for the purpose of safety. Thus, under the pervasive zero tolerance approach students are suspended or expelled not only for weapons, drugs, and violence, but also often for such minor offenses as noncompliance, insubordination, and disruption, and other behaviors that pose little or no harm but are viewed as bothersome or disrespectful to teachers and administrators. This would include behaviors such as arguing with a teacher, not following the dress code, skipping a class, being late for class, and so forth (Advancement Project/Civil Rights Project, 2000; Losen & Martinez, 2013). In too many schools the vast majority of the suspensions are not for serious violent or criminal behavior but for relatively minor misbehavior, such as disrupting class, noncompliance, tardiness, and dress code violations (Advancement Project/Civil Rights Project, 2000).

Reasonable Zero Tolerance Policies and Practices

It should be made clear that this section is not about avoiding *reasonable* zero tolerance policies and practices, including security measures, but a pervasive and *unreasonable* zero tolerance approach. That is, reasonable zero tolerance policies and security measures have a valid place in school discipline and should be one small part of a comprehensive approach that applies to serious transgressions, including most crimes, that harm others or are true threats to safety and learning. Reasonable zero tolerance policies also would apply to persistence behaviors of students that substantially interfere with the learning of others despite the school's implementation of multiple evidence-based interventions to prevent and remediate those behaviors. For those behaviors, in-school suspension might be a reasonable response. Likewise, reasonable security measures also would include locked doors, having all visitors enter one door and check into the office, and the use of security cameras in areas where threats to safety exist or are likely to occur.

These practices, however, should be one small part of a comprehensive approach to school discipline that is combined with all other elements of a positive school climate, as highlighted in previous chapters.

Research firmly supports reasonable and fair school policies that include punitive consequences for serious misbehavior and the close monitoring of student behavior. For example, fair and consistent behavioral expectations and sanctions against misbehavior characterize the most effective public schools (Arum, 2003; Catalano, Berglund, Ryan, Lonczak, & Hawkins, 2004; Gottfredson, Gottfredson, Payne, & Gottfredson, 2005; Gottfredson, Gottfredson, & Skroban, 1996). Farmer (1999) found that tough discipline policies characterize many private middle schools, much more so than public middle schools, and in those private schools the students and teachers held more positive perceptions of school climate and were much less concerned about school discipline. Farmer speculated that these findings might be attributed to private schools having a more balanced and comprehensive approach to school discipline (as well as to differences in school size, with private schools being smaller).

Do Suspensions Deter Misbehavior?

When zero tolerance policies are reasonable, viewed as fair by students, and comprising only a small part of a comprehensive approach to school discipline, suspensions seldom occur. For many students, knowing that one might be suspended serves as an effective deterrent of misbehavior. Despite claims to the contrary that suspensions fail to deter misbehavior (e.g., American Psychological Association Zero Tolerance Task Force, 2008; Chin, Dowdy, Jimerson, & Rime, 2012), there is ample research in psychology supporting the effectiveness of punishment and sanctions in deterring misbehavior (see Bandura, 1986, for review). And, as noted previously, research on effective school discipline and classroom management has consistently emphasized the importance of clear expectations, rules, and fair consequences (Gottfredson, 2001; Mayer & Leone, 1999; see Bear, 2015, for review). Although few studies exist specific to suspension as a deterrent, several indicate its effectiveness for most students (see Bear, 2012, for review; Zimmerman & Rees, 2014; Theriot, Craun, & Dupper, 2010). As reviewed in Chapter 6 on correction of behavior problems, despite their many limitations, rules and punishment are effective in deterring misbehavior. Many of their limitations are avoided when students perceive rules and their consequences as fair (Arum, 2003).

Suspensions are similar to police tickets for speeding, parking illegally, and driving under the influence of alcohol or drugs. That is, it is very likely that most individuals would commit those acts more often, especially speeding, if not for the fear of receiving a ticket; yet, a small percentage of the population receive multiple tickets, pay their fines, and continue committing the illegal act. Thus, one might very well conclude that speeding tickets and warnings (e.g., presence of police, radar, flashing warning lights that post your current speed) fail to work, citing repeating offenders as evidence while ignoring what highways would be like without those warnings and fines for speeding. The same logic applies to suspensions: If students were told that they will no longer be at risk of getting caught and suspended for fighting, bringing drugs or weapons to school, and many other criminal or disruptive acts, it is very likely that those behaviors would increase, not decrease. The author knows of no study, however, in which researchers have tested this, but such a study might silence arguments that suspensions fail to deter misbehavior among many students in most public schools.

As is true with speeding tickets given to frequent adult offenders, there is a subset of students for whom suspension fails to be an effective deterrent. In their study of 10,000 middle and high school students, Theriot et al. (2010) found that 17.1% of students were suspended two to five times and 4.5% more than five times. Other studies have shown that students who are suspended multiple times tend to be students who are lacking in social skills (Atkins et al., 2002; Morgan-D'Atrio, Northup, LaFleur, & Spera, 1996) and academic achievement (Hemphill, Toumbourou, Herrenkohl, McMorris, & Catalano, 2006; Morgan-D'Atrio et al., 1996), are highly aggressive and hyperactive (Atkins et al., 2002), associate with antisocial peers (Hemphill et al., 2006), and are more likely to have a history of antisocial behavior (Hemphill et al., 2006). These results, as well as results of a growing number of additional studies that focused on students suspended repeatedly, show that suspension does little, if anything, to help them. Instead, it often makes matters worse, increasing the likelihood of future behavior problems, including criminal behavior (Hemphill et al., 2006; Mowen & Brent, 2016). For those students, suspensions have been shown to be associated with lower academic performance and higher rates of dropout (Hwang, 2018; Noltemeyer, Marie, Mcloughlin, & Vanderwood, 2015) and increased risk of future arrest (Losen, 2013; Monahan, VanDerhei, Bechtold, & Cauffman, 2014; Mowen & Brent, 2016). Reasons for the ineffectiveness of suspensions with these students can be found in the limitations of the zero tolerance approach, as discussed next.

Limitations of the Zero Tolerance Approach

As noted earlier, in contrast to reasonable zero tolerance policies, the zero tolerance approach emphasizes safety and order via adult control of student behavior, not only using punishment, especially suspensions but also the close monitoring of student behavior to catch breaches of the code of conduct. In recent years, in many schools this has entailed the increased use of surveillance cameras and of school resource officers (Gary & Lewis, 2015). These increases occurred despite the lack of evidence that those measures actually prevent shootings or the possession of weapons and drugs (Kupchik, 2016; Tanner-Smith, Fisher, Addington, & Gardella, 2017). Both Columbine High School in Colorado and Stone Douglas High School in Florida had a school resource officer, and at Sandy Hook Elementary School in Connecticut the shooter forcefully entered the controlled access building.

Perhaps a greater limitation of a pervasive zero tolerance approach that emphasizes punishment and security measures is that the approach is not only ineffective but also counter-productive, often creating a jail- or prison-like environment (Kupchik, 2016; Mayer & Leone, 1999). As noted by Mayer and Leone (1999), "Creating an unwelcoming, almost jail-like, heavily scrutinized environment, may foster the violence and disorder school administrators hope to avoid" (p. 349). Research shows that a greater use of suspension is associated with a more negative school climate (Bear et al., 2011; Skiba, Shure, Middelberg, & Baker, 2011). Likewise, the use of resource officers tends to result in increases in crimes reported, not only for serious violent crimes and weapons and drugs, but also for less serious crimes unrelated to school violence, such as theft and vandalism (Devlin & Gottfredson, 2018). It is unlikely that these results are what many schools and parents desire. If one's aim extends beyond safety and includes creating a healthy school climate conducive to learning and the development of self-discipline, then an authoritarian zero-tolerance approach fails miserably.

Suspension shares many other limitations that characterize punishment in general, as reviewed in Chapter 6. As discussed in that chapter, a major limitation to punishment, and one that is more specific to suspension, is that punishment is often negatively and positively reinforced. For example, successfully removing a behavior (or person) that is viewed as undesirable can be quite reinforcing. Such negative reinforcement is seen when a teacher or administrator removes a student who is disruptive or annoying from the classroom or school, and then repeats the behavior because it "works" (i.e., there is less disruption and annoyance). It also is seen, however, in the actions of the student who dislikes the teacher or school: What is perceived unfavorably, annoying, or aversive (i.e., the teacher or school) is successfully eliminated or avoided by exhibiting behavior that leads to being removed from the classroom or school. The behaviors leading to the removal of something aversive are thus reinforced, and repeated. With suspension, positive reinforcement often occurs in combination with negative reinforcement: not only is something aversive removed (the student or the teacher), but something positive is often gained. For example, the student enjoys staying at home and playing video games or is praised by peers for the actions that led to the suspension; and the teacher is praised for not tolerating disobedient and disruptive students.

Many of the limitations of punishment, in general, also apply to unreasonable security measures that result in a high number of suspensions. Perhaps the foremost limitations to suspensions, extensive security measures, and a general zero tolerance approach are (a) they fail to address the multiple factors that contribute to the behaviors leading to the suspension and (b) they often produce undesirable side effects. Both of these limitations, and others, were discussed in Chapter 6. Related to the latter limitation, and more specific to the pervasive use of surveillance, school resource officers, and suspensions, is that these measures can result in an increased, not decreased, number of criminals. This happens in two major ways. First, a greater number of students are arrested in school by school resource officers and then enter the justice system (Na & Gottfredson, 2013). Second, when students are suspended they often are not provided an education, which increases the risk of academic failure, dropping out, and exposure to crime in their communities (Monahan et al., 2014).

Racial Disparities in Exclusionary Practices

During the past several decades, the zero tolerance approach, and particularly the use of suspension, has been the focus of much criticism not only because of its shortcomings and frequent use, but also largely because a disproportionate percentage of black students, compared to white students, are suspended. Compared to white males, black males are three times more likely to be suspended (Musu et al., 2019; Wright, Morgan, Coyne, Beaver, & Barnes, 2014). Research is less consistent in showing disproportionate exclusion of Latino and American Indian students (Gregory et al., 2010). Far too often a greater percentage of black students than white students receives office disciplinary referrals and suspensions not for criminal offenses and nondiscretionary offenses (e.g., fighting, alcohol, and tobacco use), but for relatively minor and discretionary offenses (e.g., noncompliance, arguing with a teacher, skipping classes) (Girvan, Gion, McIntosh, & Smolkowski, 2017; Gregory & Weinstein, 2008; Losen, 2013).

Whereas it is clear that great disparity exists in the percentages of white and black students suspended and expelled, the chief source of this disparity is less clear. The most popular explanation among educational researchers is that racial biases, either explicit or implicit, rather than differences in behavior, account for the disparities (e.g., American Civil Liberties Union, 2013; Gregory et al., 2010; Rocque, 2010; Skiba, Shure, Middelberg, & Baker, 2011; Wald & Losen, 2003). Evidence of racial bias comes from research showing that black students, compared to white students, receive harsher punishment for the same behaviors (Nicholson-Crotty, Birchmeier, & Valentine, 2009; Skiba et al., 2011). Advocates of the racial bias position argue that there is little evidence that a greater percentage of black students than white students exhibit behavior problems.

Not all researchers agree with the conclusion that racial bias is the primary root of disproportionate rates of suspensions. For example, based on their research, Wright et al. (2014) found such a conclusion "as premature if not entirely incorrect" (p. 259). In a longitudinal study, these researchers examined racial differences between black and white students in prior behavior problems (i.e., before suspensions) and current delinquent behaviors. In their study of over 21,000 students throughout the United States, they found that black students were much more likely than white students to have a history of behavior problems prior to being suspended, as rated by their teachers in kindergarten, first grade, and third grade. Parents of black students also rated their children as exhibiting more delinquent behaviors (i.e., stealing, cheating, and fighting) in eighth grade. The researchers concluded that disparities in out-of-school suspensions between the two racial groups were completely explained by differences in prior behavior problems.

It is likely that both positions are correct. That is, as noted by Wright et al. (2014), black students are at an increased risk of exhibiting behaviors that lead to suspension, which they attributed to a greater percentage of black students, compared to white students, who "are less academically prepared for school entrance and suffer from a greater range of social, emotional, and behavioral disadvantages than white or Asian youth" (p. 262). It seems reasonable that a greater percentage of black students, but particularly those living in poverty, would exhibit behavior problems in light of ample research showing that multiple factors related to poverty place children and adolescents at risk for multiple negative outcomes, including behavior problems and criminality (Sharkey, Besbris, & Friedson, 2016). However, researchers also are correct in arguing that racial biases, which often are implicit (Gregory & Mosely, 2004; Gregory et al., 2010), account for disparities in suspension rates, and that suspending students, regardless of race, does little to help those who are repeatedly suspended or who are expelled.

Recommended Strategies and Interventions for Improving School Safety

As emphasized earlier, strategies and interventions for improving all other domains and dimensions of school climate apply to improving school safety. One might improve school safety without improvements in other areas, such as in teacher-student relationships or student engagement, but school climate would be poor. Students might be safer, but like school less. Thus, if one's aim is to make the school safe, while also making it a caring environment conducive to student learning and social-emotional well-being, the following strategies and interventions should always be combined with those found in previous chapters. The following recommendations are ones that are not redundant with those chapters.

1. *Analyze data, including school climate data, related to school safety.* A comprehensive needs assessment should guide decision-making about the need for changes in current policies and practices pertaining to school safety. The needs assessment should include data from multiple sources, especially those consistent with indicators of school safety discussed earlier in this chapter. Especially important indicators of school safety are:
   - office disciplinary referrals
   - suspensions and expulsions
   - police reports and arrests
   - surveys of school climate and safety completed by students, teachers/staff, and parents or caregivers (see Chapter 10)

   Interventions and safety measures should match the needs of the individual school, with those needs reflected in school safety indicators. For example, if data indicate that students are bringing weapons or drugs into the school, then increased security measures such as security cameras, drug sniffing dogs, locker searchers, and metal detectors should be considered (and should be viewed as fair by students). If a school experiences none of the above problems, or minor ones (e.g., infrequent theft, vandalism, bullying), it is unlikely that additional interventions and safety measures are necessary. It is likely, however, that their adoption would lead to students perceiving the school's climate less favorably.

   Although this depends on the type of data collected, in general, the data should be disaggregated by: (a) behavior of concern (e.g., defiance, noncompliance, drugs, fighting); (b) the location where the behavior occurred (e.g., hallway, cafeteria, bus, playground, or parking lot); (c) the person making the referral; and (d) race/ethnicity of the student. More about the general use of disaggregated data is presented in Chapter 10. However, with respect to school safety, the use of disaggregated data is especially valuable when examining for disproportionality in suspension rates, and the likelihood of related implicit bias. As discussed previously, implicit bias is more likely to be found in ODRs and suspensions for noncriminal behaviors, such as defiance and noncompliance. However, data might show that it also is reflected in calls to the police or arrests by school resource officers. For example, the data might show that for the same behavior, police are called more for one racial group than another.

2. *Avoid the lure of simple "quick fixes" to the complex problem of school safety.* The recommendation of avoiding quick fixes applies to all aspects of school climate, but it is perhaps most applicable to school safety. In addition to being ineffective, quick fixes for school safety are often more expensive than quick fixes for other aspects of school climate. Perhaps more importantly, the negative consequences of falsely assuming that the quick fix "works" are more dire: Not only is it likely to fail to improve school safety, it may result in a less positive school climate. Some common, and ineffective, quick fixes *to be avoided* follow:
    - *Student profiling.* This consists of creating a list of characteristics of students most likely to engage in a given act, such as a school shooting. Student profiling became popular shortly after the Columbine shooting, but shortly thereafter studies of school shootings by the U.S. Department of Education, U.S. Secret Service, and the Federal Bureau of Investigation found it to be unreliable and of little usefulness (Fein et al., 2002; Vossekuil, Fein, Reddy, Borum, & Modzeleski, 2002). Those studies showed that although a large number of shooters had been bullied and sought revenge, the shooters did not fit any one profile. Moreover, the studies concluded that attempts to create a profile were leading schools to falsely identify far too many students as being threats to safety.
    - *School uniforms, strict dress code, and ID badges.* Those practices may have other value and be adopted for those reasons (for students to look nicer, and to learn the names of students), but there is little empirical evidence that they make schools any safer. Rarely do they reduce suspensions, and often they greatly increase them, such as when students are suspended for dress code violations or failing to wear an ID badge.
    - *Simply suspending more or fewer students, while doing nothing else.* The number of suspensions varies greatly across schools, and often within the same school over time (Morrison, Redding, Fisher, & Peterson, 2006). It is very easy for a school principal to change the number of suspensions, either reducing or increasing them by simply telling teachers not to refer students, or rarely refer students, to the office. Although the suspension rate declines, this does not necessarily mean that student behavior, school safety, or school climate has improved. To be sure, schools should use suspensions as a last resort and for the most serious rule violations. When used otherwise, their usage should be curtailed, but this should be done in combination with other strategies that address factors contributing to their overuse. These would include student, teacher, and school factors.
    - *Alternative schools and interim alternative educational settings.* The practice of placing students in alternative schools and interim alternative educational placements (IAES) as a consequence of rule violations leading to long-term suspension or expulsion has grown greatly over the past decade. In addition to the popularity of the zero tolerance approach to school discipline, an impetus for such growth has been the provision in the Individuals with Disabilities Education Act that allows schools to remove students with disabilities from their current setting, and without parent approval, and place them in an IAES in special circumstances that threaten school safety. Ordinarily, parent permission

is required to change the placement of a child with a disability. But, to balance the right of students with disabilities to a free and appropriate education with the right of all students to safety this provision was added to the law. In brief, students with disabilities may be removed from their current placement, and without parent approval, and placed into an IAES for the possession of weapons or illegal drugs, serious bodily injury, and substantial likelihood of injury (note that the latter requires a ruling by a hearing officer). An IAES is not defined in the law and can comprise a variety of settings. However, an alternative school is often used as an IAES.

As with suspensions per se, one might argue that removing students under the above circumstances makes schools safer. However, as stated earlier in this chapter, this does little if anything to improve school climate or to help students who are suspended.

Characteristics of an IAES or alternative school that are likely to be effective include: (a) qualified teachers and staff; (b) on-site counseling and related services; (c) a case management and multi-disciplinary team approach to student services; (d) flexibility in program management, decision-making, and role functions; (e) sensitivity to individual and cultural differences; (f) evidence-based practices, linked to assessment, that target social-emotional and academic-vocational behaviors; (g) clear individual and behavioral program goals; (h) sufficient funding and resources; and (i) program evaluation (Bear, Quinn, & Burkholder, 2002). The primary aim of the placement should be to help prevent the reoccurrence of the behavior leading to their removal from school. Unfortunately, too often alternative placements are not characterized by the above, and there is little research showing that they are effective in preventing the reoccurrence of behaviors that led to student removals.

- *Matching teachers and students of same race/ethnicity.* This quick fix is more specific to reducing suspensions than to improving safety and is based on the belief that white teachers are more inclined than black teachers to suspend black students. Bradshaw, Mitchell, O'Brennan, and Leaf (2010) found that black students received no greater office disciplinary referrals from white than from black teachers.
- *Current bandwagons and programs that offer a piecemeal approach with little evidence or no evidence of effectiveness in reducing behavior problems and improving school safety.* Unfortunately, far too often schools adopt strategies and programs that are lacking in evidence of effectiveness beyond testimonials of participants and improvement in areas that might be highly valued but do not translate into reduced behavior problems or greater student safety (e.g., changes in knowledge or awareness of behavioral expectations or emotions). It is not effectiveness research that attracts those schools but instead persuasive and entertaining presenters at workshops and the fear of failing to jump on the current bandwagon and being left behind.

Many of those programs and approaches include strategies that *are* supported by research, such as building and maintaining supportive teacher-student relationships, modeling, and teaching socio-emotional competencies. What is typically lacking, however, is evidence that the programs and approaches offer anything new and that they are more effective than current practices found in many classrooms and evidence-based programs. Examples in the past have been programs focusing on self-esteem, character traits and specific social skills, values clarification, moral education, zero tolerance, and the systematic use of rewards (Bear, 2010). A more recent example appears to be what is referred to as *restorative practices* or the *restorative justice approach* (Advancement Project, 2014). As noted by Song and Swearer (2016, p. 315)

> Schoolwide approaches to RJ [Restorative Justice] are very similar (if not identical in many cases) to other whole-school approaches to intervention such as those found in schoolwide bullying programs and trauma-informed schools; the primary difference is the use of the restorative circle.

Even within the restorative circle, however, it is a great challenge to find any unique strategies, as the strategies employed in the restorative circle are strategies found in active listening (e.g., use of "I" messages) and inductive discipline to foster understanding, expression of emotions, empathy-based guilt, and the assumption of responsibility for one's actions. To be sure, the strategies recommended as restorative practices are often associated with improvements in school climate. However, randomized control group studies are lacking in showing that those practices are more effective in reducing behavior problems and promoting safety when compared to other programs or to practice as normal. In a recent two-year randomized control group study of the effectiveness of restorative practices intervention (including 11 restorative practices), the intervention was found to have no significant impact on any of the outcome measures, including students' perceptions of school climate, connectedness, peer attachment, social skills, and bullying victimization (Acosta et al., 2019).

3. *Adopt a comprehensive and authoritative approach to school discipline and school climate.* This follows on from the above recommendation: Quick fixes do not work. As emphasized throughout this book, if one's aims are the management of student behavior and the development of social and emotional competencies that underlie self-discipline, a comprehensive and authoritative approach is needed. As such, all four critical components of classroom management and school discipline need to be in place (Bear, 2005, 2010): (a) strategies for developing social and emotional competencies, especially those related to self-discipline; (b) strategies for preventing behavior problems; (c) strategies for correcting common behavior problems; and (d) programs and strategies for responding to serious and chronic behavior problems. Practices and strategies within each of those components should be guided by the authoritative approach to classroom management, school discipline, and school climate, as reviewed in Chapter 1, which balances social-emotional support and structure. Research shows that the authoritative approach not only characterizes effective classroom management and school discipline (Bear, 2015), but also high schools with fewer suspensions and smaller racial disproportionality in suspensions (Gregory, Cornell, & Fan, 2011).

4. ***Assure that students are taught social and emotional competencies that promote prosocial behavior and inhibit antisocial behavior.*** Developing social and emotional competencies, especially those most directly related to self-discipline and school safety, should not be viewed as synonymous with preventing and correcting behavior problems, but as a separate component of a comprehensive and authoritative approach to school discipline and school climate (Bear, 2005, 2010). As discussed in Chapter 4, the teaching of social and emotional competencies should be integrated throughout the curriculum and everyday practices of classroom management. Among the competencies most directly related to safety are social and moral decision-making, empathy, impulse control, resisting peer pressure, and getting along with others.
5. ***Ensure that students are aware of threats to safety and understand how to report them, and why they should do so.*** In the majority of student school shootings (and in many suicides), at least one classmate knew about the act of violence ahead of time but failed to inform an adult (Borum et al., 2010). Many other school shootings have been averted by classmates informing adults ahead of time of potential threats (Madfis, 2014). Thus, as has been shown to be true with bullying (Garandeau, Poskiparta, & Salmivalli, 2014), bystanders can play a critical role in preventing many acts of violence. Common reasons why bystanders fail to intervene and report potential acts of violence are the following:
    - They fail to recognize or foresee the seriousness of the threat. For example, they don't think the person is serious about committing the act or is unable to carry it out, or they fail to understand the consequences of the act and not intervening.
    - They do not perceive or accept moral responsibility for intervening. For example, they feel that others should do something about it, such as parents, teachers, or other peers. They fail to recognize a moral and social responsibility to help others—both the perpetrator and potential victims.
    - They fear retaliation or other psychological costs if they report it. This would include physical retaliation, but also emotional and social costs, such as perceived personal distress and being viewed by peers as a "snitch."
    - The belief that no one will or can do anything about it. For example, they found that no one took actions previously when concerns were expressed or they believe that the school can't do much about the threat.
    - Do not know how to help or report it.

    Each of those reasons should be addressed in the contexts of the social and emotional curriculum and school climate. This would include SEL lessons in responsible decision-making and social awareness, especially those focusing on recognizing and understanding the emotions of others, empathy, social perspective-taking, moral responsibility, and social problem-solving. It also would include direct instruction on when and how to intervene and exactly how to report threats of violence and to seek support or help. Such lessons and instructions might be taught in a package curriculum and/or integrated throughout the general curriculum and reinforced in assemblies, school announcements (e.g., on importance of helping others, empathy, kindness), media, pledges taken by students, and so forth.

6. ***Provide resources and supports for students who threaten safety and those who are victims of aggression or violence.*** This applies to all students, but particularly students who are at-risk of engaging in, or have exhibited acts that make schools unsafe, such as students who possess or use drugs, threaten or physically harm others, engage in bullying, or are depressed or suicidal (i.e., students commonly referred to as being at Tiers 2 and 3, or the selective and indicated levels of mental health prevention and intervention). It also would include the victims of acts of aggression, including bullying, who need services. Resources and supports should:
    - Provide for a full range of needs of students and staff, including:
        o mental health evaluations
        o evidence-based interventions
        o threat assessments
        o consultation to teachers, staff, and parents
        o professional training of teachers and staff
        o assessment of school needs, strengths, and weaknesses
    - Be readily available in-school and out-of-school. In-school services are likely to be provided by school counselors, school psychologists, school social workers, and school resources officers. Out-of-school services are likely to be provided by private and public agencies, including mental health, social services, and law enforcement agencies. Close coordination and collaboration of services and supports should exist between the school and outside agencies. Teachers, staff, and parents need to be aware of the availability of services and supports, and how to obtain them.
    - Be sufficient to meet the needs of all students and teachers. This would include having a sufficient number of support staff, and the staff having sufficient time. It also includes assistance in helping provide services to the home, when needed.
7. ***Establish protocols for assessing the seriousness of threats of violence.*** Not all threats are serious, but all should be taken seriously. A particular challenge to schools is to screen out threats that have a low probability of resulting in actual harm or disruption, while devoting much greater attention to serious threats. Threat assessment interview protocols exist to help schools with this challenge. When conducted successfully, threat assessments avoid schools over-reacting to many threats that are not serious or pose an actual threat and avoid under-reacting to serious threats and students in need of mental health services (Flannery et al., 2019). Threat assessment interviews also are often effective in deterring others from acts of violence by making them aware that their threats are noticed and taken seriously (Amman et al., 2017). Research indicates that schools using threat assessments, compared to those not using them, have fewer suspensions and reports of aggression and bullying; have students who are more willing to report concerns about threatening behavior to school authorities; and have teachers who report more positive perceptions of school safety (Cornell, 2015; Cornell, Allen, & Fan, 2012; Cornell, Sheras, Gregory, & Fan, 2009).

    Most often, the student interview is conducted by a school psychologist, school counselor, or school resource officer. Ideally, there should be more than one individual in the school at all times who is trained in threat assessment. Interview questions typically address the student's motives, goals, and intentions; interests in weapons and earlier school attacks, and other aggressive and violent acts; the student's violence-related behavior; availability of weapons; relationships with others, including having at least one adult he or she trusts and confides in; and circumstances surrounding the threat and the likelihood of the violent act of occurring (Vossekuil et al., 2002).

The interview protocol with the most supporting research is that of the Virginia threat assessment model (Cornell, 2018). Studies show that schools using the protocol, compared to those not using it, have fewer suspensions and reports of aggression and bullying (Cornell, 2015; Cornell et al., 2012, 2009); students in those schools are more likely to view school discipline as fair and more willing to report concerns about threatening behavior to school authorities (Cornell, 2015; Cornell et al., 2009); and teachers in those schools are more likely to report feeling safe (Cornell, 2015). In this model, results of student interviews and other sources of information are guided by a step-by-step decision tree used to evaluate threats of violence, ranging from fights to shootings. A key element is differentiating substantive or serious and very serious threats from transient threats (i.e., threats not likely to be serious). Guidelines are provided as to how to respond to either type of threat. For all serious and very serious threats, schools are advised to take immediate precautions for potential victims; notify the student's parents; contact or consult with law enforcement; seek a mental health evaluation; initiate counseling and/or other interventions; and discipline the student, as appropriate, based on the seriousness of the threat.

8. *When students are referred to the office for misbehavior, develop a plan with the student to help prevent the misbehavior from reoccurring.* This applies to all referrals to the office, but especially those resulting in suspension (in school or out of school), placements in alternative settings, and other placements outside of school. As discussed in Chapter 7 on correcting behavior problems, the plan, either formal or informal, should consist of two major parts: (1) what the teacher, others in the school, and the home will do to help prevent the behavior from reoccurring and (2) what the student will do to help prevent the behavior from reoccurring.

9. *Ensure that a comprehensive crisis response plan is in place and the school is prepared for a crisis.* Despite the best efforts for making school safe, acts of violence nevertheless occur; thus, schools must be prepared to respond. Every school and school district should have a crisis plan in place and a crisis response team ready to implement it. Many states require this by law, including annual reviews of the plan and practice drills. The four most common components of a plan are prevention, preparedness, response, and recovery.
   - **Prevention** includes strategies throughout this book for promoting a positive school climate.
   - **Preparedness** entails having a crisis intervention plan, with teachers, staff, and students trained in its implementation; having highly trained staff available to conduct threat assessments and to respond to a crisis; and ensuring that outside agencies and supports (especially law enforcement) are prepared to respond immediately to a crisis.

- **Response** refers to how the crisis plan is actually implemented during the time of a crisis. It includes the communication and coordination between the school, district office, and outside agencies; securing and evacuating the building; preventing or curtailing harm; arranging medical and mental health care; notifying parents; and working with the media and others to inform the public.
- **Recovery** refers to actions needed after the crisis has occurred: meeting the full range of mental health needs of students and staff by providing support and counseling to individuals and groups. As with preparation and response, this component of crisis response should be planned well before a crisis occurs.

Specific steps, recommendations, and practical tools for implementing each of these components can be found in the comprehensive (and free) *NEA's School Crisis Guide* (National Education Association, 2018). Another very useful model for crisis response is the PREPaRE model (Brock et al., 2009) of the National Association of School Psychologists (NASP). This model, however, is more useful for mental health workers than for general educators and is designed particularly for providing training. As with the NEA model, the NASP model incorporates security and safety recommendations from the U.S. Department of Education and Homeland Security. In this model PREPaRE refers to: *Prevent* crisis and psychological trauma, *Reaffirm* physical health and perceptions of security and safety, *Evaluate* psychological trauma risks, *Provide* interventions, *Respond* to psychological needs, and *Examine* the effectiveness of crisis prevention and intervention.

10. *Provide professional development on school safety and on-going support and resources.* Training for all teachers and staff should be both general and specific. Whereas all staff should be trained in preventing, preparing, and responding to a crisis, the level of training should vary depending on each staff member's role, responsibility, and individual training needs. Whereas all staff should be skilled in strategies for preventing a crisis and in implementing their school's response plan during a crisis, school administrators should receive additional training in the coordinating services and communicating with outside agencies and the media. Likewise, mental health professionals should receive greater training in such areas as threat assessment, trauma-informed interventions, and mental health consultation. However, professional development should be based on each individual's skills and needs, as well as on the general needs, strengths, and weaknesses of the school. It also should not be a one-time occurrence, but should include on-going training, supervision, and support, which should include necessary resources. Among topics that should be considered for professional development are:
    - Conflict resolution and aggression de-escalation techniques.
    - Trauma-informed interventions.
    - Suicide prevention and intervention.
    - Bullying prevention and intervention (including cyberbullying).
    - Home-school collaboration and communication.
    - Ethical and legal use of physical restraint, such as for student fights.
    - Procedures for reporting and receiving help and support before, during, and after a crisis.

- Resources and supports for students, teachers/staff, and parents, especially availability of mental health services for students who threaten or act violently and for victims of violence. This should include roles and responsibilities of support staff, such as school counselors, school psychologists, and school resource officers.
- The relation of school climate in all aspects of school crisis: prevention, preparation, response, and recovery, but especially in prevention (e.g., the importance of positive teacher-student and student-student relationships and the teaching of social and emotional competencies).
- Ethical and legal responsibilities in responding to threats and acts of violence, especially suicide and bullying.
- Security measures in the building; their purpose, limitations, and how to use them most effectively.
- Where appropriate (e.g., urban high schools), the role of gang affiliation in matters of school safety, especially for preventing weapon use. Training should include helping students resist peer pressure to join a gang and how to get out of a gang (see Sharkey & Janes, 2019).

Summary

Whether or not schools are safe depends largely on how one defines safety. However, with respect to being safe from acts of violence, including physical assault and shootings, students (and teachers) are much safer in school than most other places (Mayer & Jimerson, 2019). This includes restaurants, highways, and homes—places where calls for increased security are rarely if ever heard. On average, one should expect a school shooting to occur in a given school about once every 6,000 years (Borum et al., 2010).

One might argue, however, that few schools are safe based on other common indicators of school safety, such as bullying, fights, drug possession, school suspensions, and other indicators discussed in this chapter. Regardless, if one concludes that schools are safe or unsafe, it is well established that school safety, and particularly perceptions of safety on the part of students and staff, is a critical dimension of school climate. It is closely related to all other domains and dimensions of school climate. Thus, if one's goal is to create and maintain a safe school, it behooves schools to target all areas of school climate for improvement. In doing so, schools need to strive to adopt an authoritative approach, rather than an authoritarian or zero tolerance approach, to school discipline; one that focuses much more on relationships and building social and emotional competencies than on the use of suspensions and other forms of punishment. Strategies and interventions for doing so were presented in this chapter, as well as throughout the book.

CHAPTER 10

ASSESSING SCHOOL CLIMATE AND LINKING RESULTS TO EFFECTIVE PRACTICES

In light of research presented throughout this book associating multiple and various aspects of school climate to highly valued educational outcomes including student behavior and academic achievement, it is no wonder that the number of instruments for assessing school climate have increased greatly during the past decade. As noted in Chapter 1, the recent interest among educators in assessing school climate also has been sparked by school climate frequently being targeted for improvement in universal-level prevention and promotion programs. As also discussed in that chapter, growing interest in school climate and its assessment can be linked to the following actions or initiatives by the U.S. Department of Education: (a) funding School Climate Transformation Grants for states and local educational agencies to improve (and assess) school climate; (b) creating and disseminating school climate materials and resources to schools, including a web-based measure of school climate and a guide for improving school climate (see https://safesupportivelearning.ed.gov/SCIRP/Quick-Guide); and (c) including a provision in the Every Student Succeeds Act that requires schools to use a minimum of four accountability indicators, with one indicator being of school quality, which may consist of "school climate and safety" (see www.ed.gov/essa).

This chapter discusses the Delaware School Surveys and how they are used to help schools identify areas of school climate in need of improvements and to persuade major stakeholders (e.g., teachers, support staff, students, and parents) that there is a *need* for change. The Delaware School Surveys consist of the Delaware School Climate Surveys, which focus on the major domains of school climate, and four additional supplemental surveys that assess factors often viewed as school climate inputs or outcomes (or both)—factors that influence and are influenced by school climate, as discussed in Chapter 1. Those factors include bullying victimization, student engagement, social and emotional competencies, and teachers' use of positive, punitive, and social and emotional learning techniques for classroom management. The surveys were developed at the University of Delaware's Center for Disabilities Studies, with funding from the Delaware Department of Education (DDOE) and a 5-year School Climate Transformation Grant from the U.S. Department of Education. The surveys are administered annually in Delaware schools, with participation being voluntary (although many school districts require them). Administration, scoring, data processing, school reports, and professional training workshops related to the surveys and improving school climate are provided by the DDOE.

Although other good instruments (and many poor ones) exist for assessing school climate, the Delaware surveys are the focus in this chapter for several reasons. First, the surveys include one or more scales that align with the topics of eight chapters in this book (i.e., teacher-student relationships, student-student relationships, student engagement, social and emotional competencies, preventing behavior problems, correcting behavior problems, bullying, and school safety). Thus, they provide educators and researchers with useful tools for assessing each of those aspects of school climate to help determine a school's strengths and weaknesses and need for change. Without demonstrating a need for change, the greatest resistance to change should be expected (Curtis, Castillo, & Cohen, 2008; Fullan, 2007). Second, as discussed in the following section, the surveys are designed to be of high practical utility. Third, the surveys are among the few tools for assessing school climate that are guided by theory and supported by multiple published studies presenting evidence of validity and reliability of their scores. The guiding theory and research are discussed later in this chapter.

Delaware School Surveys

The Delaware School Surveys were designed to provide schools with psychometrically sound instruments for assessing a school's strengths and needs in the most commonly recognized areas of school climate. Schools find the survey data of value when developing school improvement plans by helping them identify areas needing improvement. Having been used by approximately 70% of public schools in Delaware for over 10 years, the surveys have been continually revised in response to feedback from schools and studies of their psychometric properties. The surveys offer the following practical features that schools find appealing:

- *Free to the public.* Because their development was funded by state and federal funds, schools may make copies for non-profit use. Copies of the surveys, a technical manual, and additional related resources can be downloaded from: http://wh1.oet.udel.edu/pbs/school-climate/de-school-climate-survey/.
- *Student, teacher/staff, and home versions.* The student version is for grades 3–12, except for the Delaware Bullying Victimization Survey which is for grades 6–12. However, a reading level of third grade or above is required, unless the items are read aloud. The teacher/staff and home versions are for all grades, preschool–12.
- *Flexibility in choice of scales and subscales.* Whereas the multiple scales on the surveys are typically administered together (e.g., the five scales on the student survey), each scale can be administered alone. For example, a school interested in assessing only school climate and bullying victimization might choose to administer the Delaware School Climate Scale and Delaware Bullying Victimization Scale, but not the other three scales on the student version. Likewise, a school might stagger the administration of the scales, administering selected scales and subscales (or student, teacher, and home versions) one year, and others another year.

- *Brevity: Each scale requires little time to complete.* Completion of the School Climate Scale takes about 10 minutes for most students to complete (less time for teachers and parents). The four supplemental scales take approximately 3–5 minutes each.
- *The same or very similar items are found on all three versions and at all grade levels.* This allows schools to compare scores on the same scales, subscales, and items between groups, such as between students, teachers/staff, and parents; between students at different grade levels; and between respondents of different racial/ethnic groups. This feature also allows for comparisons, using the same items, from year to year.
- *Scales and subscales align with the goals commonly targeted in most programs for preventing behavior problems, promoting mental health, and improving school climate.* With 5 scales and 23 subscales, the surveys tap multiple aspects of school climate and related outcomes commonly targeted in the SEL and SWPBIS approaches.
- *Completed via computer device (i.e., computer, tablet, or cellphone) or hard copy.* In Delaware, the teacher/staff version is completed only via computer device, whereas both computer and print options (using Scantron forms) are used for completion of the student and home versions.
- *Detailed data reports and guidelines for interpreting the data.*[1] The DDOE provides schools in Delaware with scoring of the surveys and extensive score reports. The reports help schools examine differences in scores between groups (e.g., grade, gender, and racial/ethnic groups) and determine specific strengths and weaknesses.
- *Staff development and training modules.* Schools are encouraged to address identified areas of strength and weakness. The DDOE has developed eight staff development and training modules that provide schools with evidence-based strategies for addressing unfavorable scores in the areas of teacher-student relationships, student-student relationships, student engagement, school safety, bullying victimization, fairness of rules, and social and emotional competencies. Another module provides guidance on integrating the SEL and SWPBIS approaches to improve school climate.

As shown in Table 10.1, the Delaware School Surveys include the Delaware School Climate Scale (DSCS) and four supplemental scales: the Delaware Bullying Victimization Scale (DBVS), Delaware Student Engagement Scale (DSES), Delaware Positive, Punitive, and SEL Techniques Scale (DTS), and the Delaware Social and Emotional Competencies Scale (DSECS). Only the student version includes all five scales. The home survey includes three scales (DSCS, DBVS, DSES) and the teacher/staff survey includes two scales (DSCS, DTS). A description of each scale follows. After the scales are described, evidence supporting the validity and reliability of scores on the scales is summarized. That evidence is presented separately for the DSCS because it is more extensive. For the four supplemental scales, the evidence of validity and reliability is summarized together for all four scales since the evidence is similar across the scales. Readers are referred to the technical manual for more information about each scale, especially for evidence supporting the validity and reliability of scores, as well as for norms based on students in Delaware schools (presented for grade levels, race/ethnicity, and gender).

Table 10.1 Scales and Subscales of the Delaware School Surveys (number of items is in parentheses)

Student Survey	Teacher/Staff Survey	Home Survey
\multicolumn{3}{c}{**Delaware School Climate Scale**}		
Teacher-Student Relationships (5)	Teacher-Student Relationships (5)	Teacher-Student Relationships (5)
Student-Student Relationships (5)	Student-Student Relationships (5)	Student-Student Relationships (5)
Clarity of Expectations (4)	Clarity of Expectations (4)	Clarity of Expectations (4)
Fairness of Rules (4)	Fairness of Rules (4)	Fairness of Rules (4)
School Safety (3)	School Safety (3)	School Safety (3)
Student Engagement-Schoolwide (6)	Student Engagement-Schoolwide (6)	
Bullying Schoolwide (3)	Bullying Schoolwide (3)	
	Teacher-Home Communications (4)	Teacher-Home Communications (4)
	Teacher/Staff Relationships (4)	
Total School Climate (30)	Total School Climate (38)	Total School Climate (25)
		Parent Satisfaction[1] (4)
\multicolumn{3}{c}{**Delaware Positive, Punitive, and SEL Techniques Scale**}		
Positive Behavior Techniques (5)	Positive Behavioral Techniques (5)	
Punitive Techniques (5)	Punitive Techniques (5)	
Social Emotional Learning Techniques (6)	Social Emotional Learning Techniques (6)	
Total Score (16)	Total Score (16)	
\multicolumn{3}{c}{**Delaware Bullying Victimization Scale**}		
Physical Bullying[2] (4)		Physical Bullying (4)
Verbal Bullying[2] (4)		Verbal Bullying (4)
Social/Relational Bullying[2] (4)		Social/Relational Bullying (4)
Cyberbullying[3] (4)		Cyberbullying[3] (4)
Total Score (16 items, with Cyberbullying subscale)		Total Score (16 items, with Cyberbullying subscale)
\multicolumn{3}{c}{**Delaware Student Engagement Scale**}		
Cognitive (4)		Cognitive (4)
Behavioral (4)		Behavioral (4)
Emotional (4)		Emotional (4)
Total Score (12)		Total Score (12)

(continued)

Assessing School Climate   171

Table 10.1 (continued)

Student Survey	Teacher/Staff Survey	Home Survey
Delaware Social and Emotional Competencies Scale		
Self-Management (4)		
Responsible Decision-making (4)		
Social Awareness (4)		
Relationship Skills (4)		
Total Score (16)		

Note: The number of items on each subscale and scale is in parenthesis.
[1] The score on the Parent Satisfaction subscale is not included in the total school climate score.
[2] Grades 6–12 only for the printed version. Optional for grades 4–5 with computer version.
[3] Grades 6–12 only.

Delaware School Climate Scale (DSCS)

As shown in Table 10.1, the DSCS has five subscales and 25 items in common across the student, teacher/staff, and home versions. The student and teacher/staff versions include two additional subscales not found on the home version: Student Engagement Schoolwide and Bullying Schoolwide. These two subscales were not included on the home version because it is thought that students and teachers/staff are better judges than parents of schoolwide student engagement and bullying victimization. Although parents are not asked to complete the Schoolwide Student Engagement and Bullying Victimization subscales of the DSCS, they are administered two other scales in which they are asked to rate the engagement and bullying victimization for their *individual* child (i.e., the Delaware Student Engagement Scale and the Delaware Bullying Victimization Scale).

Items on the seven subscales of the student version of the DSCS appear in Table 10.2. Students respond to each item using a Likert scale of 1 = Disagree a lot, 2 = Disagree, 3 = Agree, and 4 = Agree a lot. A score for each subscale is derived by averaging responses across the subscale's five items, with possible scores ranging from 1 to 4. Higher scores reflect more favorable perceptions, with the exception of scores on the Bullying Schoolwide subscale wherein lower scores are more favorable (i.e., there is less bullying). A total school climate score is derived by averaging all item scores (with scores for Bullying Schoolwide reverse scored). The same response and scoring formats are used for the teacher/staff and home versions.

In addition to the five subscales that all three versions have in common, the teacher/staff version includes two subscales not found on the student version: Teacher/Staff Relations and Teacher-Home Communications. The following items are on Teacher/Staff Relations subscale:

- Teachers, staff, and administrators function as a good team.
- There is good communication among teachers, staff, and administrators.

Table 10.2 Items on the Delaware School Climate Scale (Student Version)

Subscale	Items
Teacher-Student Relations	Teachers treat students of all races with respect. Teachers care about their students. Teachers listen to students when they have problems. Adults who work here care about the students. Teachers like their students.
Student-Student Relations	Students are friendly with each other. Students care about each other. Students respect others who are different. Students treat each other with respect. Students get along with each other.
Student Engagement Schoolwide[1]	Most students turn in their homework on time. Most students try their best. Most students follow the rules. Most students like this school. Most students work hard to get good grades. Most students feel happy.
Clarity of Expectations	Rules are made clear to students. Students know how they are expected to act. Students know what the rules are. It is clear how students are expected to act.
Fairness of Rules	The school rules are fair. The consequences of breaking rules are fair. The school's Code of Conduct is fair. Classroom rules are fair.
School Safety	Students are safe in the hallways. Students feel safe. Students know they are safe in this school.
Bullying Schoolwide[1]	Students threaten and bully others. Students worry about others bullying them. Students bully one another.
Validity Screening Item (not scored)	I am lying on this survey.

[1] Subscales included on the teacher/staff version, but not on the home version of the survey.

- Teachers, staff, and administrators work well together.
- Administrators and teachers support one another.

The following items are on the Teacher-Home Communications subscale:

- Teachers work closely with parents to help students when they have problems.
- Teachers do a good job communicating with parents.
- Teachers show respect toward parents.
- Teachers listen to the concerns of parents.

The home version includes two subscales not found on the student version: the Teacher-Home Communications subscale and the Parent Satisfaction subscale. Items on the Teacher-Home Communications subscale are the same as those listed previously for the Teacher/Staff subscale. Items on the Parent Satisfaction subscale are:

- Overall, the climate is positive.
- I am satisfied with the education students get.
- I am pleased with school discipline.
- I like this school.

Items on the Parent Satisfaction subscale are not calculated into the total school climate score. This is because that subscale does not assess a distinct domain of school climate, but parents' overall satisfaction with the school's climate based on perceptions across all domains of school climate.

Theoretical Roots. As with each of the other scales on the Delaware School Surveys, the DSCS is grounded in social-cognitive theory (Bandura, 1986; Bandura, Capara, Barbaranelli, Pastorelli, & Regalia, 2001) and ecological systems theory (Bronfenbrenner, 1979), which recognize that multiple factors operate at different system levels (e.g., individual, classroom, school, home, community), and in reciprocal fashions, in determining human behavior. Both theories view an individual's perceptions of the social environment (especially social transactions), rather than objective reality per se, as of primary importance in understanding human behavior. Thus, how students perceive the school environment is a stronger predictor of important social, emotional, and academic outcomes for students than what actually *occurs* in school.

The DSCS also is based on two theoretical frameworks more specific to school discipline and school climate, yet consistent with social-cognitive and ecological systems theories: (a) authoritative discipline theory (Baumrind, 1971, 1996, 2013; Bear, 2005; Brophy, 1996; Gregory & Cornell, 2009) and (b) Stockard and Mayberry's (1992) theoretical framework of school climate. Those two frameworks were discussed in Chapter 1. To one extent or another, each of the subscales align with one or both of the two dimensions in the two frameworks. Some subscales align more closely with one dimension than another, whereas others tend to incorporate aspects of both dimensions in the two frameworks. For example, two subscales of the DSCS align conceptually well with the responsiveness dimension in authoritative discipline theory and the social action dimension in Stockard and Mayberry's framework: Teacher-Student Relationships and Student-Student Relationships. Additionally, the Social Emotional Learning Techniques subscale of the Delaware Positive, Punitive/Corrective, and Social-Emotional Learning Techniques Scale also aligns well with the construct of responsiveness/social action. High scores on those subscales indicate high responsiveness/social action. Three other subscales of the DSCS align closely with the structure dimension in school discipline theory and with social order in Stockard and Mayberry's framework: Clarity of Expectations, Fairness of Rules, and Home-School Communication. Other subscales, however, are better viewed as representing a combination of both responsiveness/social action and demandingness/social order, or as outcomes of those two dimensions: Student Engagement Schoolwide, School Safety, and Bullying Schoolwide.

Two additional scales were not designed to assess either responsiveness/social action or demandingness/social action: Teacher/Staff Relations (found only on the Teacher/Staff survey) and Parent Satisfaction (found only on the Home survey). The Teacher/Staff Relations subscale was added in response to observations voiced by teachers and school staff (and by DDOE) that the relations between teachers and staff are an important part of school climate, as recognized on several other teacher surveys of school climate (Cohen, McCabe, Michelli, & Pickeral, 2009; Zullig, Koopman, Patton, & Ubbes, 2010). Although recognized as important in school climate, there is not a strong case for teacher/staff relations clearly constituting responsiveness or structure. Indeed, one might argue that it aligns with both or neither.

Evidence of Validity and Reliability. Face and content validity of the DSCS is supported by the scale being grounded in theory and research, supporting the importance of each of the multiple domains of school climate assessed, as well as their inclusion in most conceptualizations and measures of school climate. Research evidence of validity and reliability of scores on the student, teacher/staff, and home versions of the school climate scale can be found in the instrument's technical manual (Bear et al., 2019). Additional evidence from research studies appears in peer-reviewed journals reporting on the psychometric properties of the student version (Bear, Gaskins, Blank, & Chen, 2011; Bear et al., 2019), teacher/staff version (Bear, Yang, Pell, & Gaskins, 2014), and home version (Bear, Yang, & Pasipanodya, 2014). Those sources provide evidence of construct validity and criterion-related validity of scores on the scales and subscales.

Construct validity refers to the extent to which a scale assesses what it claims to assess, whereas criterion-related validity refers to the extent to which a scale relates to important outcomes. With respect to construct validity, results of confirmatory factor analyses (CFA) support the factor structure of the surveys and measurement invariance across grade levels (elementary, middle, and high school), racial/ethnic groups, and gender. Such results are necessary for schools to accurately compare scores between groups. Evidence of criterion-related validity is seen in scores across the student, teacher/staff, and home versions correlating positively with student academic achievement and negatively with school suspensions. Scores on the student version also have been shown to relate positively with student engagement (Bear et al., 2019; Yang, Bear, & May, 2018) and negatively with disciplinary infractions (Fefer & Gordon, 2018). For the home version, in addition to correlating positively with academic achievement and negatively with suspensions, Bear et al. (2014) found that school climate scores correlated negatively with parents reporting that their child was bullied in school. Finally, low scores on the teacher/staff version were found to be associated with teachers reporting greater emotional exhaustion and depersonalization, less personal accomplishment, and more negative overall well-being (Xie, Peng, Zhu, Yang, & Bear, 2018).

With respect to the reliability of scores, the technical manual (Bear et al., 2019) reports acceptable coefficients of internal consistency for subscale and scale scores. Across grade levels (i.e., elementary, middle, and high school), coefficients range from .86 to .89 for the total score and .70 to .87 for subscale scores on the student version; .92 to .94 for the total score and .82 to .96 for subscale scores on the teacher/staff version; and .96 to .98 for the total score and .86 to .93 for subscale scores on the home version. Alpha coefficients also are reported for each grade, grades 3–12 for the student version range from .85 to .90 for the total score and from .62 to .87 for subscale scores. Coefficients for subscale scores fell below .70 only at grade 3 (ranging from .62 to .84), warranting caution in the use of subscale scores at that grade level.

Delaware Positive, Punitive, and Social-Emotional Learning Techniques Scale

As discussed and reviewed throughout this book, how teachers and staff manage student behavior is widely recognized as a major determinant of school climate. The Delaware Positive, Punitive, and SEL Techniques Scale (DTS) assesses perceptions among students and teachers/staff of the extent to which positive, punitive, and social-emotional techniques are used in their school to manage student behavior and develop self-discipline. The scale consists of three subscales: Positive Behavioral Techniques, Punitive Disciplinary Techniques, and Social Emotional Learning Techniques. Items on the three subscales are shown in Table 10.3. Students respond to each item using the same 4-point Likert scale used on the school climate scale, and subscale scores (ranging from 1 to 4) are derived in the same manner as on that scale. Whereas higher scores on Positive Behavioral Techniques and SEL techniques are favorable, high scores on the Punitive Techniques subscale are unfavorable.

The Positive Behavioral Techniques subscale consists of five items that assess the extent to which students, teachers, and staff recognize students' behavior with praise and rewards. As discussed in Chapter 5, when used wisely and strategically, praise and rewards provide invaluable feedback to students, reinforce student behavior, and foster positive teacher-student relationships.

The Punitive Techniques subscale consists of five items that assess the perceived use of harsh punitive consequences of behavior, as often associated with the zero tolerance approach to school discipline and with a *negative* school climate. The scale is not intended to assess milder punitive consequences that *are* commonly used by the most effective classroom teachers and schools, in combination with positive behavioral techniques, to manage student behavior, such as taking away privileges, verbal reprimands, and physical proximity.

The *Social-Emotional Learning Techniques* subscale is comprised of six items that assess the perceived use of SEL techniques commonly associated with the Social and Emotional Learning approach (as reviewed in Chapter 4) and particularly for developing responsible decision-making, self-management, social awareness, and relationship skills.

Table 10.3 Items on the Positive, Punitive, and SEL Techniques Scale

Positive Behavioral Techniques	Students are praised often.
	Students are often given rewards for being good.
	Teachers often let students know when they are being good.
	Classes get rewards for good behavior.
	Teachers use just enough praise and rewards; not too much or too little.
Punitive Techniques	Students are punished a lot.
	Students are often sent out of class for breaking rules.
	Students are often yelled at by adults.
	Many students are sent to the office for breaking rules.
	Students are punished too much for minor things.
SEL Techniques	Students are taught to feel responsible for how they act.
	Students are taught to understand how others think and feel.
	Students are taught that they can control their own behavior.
	Students are taught how to solve conflicts with others.
	Students are taught they should care about how others feel.
	Students are often asked to help decide what is best for the class or school.

Delaware Bullying Victimization Scale

The *Delaware Bullying Victimization Scale* (DBVS), which is included on the student and home surveys, is comprised of four subscales: Verbal Bullying, Physical Bullying, Social/Relational Bullying, and Cyberbullying. Students respond on a 6-point Likert scale by indicating the degree to which they have been victims of the given bullying behavior in school since the beginning of the school year. On the home version, parents complete the same items while referring to their child's bullying victimization. Scores for the item choices are: 1 = Never, 2 = Sometimes, 3 = Once or Twice a Month, 4 = Once a Week, 5 = Several Times a Week, and 6 = Every Day.

Items for the verbal, physical, and social/relational subscales were adapted from the Adolescent Peer Relations Instrument: Bully/Target (Marsh et al., 2011; Parada, 2000). In Delaware, the cyberbullying items are administered to all students in grades 6–12 and are optional for grades 4–5 when completed via computer. Subscale scores are derived for each of the four subscales by averaging item responses on the respective subscale, and a total scale score is computed by averaging item responses across the three (or four) subscales. Two separate total scores are calculated for the student version: one includes the cyberbullying subscale and the other excludes it. Computing a total score without cyberbullying allows schools to compare total scores across grade levels while using the same three subscales administered in all grades. Providing two different total scores also is consistent with a current debate among researchers over whether or not cyberbullying is best viewed as the same construct as the other three forms of bullying, especially since it most often occurs outside of the school (e.g., Olweus, 2012). Because cyberbullying items do not appear on the home version, that total score does not include cyberbullying.

Table 10.4 Items on the Delaware Bullying Victimization Scale

Verbal Bullying	I was teased by someone saying hurtful things to me. A student said mean things to me. I was called names I didn't like. Hurtful jokes were made up about me.
Physical Bullying	I was pushed or shoved on purpose. I was hit or kicked and it hurt. A student stole or broke something of mine on purpose. A student threatened to harm me.
Social/Relational Bullying	Students left me out of things to make me feel badly. A student told/got others not to like me. A student got others to say mean things about me. Students told another student not to be friends with me because the other students didn't like me.
Cyberbullying	A student *sent me* a mean or hurtful message about me using email, text messaging, instant messaging, or similar electronic messaging. A student *sent to others* a mean or hurtful message about me using email, text messaging, instant messaging, or similar electronic messaging. A student *posted* something mean or hurtful about me on a social media website such as Facebook, Twitter, or Instagram. A student *pretending to be me* sent or posted something hurtful or mean *about me or others* using text messaging, a social media website, email, or a similar method.
Items Not Scored	I was bullied in this school.

In addition to the items assessing verbal, social/relational, physical, and cyberbullying behaviors (see Table 10.4), there is an additional single item referring to being bullied in general: "I was bullied in this school" on the student version, and "My child was bullied in this school" on the home version. Responses to this item are not included on the subscale or full-scale score. The item was designed to stand alone for schools to examine if students and parents who report specific bullying behaviors also report "bullying." Research shows that survey respondents are much more likely to report bullying behaviors, such as teasing, than bullying per se (Bear, Whitcomb, Elias, & Blank, 2015).

Delaware Student Engagement Scale

The Delaware Student Engagement Scale (DSES), included on the student and home versions of the surveys, assesses three types of student engagement: cognitive, behavioral, and emotional. A description of each type and supporting research as to their importance are presented in Chapter 7. As with the bullying victimization scale, items target the individual student, either the student completing the scale or the child of the parent completing it. Items on the three subscales of the student version appear in Table 10.5. The same items appear on

Table 10.5 Items on the Delaware Student Engagement Scale (Student Version)

Behavioral Engagement	I pay attention in class.
	I follow the rules at school.
	When I don't do well, I work harder.
	I stay out of trouble at school.
Cognitive Engagement	I try my best in school.
	I turn in my homework on time.
	I get good grades in school.
	I have plans for more school or training after high school.
Emotional Engagement	I feel happy in school.
	My school is a fun place to be.
	I like the students who go to this school.
	I like this school.

the home version but are worded to refer to the child of the parent (e.g., "My child pays attention in class.") Participants respond on the same 4-point Likert scale used with the school climate and classroom management techniques scales, and subscale and total scale scores are computed in the same manner as on those two scales.

Delaware Social and Emotional Competencies Scale

The *Delaware Social and Emotional Competencies Scale* (DSECS) assesses four of the five social and emotional competencies identified by the Collaborative for Academic, Social, and Emotional Learning (CASEL, 2019) and targeted in many SEL programs: *responsible decision-making, relationship skills, self-management,* and *social awareness*. Those competencies, as described in Chapter 4, have been shown to be important to students' academic achievement and mental health. The social-emotional competency of *self-awareness* is not included on the current edition of the DSECS.[2] Several reasons are given in the manual for its exclusion. The first concerns the appropriateness of schools surveying students' feelings of self-esteem, depression, and overall emotional well-being without obtaining active consent from students and parents. In Delaware schools, active consent is not required for the Delaware surveys. It is very likely that requiring it would greatly reduce student participation. This is not only because many students and parents would decline to participate or fail to return consent forms, but also because some school districts are likely to view administering the surveys as not worth the hassle of obtaining consent. Although screening for mental health concerns is important, this is not a purpose of the Delaware surveys.

Another reason for excluding self-awareness is that although it is typically included in state SEL standards for preschool and early elementary school, it is less often included in higher grades. Thus, it is unclear what items for assessing self-awareness might be included across all grade levels. Finally, the authors argue that several items assessing the important aspects of self-awareness are already included on the surveys, as found on the Delaware Student Engagement Scale and other subscales of the DSECS. These include such items on the DSES

Table 10.6 Items on the Delaware Student Social and Emotional Competencies Scale

Responsible Decision-making/ Responsibility	I feel responsible for how I act.
	I am good at deciding right from wrong.
	I make good decisions.
	I think about the consequences of what I do.
Understanding How Others Think and Feel/Social Awareness	I think about how others feel.
	I care about how others feel.
	I respect what others think.
	I try to understand how others think and feel.
Self-management of Emotions and Behavior	I can control how I behave.
	I think before I act.
	I can control my anger.
	I can calm myself when upset.
Relationship Skills	I am good at solving conflicts with others.
	I get along well with others.
	I am kind to others.
	I help others.

as: "I follow the rules at school." "I try my best in school." and "I feel happy in school." Self-awareness, particularly self-efficacy, also is captured in multiple items on the other four DSECS subscales, including: "I am good at solving conflicts with others." "I am good at waiting for what I want." and "I am good at deciding right from wrong."

The four subscales, and the respective items, are shown in Table 10.6. Students respond to each of the 16 items item using a 4-point Likert scale, with 4 = Very much like me, 3 = Somewhat like me, 2 = Not much like me, and 1 = Not like me at all. Subscale scores are calculated by averaging scores across items for the respective subscale. A total scale score consists of the average scores across all 16 items.

Evidence of Validity and Reliability for the Four Supplemental Scales

As noted previously, extensive evidence of the validity and reliability of scores on each of the scales is presented in the technical manual for the surveys. Such evidence includes the results of the confirmatory factor analyses (CFA) conducted on each scale and across student, teacher/staff, and home versions. Results supported either a bifactor or second-order factor for each of the four supplementary scales (and also for the School Climate Scale). The advantages of these two models is that they allow for the use of both subscale and full scale scores. Results of the CFA conducted on the Positive, Punitive, and SEL Techniques Scale supported a three-factor model and was chosen as the preferred model. This model does not support combining subscale scores to create a total score; thus, a total score is not computed for this scale.

With respect to criterion-related validity, with a few exceptions as reported in the manual, scores on each of the scales and subscales correlated, as predicted, with the total school climate score. Additional evidence of criterion-related validity is reported in school climate scores, at the school-level, correlating with the school's academic achievement and number of suspensions. All correlations were in the direction predicted and statistically significant, with only several exceptions.

Additional evidence of criterion-related validity is presented in the technical manual for scores on the Delaware Bullying Victimization Scale and the Delaware Social and Emotional Competencies Scale (student versions). As predicted, higher scores for bullying victimization and lower scores for social and emotional competencies were found to be associated with students' perceptions of poorer school climate and a lack of student engagement. As further evidence of criterion-related validity of scores on the bullying victimization scale, Marsh et al. (2011) found higher scores for verbal, social, and physical bullying victimization to be associated with depression and negative self-concept among adolescents. In another study of adolescents, Xie, Wei, and Bear (2018) found high scores on the four bullying victimization subscales to be associated with students' self-ratings of greater anxiety and negative overall mental health.

As additional evidence of the validity of scores on the Social and Emotional Competencies Scale, in a study of over 30,000 students, Mantz, Bear, Yang, and Harris (2016) reported that the total social-emotional competency score correlated significantly and positively with individual students' self-reported cognitive, behavioral, emotional, and total engagement. Moreover, at the school level, the total social-emotional competence score correlated positively with school-level academic achievement and negatively with suspensions/expulsions.

As evidence of reliability of scores on the three versions of the four scales and their subscales, coefficients of internal consistency are presented in the manual for each grade level (elementary, middle, and high school), gender, and for racial/ethnic groups. Across each of those groups and for all scales and subscales the coefficients exceed .70, indicating acceptable reliability. As expected given the larger number of items, coefficients are much higher for total scores, ranging from .85 (school climate score for third grade students) to .97, with most exceeding .90. For the student version, coefficients also are presented for each grade (3–12). Those coefficients exceed .70, with the following exceptions on the student version. On the Positive, Punitive, and SEL subscales of the student version two coefficients fell below .70: positive techniques at grade 3 (.67) and punitive disciplinary techniques at grade 12 (.69). On the Cognitive Engagement subscale of the DSES-S coefficients were .63, .64, and .69 for grades 3, 4, and 5, respectively. Caution is warranted in interpreting results for those subscales.

Validity Screening Items

Previous research indicates that approximately 8% of students respond inaccurately to surveys (Cornell, Klein, Konold, & Huang, 2012). Whereas some students respond randomly, others simply respond the same to every item and likely without reading the items. Cornell and colleagues found these response patterns to be especially common among adolescents with negative perceptions toward school. To increase the validity of student responses, the student version of the Delaware surveys contains two validity screening items. The first item is "I am lying on this survey," which appears as the last item on the DSCS-S. The second one is "I am telling the truth on this survey" and appears as the final item on the DSES. Responses to the survey are considered to be valid only if the student disagrees with the first item and agrees with the second item.

Recommendations for Using Data to Improve School Climate

In this section, guidance is provided on using the Delaware surveys for needs assessment, as they are most commonly used in Delaware schools. Although the focus is on the Delaware surveys, the guidance provided applies to other instruments that assess school climate.

1. *Establish a school team to analyze and report on the data.* Many schools already have a team that is well suited for collecting, managing, analyzing and reporting the data, such as a school climate, SWPBIS, or SEL team. If not, one should be established. The team should be multidisciplinary, including teachers, support staff, and school administrators (especially the principal or assistant principal). A school psychologist, with expertise in both mental health and assessment, should be a member, where feasible. The team might also include students (as age appropriate), parents, and other members of the community. Among the team's responsibilities are promoting initiatives for improving school climate by garnering support from major stakeholders, coordinating the administration of the surveys, arranging for scoring and summary reports, helping to interpret the data, sharing the data with others, and linking the findings to any interventions, including staff development, and programs that might be needed based on the data.

2. *Take precautions to ensure confidentiality.* The Delaware surveys are not intended to identify any respondent to the surveys (i.e., an individual student, teacher/staff member, or parent). If respondents are to be identified, this should be done only with clear written consent of the respondent, and of the parent/guardian of a student. To prevent identification of respondents, they should not be asked to record their names, and only nontraceable ID numbers should be used when coding data. Schoolwide data should not be reported at the class level (e.g., Class 101), and especially data for the teacher survey since the teacher of that class would be known. Likewise, no group data should be reported if any individual member might be identified. For this reason, data are not reported on the Delaware surveys for any group with less than five individuals.

3. *Analyze and interpret the data.* Data should be analyzed and interpreted in a planned and systematic manner. Each May, the Delaware Department of Education provides schools in Delaware with an extensive detailed report of the results of the surveys. The report includes three types of scores on each scale and subscale that are used in analyzing the data and detecting a school's strengths and weaknesses. Those scores are:

    Average item score. This score consists of the average score across items on the given scale or subscale. It is most valuable for comparing scores within a school and its determining strengths and weaknesses irrespective of how other schools score on the same measure.

Individual item score. This score consists of the percentage of students, teacher/staff, or parents selecting each of the given responses to a specific item on a subscale (e.g., 33% responded "Agree a Lot" and 20% "Disagree" to "I feel safe in this school."). This score allows teams to investigate what particular responses contributed more or less to any strengths and weaknesses indicated in scale and subscale scores.

Standard Score. This score is based on norms established in Delaware, allowing a school to compare its scores to similar schools and populations in the state. The average score is set at 100, with a standard deviation of 10. Standard scores are provided for all groups for which data are reported. For example, for the student version, standard scores (and norms) are provided by grade level (elementary, middle, and high school), grades (3–12), race/ethnicity, and gender. Standard scores are invaluable in understanding if a school's average item scores are normal or common in similar schools. For example, average item scores on the Delaware surveys tend to be lowest on the Student-Student Relationships and Student Engagement Schoolwide subscales, especially after elementary school, and highest on the Teacher-Student Relationships and Clarity of Expectations subscales. By comparing average item scores with standard scores on those subscales, a middle school with this pattern of scores might discover that the pattern is commonly found in other middle schools.

In addition to comprehensive data reports, schools are provided with the Delaware School Climate Survey Interpretation Worksheets which guide school climate leadership teams through specific steps for interpreting their scores. These worksheets are available for free to all schools (see http://wh1.oet.udel.edu/pbs/school-climate/use-of-school-climate-data/). Using the worksheets, schools are guided in analyzing and interpreting scores both within and between the student, teacher/staff, and home surveys, beginning with scale and subscale scores and progressing to responses to individual items. This includes examining data for each identified group of respondents. For example, on the five scales of the student version, and each of their subscales, scores are examined by race/ethnicity, grade, and gender.

4. **Recognize common demographic and group differences when interpreting the data.** It is well established that various demographic factors influence school climate. This includes race/ethnicity, gender, and socioeconomic status (SES). In general, African-American students score lower than other racial/ethnic groups and males score lower than females (Bear et al., 2019; Koth, Bradshaw, & Leaf, 2008). Scores also tend to be less favorable in low SES schools than high SES schools (Berkowitz, Moore, Astor, & Benbenishty, 2016), and when reported by students rather than by either teachers/staff or parents (Bear et al., 2018; Ramsey, Spira, Parisi, & Rebok, 2016). As noted previously, by using both average item scores and standard scores, a school can determine if a low score for a given group is normative and thus commonly found in other schools that are similar. For example, a middle school has an average item score of 2.8 on the Student-Student Relationships subscale, which reflects unfavorable student perceptions. However, if that score translates into a standard score of 100, it would indicate that the students' perceptions are average compared to students in other middle schools.

5. *Recognize developmental differences when interpreting the data.* A consistent finding among researchers is that school climate scores are much higher in elementary school than secondary school. Scores drop precipitously when students transition to middle school (Coelho, Romão, Brás, Bear, & Prioste, 2019; Madjar & Cohen-Malayev, 2016).
6. *Consider the validity and reliability of scores for the school and groups within it.* Although studies support the validity and reliability of scores on the Delaware surveys, schools should be cognizant of factors that can greatly lower the validity and reliability of scores on any instrument. A major source of unreliable and invalid data is respondents not taking the survey seriously. This is especially found among student respondents. Each year approximately 13% of Delaware student surveys are purged based on responses to the two validity screening items. The item "I am lying on this survey," in particular, draws a large number of non-validating responses of "I agree" or "I agree a lot" responses (approximately 10%; compared to 5% of students disagreeing with "I am telling the truth on this survey"). This item tends to catch many students who simply agree to every item on the survey.

    Other common sources of unreliable data are small sample sizes and a nonrandom selection of respondents. Schools are cautioned not to generalize findings to the whole school, or a subgroup, based on sampling a small number of respondents (e.g., only 15 Hispanic students, of a total of 100 in the school, complete the survey), especially when the sample is not random (e.g., the 15 students came from only two classes or one grade level). Small sample sizes are particularly problematic when comparisons are made between groups, as this entails comparing one unreliable data set with another one (e.g., comparing across racial/ethnic groups or grade levels when sample sizes are small).
7. *Examine data from other sources to help validate survey findings and to provide a more comprehensive assessment of school climate.* In addition to comparing data across respondents, both within and across student, teacher/staff, and home versions, the findings should be compared to other sources of data and information related to school climate and school discipline. This might include the number of office disciplinary referrals, in-school and out-of-school suspensions, and expulsions; and where they occurred and for what offenses. Additional data might include school completion rates (high school), absences, report card grades, academic achievement scores, teacher/staff turn-over rate, and complaints from parents and teachers/staff. In addition to examining those sources of data, further confirmatory information might be obtained by conducting follow-up surveys or focus groups to help pinpoint factors contributing to either unfavorable or favorable responses.
8. *Share and discuss results with stakeholders.* The school climate leadership team should communicate the school climate findings, especially with major stakeholders. Major stakeholders should consist of those most concerned about and affected by the school's climate. This would include not only groups who completed the surveys (i.e., students, teachers/staff, and parents) but also other members of the community. District-level administrators and school boards should be presented with the findings, especially when the surveys are administered district wide (as done in Delaware). At the building level, findings should be shared and discussed with teachers and staff

(including administrators) such as in professional learning community meetings, staff meetings, or professional development meetings; with students in classroom and student government meetings; and with parents and other community members in PTA meetings. (For a useful PowerPoint for sharing results of Delaware surveys, see: http://wh1.oet.udel.edu/pbs/school-climate/use-of-school-climate-data/.)

Consideration also should be given to sharing results in the context of focus groups with specific groups, especially those reporting unfavorable perceptions of school climate. For example, if a large number of Hispanic/Latino students in a school responded more negatively than other groups to items on a scale or subscale, such as for bullying victimization, the school leadership team should consider meeting with those students, or their representatives, to gain insight into responses on the survey and to explore suggestions for reducing bullying and improving school climate.

9. **Link findings to evidence-based strategies for improving school climate.** Some schools find favorable scores across all scales and subscales and thus no need for change, which is a good reason to celebrate. Those schools should highlight and continue implementing strategies that likely contribute to their success. Many schools, however, find one or more weaknesses on the subscales, either schoolwide or more specific to one or more groups of respondents. If found to be schoolwide, strategies at that level (i.e., universal, or Tier 1) should be considered. If low scores are specific to one or more groups of respondents (and believed to be valid based on confirmatory evidence), consideration should be given to strategies that target the low scoring group(s), or individuals within it. For example, this might entail strategies for fostering student engagement, improving teacher-student relationships, or reducing bullying victimization that are to be implemented in sixth grade or with a particular racial/ethnic group in the school. Those strategies would be both teacher- and student-centered, addressing what students *and* teachers/staff (and perhaps the home) can do to improve scores in the given area of need.

Because individuals are not identified on the surveys, other methods would be needed to identify individual students who might need and benefit from more focused and intensive interventions and supports, as commonly associated with Tiers 2 and 3 in a multitiered system. This applies to some scales more so than others, and especially to the scales that assess student engagement, bullying victimization, and students' social and emotional competencies. Depending on the area of identified need, the methods for identifying students might include teacher, parent, or student (i.e., self) nominations or ratings (with parent consent) of individual students on screening instruments that focus on the specific area of need, or a review of other existing individual-level data (e.g., office referrals, student grades).

Strategies that address low scores for teacher-student relationship, student-student relationships, student engagement, bullying victimization, school safety, behavioral expectations and fairness of rules, and social and emotional competencies were presented in previous chapters of this book. Another good resource is training modules developed by the Delaware Department of Education that align with many of the school climate subscales (see http://wh1.oet.udel.edu/pbs/school-climate-modules/).

Whereas the school climate leadership team should assume primary responsibility for analyzing and interpreting survey results and sharing them with the school community, it is important that a much larger group, such as those with whom the data are shared, participate in the process of brainstorming, reviewing, and selecting strategies, and especially any programs, for implementation. Failure to involve those who will be asked to implement the strategies and programs is likely to result in resistance and lack of commitment to change, which is the most common cause for the failure of most school reform efforts (Curtis et al., 2008; Fullan, 2007).

10. *Consider adopting a schoolwide and evidence-based program for improving school climate.* Implementing selected evidence-based strategies in response to identified needs, such as those strategies recommended throughout this book, may not be sufficient for improving school climate. This is particularly true when needs are multiple or substantial (as indicated in very low scores) and thus warrant more intensive and systemic change, including staff development. Consistent with the authoritative approach, and its emphasis on providing a balance of social-emotional support and structure to achieve the dual aims of managing student behavior and developing social and emotional competences that underlie self-discipline, consideration should be given to adopting an evidence-based SEL program that shares such emphasis. Another option consistent with the authoritative approach is integrating evidence-based strategies found in the SEL and SWPBIS approaches, and thus providing a healthy balance of responsiveness and structure (Bear, 2010; Bear et al., 2015; Sprague et al., 2018).

As noted in Chapter 4, a large number of evidenced-based packaged SEL programs are available, and readers are encouraged to read reviews of those programs on the CASEL website (https://casel.org/guide/) before choosing among them. In their comprehensive review of the effectiveness of SEL programs, Durlak et al. (2011) identified four practices found to be associated with program effectiveness. Following the acronym SAFE, effective programs consisted of Sequenced activities that were planned and taught in a step-by-step manner; emphasized Active forms of learning, such as role plays, discussions, and rehearsal with feedback; Focused on developing social and emotional skills and providing sufficient time to teach and practice those skills; and targeted Explicit and specific social and emotional skills. In addition to having SAFE features, answers to the following questions should help guide the choice of a SEL program (Bear, 2010):

- Are the program's philosophy, goals, and strategies consistent with the philosophy and mission of the school and supported by teachers, administrators, support staff, and parents?
- Does empirical research show that the program leads to important outcomes that the school hopes to achieve, and particularly those reflecting the areas of identified need? Were the schools in the studies that demonstrated program effectiveness similar to the school considering adoption of the program?
- Does the program provide tools of demonstrated usefulness to evaluate the program's effectiveness? Do the tools clearly align with the goals of the program and with the outcomes valued by the school? If not, are such measures readily available (and free or inexpensive)?

- Does the program provide tools, such as guides and checklists, that can be used to help ensure that the program is implemented as intended and with fidelity?
- In addition to curriculum lessons, does the program provide support materials that help to maintain skills that are taught and to promote the generalization of skills beyond the classroom? This might include information to parents, homework, schoolwide activities, morning announcements, etc.
- Does the program offer professional development training (for before and after implementation begins) on ongoing support? Are teachers/staff willing and able to attend the training?
- Will adequate funds and resources be available to support the program? This should include funds for materials and professional development.
- Are there schools, preferably nearby, that school administrators, teachers, and staff can visit that have already implemented the program successfully? Visiting those schools is often invaluable in learning of the program's advantages and disadvantages and of any obstacles that a school might encounter in the program's implementation.

Summary

Hopefully, educators reading this book will implement many of the strategies presented throughout it—ones they are not already implementing—to improve school climate and reduce behavior problems. However, they should not embark upon major schoolwide improvement efforts without first conducting a needs assessment that identifies areas of need. Many excellent school climate surveys are available for conducting a needs assessment. This chapter focused on the Delaware School Surveys, used by most schools in Delaware for over ten years. Consisting of 5 scales and 23 subscales, the Delaware surveys are comprehensive in scope, assessing the most widely recognized domains and dimensions of school climate, as well as major constructs that influence and are influenced by school climate. Evidence that the surveys are psychometrically sound and of high practical utility was presented, including recommendations and resources for linking scores to evidence-based strategies for school improvement.

Notes

1 Although scoring and detailed reports are not available to non-Delaware schools from the Delaware Department of Education, those schools may complete the surveys via an App that scores and reports the data. The App is available from www.mosaic-network.com/Covitality

2 The Delaware Department of Education plans to field test items designed to assess self-awareness in Spring 2020.

REFERENCES

Abbott-Chapman, J., Martin, K., Ollington, N., Venn, A., Dwyer, T., & Gall, S. (2013). The longitudinal association of childhood school engagement with adult educational and occupational achievement: Findings from an Australian national study. *British Educational Research Journal, 40*, 102–120. doi:10.1002/berj.3031

Aboud, F. E., & Doyle, A. B. (1996). Parental and peer influences on children's racial attitudes. *International Journal of Intercultural Relations, 20*, 371–383. doi:10.1016/0147-1767(96)00024-7

Ackert, E. (2018). Segregation paradox? School racial/ethnic and socioeconomic composition and racial/ethnic differences in engagement. *Social Science Research, 70*, 144–162. doi:10.1016/j.ssresearch.2017.10.010

Acosta, J., Chinman, M., Ebener, P., Malone, P., Phillips, A., & Wilks, A. (2019). Evaluation of a whole-school change intervention: Findings from a two-year cluster randomized trial of the restorative practices intervention. *Journal of Youth and Adolescence, 48*, 876–890. doi:10.1007/s10964-019-01013-2

Adams, R. E., & Bukowski, W. M. (2007). Relationships with mothers and peers moderate the association between childhood sexual abuse and anxiety disorders. *Child Abuse & Neglect, 31*, 645–656. doi:10.1016/j.chiabu.2006.12.011

Adelman, H. S., & Taylor, L. (2006). *The school leader's guide to student learning supports: New directions for addressing barriers to learning*. Thousand Oaks, CA: Corwin Press.

Advancement Project. (2014). *Restorative practices: Fostering healthy relationships & promoting positive discipline in schools*. Retrieved from https://advancementproject.org/resources/restorative-practices-fostering-healthy-relationships-promoting-positive-discipline-in-schools/

Advancement Project/Civil Rights Project. (2000). *Opportunities suspended: The devastating consequences of zero tolerance and school discipline policies*. Cambridge, MA: Harvard University Press.

Ahnert, L., Harwardt-Heinecke, E., Kappler, G., Eckstein-Madry, T., & Milatz, A. (2012). Student-teacher relationships and classroom climate in first grade: How do they relate to students' stress regulation? *Attachment and Human Development, 14*, 249–263. doi 10.1080/14616734.2012.673277

Ainsworth, M. D. S. (1989). Attachments beyond infancy. *American Psychologist, 44*, 709–716. doi:10.1037/0003-066X.44.4.709

Akin-Little, K. A., & Little, S. G. (2009). The true effects of extrinsic reinforcement on "intrinsic" motivation. In A. Akin-Little, S. G. Little, S. G. Bray, M. A. Kehle, & J. Thomas (Eds.), *Behavioral interventions in schools: Evidence-based positive strategies* (pp. 73–91). Washington, DC: American Psychological Association.

Alberto, P. A., & Troutman, A. C. (2013). *Applied behavior analysis for teachers* (9th ed.). Upper Saddle River, NJ: Merrill Prentice-Hall.

References

Allan, N. P., Hume, L. E., Allan, D. M., Farrington, A. L., & Lonigan, C. J. (2014). Relations between inhibitory control and the development of academic skills in preschool and kindergarten: A meta-analysis. *Developmental Psychology, 50*, 2368–2379. doi:10.1037/a0037493

Álvarez-García, D., García, T., & Núñez, J. C. (2015). Predictors of school bullying perpetration in adolescence: A systematic review. *Aggression and Violent Behavior, 23*, 126–136. doi:10.1016/j.avb.2015.05.007

American Civil Liberties Union. (2013). *School-to-prison pipeline*. Retrieved from www.aclu.org/racial-justice/school-prison-pipeline

American Psychological Association Zero Tolerance Task Force. (2008). Are zero tolerance policies effective in the schools? An evidentiary review and recommendations. *American Psychologist, 63*, 852–862. doi:10.1037/0003-066X.63.9.852

Amman, M., Bowlin, M., Buckles, L., Burton, K. C., Brunell, K. F., Gibson, K. A., & Robins, C. J. (2017). *Making prevention a reality: Identifying, assessing, and managing the threat of targeted attacks*. Washington, DC: U.S. Department of Justice.

Analitis, F., Velderman, M. K., Ravens-Sieberer, U., Detmar, S., Erhart, M., & Herdman, M.; European Kidscreen Group. (2009). Being bullied: Associated factors in children and adolescents 8 to 18 years old in 11 European countries. *Pediatrics, 123*, 569–577. doi:10.1542/peds.2008-0323

Anderson, C. S. (1982). The search for school climate: A review of the research. *Review of Educational Research, 52*, 368–420. doi:10.3102/00346543052003368

Antoniadou, N., & Kokkinos, C. M. (2015). Cyber and school bullying: Same or different phenomena? *Aggression and Violent Behavior, 25*, 363–372. doi:10.1016/j.avb.2015.09.013

Anyon, Y., Zhang, D., & Hazel, C. (2016). Race, exclusionary discipline, and connectedness to adults in secondary schools. *American Journal of Community Psychology, 57*, 342–352. doi:10.1002/ajcp.12061

Archambault, I., Janosz, M., Fallu, J., & Pagani, L. S. (2009). Student engagement and its relationship with early high school dropout. *Journal of Adolescence, 32*, 651–670. doi:10.1016/j.adolescence.2008.06.007

Arum, R. (2003). *Judging school discipline: The crisis of moral authority*. Cambridge, MA: Cambridge University Press.

Asher, S., & Mcdonald, K. L. (2009). The behavioral basis of acceptance, rejection, and perceived popularity. In K. H. Rubin, W. M. Bukowski, & B. Laursen (Eds.), *Handbook of peer interactions, relationships, and groups* (pp. 232–233). New York: Guilford Press.

Aspen Institute National Commission on Social, Emotional, and Academic Development. (2019). *From a nation at risk to a nation at hope*. Retrieved from http://nationathope.org/

Astor, R. A., Benbenishty, R., Marachi, R., & Meyer, H. A. (2006). In S. R. Jimerson & M. J. Furlong (Eds.), *Handbook of school violence and school safety: From research to practice* (pp. 221–233). Mahwah, NJ: Erlbaum.

Atkins, M. S., McKay, M. M., Frazier, S. L., Jakobsons, L. J., Arvanitis, P., Cunningham, T., & Lambrecht, L. (2002). Suspensions and detentions in an urban, low-income school: Punishment or reward? *Journal of Abnormal Child Psychology, 30*, 361–371. doi:10.1023/A:1015765924135

Responsive Classroom (with Badge, L., Ghosh, S., Hunter II, E., Meehan, C., & Wade, C.). (2018). *Teaching self-discipline: The responsive classroom guide to helping students dream, behave, and achieve in elementary school*. Turner Falls, MA: Center for Responsive Schools, Inc.

Baker, J. (1999). Teacher-student interaction in urban, at-risk classrooms: Differential behavior, relationship quality, and student satisfaction with school. *The Elementary School Journal, 100*, 57–70. doi:10.1086/461943

Baker, J. A., Grant, S., & Morlock, L. (2008). The teacher-student relationship as a developmental context for children with internalizing or externalizing behavior problems. *School Psychology Quarterly, 23*, 3–15. doi:10.1037/1045-3830.23.1.3

Balfanz, R., Herzog, L., & Mac Iver, D. J. (2007). Preventing student disengagement and keeping students on the graduation path in urban middle-grades schools: Early identification and effective interventions. *Educational Psychologist, 42*, 223–235. doi:10.1080/00461520701621079

Balliet, D., Mulder, L. B., Lange, V., & Paul, A. M. (2011). Reward, punishment, and cooperation: A meta-analysis. *Psychological Bulletin, 137*, 594–615. doi:10.1037/a0023489

Baly, M. W., Cornell, D. G., & Lovegrove, P. (2014). A longitudinal investigation of self- and peer reports of bullying victimization across middle school. *Psychology in the Schools, 51*, 217–240. doi:10.1002/pits.21747

Bandura, A. (1986). *Social foundations of thought and action: A social cognitive theory.* Upper Saddle River, NJ: Prentice-Hall.

Bandura, A. (2016). *Moral disengagement: How people do harm and live with themselves.* New York: Worth Publishers.

Bandura, A., Capara, G. V., Barbaranelli, C., Pastorelli, C., & Regalia, C. (2001). Sociocognitive self-regulatory mechanisms governing transgressive behavior. *Journal of Personality and Social Psychology, 80*, 125–135. doi:10.1037/0022-3514.80.1.125

Bannink, R., Broeren, S., van de Looij – Jansen, P. M., de Waart, F. G., & Raat, H. (2014). Cyber and traditional bullying victimization as a risk factor for mental health problems and suicidal ideation in adolescents. *Plos One, 9*, e94026. doi:10.1371/journal.pone.0094026

Barboza, G. E., Schiamberg, L. B., Oehmke, J., Korzeniewski, S. J., Post, L. A., & Heraux, C. G. (2009). Individual characteristics and the multiple contexts of adolescent bullying: An ecological perspective. *Journal of Youth and Adolescence, 38*, 101–121. doi:10.1007/s10964-008-9271-1

Barofsky, L. A., Kellerman, I., Baucom, B., Oliver, P. H., & Margolin, G. (2013). Community violence exposure and adolescents' school engagement and academic achievement over time. *Psychology of Violence, 3*, 381–395. doi:10.1037/a0034121

Baroody, A. E., Rimm-Kaufman, S., Larsen, R. A., & Curby, T. W. (2016). A multi-method approach for describing the contributions of student engagement on fifth grade students' social competence and achievement in mathematics. *Learning and Individual Differences, 48*, 54–60. doi:10.1016/j.lindif.2016.02.012

Barrish, H. H., Saunders, M., & Wolf, M. M. (1969). Good Behavior Game: Effects of individual contingencies for group consequences on disruptive behavior in a classroom. *Journal of Applied Behavior Analysis, 2*, 119–124. doi:10.1901/jaba.1969.2-119

Barth, J. M., Dunlap, S. T., Dane, H., Lochman, J. E., & Wells, K. C. (2004). Classroom environment influences on aggression, peer relations, and academic focus. *Journal of School Psychology, 42*, 115–133. doi:10.1016/j.jsp.2003.11.004

Barton, L. E., Brulle, A. R., & Repp, A. C. (1983). Aversive techniques and the doctrine of the least restrictive alternative. *Exceptional Education Quarterly, 3*, 1–8. doi:10.1177%2F074193258300300407

Batanova, M., & Loukas, A. (2016). Empathy and effortful control effects on early adolescents' aggression: When do students' perceptions of their school climate matter? *Applied Developmental Science, 20*, 79–93. doi:10.1080/10888691.2015.1067145

Baumrind, D. (1971). Current patterns of parental authority. *Developmental Psychology, 4*, 1–103. doi:10.1037/h0030372

Baumrind, D. (1996). The discipline controversy revisited. *Family Relations, 45*, 405–414. doi:http://dx.doi.org/10.2307/585170

Baumrind, D. (2013). Authoritative parenting revisited: History and current status. In R. E. Larzelere, A. S. Morris, & A. W. Harrist (Eds.), *Authoritative parenting: Synthesizing nurturance and discipline for optimal child development* (pp. 11–34). Washington, DC: American Psychological Association.

Bear, G. G. (with A. Cavalier & M. Manning). (2005). *Developing self-discipline and preventing and correcting misbehavior.* Boston, MA: Allyn & Bacon.

Bear, G. G. (2010). *School discipline and self-discipline: A practical guide to promoting prosocial student behavior.* New York: Guilford Press.

Bear, G. G. (2012). Both suspension and alternatives work, depending on one's aim. *Journal of School Violence, 11*, 174–186. doi:10.1080/15388220.2012.652914

Bear, G. G. (2013). Teacher resistance to frequent rewards and praise: Lack of skill or a wise decision? *Journal of Educational & Psychological Consultation, 23*, 318–340. doi:10.1080/10474412.2013.845495

Bear, G. G. (2015). Preventive classroom management. In E. T. Emmer & E. J. Sabornie (Eds.), *Handbook of classroom management* (2nd ed., pp. 15–39). New York: Routledge.

Bear, G. G., Biondi, T., & Morales, S. (2019). Implementing the Good Behavior Game: Helping handout for school. In G. G. Bear & K. M. Minke (Eds.), *Helping handouts: Supporting students at school and home* (pp. S6H1, 1–7). Bethesda, MD: National Association of School Psychologists.

Bear, G. G., Gaskins, C., Blank, J., & Chen, F. F. (2011). Delaware school climate survey-student: Its structure, concurrent validity, and reliability. *Journal of School Psychology, 49*, 157–174. doi:10.1016/j.jsp.2011.01.001

Bear, G. G., Homan, J., & Harris, A. (2019). Bullying: Helping handout for school. In G. G. Bear & K. M. Minke (Eds.), *Helping handouts: Supporting students at school and home* (pp. S2H5, 1–7). Bethesda, MD: National Association of School Psychologists.

Bear, G. G., Homan, J., & Morales, S. (2019). Using praise and rewards wisely: Helping handout for school and home. In G. G. Bear & K. M. Minke (Eds.), *Helping handouts: Supporting students at school and home* (pp. S6H4, 1–6). Bethesda, MD: National Association of School Psychologists.

Bear, G. G., Mantz, L. S., Glutting, J. J., Yang, C., & Boyer, D. E. (2015). Differences in bullying victimization between students with and without disabilities. *School Psychology Review, 44*, 98–116. doi:10.17105/SPR44-1.98-116

Bear, G. G., Quinn, M., & Burkholer, S. (2002). *Interim alternative educational settings and children with disabilities*. Bethesda, MD: National Association of School Psychologists.

Bear, G. G., Slaughter, J., Mantz, L., & Farley-Ripple, L. (2017). Rewards, praise, and punitive consequences: Relations with intrinsic and extrinsic motivation. *Teaching and Teacher Education, 65*, 10–20. doi:10.1016/j.tate.2017.03.001

Bear, G. G., Webster-Stratton, C., Furlong, M., & Rhee, S. (2000). Preventing aggression and violence. In K. M. Minke & G. G. Bear (Eds.), *Preventing school problems—Promoting school success: Strategies and programs that work* (pp. 1–69). Bethesda, MD: National Association of School Psychologists.

Bear, G. G., Whitcomb, S., Elias, M., & Blank, J. (2015). SEL and schoolwide positive behavioral interventions and supports. In J. Durlak, T. Gullotta, C. Domitrovich, P. Goren, & R. Weissberg (Eds.), *Handbook of social and emotional learning* (pp. 453–467). New York: Guilford Press.

Bear, G. G., Yang, C., Chen, D., He, X., Xie, J., & Huang, X. (2018a). Differences in school climate and student engagement in China and the United States. *School Psychology Quarterly, 33*, 323–335. doi:10.1037/spq0000247

Bear, G. G., Yang, C., Harris, A., Mantz, L., Hearn, S., & Boyer, D. (2018b). *Technical manual for Delaware surveys of school climate; bullying victimization, student engagement, and positive, punitive, and social emotional learning techniques; and social and emotional competencies*. Retrieved from University of Delaware, Center for Disabilities Studies, Positive Behavioral Supports and School Climate Project website: http://wh1.oet.udel.edu/pbs/technical-manual-for-school-climate-surveys

Bear, G. G., Yang, C., Mantz, L. S., & Harris, A. B. (2017). School-wide practices associated with school climate in elementary, middle, and high schools. *Teaching and Teacher Education, 63*, 372–383. doi:10.1016/j.tate.2017.01.012

Bear, G. G., Yang, C., & Pasipanodya, E. (2014). Assessing school climate: Validation of a brief measure of the perceptions of parents. *Journal of Psychoeducational Assessment, 32*, 1–15. doi:10.1177%2F0734282914545748

Bear, G., Yang, C., Pell, M., & Gaskins, C. (2014). Validation of a brief measure of teachers' perceptions of school climate: Relations to student achievement and suspensions learning environments research, *Learning Environments Research, 17*, 339–354. doi:10.1007/s10984-014-9162-1

Belfield, C., Bowden, A., Klapp, A., Levin, H., Shand, R., & Zander, S. (2015). The economic value of social and emotional learning. *Journal of Benefit-Cost Analysis, 6,* 508–544. doi:10.1017/bca.2015.55

Benner, A. D., Graham, S., & Mistry, R. S. (2008). Discerning direct and mediated effects of ecological structures and processes on adolescents' educational outcomes. *Developmental Psychology, 44,* 840–854. doi:10.1037/0012-1649.44.3.840

Berg, J. K., & Cornell, D. (2016). Authoritative school climate, aggression toward teachers, and teacher distress in middle school. *School Psychology Quarterly, 31,* 122–139. doi:10.1037/spq0000132

Berger, C., Batanova, M., & Cance, J. D. (2015). Aggressive and prosocial? Examining latent profiles of behavior, social status, machiavellianism, and empathy. *Journal of Youth and Adolescence, 44,* 2230–2244. doi:10.1007/s10964-015-0298-9

Berkowitz, L. (1989a). Situational influences on aggression. In J. Groebel & R. A. Hinde (Eds.), *Aggression and war: Their biological and social bases* (pp. 91–100). Thousand Oaks, CA: Sage.

Berkowitz, L. (1989b). Frustration–Aggression hypothesis: Examination and reformulation. *Psychology Bulletin, 106,* 59–73. doi:10.1037/0033-2909.106.1.59

Berkowitz, R., Moore, H., Astor, R. A., & Benbenishty, R. (2016). A research synthesis of the association between socioeconomic background, inequality, school climate, and academic achievement. *Review of Educational Research, 87,* 425–469. doi:10.3102/0034654316669821

Bierman, K. L., Coie, J. D., Dodge, K. A., Foster, E. M., Greenberg, M. T., Lochman, J. E., & Pinderhughes, E. E. (2007). Fast track randomized controlled trial to prevent externalizing psychiatric disorders: Findings from grades 3 to 9. *Journal of the American Academy of Child and Adolescent Psychiatry, 46,* 1250–1262. doi:10.1097/chi.0b013e31813e5d39

Bingham, G. E., & Okagaki, L. (2012). Ethnicity and student engagement. In S. L. Christenson, A. L. Reschly, & C. Wylie (Eds.), *Handbook of research on student engagement* (pp. 65–95, Chapter xxvii, 840 Pages). New York: Springer Science + Business Media.

Birch, S. H., & Ladd, G. W. (1998). Children's interpersonal behaviors and the teacher-child relationship. *Developmental Psychology, 34,* 934–946. doi:10.1037/0012-1649.34.5.934

Birkett, M., Espelage, D. L., & Koenig, B. (2009). LGB and questioning students in schools: The moderating effects of homophobic bullying and school climate on negative outcomes. *Journal of Youth and Adolescence, 38,* 989–1000. doi:10.1007/s10964-008-9389-1

Blake, J. J., Lund, E. M., Zhou, Q., Kwok, O., & Benz, M. R. (2012). National prevalence rates of bully victimization among students with disabilities in the United States. *School Psychology Quarterly, 27,* 210–222. doi:10.1037/spq0000008

Bodovski, K., & Farkas, G. (2007). Mathematics growth in early elementary school: The roles of beginning knowledge, student engagement, and instruction. *The Elementary School Journal, 108,* 115–130. doi:10.1086/525550

Boivin, M., & Bégin, G. (1989). Peer status and self-perception among early elementary school children: The case of the rejected children. *Child Development, 60,* 591–596. doi:10.2307/1130725

Boman, J. H., Krohn, M. D., Gibson, C. L., & Stogner, J. M. (2012). Investigating friendship quality: An exploration of self-control and social control theories' friendship hypotheses. *Journal of Youth and Adolescence, 41,* 1526–1540. doi:10.1007/s10964-012-9747-x

Bond, L., Butler, H., Thomas, L., Carlin, J., Glover, S., Bowes, G., & Patton, G. (2007). Social and school connectedness in early secondary school as predictors of late teenage substance use, mental health, and academic outcomes. *Journal of Adolescent Health, 40,* 357.e9–357.e18. doi:10.1016/j.jadohealth.2006.10.013

Booren, L. M., Handy, D. J., & Power, T. G. (2011). Examining perceptions of school safety strategies, school climate, and violence. *Youth Violence and Juvenile Justice, 9,* 171–187. doi:10.1177/1541204010374297

Booth, M. Z., & Gerard, J. M. (2014). Adolescents' stage-environment fit in middle and high school: The relationship between students' perceptions of their schools and themselves. *Youth & Society, 46,* 735–755. doi:10.1177/0044118X12451276

Borum, R., Cornell, D. G., Modzeleski, W., & Jimerson, S. R. (2010). What can be done about school shootings? A review of the evidence. *New Perspectives on School Safety and Violence Prevention, 39*, 27–37. doi:10.3102/0013189X09357620

Bosworth, K., Ford, L., & Hernandaz, D. (2011). School climate factors contributing to student and faculty perceptions of safety in select Arizona schools. *Journal of School Health, 81*, 194–201. doi:10.1111/j.1746-1561.2010.00579.x

Boulton, M. J., Duke, E., Holman, G., Laxton, E., Nicholas, B., Spells, R., & Woodmansey, H. (2009). Associations between being bullied, perceptions of safety in classroom and playground, and relationship with teacher among primary school pupils. *Educational Studies, 35*, 255–267. doi:10.1080/03055690802648580

Boulton, M. J., Trueman, M., Chau, C., Whitehand, C., & Amatya, K. (1999). Concurrent and longitudinal links between friendship and peer victimization: Implications for befriending interventions. *Journal of Adolescence, 22*, 461–466. doi:10.1006/jado.1999.0240

Boulton, M. J., Woodmansey, H., Williams, E., Spells, R., Nicholas, B., Laxton, E., & Duke, E. (2012). Associations between peer bullying and classroom concentration: Evidence for mediation by perceived personal safety and relationship with teacher. *Educational Psychology, 32*, 277–294. doi:10.1080/01443410.2011.648903

Bowlby, J. (1969). Attachment and loss: Volume 1: Attachment. In *The international psycho-analytical library* (Vol. 79, pp.1–401). London: The Hogarth Press and the Institute of Psycho-Analysis.

Bradshaw, C. P., Mitchell, M. M., O'Brennan, L. M., & Leaf, P. J. (2010). Multilevel exploration of factors contributing to the overrepresentation of black students in office disciplinary referrals. *Journal of Educational Psychology, 102*, 508–520. doi:10.1037/a0018450

Bradshaw, C. P., Waasdorp, T. E., Goldweber, A., & Johnson, S. L. (2013). Bullies, gangs, drugs, and school: Understanding the overlap and the role of ethnicity and urbanicity. *Journal of Youth and Adolescence, 42*, 220–234. doi:10.1007/s10964-012-9863-7

Bradshaw, C. P., Waasdorp, T. E., & Leaf, P. J. (2012). Effects of school-wide positive behavioral interventions and supports on child behavior problems. *Pediatrics, 130*, e1136–e1145. doi:10.1542%2Fpeds.2012-0243

Brand, S., Felner, R., Shim, S., Seitsinger, A., & Dumas, T. (2003). Middle school improvement and reform: Development and validation of a school-level assessment of climate, cultural pluralism, and school safety. *Journal of Educational Psychology, 95*, 570–588. doi:10.1037/0022-0663.95.3.570

Bray, M. A., & Root, M. M. (2016). *Picture perfect: Video self-modeling for behavior change.* Eugene, OR: Ancora Publishing.

Brock, S. E., Nickerson, A. B., Reeves, M. A., Jimerson, S. R., Lieberman, R. A., & Feinberg, T. A. (2009). *School crisis prevention and intervention: The PREPaRE model.* Washington, DC: National Association of School Psychologists.

Brock, L. L., Nishida, T. K., Chiong, C., Grimm, K. J., & Rimm-Kaufman, S. E. (2008). Children's perceptions of the classroom environment and social and academic performance: A longitudinal analysis of the contribution of the responsive classroom approach. *Journal of School Psychology, 46*, 129–149. doi:10.1016/j.jsp.2007.02.004

Bronfenbrenner, U. (1979). *The ecology of human development.* Cambridge, MA: Harvard University Press.

Bronfenbrenner, U., & Ceci, S. J. (1994). Nature-nurture reconceptualized in developmental perspective: A bioecological model. *Psychological Review, 101*, 568–586. doi:10.1037/0033-295X.101.4.568

Brophy, J. E. (1981). On praising effectively. *Elementary School Journal, 81*, 269–278. doi:10.1086/461229

Brophy, J. E. (1996). *Teaching problem students.* New York: Guilford Press.

Brophy, J. E. (2010). *Motivating students to learn* (3rd ed.). New York: Routledge.

Brophy, J. E., & McCaslin, M. (1992). Teachers' reports of how they perceive and cope with problem students. *Elementary School Journal, 93*, 3–68. doi:10.1086/461712

Bruni, T. P., Drevon, D., Hixson, M., Wyse, R., Corcoran, S., & Fursa, S. (2017). The effect of functional behavior assessment on school-based interventions: A meta-analysis of single-case research. *Psychology in the Schools, 54*, 351–369. doi:10.1002/pits.22007

Bryce, C. I., Bradley, R. H., Abry, T., Swanson, J., & Thompson, M. S. (2018). Parents' and teachers' academic influences, behavioral engagement, and first- and fifth-grade achievement. *School Psychology Quarterly.* doi:10.1037/spq0000297

Bub, K. L., Robinson, L. E., & Curtis, D. S. (2016). Longitudinal associations between self-regulation and health across childhood and adolescence. *Health Psychology, 35*, 1235–1245. doi:10.1037/hea0000401

Buhs, E. S., Koziol, N. A., Rudasill, K. M., & Crockett, L. J. (2018). Early temperament and middle school engagement: School social relationships as mediating processes. *Journal of Educational Psychology, 110*, 338–354. doi:10.1037/edu0000224

Buhs, E. S., Ladd, G. W., & Herald, S. L. (2006). Peer exclusion and victimization: Processes that mediate the relationship between peer group rejection and children's classroom engagement and achievement. *Journal of Educational Psychology, 98*, 1–13. doi:10.1037/0022-0663.98.1.1

Buhs, E. S., Ladd, G. W., & Herald-Brown, S. (2010). Victimization and exclusion: Links to peer rejection, classroom engagement, and achievement. In S. R. Jimerson, S. M. Swearer, & D. L. Espelage (Eds.), *Handbook of bullying in schools: An international perspective* (pp. 163–171). New York: Routledge.

Bullis, M., Walker, H., & Sprague, J. R. (2001). A promise unfulfilled: Social skills training with at-risk and antisocial children and youth. *Exceptionality, 9*, 67–90. doi:10.1207/S15327035EX0918&2_6

Burnett, P. C. (2002). Teacher praise and feedback and students' perceptions of the classroom environment. *Educational Psychology, 22*, 1–16. doi:10.1080/01443410120101215

Burns, E. C., Martin, A. J., & Collie, R. J. (2018). Understanding the role of personal best (PB) goal setting in students' declining engagement: A latent growth model. *Journal of Educational Psychology, 111*, 557–572. doi:10.1037/edu0000291

Buyse, E., Verschueren, K., Verachtert, P., & Van Damme, J. (2009). Predicting school adjustment in early elementary school: Impact of teacher-child relationship quality and relational classroom climate. *Elementary School Journal, 110*, 119–141. doi:10.1086/605768

Canter, L. (1976). *Assertive discipline: A take charge approach for today's educator.* Santa Monica, CA: Canter and Associates.

Canter, L., & Canter, M. (2001). *Assertive discipline: Positive behavior management for today's classroom.* Los Angeles, CA: Canter and Associates.

Cappella, E., Kim, H. Y., Neal, J. W., & Jackson, D. (2013). Classroom peer relationships and academic engagement in elementary school: The role of social network equity. *American Journal of Community Psychology, 52*, 367–379. doi:10.1007/s10464-013-9603-5

Caprara, G. V., Barbaranelli, C., Pastorelli, C., Bandura, A., & Zimbardo, P. G. (2000). Prosocial foundations of children's academic achievement. *Psychological Science, 11*, 302–306. doi:10.1111/1467-9280.00260

Caraway, K., Tucker, C. M., Reinke, W. M., & Hall, C. (2003). Self-efficacy, goal orientation and fear of failure as predictors of school engagement in high school students. *Psychology in the Schools, 40*, 417–427. doi:10.1002/pits.10092

Card, N. A., & Hodges, E. V. E. (2008). Peer victimization among schoolchildren: Correlations, causes, consequences, and considerations in assessment and intervention. *School Psychology Quarterly, 23*, 451–461. doi:10.1037/a0012769

Carlo, G., Mestre, M. V., Samper, P., Tur, A., & Armenta, B. E. (2010). Feelings or cognitions? Moral cognitions and emotions as longitudinal predictors of prosocial and aggressive behaviors. *Personality and Individual Differences, 48*, 872–877. doi:10.1016/j.paid.2010.02.010

Carney, J. V. (2000). Bullied to death: Perceptions of peer abuse and suicidal behavior during adolescence. *School Psychology International, 21*, 213–223. doi:10.1177/0143034300212007

Carter, M., McGee, R., Taylor, B., & Williams, S. (2007). Health outcomes in adolescence: Associations with family, friends and school engagement. *Journal of Adolescence, 30*, 51–62. doi:10.1016/j.adolescence.2005.04.002

Cassidy, T. (2009). Bullying and victimisation in school children: The role of social identity, problem-solving style, and family and school context. *Social Psychology of Education, 12*, 63–76. doi:10.1007/s11218-008-9066-y

Catalano, R. F., Berglund, M. L., Ryan, J. A. M., Lonczak, H. S., & Hawkins, J. D. (2004). Positive youth development in the United States: Research findings on evaluations of positive youth development programs. *Annals of the Academy of Political and Social Science, 591*, 98–124. doi:10.1177/0002716203260102

Catalano, R. F., Haggerty, K. P., Oesterle, S., Fleming, C. B., & Hawkins, D. J. (2004). The importance of bonding to school for healthy development: Findings from the social development research group. *Journal of School Health, 74*, 252–261. doi:10.1111/j.1746-1561.2004.tb08281.x

Center for Responsive Schools. (2019). *About Responsive Classroom*. Retrieved from www.responsiveclassroom.org/about-responsive-classroom

Center for the Collaborative Classroom. (2018). *Caring school community* (2nd ed.). Alameda, CA: Author.

Cheng, H., & Furnham, G. (2002). Personality, peer relations, and self-confidence as predictors of happiness and loneliness. *Journal of Adolescence, 25*, 327–339. doi:10.1006/jado.2002.0475

Cheung, C. S. (2019). Parents' involvement and adolescents' school adjustment: Teacher-student relationships as a mechanism of change. *School Psychology, 34*, 35–362. doi:10.1037/spq0000288

Cheung, C. S., & Pomerantz, E. M. (2012). Why does parents' involvement enhance children's achievement? The role of parent-oriented motivation. *Journal of Educational Psychology, 104*, 820–832. doi:10.1037/a0027183

Chin, J. K., Dowdy, E., Jimerson, S. R., & Rime, W. J. (2012). Alternatives to suspensions: Rationale and recommendations. *Journal of School Violence, 11*, 156–173. doi:10.1080/15388220.2012.652912

Christenson, S. L., & Havsy, L. H. (2004). Family-school-peer relationships: Significance for social, emotional, and academic learning. In J. E. Zins, R. P. Weissberg, M. C. Wang, & H. J. Walberg (Eds.), *Building academic success on social and emotional learning: What does the research say?* (pp. 59–75). New York: Teachers College Press.

Chu, X., Fan, C., Lian, S., & Zhou, Z. (2019). Does bullying victimization really influence adolescents' psychosocial problems? A three-wave longitudinal study in China. *Journal of Affective Disorders, 246*, 603–610. doi:10.1016/j.jad.2018.12.103

Cigala, A., Mori, A., & Fangareggi, F. (2015). Learning others' point of view: Perspective taking and prosocial behaviour in preschoolers. *Early Child Development and Care, 185*, 1199–1215. doi:10.1080/03004430.2014.987272

Cillessen, A. H., & Mayeux, L. (2007). Expectations and perceptions at school transitions: The role of peer status and aggression. *Journal of School Psychology, 45*, 567–586. doi:10.1016/j.jsp.2007.05.004

Claes, L., Luyckx, K., Baetens, I., Van de Ven, M., & Witteman, C. (2015). Bullying and victimization, depressive mood, and non-suicidal self-injury in adolescents: The moderating role of parental support. *Journal of Child and Family Studies, 24*, 3363–3371. doi:10.1007/s10826-015-0138-2

Coelho, V. A., Romão, A. M., Brás, P., Bear, G., & Prioste, A. (2019). Trajectories of students' school climate dimensions throughout middle school transition: A longitudinal study. *Child Indicators Research*. doi:10.1007/s12187-019-09674-y

Cohen, J., McCabe, E. M., Michelli, N. M., & Pickeral, T. (2009). School climate: Research, policy, practice, and teacher education. *Teachers College Record, 111*(1), 180–213. Retrieved from www.tcrecord.org/Content.asp?ContentId=15220

Coie, J. D., & Dodge, K. A. (1983). Continuities and changes in children's social status: A five-year longitudinal study. *Merrill-Palmer Quarterly, 29*(3), 261–282. Retrieved from www.jstor.org/stable/pdf/23086262.pdf?seq=1#page_scan_tab_contents

Collaborative for Academic, Social, and Emotional Learning (2019). *Core SEL Competencies.* Retrieved from https://casel.org/core-competencies/
Committee for Children. (2019). *Second Step Social-Emotional Learning.* Seattle, WA: Author.
Conduct Problems Prevention Research Group. (2010). The effects of a multiyear universal social-emotional learning program: The role of student and school characteristics. *Journal of Consulting and Clinical Psychology, 78,* 156–168. doi:10.1037/a0018607
Conners-Burrow, N., Johnson, D. L., Whiteside-Mansell, L., McKelvey, L., & Gargus, R. A. (2009). Adults matter: Protecting children from the negative impacts of bullying. *Psychology in the Schools, 46,* 593–604. doi:10.1002/pits.20400
Cook, C. R., Coco, S., Zhang, Y., Fiat, A. E., Duong, M. T., Renshaw, T. L., & Frank, S. (2018). Cultivating positive teacher-student relationships: Preliminary evaluation of the establish–Maintain–Restore (EMR) method. *School Psychology Review, 47,* 226–243. doi:10.17105/SPR-2017-0025.V47-3
Cook, C. R., Williams, K. R., Guerra, N. G., Kim, T. E., & Sadek, S. (2010). Predictors of bullying and victimization in childhood and adolescence: A meta-analytic investigation. *School Psychology Quarterly, 25,* 65–83. doi:10.1037/a0020149
Cormier, R. (1974). *The Chocolate War.* New York: Pantheon Books.
Cornell, D. (2015). Our schools are safe: Challenging the misperception that schools are dangerous places. *American Journal of Orthopsychiatry, 85,* 217–220. doi:10.1037/ort0000064
Cornell, D. (2018). *Comprehensive School Threat Assessment Guidelines.* Charlottesville, VA: School Threat Assessment Consultants LLC.
Cornell, D., Allen, K., & Fan, X. (2012). A randomized controlled study of the Virginia student threat assessment guidelines in grades K-12. *School Psychology Review, 41*(1), 100–115.
Cornell, D., & Huang, F. (2016). Authoritative school climate and high school student risk behavior: A cross-sectional multi-level analysis of student self-reports. *Journal of Youth and Adolescence, 45,* 2246–2259. doi:10.1007/s10964-016-0424-3
Cornell, D., & Huang, F. (2019). Collecting and analyzing local school safety and climate data. In M. J. Mayer & S. R. Jimerson (Eds.), *School safety and violence prevention: Science, practice, and policy* (pp. 151–175). Washington, DC: American Psychological Association. doi:10.1037/0000106-003
Cornell, D., Klein, J., Konold, T., & Huang, F. (2012). Effects of validity screening items on adolescent survey data. *Psychological Assessment, 24,* 21–35. doi:10.1037/a0024824
Cornell, D., Sheras, P., Gregory, A., & Fan, X. (2009). A retrospective study of school safety conditions in high schools using the Virginia threat assessment guidelines versus alternative approaches. *School Psychology Quarterly, 24,* 119–129. doi:10.1037/a0016182
Cornell, D., Shukla, K., & Konold, T. (2015). Peer victimization and authoritative school climate: A multilevel approach. *Journal of Educational Psychology, 107,* 1186–1201. doi:10.1037/edu0000038
Cornell, D., Shukla, K., & Konold, T. R. (2016). Authoritative school climate and student academic engagement, grades, and aspirations in middle and high schools. *AERA Open, 2,* 1–18. doi:10.1177%2F2332858416633184
Cortes, K. I., & Kochenderfer-Ladd, B. (2014). To tell or not to tell: What influences children's decisions to report bullying to their teachers? *School Psychology Quarterly, 29,* 336–348. doi:10.1037/spq0000078
Côté-Lussier, C., & Fitzpatrick, C. (2016). Feelings of safety at school, socioemotional functioning, and classroom engagement. *Journal of Adolescent Health, 58,* 543–550. doi:10.1016/j.jadohealth.2016.01.003
Covell, K., McNeil, J. K., & Howe, R. B. (2009). Reducing teacher burnout by increasing student engagement: A children's rights approach. *School Psychology International, 30,* 282–290. doi:10.1177/0143034309106496

Craig, W. M., Pepler, D., & Atlas, R. (2000). Observations of bullying in the playground and in the classroom. *School Psychology International, 21*, 22–36. doi:10.1177/0143034300211002

Crean, H. F., & Johnson, D. B. (2013). Promoting alternative thinking strategies (PATHS) and elementary school aged children's aggression: Results from a cluster randomized trial. *American Journal of Community Psychology, 52*, 56–72. doi:10.1007/s10464-013-9576-4

Crick, N. R., & Dodge, K. A. (1994). A review and reformulation of social information-processing mechanisms in children's social adjustment. *Psychological Bulletin, 115*, 74–101. doi:10.1037/0033-2909.115.1.74

Crone, D. A., Horner, R. H., & Hawken, L. S. (2004). *Responding to problem behavior in schools: The Behavior Education Program*. New York: Guilford Press.

Crone, D. A., Horner, R. H., & Hawken, L. S. (2010). *Responding to problem behavior in schools: The Behavior Education Program* (2nd ed.). New York: Guilford Press.

Croninger, R. G., & Lee, V. E. (2001). Social capital and dropping out of high school: Benefits to at-risk students of teachers' support and guidance. *Teachers College Record, 103*, 548–581. doi:10.1111/0161-4681.00127

Cunningham, C. E., Mapp, C., Rimas, H., Cunningham, L., Mielko, S., Vaillancourt, T., & Marcus, M. (2016). What limits the effectiveness of antibullying programs? A thematic analysis of the perspective of students. *Psychology of Violence, 6*, 596–606. doi:10.1037/a0039984

Curran, F. C. (2016). Estimating the effect of state zero tolerance laws on exclusionary discipline, racial discipline gaps, and student behavior. *Educational Evaluation and Policy Analysis, 38*, 647–668. doi:10.3102/0162373716652728

Curtis, J. C., Castillo, J. M., & Cohen, R. M. (2008). Best practices in system-level change. In A. Thomas & J. Grimes (Eds.), *Best practices in school psychology* (Vol. 3, 5th ed., pp. 887–902). Bethesda, MD: National Association of School Psychologists.

Curtis, M. J., Batsche, G. M., & Mesmer, E. M. (2000). Implementing the IDEA 1997 amendments: A compelling argument for systems change. In C. F. Telzrow & M. Tankersley (Eds.), *IDEA amendments of 1997: Practice guidelines for school-based teams*. Bethesda, MD: National Association of School Psychologists.

Curwin, R. L., Mendler, A. N., & Mendler, B. D. (2008). *Discipline with dignity: New challenges, new solutions*. Alexandria, VA: Association for Supervision and Curriculum Development.

Danielsen, A. G., Wiium, N., Wilhelmsen, B. U., & Wold, B. (2010). Perceived support provided by teachers and classmates and students' self-reported academic initiative. *Journal of School Psychology, 48*, 247–267. doi:10.1016/j.jsp.2010.02.002

Davis, M. H., & McPartland, J. M. (2012). High school reform and student engagement. In S. L. Christenson, A. L. Reschly, & C. Wylie (Eds.), *Handbook of research on student engagement* (pp. 515–540). New York: Springer.

De Laet, S., Colpin, H., Vervoort, E., Doumen, S., Leeuwen, K. V., Goossens, L., & Verschueren, K. (2015). Developmental trajectories of children's behavioral engagement in late elementary school: Both teachers and peers matter. *Developmental Psychology, 51*, 1292–1306. doi:10.1037/a0039478

de Luque, M. F. S., & Sommer, S. M. (2000). The impact of culture on feedback-seeking behavior: An integrated model and propositions. *The Academy of Management Review, 25*, 829–849. doi:10.2307/259209

Deci, E. L., Koestner, R., & Ryan, R. M. (1999). A meta-analytic review of experiments examining the effects of extrinsic rewards on intrinsic motivation. *Psychological Bulletin, 125*, 627–668. doi:10.1037/0033-2909.125.6.627

Deci, E. L., Koestner, R., & Ryan, R. M. (2001). Extrinsic rewards and intrinsic motivation in education: Reconsidered once again. *Review of Educational Research, 71*, 1–27. doi:10.3102/00346543071001001

Decker, D. M., Dona, D. P., & Christenson, S. L. (2007). Behaviorally at-risk African American students: The importance of student-teacher relationships for student outcomes. *Journal of School Psychology, 45*, 83–109. doi:10.1016/j.jsp.2006.09.004

Demaray, M. K., & Malecki, C. K. (2002). Critical levels of perceived social support associated with student adjustment. *School Psychology Quarterly*, 17, 213–241. doi:10.1521/scpq.17.3.213.20883

Devlin, D. N., & Gottfredson, D. C. (2018). The roles of police officers in schools: Effects on the recording and reporting of crime. *Youth Violence and Juvenile Justice*, 16, 208–223. doi:10.1177/1541204016680405

Dewey, J. (1938). *Experience & Education*. New York: Kappa Delta Pi.

Doll, B., Brehm, K., & Zucker, S. (2014). *Resilient classrooms: Creating healthy environments for learning* (2nd ed.). New York: Guilford Press.

Domitrovich, C. E., Cortes, R., & Greenberg, M. T. (2007). Improving young children's social and emotional competence: A randomized trial of the preschool PATHS curriculum. *Journal of Primary Prevention*, 28, 67–91. doi:10.1007/s10935-007-0081-0

Donohue, K. M., Perry, K. E., & Weinstein, R. S. (2003). Classroom instructional practices and children's rejection by their peers. *Journal of Applied Developmental Psychology*, 24, 91–118. doi:10.1016/S0193-3973(03)00026-1

Doramajian, C., & Bukowski, W. M. (2015). A longitudinal study of the associations between moral disengagement and active defending versus passive bystanding during bullying situations. *Merrill-Palmer Quarterly*, 61, 144–172. doi:10.13110/merrpalmquar1982.61.1.0144

Dornbusch, S. M., Ritter, P. L., Leiderman, P. H., Roberts, D. F., & Fraleigh, M. J. (1987). The relation of parenting style to adolescent school performance. *Child Development*, 58, 1244–1257. doi:10.2307/1130618

Doumen, S., Verschueren, K., Buyse, E., Germeijs, V., Luyckx, K., & Soenens, B. (2008). Reciprocal relations between teacher-child conflict and aggressive behavior in kindergarten: A three-wave longitudinal study. *Journal of Clinical Child and Adolescent Psychology*, 37, 588–599. doi:10.1080/15374410802148079

Doyle, W. (2006). Ecological approaches to classroom management. In C. Evertson & C. Weinstein (Eds.), *Handbook of classroom management: Research, practice, and contemporary issues* (pp. 97–125). New York: Lawrence Erlbaum.

Dreikurs, R. (1968). *Psychology in the classroom: A manual for teachers*. New York: Harper & Row.

Driscoll, K. C., & Pianta, R. C. (2010). Banking time in head start: Early efficacy of an intervention designed to promote supportive teacher-child relationships. *Early Education & Development*, 21, 38–64. doi:10.1080/10409280802657449

Dubow, E. F., Tisak, J., Causey, D., Hryshko, A., & Reid, G. (1991). A two-year longitudinal study of stressful life events, social support, and social problem-solving skills: Contributions to children's behavioral and academic adjustment. *Child Development*, 62, 583–599. doi:10.2307/1131133

Duckworth, A. L., & Seligman, M. E. (2005). Self-discipline outdoes IQ in predicting academic performance of adolescents. *Psychological Science*, 16, 939–944. doi:10.1111/j.1467-9280.2005.01641.x

Duckworth, A. L., & Seligman, M. E. (2017). The science and practice of self-control. *Perspectives on Psychological Science*, 12, 715–718. doi:10.1177/1745691617690880

Duckworth, A. L., Tsukayama, E., & Kirby, T. A. (2013). Is it really self-control? Examining the predictive power of the delay of gratification task. *Personality and Social Psychology Bulletin*, 39, 843–855. doi:10.1177/0146167213482589

Duckworth, A. L., Tsukayama, E., & May, H. (2010). Establishing causality using longitudinal hierarchical linear modeling: An illustration predicting achievement from self-control. *Social Psychological and Personality Science*, 1, 311–317. doi:10.1177/1948550609359707

Duffy, A., & Nesdale, D. (2009). Peer groups, social identity, and children's bullying behaviour. *Social Development*, 18, 121–139. doi:10.1111/j.1467-9507.2008.00484.x

Duke, D. (1989). *Strategies to reduce student misbehavior*. (O. Moles, edited by). Washington, DC: Office of Educational Research and Improvement, US. Department of Education.

Duke, D. L. (2002). *Creating safe schools for all children*. Boston, MA: Allyn & Bacon.

References

Duong, M. T., Pullmann, M. D., Buntain-Ricklefs, J., Lee, K., Benjamin, K. S., Nguyen, L., & Cook, C. R. (2019). Brief teacher training improves student behavior and student-teacher relationships in middle school. *School Psychology, 34,* 212–221. doi:10.1037/spq0000296

Durlak, J. A., & DuPre, E. P. (2008). Implementation matters: A review of research on the influence of implementation on program outcomes and the factors affecting implementation. *American Journal of Community Psychology, 41,* 237–350. doi:10.1007/s10464-008-9165-0

Durlak, J. A., Weissberg, R. P., Dymnicki, A. B., Taylor, R. D., & Schellinger, K. B. (2011). The impact of enhancing social and emotional learning: A meta-analysis of school-based universal interventions. *Child Development, 82,* 405–432. doi:10.1111/j.1467-8624.2010.01564.x

Dweck, C. S. (2012). *Mindset: How you can fulfill your potential.* London: Constable & Robinson Limited.

Eccles, J. S., & Midgley, C. (1989). Stage/environment fit: Developmentally appropriate classrooms for early adolescents. In R. Ames & C. Ames (Eds.), *Research on motivation in education* (Vol. 3, pp. 139–181). New York: Academic Press.

Eisenberg, N., Eggum, N. D., & Di Giunta, L. (2010). Empathy-related responding: Associations with prosocial behavior, aggression, and intergroup relations. *Social Issues and Policy Review, 4,* 143–180. doi:10.1111/j.1751-2409.2010.01020.x

Eisenberg, N., Fabes, R. A., Karbon, M., Murphy, B. C., Wosinski, M., Polazzi. L., & Juhnke, C. (1996). The relations of children's dispositional prosocial behavior to emotionality, regulation, and social functioning. *Child Development, 67,* 974–992. doi:10.1037/0012-1649.32.2.195

Eisenberg, N., Fabes, R. A., & Spinrad, T. L. (2006). Prosocial behavior. In W. Damon, R. M. Learner (Series Eds.), & N. Eisenberg (Vol. Ed.), *Handbook of child psychology: Vol. 3. Social, emotional, and personality development* (6th ed., pp. 646–718). Hoboken, NJ: John Wiley & Sons Inc.

Eisenberg, N., Spinrad, T. L., & Eggum, N. D. (2010). Emotion-related self-regulation and its relation to children's maladjustment. *Annual Review of Clinical Psychology, 6,* 495–525. doi:10.1146/annurev.clinpsy.121208.131208

Eisenberg, N., Zhou, Q., & Koller, S. (2003). Brazilian adolescents' prosocial moral judgment and behavior: Relations to sympathy, perspective taking, gender-role orientation, and demographic characteristics. *Child Development, 72,* 518–534. doi:10.1111/1467-8624.00294

Eliot, M., Cornell, D., Gregory, A., & Fan, X. (2010). Supportive school climate and student willingness to seek help for bullying and threats of violence. *Journal of School Psychology, 48,* 533–553. doi:10.1016/j.jsp.2010.07.001

Elledge, C. L., Elledge, A. R., Newgent, R. A., & Cavell, T. A. (2016). Social risk and peer victimization in elementary school children: The protective role of teacher-student relationships. *Journal of Abnormal Child Psychology, 44,* 691–703. doi:10.1007/s10802-015-0074-z

Elliott, S. N., Frey, J. R., & DiPerna, J. C. (2014). Improving social skills: Enabling academic and interpersonal successes. In S. Brock & S. R. Jimerson (Eds.), *Best practices in school crisis prevention and intervention* (2nd ed., pp. 55–77). Bethesda, MD: National Association of School Psychologists.

Elsaesser, C., Gorman-Smith, D., & Henry, D. (2013). The role of the school environment in relational aggression and victimization. *Journal of Youth and Adolescence, 42,* 235–249. doi:10.1007/s10964-012-9839-7

Emmer, E. T., & Evertson, C. M. (2017). *Classroom management for middle and high school teachers* (10th ed.). Boston, MA: Pearson.

Emmons, C., Haynes, N. M., & Comer, J. P. (2002). *School climate survey: Elementary and middle school version (Revised Edition).* New Haven, CT: Yale University Child Study Center.

Epstein, M., Atkins, M., Cullinan, D., Kutash, K., & Weaver, R. (2008). *Reducing behavior problems in the elementary school classroom: A practice guide (NCEE #2008-012).*

Washington, DC: National Center for Education Evaluation and Regional Assistance, Institute of Education Sciences, U.S. Department of Education. Retrieved from https://ies.ed.gov/ncee/wwc/Docs/PracticeGuide/behavior_pg_092308.pdf

Epstein, R. A., Fonnesbeck, C., Potter, S., Rizzone, K. H., & McPheeters, M. (2015). Psychosocial interventions for child disruptive behaviors: A meta-analysis. *Pediatrics, 136*, 947–960. doi:10.1542/peds.2015-2577

Espelage, D. L., & Hong, J. S. (2019). School climate, bullying, and school violence. In M. J. Mayer & S. R. Jimerson (Eds.), *School safety and violence prevention: Science, practice, and policy* (pp. 45–70). Washington, DC: American Psychological Association.

Espelage, D. L., Low, S., Polanin, J. R., & Brown, E. C. (2015). Clinical trial of Second Step middle-school program: Impact on aggression & victimization. *Journal of Applied Developmental Psychology, 37*, 52–63. doi:10.1016/j.appdev.2014.11.007

Espelage, D. L., Low, S., Polanin, J. R., & Brown, R. (2013). First year outcomes from a trial of the Second Step student success through prevention program. *Journal of Adolescent Health, 53*, 180–186. doi:10.1016/j.jadohealth.2013.02.021

Espelage, D. L., & Swearer, S. M. (Eds.). (2004). *Bullying in American schools: A social-ecological perspective on prevention and intervention*. Mahwah, NJ: Erlbaum.

Espelage, D. L., Low, S., Van Ryzin, M. J., & Polanin, J. R. (2015). Clinical trial of Second Step middle school program: Impact on bullying, cyberbullying, homophobic teasing, and sexual harassment perpetration. *School Psychology Review, 44*, 464–479. doi:10.17105/spr-15-0052.1

Estell, D. B., & Perdue, N. H. (2013). Social support and behavioral and affective school engagement: The effects of peers, parents, and teachers. *Psychology in the Schools, 50*, 325–339. doi:10.1002/pits.21681

Evans, C. B. R., Fraser, M. W., & Cotter, K. L. (2014). The effectiveness of school-based bullying prevention programs: A systematic review. *Aggression and Violent Behavior, 19*, 532–544. doi:10.1016/j.avb.2014.07.004

Evertson, C. M., & Emmer, E. T. (2017). *Classroom management for elementary teachers* (10th ed.). Boston, MA: Pearson.

Faris, R., & Felmlee, D. (2014). Casualties of social combat: School networks of peer victimization and their consequences. *American Sociological Review, 79*, 228–257. doi:10.1177/0003122414524573

Farmer, G. L. (1999). Disciplinary practices and perceptions of school safety. *Journal of Social Service Research, 26*, 1–38. doi:10.1300/J079v26n01_01

Fearon, R., Bakermans-Kranenburg, M., van Ijzendoorn, M., Lapsley, A., & Roisman, G. (2010). The significance of insecure attachment and disorganization in the development of children's externalizing behavior: A meta-analytic study. *Child Development, 81*. doi:10.1111/j.1467-8624.2009.01405.x

Fefer, S. A., & Gordon, K. (2018). Exploring perceptions of school climate among secondary students with varying discipline infractions. *International Journal of School & Educational Psychology*. doi:10.1080/21683603.2018.1541033

Fein, R., Vossekuil, B., Pollack, W., Borum, R., Modzeleski, W., & Reddy, M. (2002). *Threat assessment in schools: A guide to managing threatening situations and to creating safe school climates*. Washington, DC: U.S. Secret Service and Department of Education.

Ferguson, C. J., San Miguel, C., Kilburn, J. C., Jr., & Sanchez, P. (2007). The effectiveness of school-based anti-bullying programs: A meta-analytic review. *Criminal Justice Review, 32*, 401–414. doi:10.1177/0734016807311712

Findlay, L. C., Girardi, A., & Coplan, R. J. (2006). Links between empathy, social behavior, and social understanding in early childhood. *Early Childhood Research Quarterly, 21*, 347–359. doi:10.1016/j.ecresq.2006.07.009

Finkelhor, D., Turner, H. A., Shattuck, A., & Hamby, S. L. (2015). Prevalence of childhood exposure to violence, crime, and abuse: Results from the national survey of children's exposure to violence. *JAMA Pediatrics, 169*, 746–754. doi:10.1001/jamapediatrics.2015.0676

Fisher, B. W., Viano, S., Curran, C. F., Pearman, A. F., & Gardella, J. H. (2018). Students' feelings of safety, exposure to violence and victimization, and authoritative school climate. *American Journal of Criminal Justice*. doi:10.1007/s12103-017-9406-6

Fitzgerald, D. P., & White, K. J. (2003). Linking children's social worlds: Perspective-taking in parent-child and peer contexts. *Social Behavior and Personality*, 31, 509–522. doi:10.2224/sbp.2003.31.5.509

Fitzpatrick, S., & Bussey, K. (2014). The role of perceived friendship self-efficacy as a protective factor against the negative effects of social victimization. *Social Development*, 23, 41–60. doi:10.1111/sode.12032

Flanagan, K. S., Vanden Hoek, K. K., Shelton, A., Kelly, S. L., Morrison, C. M., & Young, A. M. (2013). Coping with bullying: What answers does children's literature provide? *School Psychology International*, 34, 691–706. doi:10.1177/0143034313479691

Flaspohler, P. D., Elfstrom, J. L., Vanderzee, K. L., Sink, H. E., & Birchmeier, Z. (2009). Stand by me: The effects of peer and teacher support in mitigating the impact of bullying on quality of life. *Psychology in the Schools*, 46, 636–649. doi:10.1002/pits.20404

Flower, A., McKenna, J. W., Bunuan, R. L., Muething, C. S., & Vega, R. (2014). Effects of the Good Behavior Game on challenging behaviors in school settings. *Review of Educational Research*, 84, 546–571. doi:10.3102/0034654314536781

Fredricks, J. A., Blumenfeld, P. C., & Paris, A. H. (2004). School engagement: Potential of the concept, state of the evidence. *Review of Educational Research*, 74, 59–109. doi:10.3102/00346543074001059

Fredricks, J. A., & Eccles, J. S. (2006). Extracurricular involvement and adolescent adjustment: Impact of duration, number of activities, and breadth of participation. *Applied Developmental Science*, 10, 132–146. doi:10.1207/s1532480xads1003_3

Fredricks, J. A., & Eccles, J. S. (2008). Participation in extracurricular activities in the middle school years: Are there developmental benefits for African American and European American youth? *Journal of Youth and Adolescence*, 37, 1029–1043. doi:10.1007/s10964-008-9309-4

Free, J. L. (2014). The importance of rule fairness: The influence of school bonds on at-risk students in an alternative school. *Educational Studies*, 40, 144–163. doi:10.1080/03055698.2013.858614

French, D., & Conrad, J. (2003). School dropout as predicted by peer rejection and antisocial behavior. *Journal of Research on Adolescence*, 11, 225–244. doi:10.1111/1532-7795.00011

Frey, K. S., Nolen, S. B., Edstrom, L., & Hirschstein, M. K. (2005). Effects of a school-based social-emotional competence program: Linking children's goals, attributions, and behavior. *Journal of Applied Developmental Psychology*, 26, 171–200. doi:10.1016/j.appdev.2004.12.002

Frick, P. J., & White, S. F. (2008). Research review: The importance of callous-unemotional traits for developmental models of aggressive and antisocial behavior. *Journal of Child Psychology and Psychiatry*, 49, 359–375. doi:10.1111/j.1469-7610.2007.01862.x

Fullan, M. (2007). *The new meaning of educational change* (4th ed.). New York: Teachers College Press.

Gable, R. A., Hester, P. H., Rock, M. L., & Hughes, K. G. (2009). Back to basics. *Intervention in School and Clinic*, 44, 195–205. doi:10.1177/1053451208328831

Gaffney, H., Farrington, D. P., Espelage, D. L., & Ttofi, M. M. (2019). Are cyberbullying intervention and prevention programs effective? A systematic and meta-analytic review. *Aggression and Violent Behavior*. doi:10.1016/j.avb.2018.07.002

Gaffney, H., Ttofi, M. M., & Farrington, D. P. (2019). Evaluating the effectiveness of school-bullying prevention programs: An updated meta-analytical review. *Aggression and Violent Behavior*. doi:10.1016/j.avb.2018.07.001

Gage, N. A., Prykanowski, D. A., & Larson, A. (2014). School climate and bullying victimization: A latent class growth model analysis. *School Psychology Quarterly*, 29, 256–271. doi:10.1037/spq0000064

Garandeau, C. F., Poskiparta, E., & Salmivalli, C. (2014). Tackling acute cases of school bullying in the KiVa anti-bullying program: A comparison of two approaches. *Journal of Abnormal Child Psychology*, 42, 981–991. doi:10.1007/s10802-014-9861-1

Gary, L., & Lewis, L. (2015). *Public school safety and discipline: 2013–14 (NCES 2015-051). U.S. department of education.* Washington, DC: National Center for Education Statistics.

Gathercoal, F. (2001). *Judicious discipline* (5th ed.). San Francisco, CA: Caddo Gap Press.

Gest, S., Madill, R., Zadzora, K., Miller, A., Requa, D., & Rodkin, P. (2014). Teacher management of elementary classroom social dynamics: Associations with changes in student adjustment. *Journal of Emotional and Behavioral Disorders, 22,* 107–118. doi:10.1177/1063426613512677

Gest, S. D., & Rodkin, P. C. (2011). Teaching practices and elementary classroom peer ecologies. *Journal of Applied Developmental Psychology, 32,* 288–296. doi:10.1016/j.appdev.2011.02.004

Gettinger, M. (1988). Methods of proactive classroom management. *School Psychology Review, 17*(2), 227–242.

Gettinger, M., & Walter, M. J. (2012). Classroom strategies to enhance academic engaged time. In S. L. Christenson, A. L. Reschly, & C. Wylie (Eds.), *Handbook of research on student engagement* (pp. 653–673). New York: Springer.

Gilman, R., Huebner, E. S., & Furlong, M. (Eds.). (2009). *Handbook of positive psychology.* New York: Routledge.

Gini, G. (2006). Social cognition and moral cognition in bullying: What's wrong? *Aggressive Behavior, 32,* 528–539. doi:10.1002/ab.20153

Gini, G. (2008). Associations between bullying behavior, psychosomatic complaints, emotional and behavioral problems. *Journal of Pediatrics and Child Health, 44,* 492–497. doi:10.1111/j.1440-1754.2007.01155.x

Gini, G., & Pozzoli, T. (2009). Association between bullying and psychosomatic problems: A meta-analysis. *Pediatrics, 123,* 1059–1065. doi:10.1542/peds.2009-1633

Gini, G., Pozzoli, T., & Hymel, S. (2014). Moral disengagement among children and youth: A meta-analytic review of links to aggressive behavior. *Aggressive Behavior, 40,* 56–68. doi:10.1002/ab.21502

Ginsburg-Block, M., Rohrbeck, C., Fantuzzo, J., & Lavigne, N. C. (2006). Peer-assisted learning strategies. In G. G. Bear & K. M. Minke (Eds.), *Children's needs III: Development, prevention, and intervention* (pp. 631–645, Chapter x, 1106 Pages). Washington, DC: National Association of School Psychologists.

Ginsburg-Block, M., Rohrbeck, C. A., & Fantuzzo, J. W. (2006). A meta-analytic review of social, self-concept, and behavioral outcomes of peer-assisted learning. *Journal of Educational Psychology, 98,* 732–749. doi:10.1037/0022-0663.98.4.732

Girvan, E. J., Gion, C., McIntosh, K., & Smolkowski, K. (2017). The relative contribution of subjective office referrals to racial disproportionality in school discipline. *School Psychology Quarterly, 32,* 392–404. doi:10.1037/spq0000178

Glasser, W. (1969). *Schools without failure.* New York: Harper & Row.

Golding, W. (1954). *Lord of the flies.* New York: The Berkley Publishing Group.

Goleman, D. (1995). *Emotional intelligence.* New York: Bantam.

Gorman-Smith, D., Tolan, P. H., & Henry, D. B. (2000). Patterns of family functioning and adolescent outcomes among urban African American and Mexican American families. *Journal of Family Psychology, 14,* 436–457. doi:10.1037/0893-3200.14.3.436

Gottfredson, D. C. (2001). *Schools and delinquency.* New York: Cambridge University Press.

Gottfredson, D. C., Gottfredson, G. D., & Skroban, S. (1996). A multimodel school-based prevention demonstration. *Journal of Adolescent Research, 11,* 97–115. doi:10.1177/0743554896111006

Gottfredson, G. D., Gottfredson, D. C., Payne, A. A., & Gottfredson, N. C. (2005). School climate predictors of school disorder: Results from a national study of delinquency prevention in schools. *Journal of Research in Crime and Delinquency, 42,* 412–444. doi:10.1177/0022427804271931

Graham, S., & Juvonen, J. (1998). Self-blame and peer victimization in middle school: An attributional analysis. *Developmental Psychology, 34,* 587–599. doi:10.1037/0012-1649.34.3.587

Grant, S., Hamilton, L. S., Wrabel, S. L., Gomez, C. J., Whitaker, A. A., Leschitz, J. T., & Ramos, A. (2017). *Social and emotional learning interventions under the Every Student*

Succeeds Act: Evidence review. Santa Monica, CA: Rand Corporation. Retrieved from www.rand.org/pubs/research_reports/RR2133.html

Gregory, A., & Cornell, D. (2009). "Tolerating" adolescent needs: Moving beyond zero tolerance policies in high school. *Theory into Practice, 48*, 106–113. doi:10.1080/00405840902776327

Gregory, A., Cornell, D., & Fan, X. (2011). The relationship of school structure and support to suspension rates for black and white high school students. *American Educational Research Journal, 48*, 904–934. doi:10.3102/0002831211398531

Gregory, A., Cornell, D., & Fan, X. (2012). Teacher safety and authoritative school climate in high schools. *American Journal of Education, 118*, 401–425. doi:10.1086/666362

Gregory, A., Cornell, D., Fan, X., Sheras, P., Shih, T., & Huang, F. (2010). Authoritative school discipline: High school practices associated with lower bullying and victimization. *Journal of Educational Psychology, 102*, 483–496. doi:10.1037/a0018562

Gregory, A., Hafen, C. A., Ruzek, E., Mikami, A. Y., Allen, J. P., & Pianta, R. C. (2016). Closing the racial discipline gap in classrooms by changing teacher practice. *School Psychology Review, 45*, 171–191. doi:10.17105/SPR45-2.171-191

Gregory, A., & Mosely, P. M. (2004). The discipline gap: Teachers' views on the overrepresentation of African American students in the discipline system. *Equity & Excellence in Education, 37*, 18–30. doi:10.1080/10665680490429280

Gregory, A., Skiba, R. J., & Noguera, P. A. (2010). The achievement gap and the discipline gap: Two sides of the same coin? *Educational Researcher, 39*, 59–68. doi:10.3102/0013189X09357621

Gregory, A., & Weinstein, R. S. (2008). The discipline gap and African Americans: Defiance or cooperation in the high school classroom. *Journal of School Psychology, 46*, 455–475. doi:10.1016/j.jsp.2007.09.001

Gresham, F. M. (1981). Assessment of children's social skills. *Journal of School Psychology, 19*, 120–133. doi:10.1016/0022-4405(81)90054-6

Gresham, F. M. (2004). Current status and future directions of school-based behavioral interventions. *School Psychology Review, 33*(3), 326–343. Retrieved from https://naspjournals.org/loi/spsr

Gresham, F. M., & Elliott, S. N. (2008). *Social skills improvement system rating scales*. Minneapolis, MN: Pearson.

Griffin, K. W., Lowe, S. R., Acevedo, B. P., & Botvin, G. J. (2015). Affective self-regulation trajectories during secondary school predict substance use among urban minority young adults. *Journal of Child & Adolescent Substance Abuse, 24*, 228–234. doi:10.1080/1067828X.2013.812530

Griffith, J. (1995). An empirical examination of a model of social climate in elementary schools. *Basic and Applied Social Psychology, 17*, 97–117. doi:10.1080/01973533.1995.9646134

Griffith, J. (1997). School climate as "social order" and "social action": A multi-level analysis of public elementary school student perceptions. *Social Psychology of Education, 2*, 339–369. doi:10.1023/A:1009657422344

Griffiths, A., Lilles, E., Furlong, M. J., & Sidhwa, J. (2012). The relations of adolescent student engagement with troubling and high-risk behaviors. In S. L. Christenson, A. L. Reschly, & C. Wylie (Eds.), *Handbook of research on student engagement; handbook of research on student engagement* (pp. 563–584). New York: Springer Science + Business Media. doi:10.1007/978-1-4614-2018-7_27

Grossman, D. C., Neckerman, H. J., Koepsell, T. D., Liu, P. Y., Asher, K. N., Beland, K., & Rivara, F. P. (1997). Effectiveness of a violence prevention curriculum among children in elementary school: A randomized controlled trial. *Journal of the American Medical Association, 277*, 1605–1611. doi:10.1001/jama.1997.03540440039030

Grusec, J. E. (2012). Socialization and the role of power assertion. *Human Development, 55*, 52–56. doi:10.1159/000337963

Haataja, A., Voeten, M., Boulton, A. J., Ahtola, A., Poskiparta, E., & Salmivalli, C. (2014). The KiVa antibullying curriculum and outcome: Does fidelity matter? *Journal of School Psychology, 52*, 479–493. doi:10.1016/j.jsp.2014.07.001

Hafen, C. A., Allen, J. P., Mikami, A. Y., Gregory, A., Hamre, B., & Pianta, R. C. (2012). The pivotal role of adolescent autonomy in secondary school classrooms. *Journal of Youth and Adolescence, 41*, 245–255. doi:10.1007/s10964-011-9739-2

Hamm, J. V., Farmer, T. W., Dadisman, K., Gravelle, M., & Murray, A. R. (2011). Teachers' attunement to students' peer group affiliations as a source of improved student experiences of the school social-affective context following the middle school transition. *Journal of Applied Developmental Psychology, 32*, 267–277. doi:10.1016/j.appdev.2010.06.003

Hamre, B. K., & Pianta, R. (2001). Early teacher-child relationships and the trajectory of children's school outcomes through eighth grade. *Child Development, 72*, 625–638. doi:10.1111/1467-8624.00301

Hamre, B. K., & Pianta, R. C. (2004). Self-reported depression in non-familial caregivers: Prevalence and associations with caregiver behavior in child-care settings. *Early Childhood Research Quarterly, 19*, 297–318. doi:10.1016/j.ecresq.2004.04.006

Hamre, B. K., & Pianta, R. C. (2005). Can instructional and emotional support in the first-grade classroom make a difference for children at risk of school failure? *Child Development, 76*, 949–967. doi:10.1111/j.1467-8624.2005.00889.x

Hamre, B. K., & Pianta, R. C. (2007). Learning opportunities in preschool and early elementary classrooms. In R. Pianta, M. Cox, & K. Snow (Eds.), *School readiness & the transition to kindergarten in the era of accountability* (pp. 49–84). Baltimore, MD: Brookes.

Hamre, B. K., & Pianta, R. C. (2009). Conceptualization, measurement, and improvement of classroom processes: Standardized observation can leverage capacity. *Educational Researcher, 38*, 109–119. doi:10.3102/0013189X09332374

Hamre, B. K., Pianta, R. C., Mashburn, A. J., & Downer, J. T. (2012). Promoting young children's social competence through the preschool PATHS curriculum and MyTeachingPartner professional development resources. *Early Education and Development, 23*, 1040–9289. doi:10.1080/10409289.2011.607360

Hardy, S. A., & Carlo, G. (2005). Identity as a source of moral motivation. *Human Development, 48*, 232–256. doi:10.1159/000086859

Hart, D., Atkins, R., & Donnelly, T. M. (2006). Community service and moral development. In M. Killen & J. Smetana (Eds.), *Handbook of moral development* (pp. 633–656). Mahwah, NJ: Erlbaum.

Hart, D., Matsuba, M. K., & Atkins, R. (2008). The moral and civic effects of learning to serve. In L. P. Nucci & D. Narvaez (Eds.), *Handbook of moral and character education* (pp. 484–499). New York: Routledge.

Harter, S. (2006). The self. In W. Damon, R. M. Lerner (Series Eds.) & N. Eisenberg (Vol. Eds.), *Handbook of child psychology: Vol. 3. Social, emotional, and personality development* (6th ed., pp. 505–570). Hoboken, NJ: John Wiley & Sons Inc.

Hay, D. F., Payne, A., & Chadwick, A. (2004). Peer relations in childhood. *Journal of Child Psychology and Psychiatry, 45*, 84–108. doi:10.1046/j.0021-9630.2003.00308.x

Haynes, N. M., Emmons, C., & Ben-Avie, M. (1997). School climate as a factor in student adjustment and achievement. *Journal of Educational and Psychological Consultation, 8*, 321–329. doi:10.1207/s1532768xjepc0803_4

Haynes, N. M., Emmons, C., & Comer, J. P. (1994). *School climate survey: Elementary and middle school version*. New Haven, CT: Yale University Child Study Center.

Haynie, D. L., Nansel, T., Eitel, P., Davis-Crump, A., Saylor, K., Yu, K., & Simons-Morton, B. (2001). Bullies, victims, and bully/victims: Distinct groups of at-risk youth. *Journal of Early Adolescence, 21*, 29–49. doi:10.1177/0272431601021001002

Hemphill, S. A., Toumbourou, J. W., Herrenkohl, T. I., McMorris, B. J., & Catalano, R. F. (2006). The effect of school suspensions and arrests on subsequent adolescent antisocial behavior in Australia and the United States. *Journal of Adolescent Health, 39*, 736–744. doi:10.1016/j.jadohealth.2006.05.010

Henderlong, J., & Lepper, M. R. (2002). The effects of praise on children's intrinsic motivation. A review and synthesis. *Psychological Bulletin, 128*, 774–795. doi:10.1037/0033-2909.128.5.774

Henry, D. B., Farrell, A. D., Schoeny, M. E., Tolan, P. H., & Dymnicki, A. (2011). Influence of school-level variables on aggression and associated attitudes during middle school. *Journal of School Psychology, 49*, 481–503. doi:10.1016/j.jsp.2011.04.007

Hernández, M. M., Eisenberg, N., Valiente, C., Spinrad, T. L., Berger, R. H., VanSchyndel, S. K., & Southworth, J. (2018). Bidirectional associations between emotions and school adjustment. *Journal of Personality, 86*, 853–867. doi:10.1111/jopy.12361

Herndon, J. S., Bembenutty, H., & Gill, M. G. (2015). The role of delay of gratification, substance abuse, and violent behavior on academic achievement of disciplinary alternative middle school students. *Personality and Individual Differences, 86*, 44–49. doi:10.1016/j.paid.2015.05.028

Hirschfield, P. J. (2018). Schools and crime. *Annual Review of Criminology, 1*, 12–28. doi:10.1146/annurev-criminol-032317-092358

Hirschfield, P. J., & Gasper, J. (2011). The relationship between school engagement and delinquency in late childhood and early adolescence. *Journal of Youth and Adolescence, 40*, 3–22. doi:10.1007/s10964-010-9579-5

Hirschi, T. (1969). *Causes of delinquency*. Berkeley, CA: University of California Press.

Hodges, E. V. E., & Perry, D. G. (1999). Personal and interpersonal antecedents and consequences of victimization by peers. *Journal of Personality and Social Psychology, 76*, 677–685. doi:10.1037/0022-3514.76.4.677

Hoffman, M. L. (2000). *Empathy and moral development: Implications for caring and justice*. Cambridge: Cambridge University Press.

Holsen, I., Smith, B. H., & Frey, K. S. (2008). Outcomes of the social competence program Second Step in Norwegian elementary schools. *School Psychology International, 29*, 71–88. doi:10.1177/0143034307088504

Hong, J. S., Espelage, D. L., Grogan-Kaylor, A., & Allen-Meares, P. (2012). Identifying potential mediators and moderators of the association between child maltreatment and bullying perpetration and victimization in school. *Educational Psychology Review, 24*, 167–186. doi:10.1007/s10648-011-9185-4

Hoover, J. H., Oliver, R., & Hazler, R. J. (1992). Bullying: Perceptions of adolescent victims in the midwestern USA. *School Psychology International, 13*, 5–16. doi:10.1177/0143034392131001

Horner, R. H. (2000). Positive behavior supports. *Focus on Autism and Other Developmental Disabilities, 15*, 97–105. doi:10.1177/108835760001500205

Horner, R. H., Sugai, G., Todd, A. W., & Lewis-Palmer, T. (2005). Schoolwide behavior support. In L. M. Bambara & L. Kern (Eds.), *Individualized supports for students with problem behaviors: Designing positive behavior plans* (pp. 359–390). New York: Guilford Press.

Houts, R. M., Caspi, A., Pianta, R. C., Arseneault, L., & Moffitt, T. E. (2010). The challenging pupil in the classroom: The effect of the child on the teacher. *Psychological Science, 21*, 1802–1810. doi:10.1177/0956797610388047

Howes, C., Hamilton, C. E., & Matheson, C. C. (1994). Children's relationships with peers: Differential associations with aspects of the teacher-child relationship. *Child Development, 65*, 253–263. doi:10.2307/1131379

Huang, F. L., & Cornell, D. (2018). The relationship of school climate with out-of-school suspensions. *Children and Youth Services Review, 94*, 378–389. doi:10.1016/j.childyouth.2018.08.013

Huang, F. L., Lewis, C., Cohen, D. R., Prewett, S., & Herman, K. (2018). Bullying involvement, teacher-student relationships, and psychosocial outcomes. *School Psychology Quarterly, 33*, 223–234. doi:10.1037/spq0000249

Hughes, J. M., Bigler, R. S., & Levy, S. R. (2007). Consequences of learning about historical racism among European American and African American children. *Child Development, 78*, 1689–1705. doi:10.1111/j.1467-8624.2007.01096.x

Hughes, J. N. (2002). Authoritative teaching: Tipping the balance in favor of school versus peer effects. *Journal of School Psychology, 40*, 485–492. doi:10.1016/S0022-4405(02)00125-5

Hughes, J. N., & Cao, Q. (2018). Trajectories of teacher-student warmth and conflict at the transition to middle school: Effects on academic engagement and achievement. *Journal of School Psychology, 67*, 148–162. doi:10.1016/j.jsp.2017.10.003

Hughes, J. N., Cavell, T. A., & Willson, V. (2001). Further support for the developmental significance of the quality of the teacher-student relationship. *Journal of School Psychology, 39*, 289–301. doi:10.1016/S0022-4405(01)00074-7

Hughes, J. N., & Kwok, O. (2006). Classroom engagement mediates the effect of teacher-student support on elementary students' peer acceptance: A prospective analysis. *Journal of School Psychology, 43*, 465–480. doi:10.1016/j.jsp.2005.10.001

Hughes, J. N., Luo, W., Kwok, O., & Loyd, L. K. (2008). Teacher-student support, effortful engagement, and achievement: A 3-year longitudinal study. *Journal of Educational Psychology, 100*, 1–14. doi:10.1037/0022-0663.100.1.1

Hughes, K., & Coplan, R. J. (2018). Why classroom climate matters for children high in anxious solitude: A study of differential susceptibility. *School Psychology Quarterly, 33*, 94–102. doi:10.1037/spq0000201

Humphrey, N., Barlow, A., Wigelsworth, M., Lendrum, A., Pert, K., Joyce, C., & Turner, A. (2016). A cluster randomized controlled trial of the Promoting Alternative Thinking Strategies (PATHS) curriculum. *Journal of School Psychology, 58*, 73–89. doi:10.1016/j.jsp.2016.07.002

Hutzell, K. L., & Payne, A. A. (2012). The impact of bullying victimization on school avoidance. *Youth Violence and Juvenile Justice, 10*, 370–385. doi:10.1177/1541204012438926

Hwang, N. (2018). Suspensions and achievement: Vary links by type, frequency, and subgroup. *Educational Researcher, 47*, 363–374. doi:10.3102/0013189X18779579

Hymel, S., & Bonanno, R. A. (2014). Moral disengagement processes in bullying. *Theory into Practice, 53*, 278–285. doi:10.1080/00405841.2014.947219

Izard, C. E. (1991). *The psychology of emotions*. New York: Plenum Press.

Jenkins, L. N., & Demaray, M. K. (2012). Social support and self-concept in relation to peer victimization and peer aggression. *Journal of School Violence, 11*, 56–74. doi:10.1080/15388220.2011.630958

Jennings, P. A., & Greenberg, M. T. (2009). The prosocial classroom: Teacher social and emotional competence in relation to student and classroom outcomes. *Review of Educational Research, 79*, 491–525. doi:10.3102/0034654308325693

Jerome, E. M., Hamre, B. K., & Pianta, R. C. (2009). Teacher-child relationships from kindergarten to sixth grade: Early childhood predictors of teacher-perceived conflict and closeness. *Social Development, 18*, 915–945. doi:10.1111/sode.2009.18.issue-410.1111/j.1467-9507.2008.00508.x

Jia, M., & Mikami, A. (2018). Issues in the assessment of bullying: Implications for conceptualizations and future directions. *Aggression and Violent Behavior, 41*, 108–118. doi:10.1016/j.avb.2018.05.004

Jiang, X., Huebner, E. S., & Siddall, J. (2013). A short-term longitudinal study of differential sources of school-related social support and adolescents' school satisfaction. *Social Indicators Research, 114*, 1073–1086. doi:10.1007/s11205-012-0190-x

Jimerson, S., Egeland, B., Sroufe, L. A., & Carlson, B. (2000). A prospective longitudinal study of high school dropouts examining multiple predictors across development. *Journal of School Psychology, 38*, 525–549. doi:10.1016/S0022-4405(00)00051-0

Johnson, D. W., & Johnson, R. T. (2006). Conflict resolution, peer mediation, and peacemaking. In C. M. Evertson & C. S. Weinstein (Eds.), *Handbook of classroom management: Research, practice, and contemporary issues* (pp. 803–832). Mahwah, NJ: Erlbaum.

Johnson, J. F., Jr., Perez, L. G., & Uline, C. L. (2013). *Teaching practices from America's best urban schools: A guide for school and classroom leaders*. Larchmont: Eye on Education.

Johnson, S. L. (2009). Improving the school environment to reduce school violence: A review of the literature. *Journal of School Health, 79*, 451–465. doi:10.1111/j.1746-1561.2009.00435.x

Jones, S. M., & Bouffard, S. M. (2012). Social and emotional learning in schools: From programs to strategies. Social policy report. *Society for Research in Child Development, 26*, 1–33.

Jones, S. M., Brown, J. L., & Aber, J. L. (2011). Two-year impacts of a universal school-based social-emotional and literacy intervention: An experiment in translational developmental research. *Child Development, 82*, 533–554. doi:10.1111/j.1467-8624.2010.01560.x

Jones, V., & Jones, L. (2010). *Comprehensive classroom management: Creating communities of support and solving problems* (9th ed.). Upper Saddle River, NJ: Merrill.

Jones, V., & Jones, L. (2016). *Comprehensive classroom management: Creating communities of support and solving problems* (11th ed.). New York: Pearson.

Juvonen, J., Espinoza, G., & Knifsend, C. (2012). The role of peer relationships in student academic and extracurricular engagement. In S. L. Christenson, A. L. Reschly, & C. Wylie (Eds.), *Handbook of research on student engagement* (pp. 387–401). New York: Springer.

Karcher, M. J. (2002). The cycle of violence and disconnection among rural middle school students: Teacher disconnection as a consequence of violence. *Journal of School Violence, 1*, 35–51. doi:10.1300/J202v01n01_03

Kärnä, A., Voeten, M., Little, T. D., Alanen, E., Poskiparta, E., & Salmivalli, C. (2013). "Effectiveness of the KiVa antibullying program: Grades 1–3 and 7–9": Correction. *Journal of Educational Psychology, 105*, 551. doi:10.1037/a0031120

Katz, J. (2013). The three block model of universal design for learning (UDL): Engaging students in inclusive education. *Canadian Journal of Education, 36*, 153–194.

Kauffman, J. M., & Brigham, F. J. (2000). Editorial: Zero tolerance and bad judgment in working with students with emotional or behavioral disorders. *Behavioral Disorders, 25*(4), 277–279.

Kauffman, J. M., Conroy, M., Gardner, R., & Oswald, D. (2008). Cultural sensitivity in the application of behavior principles to education. *Education and Treatment of Children, 31*, 239–262. doi:10.1353/etc.0.0019

Kauffman, J. M., & Landrum, T. J. (2018). *Characteristics of emotional and behavioral disorders of children and youth* (11th ed.). New York: Pearson.

Kellam, S. G., Brown, C. H., Poduska, J., Ialongo, N., Wang, W., Toyinbo, P., & Wilcox, H. C. (2008). Effects of a universal classroom behavior management program in first and second grades on young adult behavioral, psychiatric, and social outcomes. *Drug and Alcohol Dependence, 95*, S5–S28. doi:10.1016/j.drugalcdep.2008.01.004

Kern, L., & Clemens, N. H. (2007). Antecedent strategies to promote appropriate classroom behavior. *Psychology in the Schools, 44*, 65–75. doi:10.1002/pits.20206

Kim, Y. S., & Leventhal, B. (2008). Bullying and suicide: A review. *International Journal of Adolescent Medical Health, 20*, 133–154. doi:10.1515/IJAMH.2008.20.2.133

Kitsantas, A., Reiser, B., & Doster, J. (2004). Goal setting, cues, and evaluation during acquisition of procedural skills: Empowering students' learning during independent practice. *Journal of Experimental Education, 72*, 269–287. doi:10.3200/JEXE.72.4.269-287

Kitsantas, A., Ware, H. W., & Martinez-Arias, R. (2004). Students' perceptions of school safety: Effects by community, school environment, and substance use variables. *The Journal of Early Adolescence, 24*, 412–430. doi:10.1177/0272431604268712

Kiuru, K., Nurmi, J.-E., Leskinen, E., Torppa, M., Poikkeus, A.-M., Lerkkanen, M.-K., & Niemi, P. (2015). Elementary school teachers adapt their instructional support according to students' academic skills: A variable and person-oriented approach. *International Journal of Behavioral Development, 39*, 391–401. doi:10.1177/0165025415575764

Klein, J., Cornell, D., & Konold, T. (2012). Relationships between bullying, school climate, and student risk behaviors. *School Psychology Quarterly, 27*, 154–169. doi:10.1037/a0029350

Klem, A. M., & Connell, J. P. (2004). Relationships matter: Linking teacher support to student engagement and achievement. *Journal of School Health, 74*, 262–273. doi:10.1111/j.1746-1561.2004.tb08283.x

Kljakovic, M., & Hunt, C. (2016). A meta-analysis of predictors of bullying and victimisation in adolescence. *Journal of Adolescence*, 49, 134–145. doi:10.1016/j.adolescence.2016.03.002

Klomek, A. B., Marrocco, F., Kleinman, M., Schonfeld, I. S., & Gould, M. S. (2007). Bullying, depression, and suicidality in adolescents. *Journal of the American Academy of Child & Adolescent Psychiatry*, 46, 40–49. doi:10.1097/01.chi.0000242237.84925.18

Kochenderfer-Ladd, B., & Skinner, K. (2002). Children's coping strategies: Moderators of the effects of peer victimization? *Developmental Psychology*, 38, 267–278. doi:10.1037//0012-1649.38.2.267

Kohlberg, L. (1984). *Essays on moral development: Vol. 2. The psychology of moral development*. New York: Harper & Row.

Kokkinos, C. M., & Kipritsi, E. (2012). The relationship between bullying, victimization, trait emotional intelligence, self-efficacy, and empathy among preadolescents. *Social Psychology of Education*, 15, 41–58. doi:10.1007/s11218-011-9168-9

Kokkinos, C. M., & Panayiotou, G. (2007). Parental discipline practices and locus of control: Relationship to bullying and victimization experiences of elementary school students. *Social Psychology of Education*, 10, 281–301. doi:10.1007/s11218-007-9021-3

Konold, T., Cornell, D., Huang, F., Meyer, P., Lacey, A., Nekvasil, E., Heilbrun, A., Shukla, K. (2014). Multi-level multi-informant structure of the authoritative school climate survey. *School Psychology Quarterly*, 3, 238–255. doi:10.1037/spq0000062

Korpershoek, H., Harms, T., de Boer, H., van Kuijk, M., & Doolaard, S. (2016). A meta-analysis of the effects of classroom management strategies and classroom management programs on students' academic, behavioral, emotional, and motivational outcomes. *Review of Educational Research*, 86, 643–680. doi:10.3102/0034654315626799

Koth, C. W., Bradshaw, C. P., & Leaf, P. J. (2008). A multilevel study of predictors of student perceptions of school climate: The effect of classroom-level factors. *Journal of Educational Psychology*, 100, 96–104. doi:10.1037/0022-0663.100.1.96

Kounin, J. (1970). *Discipline and group management in classrooms*. New York: Holt, Rinehart & Winston.

Kounin, J. S., & Gump, P. (1974). Signal systems of lesson settings and the task-related behavior of preschool children. *Journal of Educational Psychology*, 66, 554–562. doi:10.1037/h0036748

Kupchik, A. (2016). *The real school safety problem: The long-term consequences of harsh school punishment*. Oakland, CA: University of California Press.

Kupersmidt, J. B., & DeRosier, M. E. (2004). How peer problems lead to negative outcomes: An integrative mediational model. In J. B. Kupersmidt & K. A. Dodge (Eds.), *Children's peer relations: From development to intervention* (pp. 119–138). Washington, DC: American Psychological Association.

Kusché, C. A., & Greenberg, M. T. (2012). The PATHS curriculum: Promoting emotional literacy, prosocial behavior, and caring classrooms. In S. R. Jimerson, A. B. Nickerson, M. Mayer, & M. J. Furlong (Eds.), *Handbook of school violence and school safety: International research and practice* (2nd ed., pp. 435–446). New York: Taylor & Francis.

Kwak, M., & Oh, I. (2017). Comparison of psychological and social characteristics among traditional, cyber, combined bullies, and non-involved. *School Psychology International*, 38, 608–627. doi:10.1177/0143034317729424

Kwon, K., Kim, E. M., & Sheridan, S. M. (2012). A contextual approach to social skills assessment in the peer group: Who is the best judge? *School Psychology Quarterly*, 27, 121–133. doi:10.1037/a0028696

La Greca, A. M., Boyd, B. A., Jaycox, L. H., Kassam-Adams, N., Mannarino, A. P., Silverman, W. K., & Wong, M. (2008). *Children and trauma: Update for mental health professionals*. Retrieved from www.apa.org/pi/families/resources/children-trauma-update

Landrum, T. J., & Kauffman, J. M. (2006). Behavioral approaches to classroom management. In C. M. Evertson & C. S. Weinstein (Eds.), *Handbook of classroom management: Research, practice, and contemporary issues* (pp. 47–71). Mahwah, NJ: Erlbaum.

Lansford, J. E., Malone, P. S., Dodge, K. A., Pettit, G. S., & Bates, J. E. (2010). Developmental cascades of peer rejection, social information processing biases, and aggression during middle childhood. *Development and Psychopathology*, 22, 593–602. doi:10.1017/S0954579410000301

Lee, J., & Shute, V. J. (2010). Personal and social-contextual factors in K-12 academic performance: An integrative perspective on student learning. *Educational Psychologist*, 45, 185–202. doi:10.1080/00461520.2010.493471

Lee, J. S. (2012). The effects of the teacher-student relationship and academic press on student engagement and academic performance. *International Journal of Educational Research*, 53, 330–340. doi:10.1016/j.ijer.2012.04.006

Lee, V. E., & Burkam, D. T. (2002). *Inequality at the starting gate: Social background differences in achievement as children begin school*. Washington, DC: Economic Policy Institute.

Lei, H., Cui, Y., & Zhou, W. (2018). Relationships between student engagement and academic achievement: A meta-analysis. *Social Behavior and Personality: An International Journal*, 46, 517–528. doi:10.2224/sbp.7054

Lepper, M. (1983). Social-control processes and the internalization of social values: An attributional perspective. In E. T. Higgins, D. Ruble, & W. Hartup (Eds.), *Social cognition and social development: A socio-cultural perspective* (pp. 294–330). New York: Cambridge University Press.

Lereya, S. T., Samara, M., & Wolke, D. (2013). Parenting behavior and the risk of becoming a victim and a bully/victim: A meta-analysis study. *Child Abuse & Neglect*, 37, 1091–1108. doi:10.1016/j.chiabu.2013.03.001

Lester, L., Cross, D., & Shaw, T. (2012). Problem behaviors, traditional bullying, and cyberbullying among adolescents: Longitudinal analyses. *Emotional and Behavioral Difficulties*, 17, 435–447. doi:10.1080/13632752.2012.704313

Li, X., Bian, C., Chen, Y., Huang, J., Ma, Y., Tang, L., & Yu, Y. (2015). Indirect aggression and parental attachment in early adolescence: Examining the role of perspective taking and empathetic concern. *Personality and Individual Differences*, 86, 499–503. doi:10.1016/j.paid.2015.07.008

Li, Y., & Lerner, R. M. (2011). Trajectories of school engagement during adolescence: Implications for grades, depression, delinquency, and substance use. *Developmental Psychology*, 47, 233–247. doi:10.1007/s10964-012-9857-5

Li, Y., & Lerner, R. M. (2013). Interrelations of behavioral, emotional, and cognitive school engagement in high school students. *Journal of Youth and Adolescence*, 42, 20–32. doi:10.1007/s10964-012-9857-5

Li, Y., Lynch, A. D., Kalvin, C., Liu, J., & Lerner, R. M. (2011). Peer relationships as a context for the development of school engagement during early adolescence. *International Journal of Behavioral Development*, 35, 329–342. doi:10.1177/0165025411402578

Limber, S. P. (2011). Development, evaluation, and future directions of the Olweus bullying prevention program. *Journal of School Violence*, 10, 71–87. doi:10.1080/15388220.2010.519375

Losen, D. J. (2013). Discipline policies, successful schools, racial justice, and the law. *Family Court Review*, 51, 388–400. doi:10.1111/fcre.12035

Losen, D. J., & Martinez, T. E. (2013). *Out of school and off-track: The overuse of suspensions in American middle and high schools*. Los Angeles, CA: Center for Civil Rights Remedies, The Civil Rights Project.

Low, S., Cook, C. R., Smolkowski, K., & Buntain-Ricklefs, J. (2015). Promoting social-emotional competence: An evaluation of the elementary version of Second Step. *Journal of School Psychology*, 53, 463–477. doi:10.1016/j.jsp.2015.09.002

Low, S., & Van Ryzin, M. (2014). The moderating effects of school climate on bullying prevention efforts. *School Psychology Quarterly*, 29, 306–319. doi:10.1037/spq0000073

Lubbers, M. J., Van Der Werf, M. P. C., Snijders, T. A. B., Creemers, B. P. M., & Kuyper, H. (2006). The impact of peer relations on academic progress in junior high. *Journal of School Psychology*, 44, 491–512. doi:10.1016/j.jsp.2006.07.005

Luckner, A. E., & Pianta, R. C. (2011). Teacher-student interactions in fifth grade classrooms: Relations with children's peer behavior. *Journal of Applied Developmental Psychology, 32*, 257–266. doi:10.1016/j.appdev.2011.02.010

Lynass, L., Tsai, S., Richman, T. D., & Cheney, D. (2012). Social expectations and behavioral indicators in school-wide positive behavior supports: A national study of behavior matrices. *Journal of Positive Behavior Interventions, 14*, 153–161. doi:10.1177/1098300711412076

Ma, X. (2002). Bullying in middle school: Individual and school characteristics of victims and offenders. *School Effectiveness and School Improvement, 13*, 63–89. doi:10.1076/sesi.13.1.63.3438

Maag, J. W. (2005). Social skills training for youth with emotional and behavioral disorders and learning disabilities: Problems, conclusions, and suggestions. *Exceptionality, 13*, 155–172. doi:10.1207/s15327035ex1303_2

Maag, J. W. (2006). Social skills training for students with emotional and behavioral disorders: A review of reviews. *Behavioral Disorders, 32*, 5–17. doi:10.1177/019874290603200104

Macmillan, R., & Hagan, J. (2004). Violence in the transition to adulthood: Adolescent victimization, education, and socioeconomic attainment in later life. *Journal of Research on Adolescence, 14*, 127–158. doi:10.1111/j.1532-7795.2004.01402001.x

Madfis, E. (2014). Averting school rampage: Student intervention amid a persistent code of silence. *Youth Violence and Juvenile Justice, 12*, 229–249. doi:10.1177/1541204013497768

Madjar, N., & Cohen-Malayev, M. (2016). Perceived school climate across the transition from elementary to middle school. *School Psychology Quarterly, 31*, 270–288. doi:10.1037/spq0000129

Maggin, D. M., Pustejovsky, J. E., & Johnson, A. H. (2017). A meta-analysis of school-based group contingency interventions for students with challenging behavior: An update. *Remedial and Special Education, 38*, 353–370.

Mahoney, J. L. (2000). School extracurricular activity participation as a moderator in the development of antisocial patterns. *Child Development, 71*, 502–516. doi:10.1111/1467-8624.00160

Mahoney, J. L., & Cairns, R. B. (1997). Do extracurricular activities protect against early school dropout? *Developmental Psychology, 33*, 241–253. doi:10.1037/0012-1649.33.2.241

Malti, T., & Krettenauer, T. (2013). The relation of moral emotion attributions to prosocial and antisocial behavior: A meta-analysis. *Child Development, 84*, 397–412. doi:10.1111/j.1467-8624.2012.01851.x

Mandara, J., & Murray, C. B. (2002). Development of an empirical typology of African American family functioning. *Journal of Family Psychology, 16*, 318–337. doi:10.1037/0893-3200.16.3.318

Manlove, J. (1998). The influence of high school dropout and school disengagement on the risk of school-age pregnancy. *Journal of Research on Adolescence, 8*, 187–220. doi:10.1207/s15327795jra0802_2

Manning, M. A., & Bear, G. G. (2011). Moral reasoning and aggressive behavior: Concurrent and longitudinal relations. *Journal of School Violence, 11*, 258–280. doi:10.1080/15388220.2011.579235

Manning, M. A., Bear, G. G., & Minke, K. M. (2006). Self-concept and self-esteem. In G. G. Bear & K. M. Minke (Eds.), *Children's needs III: Development, prevention, and intervention* (pp. 341–356). Bethesda, MD: National Association of School Psychologists.

Mantz, L., Bear, G. G., Yang, C., & Harris, A. (2016). The Delaware Social-Emotional Competency Scale (DSESC-S): Evidence of validity and reliability. *Child Indicators Research, 11*. Advance online publication. doi:10.1007/s12187-016-9427-6

Marsh, H. W., Nagengast, B., Morin, A. J. S., Parada, R. H., Craven, R. G., & Hamilton, L. R. (2011). Construct validity of the multidimensional structure of bullying and victimization: An application of exploratory structural equation modeling. *Journal of Educational Psychology, 103*, 701–732. doi:10.1037/a0024122

Martin, A. J. (2015). The role of personal best (PB) goal setting in students' academic achievement gains. *Learning and Individual Differences*, 45. doi:10.1016/j.lindif.2015.12.014

Martin, A. J., & Collie, R. J. (2019). Teacher-student relationships and students' engagement in high school: Does the number of negative and positive relationships with teachers matter? *Journal of Educational Psychology*, 111, 861–876. doi:10.1037/edu0000317

Marzano, R. J. (2003). *Classroom management that works: Research-based strategies for every teacher*. Alexandria, VA: Association for Supervision and Curriculum Development.

Mashburn, A. J., Hamre, B. K., Downer, J. T., & Pianta, R. C. (2006). Teacher, classroom, and child factors associated with teachers' ratings of preschoolers' relationships and behaviors. *Journal of Psychoeducational Assessment*, 24, 367–380. doi:10.1177/0734282906290594

Maslow, A. H. (1943). A theory of human motivation. *Psychological Review*, 50, 370–396. doi:10.1037/h0054346

Masten, C. L., Morelli, S. A., & Eisenberger, N. I. (2011). An fMRI investigation of empathy for 'social pain' and subsequent prosocial behavior. *Neuroimage*, 55, 381–388. doi:10.1016/j.neuroimage.2010.11.060

Mayer, M. J., & Jimerson, S. R. (2019). The importance of school safety and violence prevention. In M. J. Mayer & S. R. Jimerson (Eds.), *School safety and violence prevention: Science, practice, and policy* (pp. 4–16). Washington, DC: American Psychological Association. doi:10.1037/0000106-003

Mayer, M. J., & Leone, P. E. (1999). A structural analysis of school violence and disruption: Implications for creating safer schools. *Education and Treatment of Children*, 22(3), 333–356.

McClellan, B. E. (1999). *Moral education in America: Schools and the shaping of character from colonial times to the present*. New York: Teachers College Press.

McIntosh, K., Filter, K. J., Bennett, J. L., Ryan, C., & Sugai, G. (2010). Principles of sustainable prevention: Designing scale-up of school-wide positive behavior support to promote durable systems. *Psychology in the Schools*, 47, 5–21. doi:10.1002/pits.20448

McKnight, K., Graybeal, J., Yarbro, J., & Graybeal, L. (2016). *The heart of great teaching: Pearson global survey of educator effectiveness*. Upper Saddle River, NJ: Pearson.

Meehan, B. T., Hughes, J. N., & Cavell, T. A. (2003). Teacher-student relationships as compensatory resources for aggressive children. *Child Development*, 74, 1145–1157. doi:10.1111/1467-8624.00598

Merrell, K. W., Gueldner, B. A., Ross, S. W., & Isava, D. M. (2008). How effective are school bullying intervention programs? A meta-analysis of intervention research. *School Psychology Quarterly*, 23, 26–42. doi:10.1037/1045-3830.23.1.26

Migliaccio, T., Raskauskas, J., & Schmidtlein, M. (2017). Mapping the landscapes of bullying. *Learning Environments Research*, 20, 365–382. doi:10.1007/s10984-017-9229-x

Mikami, A. Y., Gregory, A., Allen, J. P., Pianta, R. C., & Lun, J. (2011). Effects of a teacher professional development intervention on peer relationships in secondary classrooms. *School Psychology Review*, 40(3), 367–385. Retrieved from www.ncbi.nlm.nih.gov/pmc/articles/PMC3379816/

Mikami, A. Y., Reuland, M. M., Griggs, M. S., & Jia, M. (2013). Collateral effects of a peer relationship intervention for children with attention deficit hyperactivity disorder on typically developing classmates. *School Psychology Review*, 42(4), 458–476.

Miller, C. F., Kochel, K. P., Wheeler, L. A., Updegraff, K. A., Fabes, R. A., Martin, C. L., & Hanish, L. D. (2017). The efficacy of a relationship building intervention in 5th grade. *Journal of School Psychology*, 61, 75–88. doi:101007/s10984-017-9229-x10.1016/j.jsp.2017.01.002

Mitchell, M. M., & Bradshaw, C. P. (2013). Examining classroom influences on student perceptions of school climate: The role of classroom management and exclusionary discipline strategies. *Journal of School Psychology*, 51, 599–610. doi:10.1016/j.jsp.2013.05.005

References

Moffitt, T. E., Arseneault, L., Belsky, D., Dickson, N., Hancox, R. J., Harrington, H., & Caspi, A. (2011). A gradient of childhood self-control predicts health, wealth, and public safety. *Proceedings of the National Academy of Sciences of the United States*, *108*, 2693–2698. doi: 10.1073/pnas.1010076108

Monahan, K. C., VanDerhei, S., Bechtold, J., & Cauffman, E. (2014). From the school yard to the squad car: School discipline, truancy, and arrest. *Journal of Youth and Adolescence*, *43*, 1110–1122. doi:10.1007/s10964-014-0103-1

Montuoro, P., & Lewis, R. (2015). Student perceptions of misbehavior and classroom management. In E. T. Emmer & E. J. Sabornie (Eds.), *Handbook of classroom management* (pp. 344–362). New York: Routledge.

Morgan-D'Atrio, C., Northup, J., LaFleur, L., & Spera, S. (1996). Toward prescriptive alternatives to suspensions: A preliminary evaluation. *Behavioral Disorders*, *21*, 190–200. doi:10.1177%2F019874299602100206

Morin, H. K., Bradshaw, C. P., & Berg, J. K. (2015). Examining the link between peer victimization and adjustment problems in adolescents: The role of connectedness and parent engagement. *Psychology of Violence*, *5*, 422–432. doi:10.1037/a0039798

Morris, A. S., Cui, L., & Steinberg, L. (2013). Parenting research and themes: What we have learned and where to go next. In R. E. Larzelere, A. S. Morris, & A. W. Harrist (Eds.), *Authoritative parenting: Synthesizing nurturance and discipline for optimal child development* (pp. 35–58, Chapter ix, 280 Pages). Washington, DC: American Psychological Association.

Morrison, G. M., Redding, M., Fisher, E., & Peterson, R. (2006). Assessing school discipline. In S. R. Jimerson & M. J. Furlong (Eds.), *Handbook of school violence and school safety: From research to practice* (pp. 211–220). Mahwah, NJ: Erlbaum.

Morrison, J. Q., & Jones, K. M. (2007). The effects of positive peer reporting as a classwide positive behavior support. *Journal of Behavioral Education*, *16*, 111–124. doi:10.1007/s10864-006-9005-y

Mowen, T., & Brent, J. (2016). School discipline: The cumulative effect of suspension on arrest. *Journal of Research in Crime and Delinquency*, *53*, 628–653. doi:10.1177/0022427816643135

Moy, G. E., & Hazen, A. (2018). A systematic review of the Second Step program. *Journal of School Psychology*, *71*, 18–41. doi:1016/j.jsp.2018.10.006

Multon, K. D., Brown, S. D., & Lent, R. W. (1991). Relation of self-efficacy beliefs to academic outcomes: A meta-analytic investigation. *Journal of Counseling Psychology*, *18*, 30–38. doi:10.1037/0022-0167.38.1.30

Musu, L., Zhang, A., Wang, K., Zhang, J., & Oudekerk, B. A. (2019). *Indicators of school crime and safety: 2018 (NCES 2019-047/NCJ 252571)*. Washington, DC: National Center for Education Statistics, U.S. Department of Education, and Bureau of Justice Statistics, Office of Justice Programs, U.S. Department of Justice. Retrieved from https://nces.ed.gov/pubs2019/2019047.pdf

Musu-Gillette, L., Zhang, A., Wang, K., Zhang, J., & Oudekerk, B. A. (2017). *Indicators of school crime and safety: 2016 (NCES 2017-064/NCJ 250650)*. Washington, DC: National Center for Education Statistics, U.S. Department of Education, and Bureau of Justice Statistics, Office of Justice Programs, U.S. Department of Justice. Retrieved from https://nces.ed.gov/pubs2018/2018036.pdf

Na, C., & Gottfredson, D. C. (2013). Police officers in schools: Effects on school crime and the processing of offending behaviors. *Justice Quarterly*, *30*, 619–650. doi:10.1080/07418825.2011.615754

Nansel, T. R., Overpeck, M., Pilla, R. S., Ruan, W. J., Simons-Morton, B., & Scheidt, P. (2001). Bullying behavior among U.S. youth: Prevalence and association with psychosocial adjustment. *Journal of the American Medical Association*, *285*, 2094–2100. doi:10.1001/jama.285.16.2094

Nation, M., Vieno, A., Perkins, D. D., & Santinello, M. (2008). Bullying in school and adolescent sense of empowerment: An analysis of relationships with parents, friends, and teachers. *Journal of Community and Applied Social Psychology*, *18*, 211–232. doi:10.1002/casp.921

National Center on Safe Supportive Learning Environments. (2019). *School climate.* Washington, DC: U.S. Department of Education, Office of Safe and Healthy Students. Retrieved from https://safesupportivelearning.ed.gov/safe-and-healthy-students/school-climate

National Education Association (2018). *NEA's School crisis guide.* Retrieved from www.nea.org/assets/docs/NEA%20School%20Crisis%20Guide%202018.pdf.

National Research Council. (2005). *How students learn: History, mathematics, and science in the classroom.* Washington, DC: National Academies Press.

National Research Council and Institute of Medicine. (2009). *Preventing mental, emotional, and behavioral disorders among young people: Progress and possibilities.* Washington, DC: The National Academies Press.

National School Climate Center (2019a). The national school climate inventory. Retrieved from www.schoolclimate.org/services/measuring-school-climate-csci

National School Climate Center (2019b). The *Comprehensive School Climate Inventory.* Retrieved from: www.schoolclimate.org/services/measuring-school-climate-csci

Navarro, R., Yubero, S., & Larrañaga, E. (2015). Psychosocial risk factors for involvement in bullying behaviors: Empirical comparison between cyberbullying and social bullying victims and bullies. *School Mental Health, 7,* 235–248. doi:10.1007/s12310-015-9157-9

Neal, J. W., Neal, Z., & Cappella, E. (2014). I know who my friends are, but do you? Predictors of self-reported and peer inferred relationships. *Child Development, 85,* 1366–1372. doi:10.1111/cdev.12194

Nelson, J. A., Caldarella, P., Young, K. R., & Webb, N. (2008). Using peer praise notes to increase the social involvement of withdrawn adolescents. *Teaching Exceptional Children, 41,* 6–13. doi:10.1177%2F004005990804100201

Nesdale, D., Griffith, J., Durkin, K., & Maass, A. (2005). Empathy, group norms and children's ethnic attitudes. *Journal of Applied Developmental Psychology, 26,* 623–637. doi:10.1016/j.appdev.2005.08.003

Nesdale, D., Maass, A., Durkin, K., & Griffiths, J. (2005). Group norms, threat, and children's racial prejudice. *Child Development, 76,* 652–663. doi:10.1111/j.1467-8624.2005.00869.x

Nesdale, D., & Pickering, K. (2006). Teachers' reactions to children's aggression. *Social Development, 15,* 109–127. doi:10.1111/j.1467-9507.2006.00332.x

Newcomb, A. F., & Bagwell, C. L. (1995). Children's friendship relations: A meta-analytic review. *Psychological Bulletin, 117,* 306–347. doi:10.1037/0033-2909.117.2.306

Newcomb, A. F., Bukowski, W. M., & Pattee, L. (1993). Children's peer relations: A meta-analytic review of popular, rejected, neglected, controversial, and average sociometric status. *Psychological Bulletin, 113,* 99–128. doi:10.1037/0033-2909.113.1.99

NICHD Early Child Care Research Network. (2006). The relations of classroom contexts in the early elementary years to children's classroom and social behavior. In A. C. Huston & M. N. Ripke (Eds.), *Developmental contexts in middle childhood: Bridges to adolescence and adulthood* (pp. 217–236). New York: Cambridge University Press.

Nicholson-Crotty, S., Birchmeier, Z., & Valentine, D. (2009). Exploring the impact of school discipline on racial disproportion in the juvenile justice system. *Social Science Quarterly, 90,* 1003–1018. doi:10.1111/j.1540-6237.2009.00674.x

Noltemeyer, A. L., Marie, R., Mcloughlin, C., & Vanderwood, M. (2015). Relationship between school suspension and student outcomes: A meta-analysis. *School Psychology Review, 44,* 224–240. doi:10.17105/spr-14-0008.1

Norwalk, K. E., Hamm, J. V., Farmer, T. W., & Barnes, K. L. (2016). Improving the school context of early adolescence through teacher attunement to victimization: Effects on school belonging. *The Journal of Early Adolescence, 36,* 989–1009. doi:10.1177/0272431615590230

O'Connor, E. (2010). Teacher-child relationships as dynamic systems. *Journal of School Psychology, 48,* 187–218. doi:10.1016/j.jsp.2010.01.001

O'Connor, E., Dearing, E., & Collins, B. (2011). Teacher-child relationship trajectories: Predictors of behavior problem trajectories and mediators of child and family factors. *American Educational Research Journal, 48,* 120–162. doi:10.3102/0002831210365008

O'Connor, M., Cloney, D., Kvalsvig, A., & Goldfeld, S. (2019). Positive mental health and academic achievement in elementary school: New evidence from a matching analysis. *Educational Researcher, 48*, 205–216. doi:10.3102/0013189X19848724

O'Neill, R. E., Allbin, R. W., Storey, K., Horner, R. H., & Sprague, J. R. (2014). *Functional assessment and program development for problem behavior*. Stamford, CT: Cengage Learning.

Oberle, E., & Schonert-Reichl, K. (2016). Stress contagion in the classroom? The link between classroom teacher burnout and morning cortisol in elementary school students. *Social Science & Medicine, 159*, 30–37. doi:10.1016/j.socscimed.2016.04.031

Obsuth, I., Murray, A. L., Malti, T., Sulger, P., Ribeaud, D., & Eisner, M. (2017). A non-bipartite propensity score analysis of the effects of teacher-student relationships on adolescent problem and prosocial behavior. *Journal of Youth and Adolescence, 46*, 1661–1687. doi:10.1007/s10964-016-0534-y

Oelsner, J., Lippold, M. A., & Greenberg, M. T. (2011). Factors influencing the development of school bonding among middle school students. *The Journal of Early Adolescence, 31*, 463–487. doi:10.1177/0272431610366244

Olivier, E., Archambault, I., De Clercq, M., & Galand, B. (2019). Student self-efficacy, classroom engagement, and academic achievement: Comparing three theoretical frameworks. *Journal of Youth and Adolescence*, 1–15. doi:10.1007/s10964-018-0952-0

Olweus, D. (2012). Cyberbullying: An overrated phenomenon? *European Journal of Developmental Psychology, 9*, 1–19. doi:10.1080/17405629.2012.682358

Olweus, D., & Limber, S. P. (2010a). Bullying in school: Evaluation and dissemination of the Olweus bullying prevention program. *American Journal of Orthopsychiatry, 80*, 124–134. doi:10.1111/j.1939-0025.2010.01015.x

Olweus, D., & Limber, S. P. (2010b). The Olweus bullying prevention program: Implementation and evaluation over two decades. In S. R. Jimerson, S. M. Swearer, & D. L. Espelage (Eds.), *Handbook of bullying in schools: An international perspective* (pp. 377–401). New York: Routledge/Taylor & Francis Group.

Olweus, D., & Limber, S. P. (2018). Some problems with cyberbullying research. *Current Opinion in Psychology, 19*, 139–143. doi:10.1016/j.copsyc.2017.04.012

Ongley, S. F., Nola, M., & Malti, T. (2014). Children's giving: Moral reasoning and moral emotions in the development of donation behaviors. *Frontiers in Psychology, 5*, 458. doi:10.3389/fpsyg.2014.00458

Osher, D., Bear, G. G., Sprague, J. R., & Doyle, W. (2010). How can we improve school discipline? *Educational Researcher, 39*, 48–58. doi:10.3102/0013189X09357618

Osterman, K. F. (2000). Students' need for belonging in the school community. *Review of Educational Research, 70*, 323–367. doi:10.2307/1170786

Ostrov, J. M., Perry, K. J., & Blakely-McClure, S. J. (2018). In T. Malti & K. H. Rubin (Eds.), *Handbook of child and adolescent aggression* (pp. 41–61). New York: Guilford Press.

Ozer, E. J., Wolf, J. P., & Kong, C. (2008). Sources of perceived school connection among ethnically-diverse urban adolescents. *Journal of Adolescent Research, 23*, 438–470. doi:10.1177/0743558408316725

Paget, M. (2013). Cyber-bullying and the law: What should school leaders know? Retrieved from: www.educationworld.com/a_admin/cyber-bullying-legal-issues-liability-schools.shtml

Pakaslahti, L., Karjalainen, A., & Keltikangas-Järvinen, L. (2002). Relationships between adolescent prosocial problem-solving strategies, prosocial behavior, and social acceptance. *International Journal of Behavioral Development, 26*, 137–144. doi:10.1080/01650250042000681

Parada, R. H. (2000). *Adolescent peer relations instrument: A theoretical and empirical basis for the measurement of participant roles in bullying and victimization of adolescence. An interim test manual and a research monograph: A test manual*. Penrith, Australia: University of Western Sydney, Self-Concept Enhancement and Learning Facilitation (SELF) Research Centre, Publication Unit.

References

Parker, J. G., & Asher, S. R. (1987). Peer relations and later personal adjustment: Are low-accepted children at risk? *Psychological Bulletin, 102,* 357–389. doi:10.1037/0033-2909.102.3.357

Patterson, G. R. (1982). *A social learning approach to family intervention: Vol. 3: Coercive family process.* Eugen, OR: Castalia Press.

Paunesku, D., Walton, G. M., Romero, C., Smith, E. N., Yeager, D. S., & Dweck, C. S. (2015). Mind-set interventions are a scalable treatment for academic underachievement. *Psychological Science, 26,* 784–793. doi:10.1177/0956797615571017

Pellerin, L. A. (2005). Student disengagement and the socialization styles of high schools. *Social Forces, 84,* 1159–1179. doi:10.1353/sof.2006.0027

Perdue, N. H., Manzeske, D. P., & Estell, D. B. (2009). Early predictors of school engagement: Exploring the role of peer relationships. *Psychology in the Schools, 46,* 1084–1097. doi:10.1002/pits.20446

Piaget, J. (1965). *The moral judgment of the child.* New York: Free Press (Original work published 1932).

Pianta, R. C. (1999). *Enhancing relationships between children and teachers.* Washington, DC: American Psychological Association.

Pianta, R. C., Hamre, B., & Stuhlman, M. (2003). Relationships between teachers and children. In W. M. Reynolds & G. E. Miller (Eds.), *Handbook of psychology: Educational psychology* (Vol. 7, pp. 199–234). Hoboken, NJ: John Wiley & Sons Inc.

Pianta, R. C., & Stuhlman, M. W. (2004). Teacher-child relationships and children's success in the first years of school. *School Psychology Review, 33*(3), 444–458. Retrieved from http://cx2ef4jw8j.search.serialssolutions.com.udel.idm.oclc.org/directLink?&atitle=TeacherChild+Relationships+and+Children%27s+Success+in+the+First+Years+of+School&author=Pianta%2C+Robert+C.%3BStuhlman%2C+Megan+W.&issn=02796015&title=School+Psychology+Review&volume=33&issue=3&date=2004-01-01&spage=444&id=doi:&sid=ProQ_ss&genre=article

Plank, S. B., Bradshaw, C. P., & Young, H. (2009). An application of "broken-windows" and related theories to the study of disorder, fear, and collective efficacy in schools. *American Journal of Education, 115,* 227–247. doi:10.1086/595669

Provasnik, S., & Dorfman, S. (2005). *Mobility in the teacher workforce (NCES 2005–114).* U.S. Department of Education, National Center for Education Statistics. Washington, DC: U.S. Government Printing Office.

Ramelow, D., Currie, D., & Felder-Puig, R. (2015). The assessment of school climate: Review and appraisal of published student-report measures. *Journal of Psychoeducational Assessment, 33,* 731–743. doi:10.1177/0734282915584852

Ramsey, C. M., Spira, A. P., Parisi, J. M., & Rebok, G. W. (2016). School climate: Perceptual differences between students, parents, and school staff. *School Effectiveness and School Improvement, 27,* 629–641. doi:10.1080/09243453.2016.1199436

Raufelder, D., Kittler, F., Braun, S. R., Lätsch, A., Wilkinson, R. P., & Hoferichter, F. (2014). The interplay of perceived stress, self-determination and school engagement in adolescence. *School Psychology International, 35,* 405–420. doi:10.1177/0143034313498953

Reeve, J. (2009). Why teachers adopt a controlling motivating style toward students and how they can become more autonomy supportive. *Educational Psychologist, 44,* 159–175. doi:10.1080/00461520903028990

Reeve, J. (2013). How students create motivationally supportive learning environments for themselves: The concept of agentic engagement. *Journal of Educational Psychology, 105,* 579–595. doi:10.1037/a0032690

Reeve, J. (2015). Rewards. In E. T. Emmer & E. J. Sabornie (Eds.), *Handbook of classroom management* (pp. 496–516). New York: Routledge.

Reijntjes, A., Kamphuis, J. H., Prinzie, P., Boelen, P. A., van, D. S., & Telch, M. J. (2011). Prospective linkages between peer victimization and externalizing problems in children: A meta-analysis. *Aggressive Behavior, 37,* 215–222. doi:10.1002/ab.20374

Reijntjes, A., Kamphuis, J. H., Prinzie, P., & Telch, M. J. (2010). Peer victimization and internalizing problems in children: A meta-analysis of longitudinal studies. *Child Abuse & Neglect, 34,* 244–252. doi:10.1016/j.chiabu.2009.07.009

Reinke, W. M., Smith, T. E., & Herman, K. C. (2019). Family-school engagement across child and adolescent development. *School Psychology*, 34, 346–349. doi:10.1037/spq0000322

Reschly, A. L., & Christenson, S. L. (2012). Jingle, jangle, and conceptual haziness: Evolution and future directions of the engagement construct. In S. L. Christenson, A. L. Reschly, & C. Wylie (Eds.), *Handbook of research on student engagement* (pp. 3–20). New York: Springer.

Reschly, A. L., & Christenson, S. L. (2013). Grade retention: Historical perspectives and new research. *Journal of School Psychology*, 51, 319–322. doi:10.1016/j.jsp.2013.05.002

Rest, J. R. (1983). Morality. In P. H. Musen, E. Series, J. H. Flavell, & E. M. Markman (Vol., Eds.), *Handbook of child psychology: Vol. 3. Cognitive development* (4th ed., pp. 556–629). Hoboken, NJ: John Wiley & Sons Inc.

Restorative Practices Work Group (2014). Restorative practices: *Fostering healthy relationships & promoting positive discipline in schools: A guide for educators.* https://advancementproject.org/resources/restorative-practices-fostering-healthy-relationships-promoting-positive-discipline-in-schools/

Rigby, K., & Johnson, B. (2006). Expressed readiness of australian schoolchildren to act as bystanders in support of children who are being bullied. *Educational Psychology*, 26, 425–440. doi:10.1080/01443410500342047

Rimm-Kaufman, S. E., Larsen, R. A. A., Baroody, A. E., Curby, T. W., Ko, M., Thomas, J. B., & DeCoster, J. (2014). Efficacy of the responsive classroom approach: Resuts from a 3-year, longitudinal randomized controlled trial. *American Educational Research Journal*, 51, 567–603. doi:10.3102/0002831214523821

Rivers, I., Poteat, V. P., Noret, N., & Ashurst, N. (2009). Observing bullying at school: The mental health implications of witness status. *School Psychology Quarterly*, 24, 211–223. doi:10.1037/a0018164

RMC Research Corporation. (2009). *K-12 service-learning project planning toolkit.* Scotts Valley, CA: National Service-Learning Clearinghouse. Retrieved from http://montana4h.org/documents/volunteer/volunteer_webinars/2014.11.25_AK_Service%20Learning%20Tool%20Kit.pdf

Rocque, M. (2010). Office discipline and student behavior: does race matter? *American Journal of Education*, 116, 557–581. doi:10.1086/653629

Romer, D., Duckworth, A. L., Sznitman, S., & Park, S. (2010). Can adolescents learn self-control? Delay of gratification in the development of control over risk taking. *Prevention Science*, 11, 319–330. doi:10.1007/s11121-010-0171-8

Roorda, D. L., Jak, S., Zee, M., Oort, F. J., & Koomen, H. M. (2017). Affective teacher-student relationships and students' engagement and achievement: A meta-analytic update and test of the mediating role of engagement. *School Psychology Review*, 46, 239–261. doi:10.17105/SPR-2017-0035.V46-3

Roorda, D. L., Koomen, H. M. Y., Spilt, J. L., & Oort, F. J. (2011). The influence of affective teacher-student relationships on students' school engagement and achievement: A meta-analytic approach. *Review of Educational Research*, 81, 493–529. doi:10.3102/0034654311421793

Rose, C. A., Stormont, M., Wang, Z., Simpson, C. G., Preast, J. L., & Green, A. L. (2015). Bullying and students with disabilities: Examination of disability status and educational placement. *School Psychology Review*, 44, 425–444. doi:10.17105/spr-15-0080.1

Rose, L. C., & Gallup, A. M. (2000). The 32nd annual Phi Delta Kappa/Gallup Poll of the public's attitudes toward the public schools. *Phi Delta Kappan*, 82(1), 41–66. doi:10.1177/003172170008200113

Rose-Krasnor, L., & Denham, S. (2009). Social-emotional competence in early childhood. In K. H. Rubin, W. M. Bukowski, & B. Laursen (Eds.), *Handbook of peer interactions, relationships, and groups* (pp. 162–179). New York: Guilford Press.

Rueger, S. Y., & Jenkins, L. N. (2014). Effects of peer victimization on psychological and academic adjustment in early adolescence. *School Psychology Quarterly*, 29, 77–88. doi:10.1037/spq0000036

Rumberger, R. W., & Rotermund, S. (2012). The relationship between engagement and high school dropout. In S. L. Christenson, A. L. Reschly, & C. Wylie (Eds.), *Handbook of research on student engagement* (pp. 491–513). New York: Springer Science + Business Media.

Ryan, R. M., & Deci, E. L. (2017). *Self-determination theory: Basic psychological needs in motivation, development, and wellness.* New York: Guilford Press.

Ryan, R. M., & Grolnick, W. S. (1986). Origins and pawns in the classroom: Self-report and projective assessments of individual differences in children's perceptions. *Journal of Personality and Social Psychology, 50,* 550–558. doi:10.1037/0022-3514.50.3.550

Saarento, S., Kärnä, A., Hodges, E., & Salmivalli, C. (2013). Student-, classroom-, and school-level risk factors for victimization. *Journal of School Psychology, 51,* 421–434. doi:10.1016/j.jsp.2013.02.002

Sailor, W., Dunlap, G., Sugai, G., & Horner, R. (2009). Handbook of positive behavior support. doi:10.1007/978-0-387-09632-2

Salmivalli, C., Kärnä, A., & Poskiparta, E. (2011). Counteracting bullying in Finland: The KiVa program and its effects on different forms of being bullied. *International Journal of Behavioral Development, 35,* 405–411. doi:10.1177/0165025411407457

Sandstrom, M. J. (1999). A developmental perspective on peer rejection: Mechanism of stability and change. *Child Development, 70,* 955–966. doi:10.1111/1467-8624.00069

Schonert-Reichl, K. A. (1999). Relations of peer acceptance, friendship adjustment, and social behavior to moral reasoning during early adolescence. *Journal of Early Adolescence, 19,* 249–279. doi:10.1177/0272431699019002006

Schonfeld, D. J., Adams, R. E., Fredstrom, B. K., Tomlin, R., Voyce, C., & Vaughn, L. M. (2012). Social-emotional learning in grades 3 to 6 and the early onset of sexual behavior. *Sexuality Research & Social Policy: A Journal of the NSRC, 9,* 178–186. doi:10.1007/s13178-011-0077-7

Seals, D., & Young, J. (2003). Bullying and victimization: Prevalence and relationship to gender, grade level, ethnicity, self-esteem, and depression. *Adolescence, 38*(152), 735–747.

Sentse, M., Veenstra, R., Kiuru, N., & Salmivalli, C. (2015). A longitudinal multilevel study of individual characteristics and classroom norms in explaining bullying behaviors. *Journal of Abnormal Child Psychology, 43,* 943–955. doi:10.1007/s10802-014-9949-7

Sharkey, J. D., & Janes, L. (2019). Gang involvement and getting out of it: Helping handout for school and home. In G. G. Bear & K. M. Minke (Eds.), *Helping handouts: Supporting students at school and home* (pp. S2H11, 1–6). Bethesda, MD: National Association of School Psychologists.

Sharkey, P., Besbris, M., & Friedson, M. (2016). Poverty and crime. In D. Brady & L. M. Burton (Eds.), *The Oxford handbook of the social science of poverty* (pp. 623–636). New York: Oxford University Press. doi:10.1093/oxfordhb/9780199914050.013.28

Shumow, L., Vandell, D. L., & Posner, J. (1999). Risk and resilience in the urban neighborhood: Predictors of academic performance among low-income elementary school children. *Merrill-Palmer Quarterly, 45*(2), 309–331.

Siegle, D., & McCoach, D. B. (2007). Increasing student mathematics self-efficacy through teacher training. *Journal of Advanced Academics, 18,* 278–312. doi:10.4219/jaa-2007-353

Simonsen, B., Myers, D., Everett, S., Sugai, G., Spencer, R., & LaBreck, C. (2012). Explicitly teaching social skills schoolwide: Using a matrix to guide instruction. *Intervention in School and Clinic, 47,* 259–266. doi:10.1177%2F1053451211430121

Simonsen, B., & Sugai, G. (2009). School-wide positive behavior support: A systems-level application of behavioral principles. In A. Akin-Little, S. G. Little, M. A. Bray, & T. J. Kehle Eds., *Behavioral interventions in schools: Evidence-based positive strategies* (pp. 125–140, Chapter xi, 350 Pages). Washington, DC: American Psychological Association.

Siu, A. M., & Shek, D. T. (2010). Social problem solving as a predictor of well-being in adolescents and young adults. *Social Indicators Research, 95,* 393–406. doi:10.1007/s11205-009-9527-5

Skiba, R., Shure, L. A., Middelberg, L. V., & Baker, T. L. (2011). Reforming school discipline and reducing disproportionality in suspension and expulsion. In S. R. Jimerson, A. B. Nickerson, M. J. Mayer, & M. J. Furlong (Eds.), *The handbook of school violence and school safety: International research and practice* (2nd ed.) (pp. 515–528). New York: Routledge.

Skiba, R., Simmons, A. B., Peterson, R., McKelvey, J., Forde, S., & Gallini, S. (2004). Beyond guns, drugs and gangs. *Journal of School Violence, 3*, 149–171. doi:10.1300/J202v03n02_09

Skiba, R. J., Horner, R. H., Chung, C., Rausch, M. K., May, S. L., & Tobin, T. (2011). Race is not neutral: A national investigation of African American and Latino disproportionality in school discipline. *School Psychology Review, 40*(1), 85–107.

Skinner, C. H., Cashwell, T. H., & Skinner, A. L. (2000). Increasing tootling: The effects of a peer monitored group contingency program on students' reports of peers' prosocial behaviors. *Psychology in the Schools, 37*, 263–270. doi:10.1002/(SICI)1520-6807(200005)37:3 3.0.CO;2-C

Skinner, E., Pitzer, J., & Steele, J. (2013). Coping as part of motivational resilience in school: A multidimensional measure of families, allocations, and profiles of academic coping. *Educational and Psychological Measurement, 73*, 803–835. doi:10.1177/0013164413485241

Sklad, M., Diekstra, R., Ritter, M. D., Ben, J., & Gravesteijn, C. (2012). Effectiveness of school-based universal social, emotional, and behavioral programs: Do they enhance students' development in the area of skill, behavior, and adjustment? *Psychology in the Schools, 49*, 892–909. doi:10.1002/pits.21641

Smith, D. L., & Smith, B. J. (2006). Perceptions of violence: The views of teachers who left urban schools. *The High School Journal, 89*, 34–42. doi:10.1353/hsj.2006.0004

Smith, P. K., López-Castro, L., Robinson, S., & Görzig, A. (2018). Consistency of gender differences in bullying in cross-cultural surveys. *Aggression and Violent Behavior*. doi:10.1016/j.avb.2018.04.006

Smokowski, P. R., & Kopasz, K. H. (2005). Bullying in school: An overview of types, effects, family characteristics, and intervention strategies. *Children & Schools, 27*, 101–110. doi:10.1093/cs/27.2.101

Social and Character Development Research Consortium. (2010). *Efficacy of schoolwide programs to promote social and character development and reduce problem behavior in elementary school children*. Washington, DC: National Center for Education Research, Institute of Education Sciences, US Department of Education.

Solomon, D., Watson, M. S., Delucchi, K. L., Schaps, E., & Battistich, V. (1988). Enhancing children's prosocial behavior in the classroom. *American Educational Research Journal, 25*, 527–554. doi:10.2307/1163128

Song, Y. S., & Swearer, S. M. (2016). The cart before the horse: The challenge and promise of restorative justice consultation in schools. *Journal of Educational and Psychological Consultation, 26*, 313–324. doi:10.1080/10474412.2016.1246972

Spilt, J. L., van Lier, P. A., Leflot, G., Onghena, P., & Colpin, H. (2014). Children's social self-concept and internalizing problems: The influence of peers and teachers. *Child Development, 85*, 1248–1256. doi:10.1111/cdev.12181

Spinrad, T. L., & Eisenberg, N. (2014). Empathy, prosocial behavior, and positive development in schools. In M. J. Furlong, R. Gilman, & E. S. Huebner (Eds.), *Handbook of positive psychology in schools (pp. 119–130)*. New York: Routledge.

Sprague, J. R., Whitcomb, S. A., & Bear, G. G. (2018). Mechanisms for promoting and integrating school-wide discipline approaches. In M. J. Mayer & S. R. Jimerson (Eds.), *School safety and violence prevention: Science, practice, and policy* (pp. 95–120). Washington, DC: American Psychological Association.

Stams, G. J., Brugman, D., Dekovic, M., van Rosmalen, L., van der Laan, P., & Gibbs, J. C. (2006). The moral judgment of juvenile delinquents: A meta-analysis. *Journal of Abnormal Child Psychology, 34*, 697–713. doi:10.1007/s10802-006-9056-5

Stankov, L., Lee, J., Luo, W., & Hogan, D. J. (2012). Confidence: A better predictor of academic achievement than self-efficacy, self-concept, and anxiety? *Learning and Individual Differences, 22*, 747–758. doi:10.1016/j.lindif.2012.05.013

Steinberg, L., Elmen, J. D., & Mounts, N. S. (1989). Authoritative parenting, psychosocial maturity, and academic success among adolescents. *Child Development, 60,* 1424–1436. doi:10.2307/1130932

Stewart, E. B. (2008). School structural characteristics, student effort, peer associations, and parental involvement: The influence of school- and individual-level factors on academic achievement. *Education & Urban Society, 40,* 179–204. doi:10.1177/0013124507304167

Stockard, J., & Mayberry, M. (1992). *Effective educational environments.* Newbury Park, CA: Corwin.

Sturaro, C., van Lier, P. A. C., Cuipers, P., & Koot, H. M. (2011). The role or peer relationships in the development of early school-age externalizing problems. *Child Development, 82,* 758–765. doi:10.1111/j.1467-8624.2010.01532.x

SAMHSA's Trauma and Justice Strategic Initiative. (2014). *SAMHSA's concept of trauma and guidance for a trauma-informed approach.* [HHS Publication No. (SMA) 14-4884.]. Rockville, MD: U.S. Department of Health and Human Services Substance Abuse and Mental Health Services Administration.

Sugai, G., & Horner, R. H. (2008). What we know and need to know about preventing problem behavior in schools. *Exceptionality, 16,* 67–77. doi:10.1080/09362830801981138

Sugai, G., & Horner, R. H. (2009). Defining and describing schoolwide positive behavior support. In W. Sailor, G. Dunlap, G. Sugai, & R. Horner (Eds.), *Handbook of positive behavior support* (pp. 307–326). New York: Springer.

Sugai, G., & Horner, R. (2010). Schoolwide positive behavior supports: Establishing a continuum of evidence-based practices. *Journal of Evidence-Based Practices for Schools, 11*(1), 62–83.

Swearer, S. M., & Hymel, S. (2015). Understanding the psychology of bullying: Moving toward a social-ecological diathesis-stress model. *American Psychologist, 70,* 344–353. doi:10.1037/a0038929

Swearer, S. M., Wang, C., Berry, B., & Myers, Z. R. (2014). Reducing bullying: Application of social cognitive theory. *Theory into Practice, 53,* 271–277. doi:10.1080/00405841.2014.947221

Swearer, S. M., Wang, C., Maag, J. W., Siebecker, A. B., & Frerichs, L. J. (2012). Understanding the bullying dynamic among students in special and general education. *Journal of School Psychology, 50,* 503–520. doi:10.1016/j.jsp.2012.04.001

Tamnes, C. K., Overbye, K., Ferschmann, L., Fjell, A. M., Walhovd, K. B., Blakemore, S. J., & Dumontheil, I. (2018). Social perspective taking is associated with self-reported prosocial behavior and regional cortical thickness across adolescence. *Developmental Psychology, 54,* 1745–1757. doi:10.1037/dev0000541

Tangney, J. P., Baumeister, R. F., & Boone, A. L. (2004). High self-control predicts good adjustment, less pathology, better grades, and interpersonal success. *Journal of Personality, 72,* 271–324. doi:10.1111/j.0022-3506.2004.00263.x

Tanner-Smith, E. E., Fisher, B. W., Addington, L. A., & Gardella, J. H. (2017). Adding security, but subtracting safety? Exploring schools' use of multiple visible security measures. *American Journal of Criminal Justice,* 1–18. doi:10.1007/s12103-017-9409-3

Taylor, L. C., Hinton, I. D., & Wilson, M. N. (1995). Parental influences on academic performance in African American students. *Journal of Child and Family Studies, 4,* 293–302. doi:10.1007/BF02233964

Taylor, R. D., Oberle, E., Durlak, J. A., & Weissberg, R. P. (2017). Promoting positive youth development through school-based social and emotional learning interventions: A meta-analysis of follow-up effects. *Child Development, 88,* 1156–1171. doi:10.1111/cdev.12864

Taylor, Z. E., Eisenberg, N., Spinrad, T. L., Eggum, N. D., & Sulik, M. J. (2013). The relations of ego-resiliency and emotion socialization to the development of empathy and prosocial behavior across early childhood. *Emotion, 13,* 822–831. doi:10.1037/a0032894

Teglasi, H. (2006). Temperament. In G. G. Bear & K. M. Minke (Eds.), *Children's needs: Development, prevention, and intervention* (pp. 391–403). Bethesda, MD: National Association of School Psychologists.

Thayer, A. J., Cook, C. R., Fiat, A. E., Bartlett-Chase, M. N., & Kember, J. M. (2018). Wise feedback as a timely intervention for at-risk students transitioning into high school. *School Psychology Review, 47*, 275–290. doi:10.17105/SPR-2017-0021. V47-3

Theriot, M. T., Caurn, S. W., & Dupper, D. R. (2010). Multilevel evaluation of factors predicting school exclusion among middle and high school students. *Children and Youth Services Review, 32*, 13–19. doi:10.1016/j.childyouth.2009.06.009

Thomas, D. E., & Bierman, K. L.; The Conduct Problems Prevention Research Group. (2006). The impact of classroom aggression on the development of aggressive behavior problems in children. *Development and Psychopathology, 18*, 471–487. doi:10.1017/S0954579406060251

Thornberg, R., Pozzoli, T., Gini, G., & Jungert, T. (2015). Unique and interactive effects of moral emotions and moral disengagement on bullying and defending among school children. *The Elementary School Journal, 116*, 322–337. doi:10.1086/683985

Torrente, C. E., Cappella, E., & Neal, J. W. (2014). Children's positive school behaviors and social preference in urban elementary classrooms. *Journal of Community Psychology, 42*, 143–161. doi:10.1002/jcop.21599

Tsaousis, I. (2016). The relationship of self-esteem to bullying perpetration and peer victimization among schoolchildren and adolescents: A meta-analytic review. *Aggression and Violent Behavior, 31*, 186–199. doi:10.1016/j.avb.2016.09.005

Ttofi, M. M., & Farrington, D. P. (2011). Effectiveness of school-based programs to reduce bullying: A systematic and meta-analytic review. *Journal of Experimental Criminology, 7*, 27–56. doi:10.1007/s11292-010-9109-1

Ttofi, M. M., Farrington, D. P., Losel, F., & Loeber, R. (2011). The predictive efficiency of school bullying versus later offending: A systematic/meta-analytic review of longitudinal studies. *Criminal Behaviour and Mental Health, 2*, 80–89. doi:10.1002/cbm.808

Tyler, T. (2006). Psychological perspectives on legitimacy and legitimation. *Annual Review of Psychology, 57*, 375–400. doi:10.1146/annurev.psych.57.102904.190038

Tyler, T. R., & Degoey, P. (1995). Collective restraint in social dilemmas: Procedural justice and social identification effects on support for authorities. *Journal of Personality and Social Psychology, 69*, 482–497. doi:10.1037/0022-3514.69.3.482

U.S. Department of Education, Office of Elementary and Secondary Education. (2019). *Parent and educator guide to school climate resources*. Washington, DC: Author. Retrieved from www2.ed.gov/policy/elscc/leg/essa/essaguidetoschoolclimate041019.pdf

U.S. Department of Education, Office of Safe and Healthy Students. (2016). *Quick guide on making school climate improvements*. Washington, DC: Author. Retrieved from http://safesupportivelearning.ed.gov/SCIRP/Quick-Guide

U.S. Department of Education, Office of Safe and Healthy Students. (2019). *ED School Climate Survey (EDSCLS)*. Washington, DC: Author. Retrieved from https://safesupportivelearning.ed.gov/edscls

United States Department of Education. (2019). *What is bullying?* Retrieved from www.stopbullying.gov/what-is-bullying/index.html

Valdebenito, S., Ttofi, M. M., Eisner, M., & Gaffney, H. (2017). Weapon carrying in and out of school among pure bullies, pure victims and bully-victims: A systematic review and meta-analysis of cross-sectional and longitudinal studies. *Aggression and Violent Behavior, 33*, 62–77. doi:10.1016/j.avb.2017.01.004

van Geel, M., Goemans, A., Zwaanswijk, W., Gini, G., & Vedder, P. (2018). Does peer victimization predict low self-esteem, or does low self-esteem predict peer victimization? Meta-analyses on longitudinal studies. *Developmental Review, 49*, 31–40. doi:10.1016/j.dr.2018.07.001

van Lier, P. A. C., Vuijk, P., & Crijnen, A. M. (2005). Understanding mechanisms of change in the development of antisocial behavior: The impact of a universal intervention. *Journal of Abnormal Child Psychology, 33*, 521–535. doi:10.1007/s10802-005-6735-7

Vance, M. J., Gresham, F. M., & Dart, E. H. (2012). Relative effectiveness of DRO and self-monitoring in a general education classroom. *Journal of Applied School Psychology, 28*, 89–109. doi:10.1080/15377903.2012.643758

Vansteenkiste, M., Simons, J., Lens, W., Soenens, B., Matos, L., & Lacante, M. (2004). Less is sometimes more: Goal content matters. *Journal of Educational Psychology, 96*, 755–764. doi:10.1037/0022-0663.96.4.755

Vansteenkiste, M., Timmermans, T., Lens, W., Soenens, B., & Van den Broeck, A. (2008). Does extrinsic goal framing enhance extrinsic goal-oriented individuals' learning and performance? An experimental test of the match perspective versus self-determination theory. *Journal of Educational Psychology, 100*, 387–397. doi:10.1037/0022-0663.100.2.387

Veenstra, R., Lindenberg, S., Huitsing, G., Sainio, M., & Salmivalli, C. (2014). The role of teachers in bullying: The relation between antibullying attitudes, efficacy, and efforts to reduce bullying. *Journal of Educational Psychology, 106*, 1135–1143. doi:10.1037/a0036110

Verschueren, K., Doumen, S., & Buyse, E. (2012). Relationships with mother, teacher, and peers: Unique and joint effects on young children's self-concept. *Attachment & Human Development, 14*, 233–248. doi:10.1080/14616734.2012.672263

Visconti, K. J., Sechler, C. M., & Kochenderfer-Ladd, B. (2013). Coping with peer victimization: The role of children's attributions. *School Psychology Quarterly, 28*, 122–140. doi:10.1037/spq0000014

Vitaro, F., Gagnon, C., & Tremblay, R. E. (1990). Predicting stable peer rejection from kindergarten to grade one. *Journal of Clinical Child Psychology, 19*, 257–264. doi:10.1207/s15374424jccp1903_9

Voelkl, K. E. (2012). School identification. In S. L. Christenson, A. L. Reschly, & C. Wylie (Eds.), *Handbook of research on student engagement* (pp. 193–218). New York: Springer.

Vossekuil, B., Fein, R. A., Reddy, M., Borum, R., & Modzeleski, W. (2002). *The final report and findings of the safe school initiative: Implications for the prevention of school attacks in the United States*. Washington, DC: U.S. Secret Service and U.S. Department of Education.

Vygotsky, L. (1987). Thinking and speech. In L. S. Vygotsky, R. Rieber, & A. Carton (Eds.), *The collected words of L. S. Vygotsky: Vol. 1. Problems of general psychology* (pp. 37–285). New York: Plenum Press. (Original work published 1934).

Waasdorp, T. E., Bradshaw, C. P., & Leaf, P. J. (2012). The impact of schoolwide positive behavioral interventions and supports on bullying and peer rejection: A randomized controlled effectiveness trial. *Archives of Pediatrics & Adolescent Medicine, 166*, 149–156. doi:10.1001/archpediatrics.2011.755

Wald, J., & Losen, D. J. (2003). Defining and redirecting a school-to-prison pipeline. In J. Wald & D. J. Losen (Eds.), *New directions for youth development, No. 99: Deconstructing the school-to-prison pipeline* (pp. 9–15). San Francisco, CA: Jossey-Bass.

Wang, J., Iannotti, R. J., & Nansel, T. R. (2009). School bullying among adolescents in the United States: Physical, verbal, relational, and cyber. *Journal of Adolescent Health, 45*, 368–375. doi:10.1016/j.jadohealth.2009.03.021

Wang, M., Brinkworth, M., & Eccles, J. (2013). Moderating effects of teacher-student relationship in adolescent trajectories of emotional and behavioral adjustment. *Developmental Psychology, 49*, 690–705. doi:10.1037/a0027916

Wang, M., & Degol, J. (2016). School climate: A review of the construct, measurement, and impact on student outcomes. *Educational Psychology Review, 28*, 315–352. doi:10.1007/s10648-015-9319-1

Wang, M., & Eccles, J. S. (2012a). Adolescent behavioral, emotional, and cognitive engagement trajectories in school and their differential relations to educational success. *Journal of Research on Adolescence, 22*, 31–39. doi:10.1111/j.1532-7795.2011.00753.x

Wang, M., & Eccles, J. S. (2012b). Social support matters: Longitudinal effects of social support on three dimensions of school engagement from middle to high school. *Child Development, 83*, 877–895. doi:10.1111/j.1467-8624.2012.01745.x

Wang, M., & Fredricks, J. A. (2014). The reciprocal links between school engagement, youth problem behaviors, and school dropout during adolescence. *Child Development, 85*, 722–737. doi:10.1111/cdev.12138

Wang, M., & Peck, S. C. (2013). Adolescent educational success and mental health vary across school engagement profiles. *Developmental Psychology, 49*, 1266–1276. doi:10.1037/a0030028

Wang, M., Selman, R. L., Dishion, T. J., & Stormshak, E. A. (2010). A tobit regression analysis of the covariation between middle school students' perceived school climate and behavioral problems. *Journal of Research on Adolescence, 20*, 274–286. doi:10.1111/j.1532-7795.2010.00648.x

Wang, M., & Sheikh-Khalil, S. (2014). Does parental involvement matter for student achievement and mental health in high school? *Child Development, 85*, 610–625. doi:10.1111/cdev.12153

Watson, M., & Battistich, V. (2006). Building and sustaining caring communities. In C. M. Evertson & C. S. Weinstein (Eds.), *Handbook of classroom management: Research, practice, and contemporary issues* (pp. 253–279). Mahwah, NJ: Erlbaum.

Way, S. M. (2011). School discipline and disruptive classroom behavior: the moderating effects of student perceptions. *The Sociological Quarterly, 52*, 346–375. http://dx.doi.org/10.2307/23027541

Wei, H., & Williams, J. H. (2004). Relationship between peer victimization and school adjustment in sixth grade students: Investigating mediating effects. *Violence and Victims, 19*, 557–571. doi:10.1891/vivi.19.5.557.63683

Weiner, B. (2006). *Social motivation, justice, and the moral emotions: An attributional approach.* Mahwah, NJ: Erlbaum.

Weinstein, C. S. (2006). *Secondary classroom management: Lessons from research and practice* (3rd ed.). New York: McGraw-Hill.

Weinstein, C. S., & Novodvorsky, I. (2015). *Middle and secondary classroom management: Lessons from research and practice* (5th ed.). New York: McGraw Hill Education.

Weinstein, C. S., & Romano, M. (2014). *Elementary classroom management: Lessons from research and practice* (6th ed.). New York: McGraw.

Weinstein, C. S., & Romano, M. (2019). *Elementary classroom management: Lessons from research and practice* (7th ed.). New York: McGraw Hill Education.

Welsh, W. N. (2000). The effects of school climate on school disorder. *Annals of the American Academy of Political and Social Science, 567*, 88–107. doi:10.1177/000271620056700107

Welsh, W. N. (2003). Individual and institutional predictors of school disorder. *Youth Violence and Juvenile Justice, 1*, 346–368. doi:10.1177%2F1541204003255843

Wentzel, K. (2014). Prosocial behavior and peer relations in adolescence. In L. M. Padilla Walker & G. Carlo (Eds.), *Prosocial development: A multidimensional approach* (pp. 178–200). New York: Oxford University Press.

Wentzel, K. R. (1997). Student motivation in middle school: The role of perceived pedagogical caring. *Journal of Educational Psychology, 89*, 411–419. doi:10.1037/0022-0663.89.3.411

Wentzel, K. R. (2002). Are effective teachers like good parents?: Teaching styles and student adjustment in early adolescence. *Child Development, 73*, 287–301. doi:10.1111/1467-8624.00406

Wentzel, K. R. (2005). Peer relationships, motivation, and academic performance at school. In A. J. Elliot & C. S. Dweck (Eds.), *Handbook of competence and motivation* (pp. 279–296) (pp. 619–643). New York: Guilford.

Wentzel, K. R. (2006). A social motivation perspective for classroom management. In C. M. Evertson & C. S. Weinstein (Eds.), *Handbook of classroom management: Research, practice, and contemporary issues* (pp. 619–643). Mahwah, NJ: Erlbaum.

Wentzel, K. R., Barry, C. M. N., & Caldwell, K. A. (2004). Friendships in middle school: Influences on motivation and school adjustment. *Journal of Educational Psychology, 96*, 195–203. doi:10.1037/0022-0663.96.2.195

Wentzel, K. R., & Muenks, K. (2016). Peer influence on students' motivation, academic achievement, and social behavior. In K. R. Wentzel & G. B. Ramani (Eds.), *Handbook of social influence on social-emotional, motivation, and cognitive outcomes in school contexts (pp. 13–30).* New York: Routledge.

Weyns, T., Colpin, H., De Laet, S., Engels, M., & Verschueren, K. (2018). Teacher support, peer acceptance, and engagement in the classroom: A three-wave longitudinal study in late childhood. *Journal of Youth and Adolescence, 47,* 1139–1150. doi:10.1007/s10964-017-0774-5

Wigelsworth, M., Lendrum, A., Oldfield, J., Scott, A., Ten Bokkel, I., Tate, K., & Emery, C. (2016). The impact of trial stage, developer involvement, and international transferability on universal social and emotional learning programme outcomes: A meta-analysis. *Cambridge Journal of Education, 46,* 347–376. doi:10.1080/0305764X.2016.1195791

Wigfield, A., Eccles, J. S., Schiefele, U., Roeser, R. W., & Davis-Kean, P. (2006). Development of achievement motivation. In N. Eisenberg, W. Damon, & R. Lerner (Eds.), *Handbook of child psychology: Social, emotional, and personality development.* (pp. 933–1002). Hoboken, NJ: John Wiley & Sons Inc.

Wilcox, P., Augustine, M. C., & Clayton, R. R. (2006). Physical environment and crime and misconduct in Kentucky schools. *Journal of Primary Prevention, 27,* 293–313. doi:10.1007/s10935-006-0034-z

Wilson, S. J., & Lipsey, M. W. (2007). School-based interventions for aggressive and disruptive behavior: Update of a meta-analysis. *American Journal of Preventive Medicine, 33,* S130–S143. doi:10.1016/j.amepre.2007.04.011

Winett, R. A., & Winkler, R. C. (1972). Current behavior modification in the classroom: Be still, be quiet, be docile. *Journal of Applied Behavior Analysis, 5,* 499–504. doi:10.1901%2Fjaba.1972.5-499

Wright, J. P., Morgan, M. A., Coyne, M. A., Beaver, K. M., & Barnes, J. C. (2014). Prior problem behavior accounts for the racial gap in school suspensions. *Journal of Criminal Justice, 42,* 257–266. doi:10.1016/j.jcrimjus.2014.01.001

Wyatt, J. M., & Carlo, G. (2002). What will my parents think? Relations among adolescents' expected parental reactions, prosocial moral reasoning, and prosocial and antisocial behaviors. *Journal of Adolescent Research, 17,* 646–666. doi:10.1177/074355802237468

Xie, J., Peng, Z., Zhuorong, Z., Yang, C., & Bear, G. G. (2018). Chinese version of Delaware school climate scale—Teacher/staff. *Chinese Journal of Clinical Psychology (In Chinese), 26*(2), 891–996.

Xie, J., Wei, Y., & Bear, G. G. (2018). Revision of Chinese version of the Delaware bullying victimization scale—Adolescence. *Chinese Journal of Clinical Psychology (In Chinese), 26,* 259–263. Retrieved from http://en.cnki.com.cn/Journal_en/E-E059-ZLCY-2018-02.htm

Yang, C., Bear, G., & May, H. (2018). Multilevel associations between school-wide social-emotional learning approach and student engagement across elementary, middle, and high schools. *School Psychology Review, 47,* 45–61. doi:10.17105/SPR-2017-0003.V47-1

Yang, C., Sharkey, J. D., Reed, L. A., Chen, C., & Dowdy, E. (2018). Bullying victimization and student engagement in elementary, middle, and high schools: Moderating role of school climate. *School Psychology Quarterly, 33,* 54–64. doi:10.1037/spq0000250

Yeager, D. S., Johnson, R., Spitzer, B. J., Trzesniewski, K. H., Powers, J., & Dweck, C. S. (2014). The far-reaching effects of believing people can change: Implicit theories of personality shape stress, health, and achievement during adolescence. *Journal of Personality and Social Psychology, 106,* 867–884. doi:10.1037/a0036335

Yeager, D. S., Trzesniewski, K. H., & Dweck, C. S. (2013). An implicit theories of personality intervention reduces adolescent aggression in response to victimization and exclusion. *Child Development, 84,* 970–988. doi:10.1111/cdev.12003

Yoon, J. S. (2002). Teacher characteristics as predictors of teacher-student relationships: Stress, negative affect, and self-efficacy. *Social Behavior and Personality, 30*, 485–493. doi:10.2224/sbp.2002.30.5.485

Yu, C., Li, X., Wang, S., & Zhang, W. (2016). Teacher autonomy support reduces adolescent anxiety and depression: An 18-month longitudinal study. *Journal of Adolescence, 49*, 115–123. doi:10.1016/j.adolescence.206.03.001

Zimmer-Gembeck, M. J., Chipuer, H. M., Hanisch, M. P., Creed, P. A., & Mcgregor, L. G. (2006). Relationships at school and stage-environment fit as resources for adolescent engagement and achievement. *Journal of Adolescence, 29*, 911–933. doi:10.1016/j.adolescence.2006.04.008

Zimmerman, G. M., & Rees, C. (2014). Do school disciplinary policies have positive social impacts? Examining the attenuating effects of school policies on the relationship between personal and peer delinquency. *Journal of Criminal Justice, 42*, 54–65. doi:10.1016/j.jcrimjus.2013.12.003

Zins, J. E., & Elias, M. J. (2006). Social and emotional learning. In G. G. Bear & K. M. Minke (Eds.), *Children's needs III: Development, prevention, and intervention* (pp. 1–14). Bethesda, MD: National Association of School Psychologists.

Zullig, K. J., Koopman, T. M., Patton, J. M., & Ubbes, V. A. (2010). School climate: Historical review, instrument development, and school assessment. *Journal of Psychoeducational Assessment, 28*, 139–152. doi:10.1177/0734282909344205

Zych, I., Farrington, D. P., & Ttofi, M. M. (2018). Protective factors against bullying and cyberbullying: A systematic review of meta-analyses. *Aggression and Violent Behavior*. doi:10.1016/j.avb.2018.06.008

INDEX

ABC behavioral approach 97
Aboud, F. E. 41
academic environment 6
academic outcomes 5, 7
accountability 2, 167
achievement 7, 9, 12–13, 147; authoritative parenting 14; authoritative school climate 16; bullying 133, 141; Delaware School Surveys 174, 180; ecological approach 70; empathy 50; engagement 8, 115, 127; extracurricular activities 41; PATHS 56; psychological needs 18; SEL programs 51, 52, 123–124; self-control 49; service learning 65; social and emotional competencies 13; structure 11; student-student relationships 34, 46, 55; suspended students 155; teacher-student relationships 10, 22, 24, 33
Ackert, E. 118
acting out 10, 23, 34, 147
African-Americans: engagement 115–116, 118; high expectations 123; punitive consequences 93; student-student relationships 35, 39
age 118, 134, 135
aggression 50, 147; authoritative school climate 15; engagement 115, 117; moral disengagement 53; PATHS 56; Second Step Social-Emotional Learning 57, 140; social problem-solving 48; student-student relationships 34, 35, 36, 46; support for victims 163; suspended students 155; teacher-student relationships 10, 24; threat assessment 163–164; *see also* bullying; violence

albatross metaphor 1, 2
Anderson, C. S. 1, 2
antisocial behavior: confrontative control 14; ecological systems theory 16; moral disengagement 53–54; moral reasoning 48–49; relationship skills 50; SEL programs 52, 56–57; self-discipline 52; student-student relationships 38; suspended students 155; teacher-student relationships 23, 24; *see also* behavior problems
anxiety 103, 147; bullying 132, 133, 180; engagement 117; Second Step Social-Emotional Learning 57; teacher-student relationships 23, 24
applied behavior analysis 73, 74, 89
Arum, R. 81–82
Ashurst, N. 133
Aspen Institute National Commission on Social, Emotional, and Academic Development 47
attachment theory 17, 19, 22, 38, 51
attention, giving 31
attribution theory 51
authoritarian parenting 13–14
authoritative approach 14, 15–16, 22, 91, 185; behavior problems 67, 87; bullying 137, 138, 139, 146; class meetings 45; Delaware School Surveys 173; engagement 119, 122–123; punitive consequences 93, 94, 95; safety 161, 166; self-discipline 91; student-student relationships 37, 46; teacher-student relationships 25, 27–28, 33
authoritative parenting 13–14, 52, 91, 136

autonomy 6, 10, 13, 14–15, 18; authoritative approach 91; class meetings 45; disciplinary encounters 103; engagement 117, 118, 124, 127–128; praise and rewards 29, 60, 87; prevention of behavior problems 79; punitive consequences 95, 101; teacher-student relationships 22, 24, 25, 31–32, 55

Bandura, A. 53, 90–91
Banking Time 31
Baumrind, D. 10, 11, 13–14, 15, 52
Bear, G. G. 59, 60, 82, 130–131, 174, 180
behavior problems: authoritative school climate 15; correction of 9, 89–113, 148, 161; engagement 117; prevention of 9, 67–88, 89, 148, 161, 164; racial groups 157; strategies and interventions 77–87, 96–113; student-student relationships 43, 44; teacher-student relationships 29–30; *see also* antisocial behavior
behavioral approach 68, 70–77, 89
behavioral engagement 11, 114; authoritative approach 119; Delaware School Surveys 170, 177–178, 180; individual student characteristics 116, 118; personal best goal setting 126; prevention of behavior problems 78; school safety 151; strategies and interventions 123–124
behavioral momentum 72
Belfield, C. 52
belongingness 38, 114, 116, 117, 127–128, 138
Ben-Avie, M. 3
Ben, J. 51–52
bioecological model 16–17, 19, 51
Bradshaw, C. P. 160
Brigham, F. J. 153
Bronfenbrenner, U. 16
bullying 2, 129–146, 176–177; absence of 6, 7, 9; attunement to social dynamics 42; authoritative school climate 15; definition of 129–130; Delaware School Surveys 167–168, 169, 170, 171–172, 174, 180; ecological approach 70; engagement 115, 122; KiVa Anti-Bully Program 39, 138–139, 140, 142, 146; lack of safety 147, 148, 149, 166; moral disengagement 18, 53; negative outcomes of 132–133; Olweus Bullying Prevention Program 39, 138–139, 140, 142, 146; peer support 34; prevalence of 130–131, 150; prevention programs 138–140, 142–143; protective factors 18, 135–138; relationship skills 49–50; restorative practices 161; risk factors 134–135; Safe and Supportive School Model of School Climate 4; Second Step Social-Emotional Learning 57; self-awareness 50; self-control 49; social problem-solving 48; strategies and interventions 140–146, 184; structure 11; student responses to 96; student-student relationships 10, 46; teacher-student relationships 21, 23; threat assessment 164; training 165, 166; types of 131; warning signs 131–132
burnout 33, 116
bystanders 10, 53, 133, 134, 137, 144, 162

caring: class meetings 32; social and emotional competencies 47; student-student relationships 36, 46; teacher-student relationships 22, 25, 27–28, 33
Caring School Community 45, 55, 58, 63, 100
CASEL *see* Collaborative for Social and Emotional Learning
Check and Connect 33, 111, 127
choice 79, 86, 101, 120, 124–125, 127
Class Dojo 110
class meetings 32, 45, 63, 106–107
classroom management: authoritative approach 27, 67, 161; behavioral approach 68, 70–77; bullying 139, 141; Delaware School Surveys 167; ecological approach 68–70, 71–72; engagement 119, 122, 128; meetings 32; safety 151; strategies and interventions 77–87; teacher-student relationships 25; *see also* discipline
classroom seating arrangements 38, 41, 43
cognitive engagement 11, 114; authoritative approach 119; Delaware School Surveys 170, 177–178, 180; individual student characteristics 116, 118; prevention of behavior problems 78; school safety 151; strategies and interventions 123–124
Cohen, J. 3, 6
Collaborative for Social and Emotional Learning (CASEL) 12, 47–51, 52–55, 57–58, 63, 66; Delaware Social and

Emotional Competencies Scale 178; website 39, 64, 185
Collie, R. J. 24
community 6
competence 10, 13, 18; engagement 117, 118, 127–128; teacher-student relationships 22, 25, 55
Comprehensive School Climate Inventory 3, 5
conduct problems 104, 136; *see also* behavior problems
conflict resolution 37, 55, 116, 123, 165
confrontative control 14–15
connectedness 4, 5–6; bullying 137; Check and Connect 33; engagement 114, 116; punitive consequences 92; restorative practices 161; safety 151
constructivism 51
contracts: behavioral contingency 108; bullying 142
cooperation 32, 35, 36, 109
Cornell, D. 5, 7, 8, 180
crime 149, 151, 152, 155–156
crisis response plans 164–165
cultural competence 4
cultural differences 85, 94, 95, 160
Currie, D. 6
cyberbullying 130, 131, 135; Delaware School Surveys 170, 176–177; lack of safety 149; prevention programs 138; Safe and Supportive School Model of School Climate 4; school policy 142; training 165

daily report cards (DRCs) 110, 111
data collection 74, 141, 158, 181
DBVS *see* Delaware Bullying Victimization Scale
decision-making 14–15, 120; bullying 136; class meetings 32, 45; safety 162; self-discipline 52–53; social and emotional competencies 47, 48–49; *see also* responsible decision-making
Degol, J. 6, 16
Delaware Bullying Victimization Scale (DBVS) 168, 169, 170, 176–177, 180
Delaware Positive, Punitive and SEL Techniques Scale (DTS) 169, 170, 173, 175–176, 179
Delaware School Climate Scale (DSCS) 168, 169, 170, 171–175
Delaware School Climate Surveys 15, 26, 167–186

Delaware Social and Emotional Competencies Scale (DSECS) 169, 171, 178–179, 180
Delaware Student Engagement Scale (DSES) 169, 170, 177–178
delayed gratification 36, 49
delinquency: attachment theory 17; bullying 132, 133; engagement 115, 117; racial groups 157; social control theory 17; social problem-solving 48; student-student relationships 10, 34
demandingness 10, 11, 14; authoritative approach 37, 46; correction of behavior 103; punitive consequences 95; social order 15, 173–174
depression 103, 147; bullying 129, 132, 133, 136, 180; Delaware School Surveys 178; engagement 115, 117; student-student relationships 10, 34; teacher-student relationships 23, 24; tiered approach 74
detentions 112
deterrence 90–91, 93, 152, 154–155
Dewey, J. 51
Diekstra, R. 51–52
disabilities 112, 130, 134, 135, 159–160
disaggregated data 158
discipline 5, 6; authoritative approach 27; bullying 133, 139, 141; disciplinary problems and serious disciplinary actions 149–150; engagement 122, 128; inductive 40, 63, 100, 101, 161; office disciplinary referrals 43, 76, 158, 160; Safe and Supportive School Model of School Climate 4; safety 151; social and emotional learning 63, 65; structure 7; student-student relationships 40; teacher-student relationships 29–30; threat assessment 164; zero tolerance 8, 12, 148, 152–154, 155–156; *see also* classroom management; punitive consequences
disengagement 115, 119, 127; moral 18, 53–54, 64, 101–102, 136; student-student relationships 34
diversity 6, 62–63, 65
Doyle, A. B. 41
DRCs *see* daily report cards
Dreikurs, Rudolph 21, 32, 45
dropping out: authoritative school climate 16; engagement 115, 119; student-student relationships 34; suspended students 155, 156
drugs *see* substance use

Index 227

DSES *see* Delaware Student Engagement Scale
DTS *see* Delaware Positive, Punitive and SEL Techniques Scale
Durlak, J. A. 51, 52, 185
Dymnicki, A. B. 51

ecological approach 68–70, 71–72
ecological systems theory 16–17, 19, 51, 173; *see also* social-ecological model of bullying
ED School Climate Survey 2, 4
Education World 40
Edutopia 64
effortful control 116–117
Elias, M. J. 47
Elliott, S. N. 75
emergency readiness 4; *see also* crisis response plans
Emmons, C. 3
emotional engagement 11, 114, 121; authoritative approach 119; Delaware School Surveys 170, 177–178, 180; individual student characteristics 116, 118; prevention of behavior problems 78; school safety 151; strategies and interventions 123–124
emotional safety 4, 6, 12
emotions: bullying 136; interfering 117; modeling 62; negative 116–117; praise and rewards 61–62, 87; punitive consequences 91–92, 94; self-management 49, 52, 87
empathy: bullying 144; class meetings 32; correction of behavior 100; engagement 123; inductive discipline 63; lack of 116, 136; moral behavior 53; PATHS 56; peer-assisted learning 42; praise and rewards 87; restorative practices 161; safety 162; Second Step Social-Emotional Learning 57; service learning 42, 65; social and emotional support 11; social awareness 48, 50, 162; student-student relationships 36, 40, 55; teacher-student relationships 28
engagement 4–6, 7–9, 20, 114–128; authoritative school climate 16; bullying 129, 133, 141; Check and Connect 111; Delaware School Surveys 167, 169, 170, 171–172, 174, 177–178, 180, 182; ecological approach 70; ecological systems theory 16; effective teachers 70; empathy 50; prevention of behavior problems 77–78; psychological needs 18; relationship skills 50; school safety 12, 148, 151; SEL programs 51, 55, 57; social control theory 19; strategies and interventions 122–127, 184; structure 11; student-student relationships 34, 35, 36, 46; teacher-student relationships 10, 21, 22, 33; theories 18–19
environment 6, 83; engagement 121; orderly 67; Safe and Supportive School Model of School Climate 4, 5; social 173; stage-environment fit theory 18
Espelage, D. L. 138
ethnic groups: alternative placements 160; Delaware School Surveys 182; engagement 118, 121; exclusionary practices 93, 150, 156–157; peer acceptance 38; teacher-student relationships 26
Evans, C. B. R. 138
Every Student Succeeds Act 2, 167
expectations: anti-bullying programs 138–139, 141; behavioral approach 71; correction of behavior 103; Delaware School Surveys 170, 172, 173, 182; effective teachers 69–70; engagement 122; fair school policies 154; high 120, 123; praise and rewards 87; prevention of behavior problems 79–81; safety 3, 151; social cognitive theory 18; structure 7, 9, 11, 14, 28; student perceptions 19; student-student relationships 37–38, 39–40; SWPIS 65, 75, 76, 79–80; teacher-student relationships 10, 25
expulsion 113, 148, 150, 158; Delaware School Surveys 180; racial disparities 156–157; zero tolerance approach 152
externalizing problems: bullying 132, 133, 134; engagement 117; lack of empathy 50; SEL programs 51, 57; self-control 49; student-student relationships 34, 36; teacher-student relationships 23
extinction 89, 105
extracurricular activities 31, 32, 41, 55, 121, 122
extrinsic motivation 59–61, 114, 124

facilities 5, 6
fairness 6, 81–82, 154; bullying 141; Delaware School Surveys 169, 170, 172, 173; engagement 121, 122; punitive consequences 94–95, 99, 113; safety 151; structure 28; student-student relationships 36; teacher-student relationships 25, 29

228 *Index*

Farley-Ripple, L. 60
Farmer, G. L. 154
Farrington, D. P. 138, 141
FBA *see* functional behavioral assessment
feedback: Delaware School Surveys 175; effective teachers 70; engagement 124; personal best goal setting 126; praise and rewards 62, 87; prevention of behavior problems 78
Felder-Puig, R. 6
friendships 21, 34, 35, 40; bullying 135, 136; peer-assisted learning 42; relationship skills 50; Second Step Social-Emotional Learning 57; self-efficacy 51; social problem-solving 48; *see also* student-student relationships
functional behavioral assessment (FBA) 73, 74, 97–98
funding 2, 105, 167, 186

Gaffney, H. 138
games 41
gangs 149, 166
gender 118, 121, 134–135, 182
goals 79, 115, 119, 120, 125–126
Good Behavior Game 76, 99, 109, 111
Gravesteijn, C. 51–52
Graybeal, J. 21
Graybeal, L. 21
Gresham, F. M. 75
Griffith, J. 15
group contingency interventions 108–109
growth mindset 79, 126
guilt 13, 53, 91, 100, 101, 161

Hamre, B. K. 24
Harris, A. B. 59
Haynes, N. M. 3
health: bullying 132, 134, 135; Safe and Supportive School Model of School Climate 4, 5; self-control 49; teachers 33; *see also* mental health
'hidden curriculum' 58
high probability requests 72
Hirschi, T. 17
home-school communication 170, 172–173
home support 110, 117–118, 126–127
homework 125, 126–127
homicides 148
honesty 13, 37
Horner, Rob 72–73, 74, 75
Huang, F. 5, 7, 8

ID badges 159
IDEA *see* Individuals with Disabilities Education Act
ignoring misbehavior 105
individual behavioral contingency contracts 108
individualization 104
Individuals with Disabilities Education Act (IDEA) 97, 112, 159
inductive discipline 40, 63, 100, 101, 161
institutional environment 6
instructional environment 4, 5
instructional methods: behavioral approach 71; effective teachers 69; engagement 123, 124, 128; prevention of behavior problems 79; teacher-student relationships 27; *see also* teaching
interim alternative educational settings (IAES) 159–160
internal working models 17
internalizing problems: bullying 133, 134, 136; engagement 117; friendship self-efficacy 51; SEL programs 51, 57; self-control 49; student-student relationships 10, 34; teacher-student relationships 23, 24
intrinsic motivation 59–61, 84, 86–87, 114, 124

Johnson, J. F., Jr. 120–121, 125

Kauffman, J. M. 153
KiVa Anti-Bully Program 39, 138–139, 140, 142, 146
Kong, C. 25
Koopman, T. M. 5
Korpershoek, H. 26
Kounin, J. 68–70, 83

leadership 3, 6, 121
Leaf, P. J. 160
learning 3, 4, 6; constructivist theories 51; engagement 114; peer-assisted 42, 55, 122, 123
least restrictive alternative 61, 86
Leone, P. E. 155
Lewis-Palmer, T. 75
linguistic competence 4
locus of control 61, 86
loneliness 10, 34, 49–50, 132

Mantz, L. S. 59, 60
Marsh, H. W. 180
Martin, A. J. 24

mastery 79, 119, 120–121, 124, 125, 126
Mayberry, M. 15, 173
Mayer, M. J. 155
McCabe, E. M. 3
McKnight, K. 21
meetings 32, 45, 63, 106–107
mental health 9, 147; bullying 180; Delaware School Surveys 178; Safe and Supportive School Model of School Climate 4, 5; self-control 49; serious behavior problems 103–104, 111–112; social and emotional competencies 13; teacher-student relationships 23; threat assessment 164; tiered approach 74, 103–104; training 165, 166; victims of aggression 163
mentoring 33, 111, 127
Michelli, N. M. 3
minimal sufficiency 61, 86, 99
Mitchell, M. M. 160
modeling 28, 38, 43–44, 62–63, 75, 120, 160; *see also* role models
monitoring 11, 82–83, 104, 120; behavioral approach 71; bullying 141, 143; ecological approach 69, 70; engagement 121, 122; safety 151; social skills 75; zero tolerance approach 155
moral development 50, 51, 59
moral disengagement 18, 53–54, 64, 101–102, 136
moral reasoning 48–49, 53, 60, 64, 84
motivation 10, 19, 29, 77, 84, 86–87; engagement 114, 124; personal best goal setting 126; prevention of behavior problems 67; punitive consequences 100; SEL programs 59–62
movement breaks 79
My Teacher Partner 27

National Association of School Psychologists (NASP) 165
National Center for Education Statistics (NCES) 148–150, 151
National Center on Safe Supportive Learning Environments 3–4
National School Climate Center (NSCC) 3, 5
negative affect 116–117
nonverbal communication 105
Noret, N. 133
norms: anti-bullying 136, 137, 138, 140, 141; ecological systems theory 17; engagement 114, 121; prosocial 151; safety 3; student-student relationships 38–39, 46; teacher-student relationships 14, 17
NSCC *see* National School Climate Center

Oberle, E. 52
O'Brennan, L. M. 160
office disciplinary referrals 43, 76, 158, 160
Olweus Bullying Prevention Program 39, 138–139, 140, 142, 146
optimism 30, 103
order 5, 6, 15
Ozer, E. J. 25

Paget, M. 142
PAL *see* peer-assisted learning
parenting 10, 13–14, 17, 52, 136
parents: bullying 133, 136, 139, 145; communication with 25–26, 64, 172; corrective interventions 104, 110; Delaware School Surveys 172–173; parent involvement 6; positive relationships with 32; reinforcement 106; school rules and expectations 81, 82; student-student relationships 43; support from 117–118, 126–127
participation 4, 5
partnership 6
PATHS (Promoting Alternative Thinking Strategies) 39, 56–57, 76, 124
Patton, J. M. 5
peer acceptance 34, 35, 37–38, 40, 42, 46; engagement 115; prevention of behavior problems 67; relationship skills 50; social problem-solving 48
peer-assisted learning (PAL) 42, 55, 122, 123
performance goal orientation 120
permissive parenting 13–14
personal best (PB) goal setting 126
perspective-taking 11, 48, 50; class meetings 32; correction of behavior 100; engagement 123; inductive discipline 63; lack of 116; modeling 62; SEL programs 51, 162; service learning 65; student-student relationships 37, 40, 55
phoenix metaphor 1, 2, 19
physical environment 4, 83
physical health 5; bullying 134, 135; Safe and Supportive School Model of School Climate 4; self-control 49; teachers 33
physical proximity 105
physical safety 4, 6, 12
Pianta, R. C. 24

Index

Pickeral, T. 3
positive psychology 51
positive reinforcement 71, 73, 75, 81, 156; punitive consequences 93, 97, 106; student-student relationships 38
Poteat, V. P. 133
poverty 139, 151, 157
praise 83, 104, 106; behavioral approach 71, 77; Delaware School Surveys 175; effective teachers 70; engagement 124; prevention of behavior problems 78, 83–87; SEL programs 59–62; student-student relationships 44–45; SWPIS 65; teacher-student relationships 28–29
precision requests 72
precorrection 72
prejudice 39, 41
PREPaRE model 165
prevention 9, 67–88, 89, 161, 164; behavioral approach 70–77; bullying 138–140, 142–143; crisis response plans 164; ecological approach 68–70; training 166
private schools 154
problem-solving 48–49; bullying 136; Check and Connect 127; class meetings 106–107; engagement 124; modeling 62, 63; PATHS 56; punitive consequences 102; Second Step Social-Emotional Learning 57, 140; SEL programs 51, 162; self-reflection 107; student-student relationships 37
procedures 69, 71, 80, 122, 141
professional development 6, 27, 105, 145–146, 165–166, 169, 186
profiling 159
prosocial behavior: authoritative parenting 14; confrontational control 14; ecological approach 70; ecological systems theory 16; modeling 43, 62; moral reasoning 48–49; PATHS 56–57; praise and rewards 60, 61, 87; relationship skills 50; safety 162; Second Step Social-Emotional Learning 57, 140; SEL programs 51–52; self-discipline 13, 52; service learning 42; social learning theory 38; structure 11; student-student relationships 35, 44–45, 46; teacher-student relationships 10, 22–23
prosocial development theory 51
psychological needs 7, 9, 10–11, 18, 66; bullying 138; engagement 117–118, 122, 127–128; safety 147; teacher-student relationships 22, 23, 25, 27–28, 33, 38, 55
punitive consequences 89–113; advantages of 90–91; bullying 142, 144–145; Delaware School Surveys 175–176, 180; limitations of 91–93; school safety 152, 154, 156; strategies and interventions 96–113; SWPIS 75; *see also* discipline; sanctions; suspensions

racial groups: alternative placements 160; Delaware School Surveys 182; engagement 118, 121; exclusionary practices 93, 150, 156–157; peer acceptance 38; teacher-student relationships 26
racism 39
Ramelow, D. 6
RAND Corporation 57–58
reinforcement 38, 70–71, 73, 81, 106, 120; ABC behavioral approach 97; Delaware School Surveys 175; engagement 124, 127; punitive consequences 92–93, 100, 156; self-reinforcement 86, 107; social skills 75; *see also* rewards
rejection 35–36, 41, 44, 46, 49–50, 132–133
relatedness 10, 13, 18, 22, 25, 55
relationships 5–6, 19; attachment theory 17; definitions of school climate 3, 4; Delaware School Surveys 171, 175, 178–179; disciplinary encounters 94; ecological systems theory 16–17; engagement 116, 128; with families 32; modeling relationship skills 29; praise and rewards 87; prevention of behavior problems 67, 77–78, 87; Safe and Supportive School Model of School Climate 4, 5; SEL programs 52; self-determination theory 18; self-discipline 52–53; social and emotional competencies 47, 48, 49–50, 54–55, 64, 66; social and emotional support 7, 9–10; *see also* student-student relationships; teacher-student relationships
relaxation breaks 79
resources 6, 105, 163, 167, 186
respect 13, 14; class meetings 32; prevention of behavior problems 67; service learning 65; student-student relationships 40, 46, 55, 137; teacher-student relationships 22, 25
response cost punishment 89, 107–108
responsibility: bystanders 162; correction of behavior 101–102; shared 103

responsible decision-making 2, 47, 48–49, 54, 63, 66; Delaware School Surveys 171, 175, 178–179; disciplinary encounters 94, 101; engagement 116; praise and rewards 87; SEL programs 162; self-discipline 52–53; social and emotional support 11

Responsive Classroom Approach 26–27, 32, 39, 45; benefit-cost ratio 52; embedded approach 58; inductive discipline 63, 100; research base 124; student-student relationships 55; teacher-student relationships 55

responsiveness 7, 9, 10–11, 13, 15, 19, 185; authoritative approach 46; bullying 146; Delaware School Surveys 173–174; engagement 122; student-student relationships 37; teacher-student relationships 23, 25, 33, 38, 55

restitutional overcorrection 109

restorative justice 40, 63, 100, 161

rewards: behavioral approach 71, 77; Delaware School Surveys 175; effective teachers 70; engagement 124; prevention of behavior problems 78, 83–87; SEL programs 59–62; student-student relationships 44–45; SWPIS 65, 75; systematic use of 161; teacher-student relationships 28–29

Ritter, M. D. 51–52

Rivers, I. 133

role models 41, 43–44, 62–63; *see also* modeling

routines 69, 71, 80, 122, 141

rules: behavioral approach 71; bullying 139, 141; Delaware School Surveys 169, 170, 172, 173; effective teachers 69, 70; engagement 114, 122; fairness 95, 113, 154; prevention of behavior problems 79–82; safety 151; self-discipline 13; social control theory 17; structure 9, 11, 28; student perceptions 19; student-student relationships 37–38, 39–40, 46; teacher-student relationships 10, 14, 29; zero tolerance approach 153

Safe and Supportive School Model of School Climate 4–5

safety 2, 5–6, 7–9, 12, 20, 147–166; attachment theory 17; bullying 129; definitions of school climate 3, 4; Delaware School Surveys 169, 170, 172, 174; engagement 122; factors contributing to 151–152; NCES survey 148–150, 151; physical environment 83; racial disparities 156–157; Safe and Supportive School Model of School Climate 4, 5; SEL programs 51; social order 15; strategies and interventions 158–166; student perceptions 19; student-student relationships 46; teacher-student relationships 21; theories 18–19; zero tolerance 152–154, 155–156

sanctions 15, 30, 67, 90–91, 154; bullying 142, 144–145; social and emotional learning 63; *see also* punitive consequences; suspensions

Schellinger, K. B. 51

school climate: common domains of 5–7; definitions of 3–4; measures of 2, 6–7; metaphors 1; theoretical frameworks 16–19

School Climate Scale 3

School Climate Transformation Grants 2, 167

school effectiveness 69, 121

school improvement 7

School-Wide Positive Behavioral Interventions and Supports (SWPIS) 2, 65, 71, 72–76, 79–80, 169, 185

seating arrangements 38, 41, 43

Second Step Social-Emotional Learning 56, 57, 62, 76; bullying 140, 142, 146; social problem-solving 102

security measures 150, 153, 155, 156, 158

SEL *see* social and emotional learning

self-awareness 47, 50–51, 64, 66; Delaware School Surveys 178; disciplinary encounters 94; engagement 116; self-discipline 52–53

self-concept 50, 51; bullying 180; punitive consequences 101; service learning 65; student-student relationships 34

self-confidence: bullying 136, 138; self-awareness 50; self-discipline 52; teacher-student relationships 17, 22, 23, 24

self-control 49, 56, 101

self-determination theory 13, 18, 19, 22, 51

self-discipline 9, 12–13, 14, 67, 101; aim of education 77; authoritative approach 37, 185; ecological systems theory 16; evidence-based interventions 98; extracurricular activities 41; modeling 62; monitoring by teachers 83; praise and

rewards 60; punitive consequences 91, 93, 94, 113; social and emotional learning 52–53, 54, 56, 63; teacher-student relationships 33
self-efficacy: Delaware School Surveys 179; engagement 115; self-awareness 50–51; self-discipline 52; service learning 42, 65; social cognitive theory 18; teacher-student relationships 17, 22, 24
self-esteem: attachment theory 17; bullying 132, 133, 136; Delaware School Surveys 178; engagement 115; misbehavior 29; programs on 161; self-control 49; self-determination theory 18; student-student relationships 10, 34; teacher-student relationships 23, 31–32
self-evaluation 79, 107, 126
self-management 2, 47–48, 49, 54, 64, 66; behavioral 107; Delaware School Surveys 171, 175, 178–179; disciplinary encounters 94; engagement 116; goal setting 79; praise and rewards 87; self-discipline 52–53
self-reflection 107
self-regulation 18, 53, 116
self-reinforcement 86, 107
self-sanctions 90, 91
service learning 42, 65
SES *see* socioeconomic status
sexual orientation 134, 135, 150
Simonsen, B. 75
Skinner, B. F. 70–71
Sklad, M. 51–52
Slaughter, J. 60
social action 15, 173–174
social and emotional competencies 2, 9, 11, 47–66, 160; authoritative approach 161, 185; bullying 136, 141; Delaware School Surveys 167, 169, 171, 178–179, 180; engagement 127–128; prevention of behavior problems 77–78, 87; punitive consequences 90; responsibility 101; safety 148, 151, 162, 166; self-discipline 12–13, 67, 98; strategies and interventions 54–65; structure 14; student-student relationships 46; teacher-student relationships 33
social and emotional learning (SEL) 2, 12, 68, 185–186; bystanders 162; class meetings 45; Delaware School Surveys 169, 170, 173, 175–176; effectiveness of programs 51–52; engagement 116–117, 122, 123–124; inductive discipline 100; moral disengagement 54; promoting 54–65; relationship skills 29; self-discipline 52–53; student-student relationships 39, 40
social and emotional support 7–11, 13, 20, 66; authoritative approach 27–28, 37, 91, 185; bullying 136, 137, 141; disciplinary encounters 103; engagement 119, 122; prevention of behavior problems 77–78; punitive consequences 90; teacher-student relationships 22, 33, 38
social awareness 2, 47–48, 50, 52, 54, 64, 66; Delaware School Surveys 171, 175, 178–179; disciplinary encounters 94; engagement 116; praise and rewards 87; SEL programs 162
social cognitive theory 18, 19, 51, 173
social control theory 17, 19, 51
social-ecological model of bullying 134, 135
social information processing 51
social learning theory 38
social order 15, 173–174
social perspective-taking 11, 48, 50; class meetings 32; correction of behavior 100; engagement 123; inductive discipline 63; lack of 116; modeling 62; SEL programs 51, 162; service learning 65; student-student relationships 37, 40, 55
social rejection 35–36, 41, 44, 46
social skills 35, 36–37; bullying 136, 145; class meetings 45; engagement 122, 127; Good Behavior Game 109; lack of 100, 155; peer-assisted learning 42; punitive consequences 94; restorative practices 161; Second Step Social-Emotional Learning 140; SEL programs 55–56; student-student relationships 39–40; SWPIS 75, 76; tiered approach 74
socioeconomic status (SES) 118, 121, 139, 182
sociometrics 43
Song, Y. S. 161
sports 31, 32, 35, 41, 55, 121
stage-environment fit theory 18
Stockard, J. 15, 173
stress 33, 49, 117, 119
structure 6, 7–9, 11, 13, 14, 20; authoritative approach 91, 185; bullying 141, 146; correction of behavior 103; ecological systems theory 16; engagement 119, 122–123; prevention of behavior problems 77–78, 87; social and emotional learning 65; social order

15; student-student relationships 37–38, 39; teacher-student relationships 27–28, 33; theories 18–19
student perceptions 11, 19; class meetings 45; Delaware School Surveys 182; fairness 81, 95; praise and rewards 59; punitive consequences 113; restorative practices 161
student profiling 159
student-student relationships 10, 21, 34–46; bullying 129, 133, 137–138, 141; class meetings 32; Delaware School Surveys 169, 170, 172, 182; engagement 122, 128; prevention of behavior problems 77–78, 87; safety 148, 151; SEL programs 54–55, 66; strategies and interventions 39–45
substance use 158, 163, 166; authoritative school climate 15; bullying 132, 133; engagement 115; expulsion 113; IAES 160; Safe and Supportive School Model of School Climate 4, 5; SEL programs 52; self-control 49; tiered approach 74; zero tolerance approach 153, 155
Sugai, George 72–73, 75
suicide 103, 147; bullying 129, 132, 133; prevalence of 148; student-student relationships 10, 34; tiered approach 74; training 165, 166
support 4, 5, 7–11, 20; authoritative approach 27–28, 37, 185; bullying 135–136, 137, 138, 141, 144; class meetings 45; ecological systems theory 16; home 110, 117–118, 126–127; peer 34, 35; prevention of behavior problems 67; SWPIS 74–75; teacher-student relationships 22, 33, 38; theories 18–19; victims of aggression 163; *see also* social and emotional support
suspensions 90, 150, 154–155, 158, 166; authoritative approach 15, 161; Delaware School Surveys 174, 180; effectiveness 99; engagement 115–116; limitations of 112; number of 159; racial disparities 93, 156–157; SWPIS 76; zero tolerance approach 148, 152, 153, 156
Swearer, S. M. 161
SWPIS *see* School-Wide Positive Behavioral Interventions and Supports

Taylor, R. D. 51, 52
teacher characteristics 68–70

teacher/staff relations 170, 171–172, 174
teacher-student relationships 9–10, 14, 21–33, 38, 160; attachment theory 17; behavioral approach 77; bullying 129, 133, 137–138, 141; Delaware School Surveys 169, 170, 172, 175, 182; effective teachers 70; engagement 122, 128; praise and rewards 84; prevention of behavior problems 67, 77–78, 87; punitive consequences 92, 95–96, 113; safety 148, 151; SEL programs 54–55, 66; strategies and interventions 26–33, 184
teaching 3, 6; engagement 119–120; prevention of behavior problems 67, 78; structure 11; teacher-student relationships 25, 27; *see also* instructional methods
Teaching Students to Be Peacemakers Program 55
teasing 142
Teglasi, H. 116
Theriot, M. T. 155
time-outs 99, 107, 109–110
Todd, A. W. 75
training *see* professional development
trauma 117, 119, 147, 165
truancy 16
trust: class meetings 32, 45; self-discipline 13; service learning 42, 65; student-student relationships 37, 137; teacher-student relationships 22, 25
Ttofi, M. M. 138, 141

Ubbes, V. A. 5
unicorn metaphor 1, 2
uniforms 159
United States Department of Education (USDOE) 2, 3–5, 19, 129–130, 167

values: achievement 115; cultural 30; ecological systems theory 17; engagement 8, 124; goal setting 125; safety 3; social control theory 17; student-student relationships 38; teacher-student relationships 14, 23
verbal communication 106
video recordings 110, 139
violence 2, 83, 103, 147–148, 149, 151; bystanders 162; ecological approach 70; engagement 117; expulsion 113; safety 12; support for victims 163; threat

assessment 163–164; zero tolerance approach 153; *see also* aggression; bullying
vision statements 40

Wang, M. 6, 16
warmth 25, 27–28
weapons 149, 158, 160; authoritative school climate 15; gangs 166; victims of bullying 132–133; zero tolerance approach 152, 153, 155
Wei, Y. 180
Weinstein, C. S. 82
Weissberg, R. P. 51, 52
Wigelsworth, M. 51
Winett, R. A. 92
Winkler, R. C. 92
Wolf, J. P. 25
Wright, J. P. 157

Xie, J. 180

Yang, C. 59
Yarbro, J. 21

zero tolerance 8, 12, 148, 152–154, 155–156, 161
Zins, J. E. 47
Zullig, K. J. 5
Zych, I. 136